Nemesis of Left Extremism

Studies in Critical Social Sciences

VOLUME 369

The titles published in this series are listed at *brill.com/scss*

Nemesis of Left Extremism

State, Salwa Judum and Naxalism

By

Sangit Kumar Ragi

BRILL

ISSN 1573-4234
ISBN 978-90-04-76504-7
ISBN 978-90-04-76505-4 (PDF)
DOI https://doi.org/10.1163/9789004765054

Brill and Koninklijke Brill BV are part of De Gruyter Brill.
www.degruyterbrill.com

Questions about General Product Safety Regulation: productsafety@degruyterbrill.com

Contents

Preface IX
List of Figures XI

Introduction 1
1 Chapter 1: Naxal Movement in India: A Theoretical Discourse 3
2 Chapter 2: Maoists Activities in India 4
3 Chapter 3: Political Economy of the Naxal Movement 5
4 Chapter 4: Recruitment of Cadres: Roping in Minors and Women 5
5 Chapter 5: Missionaries and the Naxal Movement in India: Is There Any Nexus between Them? 6
6 Chapter 6: Salwa Judum: People's Movement against Naxals? 7
7 Chapter 7: Intellectuals' Support of the Maoist Movement in India 8
8 Chapter 8: Maoists, Courts, and Salwa Judum 8
9 Chapter 9: National Human Rights Commission and Salwa Judum 9
10 Chapter 10: State and Political Response to the Maoists 10
11 Chapter 11: Tackling Left Extremism during Modi Regime 10

1 Naxal Movement in India: A Theoretical Discourse 12
1 Maoist Movement in India 18
2 Splits after Splits Marks the Revolutionary Movement 32
3 CPI (Maoist) 39
4 Towards Conclusion 42

2 Maoists Activities in India 47
1 Maoist Affected States and Areas 53
2 Organisation, Arms and Weapons, Leadership, Janata Darbar, Jan Adalat 57
3 Fighting against the Indian State 58
4 Naxals and Urban Areas 64

3 Political Economy of the Naxal Movement 66
1 Naxals Targeting Schools and Welfare Schemes 75
2 Emergence of Fake Naxals 77
3 NGOs Funding the Naxals 78

4 Maoist Directly into Business 79
5 Foreign Funding 81
6 Use of the Money by the Naxalites 82
7 Conclusion 83

4 **Recruitment of Cadres: Roping in Minors and Women** 84
1 Reasons for the Recruitment of the Children 93
2 Position of Women Cadre 99

5 **Missionaries and the Naxal Movement in India: Is There Any Nexus between Them?** 104
1 Maoist Not Targeting Missionaries 112
2 Missionaries at Work in Other Countries: Fuelling Fire and Conflicts 114
3 How Missionaries Support the Ultras? 116

6 **Salwa Judum: People's Movement against Naxals?** 120
1 Origin of Salwa Judum 121
2 Salwa Judum Camps 125
3 Who Joined Salwa Judum and Why? 127
4 Salwa Judum: a Short-Lived Euphoria? 132
5 Campaign against Salwa Judum 132

7 **Intellectuals' Support of the Maoist Movement in India** 141
1 Fact-Finding Reports: Facts or Bias Documents? 157

8 **Maoists, Courts, and Salwa Judum** 163

9 **National Human Rights Commission and Salwa Judum** 179
1 Salwa Judum under Scrutiny: NHRC's Observations 182
2 Ignoring Development 185
3 Cases of Rape against Salwa Judum Activists 188

10 **State and Political Response to the Maoists** 193
1 Government Going Soft on Naxals: UPA I and UPA II 194
2 Government under UPA I 195
3 Political Parties and Naxals 201
4 Bihar 205
5 Chhattisgarh 209
6 Maharashtra 210
7 Conclusion 212

11 **Tackling Left Extremism during Modi Regime** 214
1 Naxalism in the 2000s—the Soft State and Silent Surge 215
2 NDA-I: Modi Government's Response to Naxalism in First Phase 221
3 Modi 2.0: Phase II of Eliminating Naxalism 223
4 Modi 3.0: the Final Blow 225
5 Conclusion 226

Conclusion 229

Bibliography 235
Annex 1 263
Annex 2 274
Index 294

Preface

It was mid-June during the university vacation in 2010 that I started thinking of writing a manuscript on the Naxal movement in India. By then, the case against Salwa Judum had been filed in the Supreme Court of India, and a section of the intelligentsia was up in arms against it. While the state of Chhattisgarh, governed by the Bharatiya Janata Party, was lending all support to this movement, which it considered to be a people's initiative against Naxalites and their violence, Naxalites and their supporters in the media and intelligentsia depicted it as a weaponization of the masses, including children and women and using them in the battle against the Naxalites. The BJP government was in thick of controversy. The United Front Government was headed by Congressman Dr Manmohan Singh but the left components of the coalition were very powerful. The Home Minister and the Prime Minister considered left extremism as the biggest threat to the internal security of the country and started 'Operation Green Hunt' to eliminate them. But this was not liked by the Communist Party of India (CPI) and the Communist Party of India -Marxist (CPM). They considered the left extremism as an ideological and political issue and therefore to be dealt with accordingly rather than using the police force. Some of the regional parties, like Rastriya Janata Dal in Bihar, also echoed the same sentiments. And therefore, the Congress Party thought it politically prudent to disown the government position and Salwa Judum was subsequently opposed by the central government. It was sufficient to understand how political parties were taking sides on issues of national importance based on their political positions. I looked at the figure of death and casualties on both sides: civilians and police forces on the one hand, and the Naxalites or the Maoists on the other. This provoked me to read more and use my theoretical understandings and dynamics of Indian politics into account to draft a manuscript on the theme.

Several academic interruptions and other pressing demands delayed the project, and a rough draft could be possible only by the end of 2015. I gave it to a colleague in the department to read and reflect on and by the time he returned the manuscript, I moved on to another manuscript. I revived this project once again in 2024, when a journalist who has worked in the close proximity with the Naxalites met me in my department and shared several facts which I had never heard of before. He agreed with my assessment that after the abrogation of Articles 370 and 35A, which pertained to the state of Jammu and Kashmir, the BJP government, after winning the 2024 elections, would turn to eliminating the Naxalite movement in India. He agreed to further his first-hand insights into the Naxal movement.

I would like to make a special mention of my students, Raushan Thakur, Syed Insha, Deeksha Kadyan, Sagar Kadyan, Amandeep Arya and Anjani Kumar Rai for reading the entire manuscript and pinpointing errors for corrections or doing the needful where I lacked clarity. They also supported arranging the references and organizing the manuscript. I always try to ensure that the language of the book is so swift and simple that it is understandable to a common reader who does not have exposure to political science. This could be possible through students like Ashna Vinamra Jain, Shambhavi Mani Tripathy, Sandhanee Deka, Parul and Ravina who lent support in the collection of material, going through the draft and making valuable suggestions. I thank them all for extending support in the completion of the work. I also thank my colleagues in the department, especially Abhishek Choudhary and Ningthoujam Koiremba Singh, who reviewed the text, provided valuable suggestions, and encouraged me to complete it within a dedicated timeline. I am indebted to them for all the support that they extended in this journey. I also thank the staff of the Prime Minister Museum and Library for making books available to me whenever I needed them. I utilized my association with the Prime Minister's Museum and Library (PMML) to read books other than the project I was working on.

I extend my gratitude to the entire team at De Gruyter Brill, especially Christine Hededam, Melissa Henson, David Fasenfest and Tooba Shahriar for considering the work for publication. I would like to thank Ankur Rastogi to bring closer to this publication. Without their support, it would have been impossible to bring the book in time.

And last, I pay my gratitude to my wife, Reena and my children, Raghav and Madhav, who provided both intellectual and moral support in accomplishing the work. Reena would always engage in arguments and wouldn't spare until I convinced her through logic and facts. The methodological and technical support by Madhav and Raghav's help in designing the graphics and cover page has assisted in making this project a success.

I have tried my best to keep the language lucid and simple for everyone to understand an otherwise complex issue. The book is now before the wise readers.

Figures

1 Fatalities in major incidents (2004–2013) 263
2 Fatalities in major incidents (2014–2025) 264
3 Suicide attacks (2004–2013): killed vs injured 265
4 Suicide attacks (2014–2025): killed vs injured 266
5 Surrenders (2004–2025) 267
6 Killed in explosions (2004–2013) by group 268
7 Killed in explosions (2014–2025) 269
8 Security forces injured in major incidents (2004–2025) 270
9 Security forces killed in major incidents (2004–2025) 271
10 Security forces injured in explosions (2004–2025) 272
11 Security forces killed in explosions (2004–2025) 273

Introduction

The armed struggle against the Indian state, initiated in 1967 by a group of Maoist-Leninist revolutionaries in the Naxalbari area of West Bengal, India, came to be known as Naxalism, and those associated with it were referred to as Naxalites. These cadres of the CPI (ML) were dissatisfied with the parliamentary politics of the Communist Party of India (Marxist) and called them revisionists. These revolutionaries were motivated and driven by the ideology, methods, and mechanisms of Mao. They concluded that the protracted armed struggle against the class enemies and the Indian state was the only answer to liberate the exploited and toiled masses and establish an exploitation-free egalitarian society. The movement that sparked off in Bengal soon spread to other states in India and brought a vast swath of land under their influence, which popularly came to be known as the 'Red Corridor'. The 'Red Corridor' once covered the lands of several Indian provinces, including Bihar, Bengal, Odisha, Telangana, Jharkhand, Chhattisgarh, Maharashtra, Andhra Pradesh, Madhya Pradesh, and Kerala. As those who propagated Maoism as the right path to revolution, it attracted extreme radical forces within the left to its ideology. A section of the intelligentsia, comprising professors, students on campus, and journalists in the news media, lent support to the new left-wing ideology. They wrote extensively in favour of the revolutionary ideology, which was characterised by violence against the state apparatus and the wealthy feudal class. The government initially treated it as a law-and-order issue caused by a certain set of people who believed in a certain political ideology and addressed it accordingly.

However, it was soon realised that it posed a serious threat to the democratic process and the constitutional order of India. The West Bengal government, under the CPM, used ruthless force against the Naxalites and forced them to shift their bases from Bengal to other states like Kerala and Andhra Pradesh. The government in these states also did its best to contain the Maoist violence and its spread despite the use of police and paramilitary forces. This resulted in a huge loss of lives of the Naxals, security forces, and civilians. Both Naxals and the state accused each other of the state of violence and loss of lives. And this continues to date. While the Naxals charge that their violence is a response to the violence and atrocities by the state apparatus. And it is their bounden duty, as revolutionaries, to do this. The state, on the other hand, holds that it is accountable for securing the lives of the people against the violence and atmosphere of terror created by the Naxals. While the government holds that Maoist activities have been responsible for the underdevelopment of

 | HTTPS://DOI.ORG/10.1163/9789004765054-002

these areas, Maoists argue that the government's negligence towards development, betterment of lives of the people, continuous harassment and exploitation by the state agencies, and the rich and powerful have forced the poor and deprived to take up arms against the state. In the meantime, the Naxals kept swelling their strength in all senses of term, from procuring arms to recruiting cadres and training them in guerrilla war against the Indian state. They used indoctrination as well as force to rope in minors and women into the movement with the aim to shield themselves in the fight against the forces, as any casualty of women and children attracted wider condemnation of the Indian forces. They used this on several occasions to score narrative over the government, as such encounters invited criticisms from human rights organisations at home as well as outside India.

Needless to say, these contrasting narratives continued to engage the national discourse for decades. The intelligentsia and the political class remained divided on the question of how to tackle the ideology of violence perpetrated by the Naxalites. The political class took time to equate it with one kind of terrorism. The political parties, except the BJP, blew hot and cold against the menace of Naxalism based on what was suitable to their politics. Political instability and a weak coalition government at the centre provided fertile ground for the Naxalites to expand their areas of activity. Central governments standing on weak foundations of coalitions could not give sufficient attention to this problem. The BJP government in states like Madhya Pradesh and Chhattisgarh was an exception to it. The movement gained strength and momentum year after year. And over time, the government of India realised that it was the biggest threat to the country's internal security. The Congress government, under Manmohan Singh and Home Minister P. Chidambaram, recognised the threat to internal security and initiated 'Operation Green Hunt'; however, the party's political leadership, led by Sonia Gandhi, pulled them back. The Chhattisgarh government, which had supported the Salwa Judum, a movement against the Naxalites or Maoists, lost its case in court against the challengers of the Salwa Judum due to the absence of support from the centre. Some of the people who had filed the case against Salwa Judum were known sympathisers of the Naxals and lent support to their fight against the Indian state for the protection of Jal Jangal and Jameen (water, land, and the forest). The Indian state was projected as a neo-colonial oppressor of the vulnerable sections of society in conjunction with the rich corporations. The court verdict discouraged the state government from mobilising people's support against the Naxals in the areas of their influence. The charges of the National Human Rights Commission that the Naxalites force minors and women to join the movement were not widely reported in the media. Additionally, the sexual exploitation of women by the Naxals in the areas of their influence did not catch national attention. The Salwa Judum was a novel experiment towards mobilising people against the Naxalites/Maoists, but this counterinsurgency design had to be aborted due to adverse judicial pronouncements. Although the abortion of the Salwa Judum weakened the fight against the Naxals, it taught a valuable lesson: a security-centric approach using hard power would be effective if combined with the empowerment of people by improving their living conditions and eliminating the fear of the Naxals in areas of their strength.

Until 2014, state responses to Naxalism were marked by fragmented policy frameworks, inadequate inter-agency coordination, and a lack of political resolve. The electoral victory of Narendra Modi led the NDA in 2014, signalled a paradigm shift in the national counterinsurgency strategy. The government adopted a dual approach, combining aggressive counterinsurgency operations that led to the encounter of many Naxal leaders with targeted socio-economic development through the Aspirational District Programmes. Under the Modi government, the geographical footprint of Naxalism has contracted significantly, coupled with a degradation in the operational capabilities of the Maoist insurgents. The Ministry of Home Affairs, under the leadership of Amit Shah, has implemented a series of measures, including enhanced surveillance, increased security presence, and community engagement programs, which have collectively produced tangible outcomes. The Home Minister has officially announced that India will be "Naxal-free" by March 2026, an assertion supported by a consistent decline in Naxal activities across the states, their shrinking space, and the killing or surrender of their leaders on a daily basis.

This book seeks to offer a comprehensive examination of the rise, consolidation, and apparent decline of Naxalism in India. It explores the ideological foundations of the movement, the socio-political and economic contexts that facilitated its growth, and the diverse responses it elicited from the Indian state across different political regimes, as well as the explanations for the changes that occurred from 2014, which led to the almost decimation of the Naxal movement in India.

1 Chapter 1: Naxal Movement in India: A Theoretical Discourse

This chapter examines the ideological and theoretical framework of Naxalism. It explains how Naxalism or Maoism is a variant of the communist movement which seeks to achieve a classless and stateless society by capturing political power through armed revolution and converting the bourgeois rule into a proletarian rule in the period of transition. It is different from classical Marxism and Leninism-Stalinism. The Naxal movement heavily draws from the tested premise of the revolutionary armed struggle by Mao in China. Mao, though, followed the basic premise of Marxism but did not walk on dotted lines. He claimed to have tailored the premises of classical Marxism to suit the Chinese realities. And therefore, he promised that it would not be the industrial worker but intellectuals and workers in the leadership of the peasantry who would lead the revolution. Secondly, Mao held that the change cannot be wilful and peaceful. And therefore, the role of violent revolution against the state becomes the guiding political theology for the Maoists. The chapter engages with the discourses, factors, and forces which led to the divide in the international communist movement, which subsequently impacted the Indian communist movement, leading to a split first in 1964 and subsequently in 1967, wherein the radical elements within the CPM declared that the armed struggle was the correct road to Indian revolution. This resulted in the birth of CPI (ML). The discourse examines the debates that how the CPI (ML) or Maoists distinguish themselves from CPI and CPM in the characterisation of the Indian state. The study shows that with the passage of time, the movement lost its direction, and it underwent several splits one after another on frivolous grounds, and their obsession with violence and selective alignment with the political forces dented their image and allowed the Indian state to crush the movement.

2 Chapter 2: Maoists Activities in India

This chapter examines the territorial expansion of the Maoist movement and the nature of violent revolutionary activities undertaken by them. The Maoist movement originated in Naxalbari, Bengal, where they had to fight against the more moderate and parliamentary left, which utilised the repressive state apparatus to suppress the movement. The cadres of the CPM who had opted for a far more radical line of the left and formed now the CPI (ML) had to fight their parent organisation, which for them was betraying the core of socialism. The chapter explains the conflict between the two CPI and CPI (ML) and what led the Naxal movement to relocate its areas of activity by moving towards Kerala and Andhra Pradesh and then to the present Jharkhand, Chhattisgarh, and some parts of Maharashtra. The chapter also deals with the reasons and factors that have been responsible for such a territorial trajectory of the movement, with explanations of how they moved on to the areas that were mineral-rich and had dense forest cover. It examines how and why the Naxal movement, which once had greater areas under its influence, receded with time. The area under its influence was depicted as the Red Corridor, as this was the region highly under the impact zone of the Naxals. They could easily hit the police, civilians and others at their will. The author has used the data from the government sources to explain the nature of the violence and casualties of man and material from the Naxals' targets.

3 Chapter 3: Political Economy of the Naxal Movement

This chapter sheds light on the financing of left-wing groups. Furthermore, it highlights the overall sociological and political implications of these financing methods. The Naxal groups are not limited to membership fees and donations for their financing, but they also engage in a plethora of illegal activities that fund their movement. These activities, which range from but are not limited to extortion, kidnapping, and robbery, to directly engaging in the illicit business of operating black money and drug trade. Therefore, even though the organisation's ideological stance is that its fight is for the poor, its organisation and top leadership are not poor at all. This chapter also examines the overall sociological, political, and economic impact of these financing activities on the people whom the Naxals claim to be fighting for. The Naxal activities of extortion, kidnapping, and more choke out the developmental work undertaken by the government in those regions. This chapter also identifies the nexus that gets developed between the Naxals, bureaucrats, and corporate leaders solely for their mutual survival and pursuance of their interests. It also engages with ideas such as the emergence of fake Naxals, interlinkages between Naxals, NGOs, and foreign funding in the Naxal movement. The chapter, in brief, attempts to unearth a well-developed network and system that supports, sustains, and strengthens left-wing extremism in the country.

4 Chapter 4: Recruitment of Cadres: Roping in Minors and Women

The Maoists' ideal of devising an egalitarian society and their constant disagreement with the Indian state in the name of revolution garnered renewed attention within prominent sections of civil society. Naxals have successfully created a special unit of minors and a cultural wing of women within their fold.

Children and women are recruited through unconventional means for espionage, information gathering, and organising cultural programs, among other purposes. With few resources in hand and a massive support base, Naxals have managed to influence the corners of India. Both women and children play a key role in structuring the Naxals' influence and affecting the fight against the rich and the Indian state. The chapter attempts to assess the structure and dynamics of the Naxal movement by examining the condition of women and children within its fold. It primarily underlines how far Naxals are living up to their lofty ideals of constructing an equitable society and what their take is on entangling children and women in a world of violence. Subsequently, there have been squabbles between different groups over Naxals' revolutionary operations and the state's response to them. If at all, women and children are killed in a police encounter, it allows Naxals to raise the issue of human rights violations. The chapter further underlines and decodes the stoic silence of organisations that claim to be the Human rights watchdogs. In brief, it is a detailed analysis of methods and consequences of the recruitment of women and children picked up from a segment of toiling masses who, in their attempt to fill an empty stomach and driven by great futuristic goals, fall into the clutches of the Maoists, from which they will never be able to escape.

5 Chapter 5: Missionaries and the Naxal Movement in India: Is there any Nexus between Them?

This chapter primarily aims to unveil the interconnectedness of Naxals and Christian Missionaries in remote forest areas. The important questions that have been explored are whether there is a tactical understanding between the Maoists and the Missionaries. It has sought to examine this question in the context of Maoists' tolerance towards the Christian missionaries' work on the one hand and active intolerance towards the right-wing organisations working among the forest dwellers. Maoists are highly critical of the conservative customs and superstitions in practice in the Hindu society, but maintain stoic silence on the same prevalent among the Christians. The chapter analyses the means and methods applied by the missionaries to convert the innocent, illiterate, and poor tribals into Christianity and goes on to examine what makes the Naxals soft to the missionaries, whereas harsh and highly critical of the activities of the Vanvasi Kalyan Ashram, an integral unit of the Rashtriya Swayam Sevak Sangh (RSS). The Hindu nationalists, through their Vanvasi Kalyan Ashram, have put up a strong alternative against evangelical activities largely funded by the Christian world and their missionaries. The chapter has sought to explain whether the money channelled to the NGOs working under the influence of the Evangelical Church syphons off a part of it for the Naxal activities because they found in Hindutva a common enemy. This also answers why the Naxals don't awaken and arouse tribals against the foreign missionaries and allow the latter to destroy the indigenous culture of tribes. After all, the money comes from the European capitalist countries, but the Naxals go silent on the subject. Missionaries' support for Maoists is based on the principle of self-preservation, and Maoist aid helps them in achieving their far-fetched goal of converting the indigenous religion and culture of tribals. NGOs in these Naxal-infested areas also play a pertinent role in funding of these Maoists through their charitable and humanitarian-based activities. This chapter further elucidates how, after capital and military, religious conversions by Missionaries are becoming another means of colonisation, and elaborates on the nexus between Maoists and missionaries in Nepal, where they succeeded in overthrowing the existing Hindu kingdom.

6 Chapter 6: Salwa Judum: People's Movement against Naxals?

The chapter addresses a highly debated movement in the country, namely Salwa Judum, an anti-Maoist campaign initiated in 2005 by a Congress leader in Chhattisgarh. The chapter seeks to trace and analyse the birth of the movement, its nature of activities, recruitment of people and its support base. The question is whether Salwa Judum was a self-grown movement against the Naxals or was created by the state government with a clear intent of mobilising the young unemployed youth against the Maoist movement. It has tried to answer whether Salwa Judum arose out of frustration and anger arising out of uncontrolled atrocities committed by Naxals for decades. A sudden surge in local support and recruitment to the movement became a point of contention between the Maoists and their supporters. Human rights activists and their organisations also had several questions for the state regarding the issue. They alleged the atrocities of the SPOs (Special Protection Officers), who were largely underage and untrained to fight the Naxals. This chapter explains the duplicity of the Naxals and their supporters, who, on the one hand, are critical of the state on the issue of recruitment of women and children in the ranks of the Naxal movement but maintain silence about the same practice by the latter. Content analysis of the news items reported in the press and the government reports on the same subject has been employed to argue the point.

7 Chapter 7: Intellectuals' Support of the Maoist Movement in India

The chapter addresses the question of support lent to the Naxals by the intellectuals and academicians in India. There is a dominant narrative that informs that Naxals have a very powerful infiltration and reach in media, intellectuals, and academicians who support their dream of bringing a change in the present inequitable society and ending the class-driven atrocities and power relations. They criticise the violence of the state but are not equally critical of the Naxal violence. Instead, they have been fond of using retributive logic to defend the violence caused by the Maoists. The chapter has tried to throw light on whether there is an academic design in terms of course contents and teaching that creates a left-leaning ideological ecosystem, which goes to support the Maoists intellectually. Some centres of higher learning have been found making headlines in the news media on this count, which makes it important to examine this aspect. The chapter also underlines the coming together of the Maoists and separatists of Kashmir in some of the campuses of India despite their ideological incongruency. The chapter undertakes an analytical and historical approach to assess how campus politics is linked with what goes around in central politics and how a massive group of left intelligentsia provides support to Naxals as well as the Kashmiris on the grounds of their democratic rights and civil liberties. Interestingly, examination of organisations like Peoples Union for Civil Liberties and Peoples Union for Democratic Rights, though they seem to be supporting the framework of liberal democracy, in essence, they are left tilted and expel bias in favour of the Maoists, as their reports are critical of human rights violations by the state but are not equally hard against the Maoists on the issue.

8 Chapter 8: Maoists, Courts, and Salwa Judum

Often, a narrative is set into motion to suggest that the courts have been too sympathetic and lenient to the Naxals. This narrative comes from those who argue in support of the use of hard power against the Naxalites and their movement. This narrative is based on premises that Naxals are anti-development, go against the industrial set-ups, and unleash mindless violence to create terror in the minds of the people in pursuit of their cause. Their worldview is unmodern and anti-democratic. And unfortunately, they argue, courts have been too generous to weaken the state's hands that intend to defeat their war on the Indian state. This chapter examines the response of the Courts to the Naxal movement in India, keeping Salwa Judum and arrests of Naxals and court proceedings in mind. The issue captured headlines and came to the centre of discourse when one judge of the Supreme Court, while hearing the petition on the Salwa Judum, referred to the model of development that had provoked the people to take up arms. The judge had quoted at length from a book supposedly written from a left-point-of-view perspective. This observation was criticised by the media and the party in power equally. The chapter seeks to examine and analyse whether there exists such a favourable intellectual ecosystem and whether there is any merit in the arguments of those who think so. The Supreme Court had forced the state of Chhattisgarh to withdraw Salwa Judum unconditionally and had accepted the points of view of the petitioners, who leaned towards the left, that Salwa Judum was not a 'self-grown grass root people movement'. While the media and civil society remained divided over the judgment, various legal luminaries came out against it and questioned the ideological bias of the Judges involved. This was treated as judicial outreach, which favoured the ideological premise of rational violence argued by Naxals. This whole episode raised several questions—whether intellectual repute is above constitutional morality and should never be questioned their intentions. Whether judges were right to draw heavily from ideologically driven literature to blame privatisation, globalisation and neo liberal economic policies of the state for extremism? This chapter has sought to examine this discourse.

9 Chapter 9: National Human Rights Commission and Salwa Judum

This chapter deals with the human rights issues involved in the pursuit of Salwa Judum. It examines the wide range of questions pertaining to the recruitment of minors and women in Salwa Judum by the state, risking their lives in conflict zones. Since all the organisations working in the field of Human Rights, rights of the minors were highly critical of Salwa Judum, the discussion on the National Human Rights Commission Report drew a lot of attention. The report came in 2010. And it was interpreted by both the supporters and opposers of Salwa Judum in their favour. The selective passages were cited by both sides to support their arguments. Therefore, it was thought to dedicate a full chapter to it, examining the report in an objective manner. Needless to say, it was a report by one of the reputed institutional bodies, while the UPA II was in power at the centre and the state was run by the BJP. And it was a comprehensive report based on inputs from all stakeholders. A careful analysis of the report suggests that both supporters and opponents of Salwa Judum failed to read the report in its spirit and used it for their own political gains. It expressed genuine concern about the human rights violation, but admitted at the same time that Naxalites had done great harm to the people in the state, and there has been genuine anguish and anger against them in the masses. There were people who justified the state's support for the SPOs.

10 Chapter 10: State and Political Response to the Maoists

This chapter attempts to unearth the inconsistencies between political ideology and political actions of the Indian government and the political parties in their dealings with the Naxal menace. The important question that emerges is that if the Naxal movement has been one of the biggest threats to the security of the country, why have the political parties been blowing hot and cold on the issue and taking sides or opposing the Naxals, keeping in mind their political interests? This pattern has been seen with most of the political parties in India. While the CPM used brute force to stamp out Naxalism from West Bengal, they adopted a different position in the case of Chhattisgarh and Jharkhand. The dominant influence of left parties on the state actions against the Naxals during the consecutive UPA governments from 2004–2014 became very embarrassing for the party. Decisions were made in the interest of political convenience and party gain, at the expense of national security. The chapter thus highlights the dichotomy in the actions of left-leaning and non-BJP formations when dealing with Maoists in their state, as compared to other states. The hypocrisy in alleging other states' actions as 'state repression' while ignoring blood-curdling violence against Maoists in their own ruling states is quite evident. The frequently changing attitude of UPA II leaders towards Salwa Judum and Maoism underscored their sole intention of electoral gains. A further elaboration about the interlinkage between political parties and Naxals, especially during elections, for securing their win in the state elections, is provided in the chapter. This argument is elucidated with examples of how key political parties in Bengal, Bihar, Jharkhand, and Chhattisgarh used the Naxals for their electoral gains.

11 Chapter 11: Tackling Left Extremism during Modi Regime

The chapter captures the signals of changing political responses to the Naxalite insurgency in India, drawing attention to conflicting approaches adopted by successive regimes. It begins with the examination of the United Progressive Alliance, which, during its two terms, largely pursued a far more conciliatory or "soft glove" approach. Such a period was marked by policies that sought dialogue and limited developmental interventions; however, these measures proved inadequate in halting the expansion of Naxalite activity across several Indian states. The chapter later illustrates the paradigm shift post-2014 under Prime Minister Narendra Modi. The NDA government adopted a dual strategy: strong security operation juxtaposed with credible developmental initiatives, adding a new dimension to counterinsurgency thinking in India including flagship programmes like the Aspirational Districts programme as a measure to uplift the socio-economic indicators in underdeveloped and conflict-prone areas, and the establishment of Eklavya Model Residential Schools as measures to give better educational access to tribal populations, among other ameliorative measures. Moreover, it also highlights the government's much-appreciated role in fostering community participation, thereby strengthening local resistance to Maoist networks. The official data also indicates a sharp decline in both the geographical spread of Naxal influence and the incidence of violent incidents. Following a critical examination of these policy trajectories, the chapter demonstrates how the convergence of developmental imperatives with security architecture ultimately led to the near extinction of left-wing extremism in India under the Modi regime.

In brief, the book focuses on the premises of Naxalism/Maoism and how these premises evolved into a powerful movement against India's rich and feudal classes, ultimately turning towards the Indian state. For the benefit of the reader, the theoretical premises of Naxalism have been explained, but that is not the core objective of the book. Instead, it explains how, to date, different factions of the Naxal movement have been unable to agree on the composition of the class enemies and have continued to split into a dozen formations. Further, it explains how it generated wealth and used it to equip itself in its fight against the powerful state apparatus. The limitation of the work is that it does not explain how it developed networks with agencies outside Indian borders for the procurement of arms and ammunition. This was deliberately kept out of the scope of the book because it required and engaged security-centric discourses. Instead, the focus was on explaining how a violent movement not only found support in operational areas but also among the urban, educated class, which lent intellectual support and credibility to the movement. Furthermore, it was noted how the entire support baselapsed with the arrival of a powerful government at the centre, with a near Pan-Indian reach.

CHAPTER 1

Naxal Movement in India: A Theoretical Discourse

Not many years back, Naxalites recurringly used to grab the news headlines in the print and electronic media, almost on a daily basis. The reason was simple: there was hardly any day that passed without incidents of loot or abduction, explosions and killings, or blackmail or extortion by the Naxalites in one or other parts of the country, particularly in the six most Naxal-infested states of India, where they used to strike at will. Besides the material and human losses, the normal life in these states was subject to frequent demonstrations and bandh calls by the Naxals. For decades, they grew from strength to strength. There were several areas where, instead of the state, it was the writs of the Naxals that worked. Even the security forces had to think twice before entering such regions. Naxals called it by different names, such as 'liberated zones,' the 'red corridor,' and so on.

They are at war against the state, and their objective was and is to enlarge the areas of such zones before they finally could take on the Indian state. When this was or is going to happen, however, is a matter of assessment and conjectural predicament. Some claimed it would happen by 2030. The Central government assessment was that Naxalites' plan is to achieve it by 2050 (The Economic Times, 2010). All governments, be they at the centre or state, including the left government, have considered it as a threat to the democratic polity, but they failed to address the challenge that Naxals posed. For decades, the government at the centre remained confused. It lacked a clear, considered, and concerted response to this menace, blowing hot and cold, leading to chaos and policy confusion. Use of disproportionate force aroused human rights issues, whereas complacency resulted in massive casualties of the armed forces. Naxalites used this to their advantage by advancing the propaganda war against the state and strengthening their organisation.

The Naxalites' violence has receded significantly in the last few years after the BJP came into power. According to the government, as reported in Lok Sabha Parliament, the Naxalites caused death, which was 1005 in 2010 but has now come down to 98 in 2023 (The Hindu, 2023), lowering the percentage of such incidents by 77%. But they are not completely smashed or controlled. However, the menace of Naxalism has not completely disappeared or been brought under control. They are still capable of hitting civilians and armed forces. In April 2021, in the state of Chhattisgarh, Naxalites engaged the para-military forces in a gun battle for six hours and killed 22 Jawans, captured one

 | HTTPS://DOI.ORG/10.1163/9789004765054-003

and left him after three days of negotiations. Numerous examples can be cited to prove the way in which the state has been virtually compelled to act on the dictates of Naxals.

The Naxal movement is a variant of the communist movement that seeks to achieve a classless and stateless society by capturing political power through violent armed revolution. Post-revolution will be marked by the state replacing the bourgeoisie with the rule of the proletariat. This is the transitional state that Marx called the first phase of communism, whereas his followers call it the state of socialism (Sweezy, 2010:78). Though neither Marx nor Engels gave any 'definition or blueprint of this transitional state,' from 'scattered passages' it is concluded to be classless but not stateless. Thus, while the final objective is to have a classless and stateless society, it is to be achieved through the proletariat state. Lenin had rejected Kautsky's position that the proletariat can dominate but not govern. Lenin had argued that the proletariat should not only control and command the state machine but also use the old machine to smash the capitalist machine (Miliband, 2004:100).

It further holds that the change cannot be peaceful and wilful. And it cannot be left to the charity and wisdom of the dominant capitalist class, which monopolises the means of production and controls and uses the state and its different apparatus. Nor will it arrive in piecemeal. It can be possible only through violent armed revolution. It supports guerrilla warfare and stands against elections. The Naxal movement, thus, rejects any such variant of socialism that seeks to achieve socialist transition via parliamentary democratic politics. They considered the parliamentary politics and elections 'historically obsolete' (Mukherji & Chakrabarti, 1983:44). However, for the mainstream communists like CPI, those who undertook the path of Naxalite were 'impatient students and youth' (Mitra & Sen, 1971:83).

The Naxal movement draws heavily from the premise of Revolutionary Armed Struggle under the leadership of Mao in China. Mao guided and led the movement to success. Therefore, this variant within the ideology of Naxalism is also popularly termed as Maoism. Mao, though, followed the basic tenets of Marxism and Leninism, but he declined to walk on dotted lines. Mao rejected 'formula-Marxists' and exhorted that the Chinese communists should comprehend the 'Universal truth of Marxism' with 'Specific practice of Chinese revolution'[1] (Zedong, 1965:154; Mitra & Sen, 1971:34). He experimented with and used it with a great degree of variance and specificity in China. This makes Maoism distinctively different from classical Marxism, though not completely disjointed. Since it had sharper elements of violent revolution,

1 For further details see: Communist Party and Naxalites (marxists.org).

it became an attractive recipe for young youths exposed to the ideology of Marxism-Leninism.

Classical Marxism held that the societies from the state of primitive communism to now have always remained divided into two opposed classes. These opposite classes started forming when 'labour became productive enough to make it worthwhile for one human being to enslave another' (D'Mellow, 2010:58). Though such class formation drove the society forward as it could ensure the cultural, literary and material growth of the society, it also produced concentration of material wealth in the hands of few due to low productivity of the labour surplus.[2] It thus produced an inequitable and exploitative society. Every society, including capitalism, contained elements of exploitation and conflicting class formation, though every succeeding society was also at the same time more progressive and more productive than its predecessor.

Capitalism also emerged from an exploitative feudal society, but it was more progressive and productive than feudalism. Productivity did not change its exploitative character. Capitalism is not based 'on slave labour but on free labour' (Sweezy, 2010:59). It produces a society in which "the social surplus is appropriated by the owners of the means of production in the form of profit, interest, and rent" (University of Regina, 1999). The concentration of wealth and exploitation thus become intertwined and goes together. Marx held that capitalism is inherently exploitative. But it makes it possible for the civilisation to work towards realization of an exploitation-free society wherein the concentration of wealth is not in the hands of a few. In other words, capitalism produces a society that can further lay the basis for an exploitation-free society. It believes that capitalism lays the foundations for socialism (Brinkley, 1998:151). But it will not happen on its own. The working class produced out of capitalism will have to be conscious of their class interests, will have to 'organise themselves as a revolutionary force and seize power from the capitalists,' and transit the society from an exploitative to a non-exploitative society (D'Mellow, 2010:58).

Marx had predicted both the course and the components of the revolution. He argued that the proletarian revolution would take shape in a 'highly industrial society,' as only in such a society would the class differences sharpen to this effect. In an industrially advanced society, the organised working class have class consciousness of their rights because they work for the revolution. However, this did not materialise in the developed and the industrialized West.

2 P. Sweezy (2010) in 'What is Marxism and other Essays' argues that Marxism does not hanker for loss of primitive communism but the fact that "civilization was impossible without exploitation."

Capitalism did not generate the kind of class contradictions and revolutionary class consciousness that Marx had thought of and predicted. Apologists, however, continue to argue that Marx was not wrong. But this is nothing but playing with words of semantics. Actually, the dynamics of society did not playout as was predicted by Marx. The capacity of capitalism and the relative gains emanating from the flow of the capital and resources from the third world to the developed capitalist economies made the class contradictions blunt and dull in these societies. The working class in 'more developed capitalist countries were able to make enough gains by struggle within the system (Sweezy, 2010:59). Developed Europe, therefore, could not be fertile soil for revolution. Revolutions instead took place in industrially weak and agricultural societies where 'proletariat class' was yet to emerge as a distinct class in itself. It is worth to note that when the revolution took place in China, the entire working-class strength in the country was between 25 and 30 lakhs, even less than in India. Revolution necessarily was not a class revolution at all. It was rather led by the 'organised revolutionary parties' which drew cadres from different segments of the society (Sweezy, 2010:60).The same can be said about the Russian Revolution, which generally is depicted as the 'socialist revolution.' Was the Bolshevik Revolution of 1917 in Russia indeed a socialist revolution? While the predominant commentaries on the revolution consider it a socialist one, there were many who had raised the question, "Was it possible to have a socialist revolution in Russia?" (Graziosi, 2019:13). It was Lenin who made it so. There were many within the Bolsheviks who did not agree with that (Graziosi, 2019:13). It also was not a proletariat class revolution at all. The true nature of the movement could not come because of the 'iron curtain' that continued for decades, but in the post-Soviet era, a powerful argument has emerged that suggests that the so-called socialist revolution was in reality 'capitalized upon the tyranny of the Tsar rule,' which was disliked by the majority of people in the country (Billington, 1966:468). Many considered it, therefore, the beginning of the 'rebirth of the Russian nation' (Graziosi, 2019:16). And, thus, it would be wrong to call that a proletarian revolution. At the time when Russia witnessed the revolution, the society was not ripe for revolution at all in true Marxist terms. There was no advanced industrial capitalism in Russia, nor was there a powerful industrial working class, which Marx had envisaged to lead the revolution. Russian society again was a relatively peasant society, and Russia heavily depended on industrial goods imports from Europe (Imperial War Museum).

Mao took a cue from the Russian society. While the protagonists of the Russian Revolution were busy justifying the revolution as a socialist one and describing the society as industrially ripe enough for the revolution, Mao deviated from the classical Marxists on several counts, including who will lead the revolution. He assessed the situation on the ground and saw hope in peasants and the poor to lead the movement. First, he argued that the state would be needed even in communism.[3] Second, it is not the industrial worker who would lead the revolution, but this role would be discharged by the peasants, workers and intellectual class, in which peasantry would play the most important role[4] (Surjeet, 2000). Mao's assumption was based on his clear thinking on revolution. He knew that China was not an industrially developed country. The workers in the organised sector were not sufficiently numerous and conscious enough to lead the revolution. There could be two situations from there: either to wait for the situation to ripen as per Marx or to apply Marx in the new context of China. Mao chose the second option.

Mao made it clear that China had no problem in learning from the experiences of other countries, capitalist or socialist, but it was not prudent to copy and imitate anything blindly from anywhere, including Russia. We must, he argued, judge the merit of things by whether they are suited to our conditions or not, and only then should they be adopted when it is sure that they suit our conditions. Mao wrote, "Now there are two different attitudes towards learning from others. One is the dogmatic attitude of transplanting everything, whether or not it is suited to our conditions. This is not good. The other attitude is to use our heads and learn those things that suit our conditions, that is, to absorb whatever experience is useful to us. That is the attitude that we should adopt" (Zedong, 1957). Mao made it clear that if the "Chinese communists talk about Marxism apart from Chinese characteristics, that will be only Marxism in the abstract, Marxism in the void" (Zedong, 1965:195–210; Mitra & Sen, 1971:34).

Mao applied this in the case of China, indeed. He did not follow the conventional Marxist wisdom on scores of crucial issues, from leading the proletarian revolution to managing the post-revolutionary society. The experience of blindly following the basics of the Third International was there before him. It had not worked on the chartered line, which signified that there was no harm in working on socialism without being blind. The Third International, held in 1923, premised that the communists everywhere in the colonial or semi-colonial countries should support the national bourgeoisie in its struggle for independence from the colonial power. Its background was very interesting.

3 Mao argued that state would be needed even after revolution. He used the state to crush not just the elements of capitalism but also the members of the communist party which opposed him.

4 Maoist organisations in India have invoked it as a key ideological reference point underpinning their articulation of class struggle.

It was the comrades from the third world countries who opposed the idea of communists supporting the national movements in their home turf.

In the Second Congress of the Communist International, Lenin had prepared a preliminary draft on national and colonial questions in backward states and nations. Lenin had proposed in the draft that 'all the communist parties must assist the bourgeois-democratic liberation movement in these countries' (Lenin, 1920). The draft also held that the communist parties would 'fight the bourgeois-democratic movements within their own nations' after the independence (Lenin, 1957:254–55) M.N. Roy had objected to this thesis on the ground that the rise of national consciousness in these countries would weaken the rise of 'class consciousness in the masses' (Maitra, 1976:499–504) and would effectively replace the foreign imperialism with native capitalism. In other words, class consciousness was inversely proportional to national consciousness. He was not in favor of allowing the leadership of the liberation movement to slip into the 'hands of the bourgeois democrats' (Roy, 1987). Lenin did not overlook Roy's objection completely. The final draft, which was approved at the end, replaced the term 'bourgeois democratic revolution' with 'national revolutionary movement' (Lenin, 1957:265–66). It was argued that the communists would be supporting the national movement only when the movement was really revolutionary, and the exponents of the national movement do not obstruct the communists in their program of educating the masses along revolutionary lines (Lenin, 1957:265–66).

The Chinese Communist Party worked on the premise that the Bourgeoisie Democratic Revolution should precede the socialist revolution in the third world countries (Zedong). The international had argued that the feudal class in the society is in alliance with the 'foreign imperialists' power. And therefore, in order to throw off the imperialists/foreign power, there was no harm in supporting the Nationalist Bourgeoisie revolution. In China, after Sun Yat-Sen, communists supported Chiang Kai-Shek on the same ground. But this resulted in the massive defeat of the Communist Party in 1927, and the Nationalist Bourgeoisie proved to be the ally of the imperialists rather than fighting against the same. Thus, the line adopted in the Third Communist International worked adversely to the Communist Party. This was a great experience, which proved that the Communist International was not always right in its assessment of situations in different socio-economic and class settings.

Mao used this experience to apply Marxism in new ways and introduced several such principles and interpretations that were so far unknown to the dictionary of Marxism. One important aspect of his understanding of Marxism was the 'protracted people's war' in the form of armed struggle in the semi-colonial and colonial countries. Thus, no to parliamentary politics and elections, guerrilla war and armed struggle to annihilate the class enemy, and use of remote rural poor areas as social bases to build on and develop revolutionary consciousness became the core of Maoism.

1 Maoist Movement in India

The Maoist movement in India claims to draw its inspiration broadly from the Chinese experiment. It considers the Indian state to be yet a semi-colonial, semi-feudal, bourgeois state that collaborates with foreign capital and works for the capitalists' interests in India (CPI Resolution). The Indian state is, therefore, not a free state. The political freedom of the country thus is a bogus premise, as it is just formal or notional. The big bourgeoisie have allied with the imperialists who have penetrated deep into the system, and the emancipation of the proletarian class lies in the revolution manifesting through 'protracted armed struggle' before the final assault against the Indian state. The parliamentary path is not the panacea to the evils that pervade society, and the real solution lies essentially in overthrowing the present ruling class.

It is important to note that the violent revolution to such effect first started in India in 1946 in Telangana, a region in Andhra Pradesh. The movement, however, was called off in 1951 by the Communist Party of India as a result of a compromise that arrived between the CPI and the government. This is broadly now acknowledged as a truce that was reached between the communists and the government of India at the directives of the Soviet government (Katrak, 1961:138–39). The historic compromise reached by the party was not liked by a section within, which considered it as an 'accommodation with the interests of the bourgeoisie' due to 'weak and ineffective leadership' coming from the middle class (D'Mellow, 2010:05; Katrak, 1961:138). The radical elements within the left held that the CPI was not toeing the true revolutionary line, and the working-class movement was compromised by resorting to the parliamentary path.

This finally culminated in the division of the Communist Party of India and the formation of a new party with a new suffix, Communist Party of India (Marxist), in 1964. It claimed that the parent communist organisation was not moving in the right direction and was tinkering with the revolutionary movement. Therefore, splitting away from the parent organisation and the formation of a non-revisionist party of proletariats was essential. The new party declared the CPI as the revisionist and reactionary and vowed to revive and take the revolutionary struggle to a new level further. It needs to be taken into account that revisionism is an abuse in the Marxian Lexicon. Bernstein in Germany was the first to use it (Fletcher, 1982:339). While ideological position was declared to be the reason behind the division and divide, it is broadly now a settled question that it was actually a divide between the Chinese and Soviet camps within the communist party in India, which resulted from a stand on border disputes between India and China, which divided the party into pro-nationalist and pro-China. The faction under the leadership of S.A. Dange demanded a clear patriotic stand on the issue because Dange understood that the absence of it will open a pathway for disaster for the communist movement in India. However, the pro-Chinese faction within the party not just refused to do so but criticised Nehru of mishandling the border dispute (Katrak, 1961:139). Charu Mazumdar, way back in 1962, had declared that the Indian government had attacked China (Datta, 1974:420). He snatched down the photograph of Comrade Dange hanging on the wall and broke it on the surface, calling him a traitor (Marxist.org). Though he quickly said that it is not he who alone was revisionist, and it is essential to hate the revisionist in order to be revolutionary.

But instead of carrying out a revolutionary struggle for the working class and mobilising the toiling masses, the party entered into parliamentary politics and formed the government after winning the legislative election in West Bengal in 1967. The joining of the parliamentary politics and the formation of the government were defended on the grounds that they were a part of the larger objectives in mind and a mere strategic move. The new party defended that it was intended to be strengthening the democratic forces and accelerating the pace of class struggle. It held that the big bourgeoisie collaborates with imperialism for capitalist development but also fights imperialism in order to expand its own economic gains, and therefore it has a dual character. Therefore, the 'revolution should be directed against the big bourgeoisie, landlordism and imperialism through both the parliamentary and extra-parliamentary struggles'[5] (Bose, 2010:13; Mukherji, 1983:41–42).

However, the radicals within the party did not like it, and they articulated their vent without hesitation. Charu Mazumdar, in one of the eight documents which are attributed to vented this anguish, wherein he termed the CPM government revisionary (Sen et al., 1978:177). He found that the cabinet and the polit bureau of the CPM, instead of intensifying the class struggle was more interested in defending and pleading in favour of non-Congress governments in the state (Sen et al., 1978:177).

5 It was the CPI (ML) Central Committee which identified Satyanarayan Sinha to contest election after success of Janta Party in 1977.

In 1967 itself, a violent peasant revolt appeared at a place called Naxalbari in the Darjeeling district in West Bengal. This was supported by the radical group within the CPI (M). In order to quell the uprisings, which were fuelled and fired from within, the newly formed communist government used the repressive measures, which resulted into revolt in the rank and file of the CPM. The radical group led by Charu Majumdar, Kanu Sanyal and Jangal Santhal openly condemned the left government not just for the brutal use of force against the peasants and toiling people, but also for resorting to revisionist pretexts behind the use of force[6] (Charu, 1967:81–82). And finally, it culminated into split in the party and the formation of CPI (ML) in 1970.

Two factors contributed further to this split in the communist movement in India. First, there was the Chinese factor, and second, there were the ongoing ideological debates within the party. Both these factors were not disjoint but complemented each other in certain ways. It is worth to note that China in the initial years toed the Soviet line in all respects. It was not without reason. Initially, in the post-revolution period, Western countries were not ready to accept the legitimacy of the revolution and recognise China as an independent nation-state. The Soviet Union's support at that juncture was essential. For security reasons as well as for economic assistance, China was dependent on Russia. It is said that the first five-year plan was charted out in China under the Soviet guidance, from drafting to know how to execute it.

But as soon as China recovered from initial troubles, it started asserting itself, especially after de-Stalinization of Russia, which by 60s reached a new level. China started projecting itself as the true torchbearer of Marxism-Leninism. Peking started projecting itself as a new source of ideology and power in the communist movement (Katrak, 1961:139). The Chinese Communist Party started depicting Khrushchev's policy towards the US as surrendering to the imperialist forces (The Proletarian Revolution and Khrushchev's Revisionism, 1964). Though such positioning was always wrapped in ideological concerns but primary reason was how to control the leadership of the communist movement, as also to develop the proximity with the third world countries in search for new allies and market for products. China intelligently started encouraging the most radical factors in the communist parties of the third world, including India. It was in this context that the radicals and ultra-left elements got patronage from the Chinese Communist Party. China not just extended moral support but also provided material support to such groups.

6 Charu Majumdar depicted the members of the Central Committee of the CPI (M) revisionist and not against imperialism and landlordism.

This is evident from the fact that when the Bengal uprisings took place in 1967, the Chinese radio and official newspapers of the communist party of China had all appreciation for it. The official paper of the Chinese Communist Party described it as a 'Peal of Spring Thunder' as it had surfaced in the spring season. It was quickly followed by a message and direction contained in 'The *People's Daily*' which wrote in its editorial on June 5, 1967, that 'armed struggle was the correct road to Indian revolution'[7] (Bose, 2010:14; Burman, 2009). It exhorted that 'the Chinese people joyfully applaud this revolution' and it is of tremendous importance for Indians' people's revolutionary struggle (Singh, 1995:08).

It was reciprocated by the radical elements who declared openly that 'Chinese chairman was their chairman' and joined the chorus with the Chinese Communist Party (CCP) in denunciation of the Soviet Communist Party, depicting the latter as 'the epicentre and epitome of revisionism'. This element was also the one that, during the Chinese war with India in 1962, had squarely blamed the Indian government and saw the Chinese advance into India as a part of the fulfilment of long cherished dream of the march of international communism. Even though there was not a slightest trace of anything about communism and working-class revolution in such advancement, a purely nationalistic and hegemonic attempt guided by the spirit of territorial expansionism was supported by the ultra-radicals within the left in India. The left parties in India still blame Nehru for initiating hostility towards China.

The second aspect, of course, was related to the core ideological issues, which were no less important. The radical faction also visualised that the Chinese line, which entailed creating a base centre and therefrom launching a 'protracted people's war' involving armed struggle against the state, was the right course of revolution in India, as it was successful in China. Though the CPI (ML) added the suffix of Marxism-Leninism to represent its distinct identity, it was actually Marxism-Leninism-Maoism, especially Maoism. It argued that Maoism was the 'third stage of Marxism', Leninism being the second (Biswas, 2005). The Revolutionary International Movement (RIM) documents

7 Recent studies challenge the widely circulated understanding of the Naxalbari movement as a spontaneous peasant uprising rooted in agrarian class antagonism. Instead, the evidence suggests that the initial Mobilisation had a significant "outsider" character. The first confrontation reportedly involved a Rajvanshi jotedar and a Santhal individual, and on the following day, those who attacked the police with bows and arrows were predominantly Santhals who had migrated from the Chhotanagpur region of the Santhal Pargana in Bihar. Moreover, the Rajvanshi jotedars involved in these early conflicts did not conform to the traditional definition of jotedars, further complicating the conventional agrarian-class narrative associated with the movement.

of 1993 make the point clearer. It says, "Today, without Maoism, there can be no Marxism-Leninism. Indeed, to negate Maoism is to negate Marxism-Leninism itself" (Communist Party of Italy (Maoist), 2023; Rastgar, 2016). They claim to 'uphold and apply' Marxism-Leninism, but to them Marxism-Leninism of the present era is actually Maoism.

Marxism-Leninism-Maoism is not just a terminological change, they claim, but it signifies an 'ideological stage'. For them, Maoism signified the highest stage of development for the proletariat ideology and considered it to be China-specific.[8] It has a universal character as far as its application is concerned. Charu Majumdar thus wrote in the famous pamphlet 'Parties Call to Youths and Students' "... when we have got the brilliant Thought of Chairman Mao Tse-tung, the highest stage of the development of Marxism-Leninism, to guide us, it is imperative for us to judge everything anew in the light of Mao Tse-tung thought and build a completely new road along which to press ahead. We must resolutely reject the filthy path of the bourgeoisie—the path of capitulationism and uphold resolutely the path of the spirited workers and peasants—the path of revolution" (Mazumdar, 1969). Mazumdar called upon the educated youths to read, imbibe and integrate with the revolutionary thought of Chairman Mao because that alone is the path to revolution and emancipation from capitalist and imperialist exploitation (Mazumdar, 1969).

Naxalites argued that Maoism is a product of years of experiment with revolutionary practice, as it has evolved against as well as through struggle against all kinds of opportunism and revisionism which cropped up in the revolutionary ideology from time to time. The theory of New Democratic Revolution, People's War, the concept of bureaucratic capitalism, the mass line, the development of the party concept, and the idea of United Front theory, to name a few, are the product of the evolutionary growth of the ideology and out-of-the-box thinking resulting from struggle and experiences in revolutionary battle against the class enemies. Thus, Naxals rejected the very premise of Mao, who advocated applying theory keeping in mind the specificity of the context. Interestingly, while the Naxals condemned those who followed the Russian line, they eulogised being followers of the ideological line of Mao without changes. And the defence produced was that Maoism, though, was China-specific (Zedong, 1965:178), but it appears to be applicable to all, including India. How it is has no concrete answer except the citation of revolutionary practices and successes of the Peruvian Communist Party (PCP). The implied meaning of all that was that the deviation from this position,

8 The seventh Congress of Communist Party of China held that Maoism was specific to China.

i.e., Marxism-Leninism, was actually Maoism, which would mean weakening the revolutionary movement (Mazumdar, 1968:10).

The constitution of the CPI (ML) stated: "The Communist Party of India (ML) is the political party of the proletariat of India. The CPI (ML) takes Marxism-Leninism-Mao's thought as its theoretical basis, guiding its thinking. The CPI (ML) believes Mao Tse-Tung's thought is the Marxism-Leninism of our era in which imperialism is heading for a total collapse and socialism is advancing to worldwide victory." The constitution made it very clear what its inspirational point was and what it sought to achieve, as well as what it perceived of and about the Soviet line. The constitution noted further:

– "The basic programme of the CPI (M-L) is the complete overthrow of the rule of the bureaucratic bourgeoisie and the big feudal landlord classes, the agents and lackeys of US imperialism and Soviet social imperialism, and the establishment of the People's Democratic Dictatorship led by the proletariat in place of the dictatorship of the bureaucratic comprador bourgeoisie and the feudal landlord classes. The ultimate aim of the party is the realisation of socialism and communism.
– To overthrow the rule of the above enemies of the people, CPI (M-L) places the path of armed struggle before the Indian people. It rejects the parliamentary path for the whole of the strategic period" (CPI (M-L), 1970).

After the Naxalbari movement, Charu Mazumdar made four important directions and messages to the cadres. First, opposition to revisionism. Second, initiation of the class struggle. Third, Lokyudh (people's war) is important, and the peasants and the poor landless farmers would be the baseline from which the protracted guerrilla war should be waged. It is not true that the guerrilla war is possible only in the forest and hill areas, but also even on plains. Wherever the peasants are, the guerrilla war can be started (Mazumdar, 1981:190–94).

CPI (ML) took on all the Communist parties which resorted to the parliamentary path and justified all actions, including violent repression, against such trends which could possibly weaken the revolutionary movement. Thus, while the moderate left parties all across the world were questioning the prudence of the Cultural Revolution in China, which was broadly dubbed to be the repressive design against the opponents, CPI (ML) in India depicted it as a 'great leap forward' and a 'third great milestone' in the world revolutionary movement (Communist Party of Italy (Maoist), 2023). The party blamed the mainstream left for betraying the movement.

The CPI (ML) exhorted the cadre that the Telangana Movement, which coincided with the time when Mao was leading towards a decisive victory against the reactionary forces, was withdrawn by the reactionary renegade who masqueraded as a communist but whose real intentions were to enter into parliamentary politics. In the same breath, it accused the Soviet Communist Party of being revisionist and renegade in the post-Stalin era when Khrushchev extended the hands of friendship towards the US. The radical left in India described Khrushchev's alliance with the US as surrendering before the imperialist power. They found that it was a betrayal sort of as they saw the world imperialism rapidly coming to collapse (CPI (M-L), 1970). The Chinese revolution, it noted, has shown the people of the colonial world how they should advance their revolution to victory. And there was no option but to prepare for an armed struggle as Mao did in China (CPI (M-L), 1970).

It held that the parliamentary road adopted by the left parties was not in consonance with the ideology and spirit of Marxism-Leninism, particularly when the Cultural Revolution had been successful in China, and world imperialism's collapse seems to be a certainty that it had never before. The pamphlet of the Naxalites thus wrote: "It has become the main task of the Marxist-Leninists in the world over to establish bases in rural areas and to build up, on a firm foundation, the unity of workers, peasants and all other toiling people through armed struggle" (CPI (M-L), 1970).

The ideological debates thus certainly shaped the communist movement at home as they did elsewhere. Such debates have, in fact, been the core of the communist movement in which ideological and intellectual trainings moved along with proportionate activism. Marx and Engels did it during their time, and so did Lenin till the debates "degenerated into factional politics within the party and friction started glaring right into the eyes of the movement."[9] (Nash, 1990:19–32). Though the communist movement had started witnessing some trends towards shunning ideological debates from Third International itself, it fructified only after the 10th Congress of the Russian Communist Party when Lenin moved the proposal to ban the internal criticism of the party[10] (Brinkley, 1998:162).

Though Lenin had done this to save the party against too much factionalism and internal conflicts, this became the new mantra for all the leaders to invoke in the name of party discipline, which virtually converted the party forum into a monolithic feudal structure. And any voice of protest, even if correct, was silenced by depicting the person as anti-revolutionary or as one supporting the anti-revolutionary forces. Stalin did it in Russia; so was the case with Mao during the Cultural Revolution in China, where several close associates of the party who had been working for the ideology, organisation, and the movement

9 Some of the critics of Lenin has argued that Leninism is inherently undemocratic.

10 Richard Pipes' much acclaimed book 'Unknown Lenin' based on archival sources note that Lenin used force to create terror in minds of the political opponents in the party.

were met with death by declaring them revisionists and renegade[11] (Mitra & Sen, 1971:118). These ideological debates thus did not move further, particularly in the countries where communist parties came into power. On the contrary, the ruling party became the custodian of power and expected everyone to toe the line of the government, even if they were not correct.

The situations, however, took altogether a different turn in the countries where Communist parties could not occupy the seat of political power. There, the ideological debates remained very pronounced, and this has been one of the reasons behind splits after splits in the communist movement in such countries. India falls in the same category. The more radicals have always accused the lesser ones of being revisionist and renegade. And with these also emerged serious differences on a host of issues pertaining to ideology. CPI (ML) contested both the CPI and CPI (M) on issues like the identification of principle contradictions that exist in the society on the road to socialism.

Actually, there are three important factors to understand the communist movement. That applies as much to India as elsewhere. First, identifying the composition and characterisation of class and the state; second, identifying the principal contradictions that exist in society; and third, the road to change or revolution. In brief, what comprises the proletariat class and the bourgeois class as such? And how to proceed for change, and who should be taken as an ally in the course of achieving the goal of change. And thirdly, whether the parliamentary path would lead to realisation of socialistic goals at the end or not.

An objective appraisal of the class forces and their alignment before taking any political action is very essential. This appraisal is important to know the strengths and weaknesses of the forces which compose the proletarian class and also the forces which compose the bourgeoisie. If the relative strength is not known, and that too on an objective assessment basis, the proletariat may take political decisions which may be counterproductive. Since in the Marxian lexicon the state is governed by the dominant class, the class composition also tells us about the nature of the state in existence. The nature of the revolution and the allies in the revolution and against whom the revolution is to be directed all depend on the assessment of the class structure.

Though all the shades of Marxism claim to be applying Marxist methodology in understanding the class composition and the nature of the states in

11 It needs to be noted that Cultural revolution had turned out to be against the degeneration in the revolutionary mission and fervour but it was converted into a kind of repression by Mao to establish his dominance which led to killings of millions. CPI had also criticised the cultural revolution in China. It depicted this as Military Bureaucracy Dictatorship against the Dictatorship of Proletariat.

work, but they fail to arrive at a consensus. This exposes their claim of objectivity on the one hand and splits them into several shades on the other. The second important aspect has been the use of violence in revolution. There is one section which finds that violence is not essential. The application of violence depends on the situation. Marxism does not ignore revolution, but at the same time it does not essentialize it[12] (Schaff, 1973: 268–70). That means being revolutionary does not mean being always violent or subscribing to violence. It depends on expediency. It is argued that even Lenin interpreted Marxism in this sense only (Bose, 2010:12). The third issue has been participation in the democratic process of the capitalist variant, such as participation in the parliamentary elections or not. Again, there is not a definite voice on it. When a section of the Russian communists argued for it, they were abused and humiliated with the depiction as revisionists. The famous Kautsky-Lenin debate is known to all. Kautsky was declared revisionists for articulating moderate Marxism[13] (Rogers, 2015).

It would be relevant to note that the post-independence interpretation of the Indian state and the existing class structure in India has been a subject of debates, and different political formations within the communist movement in India have approached the issue differently and have also arrived at differing conclusions. Whether the bourgeoisie of all categories should be treated as one and the same and whether the revolution should be directed against all or some of them strategically be made allies against the others have been contested questions. Different communist parties take different lines on the issue. And this has made a great deal of difference in the adoption of the path to socialism.

The Communist Party of India (CPI) thus held that the Indian state was led by the 'Nationalist Bourgeoisie', which was not only anti-imperialist but also anti-feudal to some extent (Mishra, 1993). This characterisation was based on some of the steps that were taken by the Indian government after partition. Such steps included pursuing an independent foreign policy, opposing colonialism of any variant and the policy initiatives by the government, such as land reforms, land-ceiling acts, etc. These were treated as anti-imperialist stands and policy measures by the CPI, and therefore, it did not subscribe to

12 Though the Communist Manifesto clearly declares that their ends can be attained only through forcible overthrow of all existing social relations but both Marx and Lenin have argued in favour of peaceful revolution also.

13 Eduard Bernstein was a Marxist theoretician who also happened to be the colleague of Engels and Kautsky. Bernstein in January 1898 had made a statement in NEUE ZEIT that the final goal of socialism was movement.

the idea of formal independence. The way India recognised China and signed the treaty on Tibet was considered an independent decision, and in no way did it reflect the government being a puppet in the hands of the Western powers. The Communist Party of India held that the progressive efforts of the state led by the nationalist bourgeoisie, therefore, needed to be strengthened. In sum, the communists should support what came to be better described as 'Nehruvian Socialism'.

A section within the party, however, found it a deviation from the revolutionary path, which alone should define the communist movement. This section describes this stand of the party's 'revisionism and collaborationists.' The debate also intensified in 1962 when India went to war with China. The more radical section within the communist party supported the Chinese adventurism in the hope that the march of China into India would mark the expansion of the International Communist movement. Such elements encapsulated the most infamous slogan, 'Chinese Chairman is our Chairman, and the Chinese path is our path.' The moderate communists, however, adhered to the nationalist line and supported the nationalist bourgeois stand on the war vis-à-vis China.

The debate within the party culminated in the split of the Communist Party of India. The new formation, which came up in 1964, named itself 'The Communist Party of India (Marxist)' and took a different stand on the characterisation of the Indian state. It projected itself as more revolutionary and a truer adherer of Marxism, as is evident from the nomenclature too. It characterised the Indian state as a 'bourgeois-landlord state led by big bourgeois' (read as big capitalists) who were 'hand in glove with the imperialist powers for the capitalist growth' in India (CPI (M), 2019). This big bourgeois wanted to expand its own economic interests in the new politico-economic setup and, therefore, was supportive of the Indian state also. The new party, therefore, took on the Congress.

However, it also resorted to the parliamentary line. The revolutionary path for the party was not resorting to armed struggle but building a larger democratic front of 'workers, peasants and other toiling sections of the society'. Their grand alliance and their mobilisation, they visualised, would be able to capture the power. It was fine-tuning the ideology to suit the programmes rather than the ideology guiding the programmes. It sought the revolution, which it called the 'Democratic Revolution', aimed against the 'big bourgeois, landlords and imperialist forces' through both the parliamentary and extra-parliamentary processes (Bose, 2010:12).

Such an interpretation of the Indian state and charting out a parliamentary path to socialism was not accepted by the radical or ultra-left elements, for which the Maoist line was the true line for revolutionaries. This group, which, after breaking away from CPI (M), formed CPI (ML) and completely rejected the parliamentary path. It openly stood for the Chinese path for revolution and supported the Cultural Revolution drives of Mao in China, which, to them, intended to get rid of the bourgeois rot that had entered into the communist structure, causing great damage to the socialist cause.

In fact, the radicals within the CPI (ML) saw China as the base centre of the International Communist Movement, and Mao was eulogised as the one who was destined to fulfil the long-cherished historical mission of achieving socialism. It exhorted that the worldwide collapse of imperialist and capitalist forces was imminent, and the trends were telling facts in themselves (Bose, 2010:14–15). The document maintained that the revolution envisaged by the party is 'a part of the great proletarian cultural revolution.'[14] Undoubtedly, CPI (ML) banked blindly on the Chinese guidance and the Chinese line on revolution. CPI (M) reacted to this new formation by calling it a sectarian left trying to imitate Chinese know-how without thinking of the specificity of the cultural, political, social and economic conditions of India. CPI (ML) did not adhere to Mao, who made it clear that China was not Russia and therefore, the revolution in China would take its own course; it would be different from Russia.

CPI (ML) described Indian independence as 'formal independence' or nominal independence. It considers the Indian state as a 'neo-colonial state' in which there is a regime which serves the imperialists and feudal elements. It did not see a big difference between the native big bourgeoisie and the comprador bourgeoisie. To them, the native big bourgeoisie is also a comprador bourgeoisie, which acts as a puppet in the hands of US imperialism. This inference was certainly imported from Chinese interpretations of their native big bourgeoisie, where Mao depicted them as the comprador bourgeoisie. Comprador bourgeois, according to Mao, are those who directly serve the imperialist forces and are nurtured by them (Zedong, 1965:289, 320–21). These bourgeois might be native in origin, but they served the imperialist powers in the semi-colonial, backward society of China.

Mao differentiated the 'nationalist bourgeoisie' from the comprador. The nationalist bourgeoisie also promoted capitalism, but it worked more for the development of indigenous capitalism. While the comprador bourgeois benefited from exporting the raw material to the imperialist forces and selling the imported finished products, the nationalist bourgeois benefited primarily

14 The Cultural Revolution in China started in 1967 and it aimed against the bureaucratic bourgeoisie. It was condemned even by the communists because it killed millions. The revolution ended with the death of Mao.

from the surplus value accruing from wage labour. The target of the Chinese revolution was not the nationalist bourgeois but the comprador bourgeois.

This understanding of the Indian left and capitalist development in India has been rejected by the mainstream Communist parties, especially the CPM. The famous ideological debate summed up in June 1968 makes it amply clear. It alleges that the radical comrades did not make a fair assessment of the Indian bourgeoisie. In fact, there was always an existence of the comprador big bourgeoisie and the industrial nationalist bourgeoisie. The nationalist bourgeoisie not only came closer to the leaders of the national movement but also played a crucial role in it. After the Second World War, it came so much more strongly. And in post-independent India, they played a crucial role in building native capitalism without serving as a puppet of the foreign imperialist power. Even the big bourgeois, which earlier served the interests of foreign capital prior to independence, have changed a lot for the positive in the last six decades, and now they can best be placed in the industrial bourgeois category. Therefore, the implantation of a six-decade-old analogy to prove the point at the moment would not just be incorrect but also harmful to the left ideology and the communist movement as a whole.

CPM holds that the foreign collaboration of the Indian big bourgeoisie cannot and should not be equated with the comprador collaboration with foreign imperialists (Reddy, 1993:389–91). The big industrial bourgeois, though, collaborate with the foreign capitalists, but their interests are conflicting as well. They want the state to apply protectionist measures in order to protect the native industries against the dumping of goods from foreign companies. Thus, they see their interests as different from the interests of the foreign imperialists. Of course, they too have profits in mind, and they too want the growth of capitalism at home, but their role is entirely different from that of the comprador business bourgeois. The comprador bourgeois completely depends on the foreign capitalists and is subservient to the latter, which is not true in the case of the big industrial Indian bourgeois. The Indian industrial bourgeois is not just a salesman selling the products of the foreign imperialists or a trader who acts as a commission agent selling goods of the foreign imperialists in the domestic market (Grewal, 2010:25–26,37–38).

There is also a problem in drawing an analogy with the Chinese class structure existing in the pre-revolution era. While China had relatively slower economic development and was primarily an underdeveloped economy prior to the revolution, India's economy, even then, was growing at a relatively faster pace than China. Even the Communist International recognised it; Stalin articulated this idea way back in 1925 while addressing the students at the University of the Peoples of the East. He argued that putting all the colonies in one category was not correct.

There has also been contestation to the point that the Indian state has been a neo-colonial state, and the government, which is in power, is actually a puppet regime in the hands of the US. The CPI (ML) holds the position that the state is already neocolonial. Whereas the CPI (M) holds that the country would slip into 'neo-colonial domination by the USA' if the anti-people policies of the government do not get reversed. The depiction of the Indian state as the 'neo-colonial state' is primarily based on the premise that the government of India is entering into economic collaboration with the USA and is dependent on the latter for economic aid, which results in the subordination of the foreign policies to the US dictates and the latter's will. This does not seem again to be a correct assessment of the Indian state, and the factors suggested cannot be testimony to the existence of American neo-colonialism in India.

First, it can be argued that there are several European countries, such as France and Britain, which also go with the Americans on foreign policy issues. Second, they too have entered into economic collaboration. But they cannot be called a semi-colonial state at all. So is the case with India. India has entered into economic collaboration with the USA and several other countries. But that has not deterred India from taking an independent stand on foreign policy matters. Third, there are hundreds of Indian companies which today have become multinationals in a true sense and are challenging the dominance of the American or other multinationals worldwide in different sectors and areas of the economy. Be it the case of farm subsidy, environmental issues or any other. Free trade: India has taken a stand which has been best suited to its own economic and national interests. Our position is not similar to those of the Latin American countries, wherein America actually controls the economy and thereby the political structure of the country.

The CPI (ML)'s venom against the parliamentary path has also been challenged by none other than the parliamentary left, which has accused the CPI (ML) of distorting Marxism. To the CPI (ML), bourgeois parliamentary democracy does not provide a recipe for the emancipation of the working-class people and toiling masses. And therefore, it is of no use. It has therefore been giving calls to the election boycott from time to time. Participation in an election means reinforcement of the bourgeois instruments, which they claim to be a brothel or a talking shop. They use Lenin's words to prove the point. And therefore, the CPI (ML) documents have argued against participation in the election. It is another thing that one wing of this left variant has participated in the Bihar election, though they have been opposing the same in other states of India where they have a relatively effective presence, and their call for such adventurism carries very limited weight. To them, the true road to socialism lies in rejection of the bourgeois instruments and institutions of democracy and the capture of political power for the toiling masses through violent and protracted armed struggle against the Indian state.

The CPI (ML) does not buy the argument of the Communist Parties, which do see an independent foreign policy being pursued by the Indian bourgeoisie in the post-independence era. India's immediate recognition of China as a sovereign state, the joint declaration of *Panchsheel* with China, and the Bandung conference do not enthuse the radical left at all. Land reforms and progressive policies of the state are welcomed steps, but not enough.

CPI (M) considers that the first stage of the Indian revolution was completed with the political independence of the country from foreign rule. And the imperialists' intention of making our political independence formal through entrenching deep into our economy and making us dependent has not worked so far. But the danger is not over forever. CPI (M) recognises that there has been a fast entrance of US capitalists in the economy through massive investment, but yet it is imprudent to conclude that the situation has reached a level which amounts to political independence getting reduced to formal independence (CPI Constitution). Surprisingly, the party does not condemn the entries of the Chinese state and its capital into the poor countries and the exploitation of their resources. China today has come out as a big economic and military power and uses its might to dominate the regions and interfere in the domestic politics of nation-states and seeks to create a monopoly, yet it escapes the criticism of the CPI (ML).

It is worth to note that the ultra-left organisations in the India do not take out time to see the fallacy of Maoist model and its failure in China itself to provide a 'working model of socialism in the 20th century' (D'Mellow, 2010:46). These ultra-leftists do not answer that if US imperialism was and is so allergic to them then why China during Mao time itself 'entered into accommodation with US imperialism against Soviet Union?'[15] (Mitra & Sen, 1971:119). Again, in 1974, China used the 'Three World Theory' in order to justify its right-wing nationalist foreign policy during the period of Deng Xiaoping. Thus, the anti-imperialist theory was not given as much weight as was to the nationalist policy. How does the capitalist development of China not become the point of concern and criticism in the eyes of the CPI (ML)? These are some uncomfortable questions which the Naxalites ignore to answer.

Naxals hold that there are three trends of anti-imperialism at work currently. The first set of people includes social democrats, liberals, NGOs, humanists,

15 The CPI called it Ping-Pong diplomacy between Peking and Washington. CPI had also criticised the cultural revolution in China. It depicted this as Military Bureaucracy Dictatorship against the Dictatorship of Proletariat.

green activists, etc., who oppose the exploitation of resources and people by the Multinational Companies (MNCs) in the poor countries. They oppose the capturing of resources of these countries and fight for the people's rights. These people, however, do not approve of violence. They also oppose the violence by the state but fail to make a distinction between the reactionary violence and the revolutionary violence. Their approach is closer to the Gandhian model, which is not going to serve the cause of the working class. They are indeed day-dreamers and 'intoxicants in progressive wrappings'. Social democratic forums and meetings of this kind fall in this category (The Drama Unfolds, 2003).

There are second set of people like Islamists who are fighting against the US imperialism. But these people keep religion at the centre, and they are intolerant to the other sections of society. Therefore, their anti-imperialist activities would not contribute to the working-class revolution. The third set of people are revolutionaries of Peru, Turkey, Nepal, India etc. which are engaged in true emancipation, as they claim, of the working class through armed struggle, and they alone are the true Marxists of the era and true followers of Maoism (The Drama Unfolds, 2003). It held that this third trend is the genuine revolutionary movement as they have given a hard time to the 'imperialists and reactionaries in the respective countries.' It held that the coordination of the Maoist parties in South Asia and developing a communist international is the need of the time for better learning for the experiences of each party and then chalk out a suitable line of actions.[16]

2 Splits after Splits Marks the Revolutionary Movement

A careful look at the revolutionary movements in India makes it amply clear that the movement has failed to build up and sustain itself as a concerted, cohesive entity throughout its journey. It has met split after split. And this continues to date. There are at least two dozen ultra-left groups/formations which have been working under different names and under different leaders in different states of India, and they all claim to be the true inheritor of the revolutionary legacy. Interestingly, they all accuse each other of acting as revisionists. Truly speaking, the splits have less to do with the ideological differences but more so because of leadership conflicts within the organisation and other

16 There exists a Revolutionary Internationalist Movement (RIM), as an embryonic centre of Maoist, synthesizes positive negative experience of the movements and guides the movements through debates on various questions, developing the level and coming to a common understanding.

non-ideological factors at work, including pure personal and private ones[17] (Singh, 1995:140). This has been true for all the splits that fructified after the formation of CPI (ML) in the late 60s.

The CPI (ML) was formed by the All India Co-ordination Committee of Communist revolutionaries on 22 April 1969 at a mass meeting in Calcutta. The prominent leaders of the new formation were Charu Mazumdar, Kanu Sanyal, Jangal Santhal, Saroj Datta, etc. They all were active revolutionaries of the CPI (M). It was Charu Mazumdar who had, in fact, organised the peasants' uprisings in the Naxalbari Area in West Bengal. Interestingly, though the movement declared without any hesitation to follow the Maoist strategy, the new party came up formally on Lenin's birthday. Encouraged by the Naxalbari uprisings, the party organised guerrilla units in different Indian provinces such as UP, Bihar, West Bengal, Andhra Pradesh, etc. The party declared the armed struggle as the right path to the revolution and criticised the parliamentary road to socialism (Mazumdar, 1965:25).

But before the revolutionary organisation could make any further advancement and impact, it met a split in 1971. Satyanarayan Singh revolted against the leadership of Charu Mazumdar and formed a new outfit. In 1971, when India entered into war with Pakistan, the CPI (ML) group further faced a new challenge. It is argued that while China was asking the Naxalites to support Pakistan, Charu Majumdar did not accede to it. He preferred to support the East Pakistan Communist Party (ML). As a result, the CPI (ML) faced a new split, with Ashim Chatterjee forming a new group. Charu Majumdar was killed in 1972. Later on, his group further split into anti- and pro-Lin Biao factions (Singh, 1995:94). Lin Biao was a close confidante of Mao who believed that Mao's "theory of establishment of rural revolutionary base areas and encirclement of the cities from the countryside is of outstanding and universal nature" and applicable to all the third-world countries, but this was not approved by the then Chinese Communist Party, which was assumed to disapprove of the armed struggle of Charu Mazumdar. Interestingly, both these factions had allegiance to Mazumdar. The pro-Lin Biao group came to be known as CPI (ML) Shanti Pal, also known as the Central Organising Committee (CIO), whereas

17 There is no one Maoist group today. They have split into several dozen factions and operating under different names in the country. And most of the splits are not the result of ideological but the factional or organisational politics. Often there has been personality clash and conflicts over leadership which resulted into violence within. Contests over women cadre has also been the reason behind the conflict resulting into faction formation and then subsequently breaking away from the existing organisation and formation of new ones.

the anti-Lin Biao group came to be known as CPI (ML) Liberation. The Pro-Lin Biao group was led by Mahadeb Mukherjee.

CPI (ML) Liberation came up in 1974. In 1975, Vinod Mishra was elected as its General Secretary. Liberation, though, started with a commitment to armed revolution, but subsequently it resorted to reform processes. The organisation declared in 1979 to develop mass organisations in every important aspect of the social, political and economic life of the nation. Some of the mass organisations[18] which are associated to the party are Revolutionary Youth Organisation (RYA), All India Students Association (AISA), All India Agriculture Labour Association (AIALA), All India Peasants Coordination Committee, All India Central Council of Trade Union (AICCTU), All India Progressive Women's Association (AIPWA), Autonomous State Demand Committee (ASDC) etc. Such organisations initially were not welcome in the party, but subsequently, it was initiated all this in order to reach out to different sections of society. Finally, the party thought to adopt both the parliamentary and non-parliamentary tactics to revolution. The party fought parliamentary as well as legislative assembly elections in states like Assam, Jharkhand and Bihar. 'Liberation' is the monthly publication of the CPI (ML). Apart from Liberation, the Party brings out a central Hindi weekly organ too, named "*Samkaleen Lokyuddh.*" Some state party Committees bring out their own publications, like the weekly "*Ajker Deshabrati*" in West Bengal, "*Nabasphulinga*" in Tripura, "*Teeppori*" in Tamil Nadu, "*Telugu Liberation*" in Andhra Pradesh, "*Kannada Liberation*" in Karnataka, "*Samkali Lok Morcha*" in Punjab, etc.

In the early 80s (1982), there was another revolutionary party that came up, the Indian Peoples Front, popularly known as IPF. It also resorted to both parliamentary and non-parliamentary tactics. Its base was primarily in Bihar and, to an extent, in some parts of West Bengal. Even in Bihar, it was limited to a few districts of central Bihar, such as Jehanabad, Aurangabad, Gaya and Aara. The key strategists of this organisation, both political and revolutionary, were Vinod Mishra and Nagbhushan Patnaik. The organisation tried its luck in the parliamentary politics and won the Aara constituency in the 1989 Lok Sabha Elections. In 1991, it won a seat in Assam also. IPF was dissolved in 1994. IPF was to work as an umbrella of mass organisations besides organising and directing revolutionary activities.

In 1988, two major CPI (ML) formations came up, namely CPI (ML) Red Flag and CPI (ML) New Democracy. Both these formations again were the result of further splits in the existing organisations. CPI (ML) New Democracy came up

18 The mass organisations are the organisations which would be working not directly but indirectly for the revolution, and the comrades would be indirectly linked to the party.

after the split of the CPI (ML) faction of Chandra Pulla Reddy. Yatendra Kumar was made the secretary of the party. Though the party expanded its branches in West Bengal, Bihar, Orissa, Punjab, UP, Maharashtra, Delhi, Haryana, etc., they were just notional, and its support base was confined to some parts of Andhra Pradesh. The party also maintained that it would practise both the parliamentary and non-parliamentary ways of class struggle. In order to support the parliamentary politics, it opened several fronts, such as Progressive Democratic Students Union (PDSU) and Punjab Student Union (PSU), students' unions in Punjab; the Indian Federation of Trade Unions (IFTD) for the industrial workers; and also its own labour union led by its party president of the Bengal unit, Paltu Sen. It also contested assembly elections in states like Andhra Pradesh and Bihar, in which it succeeded with a single seat in each. Gummadi Narsaiah has been winning the Yellandu Constituency seats for the last five consecutive terms. However, in recent years, there has been more radicalisation of the party as it has been focusing more on guerrilla warfare.

CPI (ML) Red Flag was formed in 1988 by a section of revolutionary Marxists who broke away from the Central Reorganisation Committee of the CPI (ML). Arup Majumdar was made the Secretary of the Party. Its main support base was in Kerala, though it had also branched into Karnataka, Madhya Pradesh, Maharashtra, Chhattisgarh, West Bengal and Orissa. The party head office was located in Delhi. But this party also could not sustain itself. In 2003, the majority of the members of CPI (ML) RF under the leadership of state secretary of the party P.C. Unnichekkan and M.S. Jayakumar broke away from the party. They declared themselves as the real CPI (ML) Red Flag. The organisation started several mass organisations such as the Trade Union Centre of India (TUCI), *Yuva Janwadi, Kerala Vidyarthi Sanghatana, Janakeeya Kala Sahitya Vedi* (JKSV), and *Adivasi* Democratic Front in Madhya Pradesh. The party, though, claimed to be pursuing both the parliamentary and extra-parliamentary paths, but its activities got limited to electoral activities. In 2004, it created a joint front with other revolutionary parties such as CCR (West Bengal), MCPI, New Socialist Movement, Bhagat Singh Vichar Manch, etc., working primarily at the local or provincial level to fight parliamentary elections, but it did not bring any success to them. The party finally merged with CPI (ML) of the Kanu Sanyal faction in VIjayvada in January 2005.

In 1992, another revolutionary party came up with the same Marxist-Leninist tag with a new suffix, *Janshakti*. CPI (ML) *Janshakti* resulted from the merger of seven small factional revolutionary groups working in different provinces. The groups were CPI (ML) Resistance, CPI (ML) *AgamiYug*, CPI (ML) P.V. Rao, a faction that came up after the split of the New Democracy group, CPI (ML) Khokan Majumdar, Unity Centre of Communist Revolutionaries of India (ML)

Muktigami faction, Communist Revolutionary Group for Unity and All India Coordination Committee of Communist Revolutionaries. Chandrafulla Reddy and T.N. Reddy, two veterans of the Telangana movement, were the minds behind this outfit. The organisation also developed the mass organisations like the All India Federation of Trade Unions (AIFTD). The party vowed to work both on parliamentary and non-parliamentary lines.

The party primarily is effective only in Andhra Pradesh, where it also won the Sirsilla assembly seat in 1994. Here also, the party does not have much of a base. It is estimated that the party has 200–300 armed cadres. Its strength again suffered in 1996 when a faction broke away and formed CPI (ML) Unity Initiative, which later on merged into the CPI (ML) faction of Kanu Sanyal. The party met several splits primarily on factional lines and not on principles. The groups which emerged from it are the Communist Party of the United States of India (*Janshakti Veerana* Faction), CPI (ML) *Janshakti*, Chandra Pulla Reddy faction, and CPI (ML) *Koora Ranjana* faction. The main group, however, is the one which is led by Koora Ranjana. The party has now preferred the armed struggle, *through Dalams*, but the problem is that it is no more left with the effective strength of cadres. And that has seriously dented its revolutionary missions.

Apart from the CPI (ML) brand, there are a minimum of at least two dozen more revolutionary groups having different names and working in different states of the country. What emerges from the multiplicity of organisations is the fact that revolutionary organisations came up not just at the national or provincial level but also at the local level, primarily with the objective in mind to find the local atrocities or injustices meted out to the poor and deprived section of society. But the majority of them have been a result of factional power tussles within the organisation. This makes one conclude that the so-called revolutionaries are not as bothered about the declared noble cause of revolution as they are for their dominance within the organisation.

The present Maoist movement further strengthened after the merger of three important revolutionary organisations on September 21, 2004. The organisations that merged were CPI (ML), People's War Group (PWG) and the Maoist Communist Centre (MCC). These three organisations, though, had interstate networks, but they were primarily effective in one or at most two provinces. For example, while the People's War Group (PWG) was very effective in Andhra Pradesh, MCC was effective in Central Bihar. None of them had an all-India network at all.

The People's War Group came up on 22 April 1980 in Andhra Pradesh. Its founder, Kondapalli Seetharamaiah, one of the important leaders of the CPI (ML) and a member of the Central Organizing Committee, broke away from the party to lay the foundation of PWG. The group activity started in Karimnagar district in Northern Telangana, which subsequently spread out to other parts of the state as well as outside the state. Before its merger with other ML groups to form CPI (Maoist), the organisation had its branches in states like Bihar, Jharkhand, Madhya Pradesh, Chhattisgarh, etc.[19] However, it emerged as the most powerful group in the state of Andhra Pradesh.[20] PWG subscribed Maoist strategy of 'Organised peasant resurrection', a capturing of state power through 'protracted people war' based on 'guerrilla methods'. Instead of choosing the urban centres as base centres, it conceived of developing the base centres in the remote rural areas by developing them as liberated zones and consolidating them and encircling the cities. It termed its revolution as the New Democratic Revolution (NDR). The organisation rejected the parliamentary path to socialism and subscribed to armed struggle.

The 21-member (permanent) Central Committee was the highest decision- and policy-making body. Muppalla Lakshman Rao, alias Ganpati, was the General Secretary who also succeeded as the General Secretary of the merged outfit, CPI (ML) Maoist. The People's War Group had a distinct military wing trained in handling arms and revolutionary activities. This wing was led by Ganpati and was first founded on 2 December 2000 in Bihar and Jharkhand. A similar group was founded in other states as well. The People's Guerrilla Army (PGA) was meticulously structured. There was a Central Military Commission under which there happened to be a Regional Military Commission, which supervised and monitored the working of the State Military Commission or Zonal Military Commission. People's War Group, in a short time span, emerged as one of the most dreaded Naxal organisations in the country. It engaged in several armed struggles, which included bombing government establishments and killing individual politicians, bureaucrats and anyone whom they considered either a class enemy or not lending support to them or acting against their interests.

---

19 In Bihar, the most affected areas are Patna, Aurangabad, Gaya, Jehanabad, Rohtas, Saharsa, Buxar, Ara, Khagaria, Banka, Jamui districts etc. Palamu, Garwah, Latehar, Gumala, Chatra, Hazaribagh, and Koderma in Jharkhand; Malkangiri, Koraput, Gajpati, Raygada, Navrangapur and also in Mayurbhanj districts in Orissa; Jagadalpur, Bastar, Kanker, dantewada, Rajnadgaon, Sarguja, Kawardha and Jashpurnagar in Chhattisgarh; Midnapore, Puruliaand Bankura in West Bengal; Balaghat, Dhindoli districts in Madhya Pradesh; Gadchiroli, Bhandara and Chandrapur in Maharashtra.

20 In Khammam, Warangal, Karimnagar, Nizamabad, Adilabad in North Telangana, Mehboobnagar, Nalgonda and Medak districts in South Telangana, Anantpur and Kurnool Districts in Rayalseema Region, East Godavari, Vishakhapatnam, Vijayanagaram and Srikakulam in North Coastal Region and Guntur district in South Coastal Area.

MCC was just the renaming of *Dakshin Desh,* which was founded on October 20, 1969. *Dakshin Desh* was active in the Jangal Mahal area of Burdwan district and the Sundervan, 24 Pargana, Hoogly and Midnapore districts in West Bengal under the leadership of Amulya Sen and Kanhai Chatterjee. The organisation did not join the CPI (ML), which formed after the split in CPI (M) in 1970. Thus, it worked independently of both the CPI (M) and CPI (ML). It, however, was renamed as the Maoist Communist Centre (MCC) in 1975. In the 80s, one finds that it shifted by and large its revolutionary activities to Bihar, Jharkhand and, adjunct to them, some areas in Odisha and West Bengal.

MCC appeared to be one of the most dreaded organisations in the 80s and 90s in Bihar. It focused on the caste atrocities and selectively targeted the upper castes, primarily *Rajputs* and *Bhumihars*. In 1986, it gunned down 11 people belonging to the Rajput caste from Darmia village in Aurangabad district. On 29 May 1987, it again killed 42 people of the Rajput community in Dalelchak Baghaura village in the same district (South Asia Terrorism Portal). In 1992, on February 12, in Bara village of Gaya District, 37 members of the Bhumihar Community were massacred. Again, after seven years, on March 18, 1999, 34 members of the Bhumihar caste were killed by this organisation in the most brutal ways. Same year, on November 18, it killed 12 people from Latu village in Palamu (South Asia Terrorism Portal).

Thus, the class struggle of the MCC got subsequently degenerated into a caste war in Bihar, as in order to retaliate the MCC menace, the upper castes launched Ranveer Sena, which led to several massacres of the Dalits and landless workers in Bihar. Due to caste-oriented individual and mass annihilation, the organisation lost track and lost class support. Secondly, the areas where it was a more influential force were primarily in Bihar, Jharkhand and to some extent in Bengal. In that too, it was more active in the South Bihar and some of the districts of Central Bihar, such as Aurangabad, Jehanabad, Ara, Rohtasganj, Buxar, Gaya, Nalanda, etc. Some of the North Bihar districts too came under its influence, such as Darbhanga, Betiah, Muzaffarpur, Sitamarhi, etc. Almost all the districts were affected by the presence of the MCC in Jharkhand. In Bengal, it was confined to some area of Nadia, Burdwan, 24 North Parwana, Howrah, etc. In UP as well, it could make its presence felt in districts which were close to South Bihar as well as the Ara and Buxar belt, such as in Mirzapur, Chandauli and Sonbhadra.

MCC killed a number of police and government officials in these three states, primarily in South Bihar and almost all districts of the present Jharkhand state. It believed in individual as well as mass annihilations, which is evident from the patterns of the killings and taking on the government and police officials. Several police stations were raided to procure arms. It also affected political killings, remained engaged in landmine blasts. It had the linkage with the People's War Group (PWG) and Liberation Tigers of Tamil Eelam (LTTE) from whom they learnt the techniques of bomb making, landmine blasts, etc.

MCC also committed to the ideology of Mao Tse-tung. The organisation also floated a number of 'mass organisations' such as *Navjawan Pratirodh Sangharsh Manch, Krantikari Budhijivi Sangh, Krantikari Sanskritik Sangh, Krantikari Chhatra League*, Communist *Yuva* League, *Nari Mukti Sangh and Majdoor Mukti Sangh*, etc. MCC had also a military wing trained in guerrilla warfare, and it is understood that the comrades were trained by the LTTE, PWG and the Nepalese Maoists. The party structure was well knitted, and a well-planned organisational structure was in place down to the village level. MCC, like other revolutionary groups, also witnessed several factions within which resulted into split of the organisation. Finally, the organisation merged into the Maoist group in 2004. One reason why the left movement failed in India was continuous split from 1967, which resulted into destruction of the organisational structure and many times the group members acting against other militant groups present in the area.

3 CPI (Maoist)

It was in light of these multiple splits and weakening of the revolutionary movements across the country that the unity attempts were made, which materialised in the form of the coming of a new revolutionary political outfit in the name of CPI (Maoist). In the merger, a 'Provisional Central Committee' was constituted with Ganapati being the general secretary of the party. The ideological framework outlined in the 'Party Programme' suggests details of how it understands the class configuration in India, and how and what it aims at. Like any revolutionary party that claims to be adhering to Marxism, the CPM (Maoist) too commits to the great idea of world communism. For this, it wants unity and proximity among all the revolutionary forces working across the world. However, it wants India to develop as a strong socialist base from where it could be worked towards the ultimate goal.

The party holds that the Indian state is a 'semi-feudal, semi-colonial state' in which the 'comprador big capitalist class and landlords, who themselves are dependent on their growth and survival on imperialism, control the state (CPI (M) Constitution). To them, the British converted India into a colonial and semi-feudal state. But when they left the country, they ensured that their interests are not completely jeopardised. The 'big capitalist class', which works as the comprador bourgeois, and the landlords continue to hold their sway through the 'big administrative bourgeois', and they serve the interests of imperialist power even in the post-independence era.

Indian independence, therefore, is a farce as the imperialists and colonists continued their imperialists and colonial interests served through the landlords and the comprador bourgeois. In fact, they hold, "the direct colonial and semi-feudal system of the British imperialists was replaced with a semi-colonial and semi-feudal system under the neo-colonial form of indirect imperialist rule, exploitation and control" (CPI (M) Constitution). The landlords continue to hold a monopoly on lands as 5 percent of them control nearly 30 percent of the land holdings. The middle peasantry and rich peasantry are just 20 percent and 10 percent, respectively. Thus, 65 percent peasantry is still landless, and land reforms did not bring desired results at all (CPI (M) Constitution). And the workers in the rural area continue to be subjected to extreme semi-feudal exploitation. Thus, there is no change in the nature of the state fundamentally. There is continuity of the rule of the same class.

In fact, the Declaration of Independence was itself a design to escape the wrath of the revolutionary movement. Thus, it holds that the British left India not because the Indian National Congress forced them out, but the reason that the British were facing all-around revolts across the country in the post-Second World War period[21] which forced them to leave the country. Party notes that, unfortunately, the revolutionary activities, instead of being applied more vigorously was diluted by non-else but the communist leadership of the time, who could not make a distinct impact on the movement but got subsumed into the Gandhian ideology.

The party denounces the Indian National Congress and especially Gandhi and his techniques of *Satyagraha* and *Ahimsa* applied in the course of the national movement. Gandhi, for them, was planted by the British in the national movement to 'derail and divert' the growing anti-colonial anti-imperialists revolutionary uprisings, and he at best represented and served the interests of the 'Comprador Big Bourgeois' and the 'landlords' (CPI (M) Constitution; Sen et al., 1978). And in this whole episode, the leadership of the communist party also did not play a fair role. Instead of supporting and advancing the revolutionary battle against the colonial power, it chose to ally with it, which resulted in the derailment of the anti-imperialist people movement. It was this mindset which led the leadership to withdraw the 'Telangana armed revolt of the peasantry' and finally resorting to parliamentary politics. It was a great betrayal.

21 This is the logic many right-wing nationalists' organisations also argue.

The party holds that in contemporary India, there are four major discernible contradictions in Indian society. First, the contradiction that exists between imperialism and the Indian masses. The second contradiction exists between feudalism and the broad mass of the people. The third contradiction exists between the capital and labour, and the fourth contradiction exists among the ruling classes (CPI (M) Constitution; Sen et al., 1978). The first two contradictions are the 'basic contradictions', and they are the target of the 'New Democratic Revolution'. Out of the two major contradictions, the second is the principal contradiction and therefore needs to be accorded priority.

The party believes that the Indian economy is completely in the grip of the imperialists who control the key sector of the economy as well as the administration. International Finance Capital is forcing upon the government to enter Memorandum of Understandings (MOUs). Thousands of such MOUs have been signed by the government of India. The dependency of the country on Western capitalism for financial aid, loans, capital goods, agricultural inputs, technical know-how, and military hardwires have increased significantly (CPI (M) Constitution; Sen et al., 1978). The comprador, big capitalists and the feudal ruling classes work for them. With the privatisation and liberalisation, this control of imperialist power has increased.

What is needed to come out of this is to wage a successful democratic revolution, which they name as the New Democratic Revolution, as well as the People Democratic Revolution. The big bourgeois, comprador bourgeois, landlords, along with the 'comprador bureaucratic bourgeois' (CPI (M) Constitution; Sen et al., 1978) would be the targets of the revolution as they all are reactionary, anti-people, anti-national, and they sub-serve the interests of the imperialists' forces. And this revolution would be essentially violent. There is no space for the parliamentary path, which to them is the path of renegade and revisionists. The party document holds that the path marked by the CPI (ML) and MCC document of 1967, which suggested of 'building and advancing armed agrarian revolution through protracted peoples war (CPI (M) Constitution; Sen et al., 1978) was the correct line for the revolution in India. And it holds even for today also. They are highly critical of the parliamentary left, whom they consider have compromised the interests of the toiling masses.

The state in the post-revolution phase would be a proletarian state. Since the classes and class contradiction would remain even during the period of the rule of the proletariat, the aim of the proletarian state would be aimed at two things. First, it would work towards achieving socialism by 'resolving the class contradictions along the Marxism-Leninism-Maoism line and will make possible to enjoy democracy to the vast majority'. Secondly, it would act as a dictator towards the exploiter classes (CPI (M) Constitution; Sen et al., 1978). The state would abolish the private ownership of all kinds which feed and breed capitalism. Finance capital and the enterprises would be confiscated, and the land ownership will be transferred to the hands who till it.

The list of what the people's state would strive for is very exhaustive. But it certainly gives a sense of bringing in everyone who is deprived of in the working of modern capitalism. It includes from the peasants to the industrial workers, the daily wage earners to the tribals, to the caste untouchables, to minority. The purpose seems simple; the class proletariat to them constitute of everyone who is either a victim of the economic or social system or does not find numerically proportional representation in the cultural space of the system.

The party thus engages in intense debates over a host of crucial issues with fellow comrades who have preferred the parliamentary road to socialism. While CPI's official position is that the Capitalist bourgeois, which the CPI (Maoist) consider as the 'Comprador bourgeois', is the 'nationalist bourgeois' and cites several progressive steps which the state took up immediately after independence, such as land reforms, land ceiling acts, giving importance to the public sector undertakings, independent foreign policy, etc. Such states, to them, cannot be called as the semi-colonial, semi-feudal state. CPI (Maoist) argues, however, that the land reforms were and are not the solution and road to socialism. Public sector undertakings were again not 'to achieve socialist goals but to wear a mask of socialism in the wake of rising revolutionary tides.'

The mainstream communists like the CPI and CPI (M) continue to discount the theorisation and practices of the Naxalites. They argue that the Naxalites have done a big harm to the revolutionary struggle in India by engaging themselves in individual killings and mass murder (Zedong, 1965:154; Mitra & Sen, 1971:122–23). For them, the Naxalites have a distorted understanding of the revolution. Mao certainly justified the Guerilla war and armed struggle as an essential one for revolution, but he argued so because there were no democratic outlets for revolution.

4 Towards Conclusion

A careful reading of the documents of the CPI (Maoist) suggests a few conclusions. First, the party is still frozen in time. It has not moved beyond the late 60s, even though the state and financial market have moved miles ahead. No one would agree that the big capitalists' class in India are the puppet in the hands of American or European multinationals and the former is dependent and works for the latter. There are Indian companies which have emerged as multinationals and have aggressively positioned themselves against the

European or American giants. There are a hundred such Indian multinationals which have entered and captured the European and American market and are posing great threats to their enterprises and manufacturing base. It is not just about TATAs and Ambanis (Families running big India-based conglomerates), but there are several such companies which have left global footprints and are venturing into not just the manufacturing products but also the best use of their natural resources, like explorations of mines and oilfields. Indian oil companies are engaged in offshore oil explorations in other countries like Vietnam, the Philippines etc. India is taking the satellites of other countries in space at the most competitive price in the world. The new Indian start-ups are also giving strong competition to several large multi-national companies in the market.

Also, the argument that our foreign policy is reactionary and serves the interests of the imperialists is something inconsumable (CPI (M) Constitution). Every nation-state protects its own national interests. And their economic and military alliance or strategic friendship is governed solely by this factor. China has been supporting the worst dictators and swindlers of money in Pakistan for a simple reason: it wants India to bleed. Chinese support has not been to the progressive elements in Pakistan. China also allied with the US against the Soviet Union in the late seventies. Indian alliance with the US and its tilt towards the West is also governed by the national interests, and that cannot be treated as subservient to the interests of the imperialists.

It is interesting to note that on the one hand, the documents say that the Indian state is dependent and semi-colonial and the ruling class takes the dictates from imperialist powers, on the other, it says that the Indian state is an expansionist state which intervenes in the neighbouring countries and works against the interests of the oppressed nations (CPI (M) Constitution). Both these premises seem to be an oxymoron. How come a dependent country can venture into an expansionist adventure? It makes the formulation faulty. It is more to serve a rhetorical position than reflecting the true nature of the working of the state system. Surprisingly, China, which has been engaged in border disputes with almost all neighbouring countries and even in the far sea, frequently have been into aggressive adventuring towards India over the last few decades does not attract any criticism from the party. If there is any power in South Asia which is engaged in an expansionist design, it is China. But the party document does not say anything on Chinese adventurism at all? There is no trace of communism in China. The Communist Party carries the rhetoric communism without communism. If at all it exists, it exists only in nomenclature. It is as imperialist and expansionist as any capitalist country of the West. Yet, it is rare to find a severe criticism of China by the vanguards of proletarianism.

There seems to be an obvious bias in favour of China. If American investment in the third world countries and the signing of the MOU for the same is wrong, then how come the Chinese investment in the third world countries would be non-imperialist? The party has no answer to this. It deliberately seeks to ignore this aspect. According to the party, the privatization liberalization and globalisation are part of the imperialists' policies. If this is true, China should today be treated as one of the imperialist powers rather than the vanguard of world proletarians. But again, there is no word on China in this regard. It is not just the European Multinationals which are entering into the Indian market. Chinese companies are also doing business in India and are swallowing the indigenous small industries. CPI (Maoist) is highly critical of the Soviet leadership, especially of the post Stalin era leaders and accuse them of transforming the country into a capitalist country, which, in the garb of socialism, practised social imperialism and the cult of exploitation of the third world countries. It competed with the US imperialism for dominance and control of the oppressed nations (CPI (M) Constitution). The Chinese position is no way different today from what the Soviet Union did decades back. The CPI (Maoists) accept also that China has turned to capitalism like the former Soviet Union. But they are not as critical of China as they were of the Soviet Union. One reason is that China has been very close to the radical left in India and has been encouraging, funding and supporting them in all covert manners. Maoists treat the current wave of Liberalization, privatization and globalization (LPG) as a war on the people, as this has deepened the crisis in societies. But they fail to answer why the champions of socialism, after claiming to be practising it for decades, though not true, returned to the market ideology? They fail to explain why China, which exported Maoism elsewhere, is not working on the socialist premise at all on its home turf.

It is surprising to note that the Maoists in India also subscribe to the idea that India is one of the oldest civilizations in the world with a great cultural heritage and legacy, but the documents do not explain further what makes this country a great civilizational entity. It is known to all that it is the spiritual and Vedantic wisdom which makes it so, but the Maoists have all abuses for the same, and the whole texts have been debunked by depicting them as the texts of Brahminism, which to them bred inequality and discrimination in the society (CPI (M) Constitution). More importantly, when it comes to attacking the conservative elements and religious dogmas, they are vociferous towards Hindutva, but seldom they seldom muster the courage to hit at the fanatic elements in Islam and Christianity. They just ignore the proven linkages of Islam and terrorism, in which both have reinforced each other in a variety of ways.

The Maoists do not acknowledge the idea of India as a nation. For them, it is just a territorial living space where they are born accidentally and where they have to realise their material well-being. For them, India comprises of several nationalities and cultures, and the ruling class have captivated these nationalities and do not allow them to articulate and assert themselves in the garb of 'unity and integrity'. CPI (Maoist) supports the separatist revolutions of these nationalities, be it Kashmir or in the North-East and asserts that they should have the right to self-determination which includes even secession (CPI (M) Constitution). And who does not know that these movements are not self-grown but engineered and nurtured from outside with man, material and ideological implant? On the nationality question, they seem to be either highly confused or they fail to understand how to manage diversity. The existence of diversity is separate from nationality for them. They exhort that the comrades should lend all the support to the democratic rights of these nationalities, including their demands for autonomy and separation, especially in the case of the Northeast and J&K. In the case of these two, they hold that the communists should "extend complete and unflinching support to the demand of secession of these nationalities as long as their struggle is directed against their common enemies. They go on to suggest further that it is the responsibility and the duty of the communists to give a revolutionary orientation."[22] Who are the common enemies? Going by their document, it is feudalism, imperialism and the comprador big bourgeoisie represented by the Indian state. and therefore "each and every struggle of the nationalities should be supported if it is directed against the Indian state."[23] And once the process of overthrowing them is complete, the process of reorganising a 'voluntary Indian federation'[24] should commence, in which they should be free to secede. It is understandable that the separatists in Kashmir are against the Indian State, but do they represent the anti-imperialist, anti-feudalism forces really? They do not. In fact, the movement is not for establishing a true democratic society but based on religious intolerance towards others and creating a religious hegemony. The claim of the Maoists that what they are doing is for the larger goals of democracy and human rights does not seem to be true. Maoists have little concern for the human rights of others. They claim to be fighting for the toiling masses,

22 Legal Document submitted by the Government of India in the Supreme Court in 2013, p. 194.

23 Legal Document submitted by the Government of India in the Supreme Court in 2013, p. 193.

24 Ibid.

whereas hundreds of examples can be cited wherein their hands are soaked in the blood of the poor, innocent and deprived. Human rights and democratic values all mean to them till they supplant their ideological positions. Constitution and constitutionalism does not hold any relevance in Naxal ideology. Violence is an essential creed for them. They are not just opposed to India as a civilizational entity but also pose a threat to its territorial integrity and unity. No wonder successive governments at the centre have considered them as the biggest threat to national security.

CHAPTER 2

Maoists Activities in India

Dandakaranya is known to almost every Indian who has ever engaged with popular narratives on the Ramayana. It is a forest where Goddess Sita and Lord Ram spent most of their exile from *Ayodhya*. Ramayana depicts that this forest was an abode of several demons whose terror had made it difficult for the saints and hermits to conduct their ascetic and spiritual lives. As the story goes, Lord Ram killed them and emancipated saints and Rishis from the fear and terror of demons. This provoked the demon king of Lanka, who kidnapped *Sita* and took her to Lanka. Ram killed him in the battle, which marks the victory of good over evil, a victory of truth over untruth. *Dandakaranya* today once again has captured the popular imagination of people and security establishments for being the abode of Naxals. Spread out over 92,500 square km, starting from the Eastern Ghats in the East to the Abujhmar hills in the west, this Aranya (forest) covers not all but the majority of Naxal-infested states of India.[1] For Maoists, it is the special zone as well as the 'strategic areas' where the enemy (Indian state) is relatively weak, apart from the fact that the hilly tracts and thick forest cover provide a safe abode for the Maoists to conduct and control their activities. Dandakaranya is not the only corridor regarded as the bastion of Naxal presence. Starting from the Eastern hills and moving down to the South along the coastal Andhra is also a stretch, known as the 'red corridor', that connects the Naxal belts in West Bengal with Telangana in the South.

How many districts are under the influence of Maoists is a point of contestation. It has been at variance, and rightly so because situations are fluid and changing. In 2007, it was estimated that Naxals were active across half of India's 29 states, accounting for about 40 percent of India's geographical area. In 2009, they were active across approximately 180 of the 545 districts of India. In 2011, the government of India estimated that the decline of Maoist influence shrunk from 180 districts in 2009 to 89 districts in 2011 (SATP). After the BJP came to power, the movement has been on further decline. The Home Minister of India, Amit Shah, has made a public declaration that Naxalism will be wiped out from the Indian soil by April 2026 (Hindustan Times, 2024). This does not look like a difficult proposition, given the fact that every day, Naxals are either

1 Dandakaranya comprises of areas of states like Telangana, Chhattisgarh, Orissa, Maharashtra and Andhra Pradesh. Except for the state of Bihar and Jharkhand it comprises of all Naxal infested areas.

 | HTTPS://DOI.ORG/10.1163/9789004765054-004

being killed or forced to surrender across the states. In April 2024, the government of India reported in the parliament that the Naxal-affected districts have now come down to 38 districts of 9 states, which was earlier 10 across India (The Times of India, 2024).

This is also reflected in a significant decline in the Maoists' violence and the casualties inflicted on the civilians and armed forces by them. The number of casualties (466 civilians and 142 security forces) also marked a modest decline, if not too sharp, from 908 in 2009, 1005 in 2010, and 608 in 2011. Similarly, this trend continued in the coming years, with 415 deaths (301 civilians and 114 security personnel) in 2012 (The Indian Express, 2014). After the emergence of the BJP into power at the center, the overall number of attacks and damages declined considerably. Though still continuing, according to the Annual Report of the Ministry of Home Affairs 2023–24, it is the most potent among all the left-wing extremist (LWE) outfits in India. "It accounts for more than 90 percent of total violent incidents and 95 percent of resultant deaths" (Hindustan Times, 2024). There was a period when Maoists successfully executed and inflicted one of the most brutal attacks on civilians and paramilitary forces. In 2011, they attacked the CRPF convoy, which was returning from patrolling in the *Sukma* valley in *the Dantewada* of *Bastar* districts of Chhattisgarh. They killed 76 CRPF personnel in one go (Hindustan Times, 2024). In 2012, they again killed 17 CRPF in the same region and declared their open intention to retaliate against the state operation against the *Naxals* in the state. They carried out similar blasts in Jharkhand, Odisha, and Bihar. In 2021, again, they killed 22 paramilitary personnel in the same Sukama region towards the end of March 2021 (Mukherjee et al., 2023).

As per the report of the Ministry of Home Affairs, "Between 2004 and 2025 (31 March), 8895 people have been killed by the LWE in different parts of India" (MHA LWE Division). In another RTI reply, as reported in the Indian Express, over the last 20 years, nearly 12,183 people have been killed in 9 Naxal-infested areas (The Indian Express, 2014). Of this, 9,471 civilians and 2,712 state and central police forces lost their lives. The Home Ministry data suggests that from 2004 onward, the civilian killings were on the rise, and they reached their peak in 2010 when they killed 720 civilians. And since then, this has been in decline (MHA, 2025). Similarly, they attacked the economic infrastructure on a large scale in the areas of their strength. The same year, i.e., in 2010, Naxalites attacked 365 economic structures, which included roads to schools, hospitals, and industrial activities. Thereafter, there was a sharp decline, especially after the BJP government at the center. In 2024, it was reported that only 25 such attacks were inflicted by the Naxals, which was close to half of the number in 2023 (MHA, 2025).

The magnitude of the problem can be imagined from the fact that over 90,000 personnel (90 battalions) of central paramilitary forces once were engaged in anti-Naxal operations across 9 states of India. In addition, a special Reserve Naga Battalion of 1,000 was also deployed in anti-Naxal operations in India (The Indian Express, 2014). The nature of the threat that emerges from it can be seen from the fact that the Ministry of Home Affairs in the government of India carved out a separate division to monitor the Naxal activities. More importantly, both then Prime Minister Manmohan Singh and the Home Minister of India, P. Chidambaram, once openly admitted that Naxalism was the biggest threat to the security of the country. The meeting in which the prime minister said so was attended by all the chief ministers of the states, and they all concurred with this fact. Prime Minister Manmohan Singh had said, "It would not be an exaggeration to say that the problem of Naxalism is the single biggest internal security challenge ever faced by our country" (PMO, 2006; Hindustan Times, 2006). The prime minister and the chief ministers of the Naxal-infested states were unanimous on the point that this was the problem that required the topmost priority.

Long before this meeting, the then Home Minister of India, P. Chidambaram, was of the opinion that given the range and degree of violence perpetrated by the Maoists, the national security of the country was at risk and, however, explicitly ruled out any military response (One India, 2009; The Indian Express, 2009). Understanding this as a law-and-order problem or a problem that emanates from poverty, or treating it as an act of misguided youths, would be an oversimplification of a phenomenon that is driven by an ideology that trains, motivates, and molds the minds into an armed squad to overthrow the existing political and economic structures.

Violence is the creed that the Maoists follow without confusion. To them, the transformation of society to socialism cannot be peaceful and incremental through the parliamentary mechanism. The only solution before the proletariat/working class is to overthrow the existing state system. Revolutionary struggle is the only way to accomplish it. The party of the proletariat should form mass organisations of different forms and train the members and inculcate in them the revolutionary spirit. Still, they must not forget that the ultimate objective can come through violent revolution only. It must be recognised that the state is the principal enemy, and therefore, they have been ruthless in attacking the instruments of the state, especially the military and paramilitary forces. However, a careful reading of the violence and patterns of strikes suggests that civilians and the poor and uneducated ones who have been struggling for their daily meals have been the most significant casualties. The majority of civilians killed by the Naxals come from the lowest rung of society. Because it happens in villages and tribal areas, which are way behind in the matrix of development. Thus, the people who otherwise should have been on the Maoists' side in their revolution are the victims of the latter.

The civilians tortured by the Maoists fall into three categories. The first set of people comprises those who did not cooperate with the Maoists and refused to oblige them in terms of money or shelter as demanded. The Maoists punish them. The support that came to the Maoists in the villages was the result of both the people's reaction to the apathy, neglect, and atrocities of the state and the atmosphere of fear that the Maoists unleashed in the areas of their dominance. While a section of the people supports them because they genuinely think that the Naxals are advancing and fighting for their cause, an equally and numerically significant segment of the village population does not believe in the acts and philosophy of the Naxals. Still, they do not muster the courage to oppose them because of the threat to their lives. After entering the village, Maoists want to exercise complete control of villages and often start deciding dos and don'ts. Anyone who dares to differ or oppose them is punished. Therefore, those who champion the cause and modus operandi of the Naxals and go overboard to accuse the state only need to understand that the Maoists' support in the villages is not always wilful. On the contrary, they are but under duress in the majority of cases. All the reports, by and large, whether they have been based on individual surveys or Organised data collection from the conflict areas, including the National Human Rights Commission and Independent Citizens' Initiatives, have comprehensively documented this (Guha, 2007). Innocent people are sandwiched between the Maoists and the state. When people refuse to toe the line of the Maoists, they are punished by the latter. The nature of punishment is so harsh that it is difficult for the poor villagers to deny help and hospitality to the Maoists. And, when they oblige them through hospitality or other means, these people are tortured by the police for being Maoist supporters. Thus, the innocent people suffer doubly because they have to pay the price either way for giving shelter to the Maoist cadres, even though they do it under duress. If they cooperate with the police, they are subjected to the Maoists' mode of punishment, often unfolding into the killing of such persons after branding them as 'police informers'[2] (Guha, 2007).

Apart from the common innocent villagers, the Maoists have been infrequently targeting politicians and frequently targeting the contractors and bureaucrats. The target groups are well thought out, and the specific purpose is kept in mind. While they all represent the class enemy in the radical Marxian

---

2 Both the National Human Rights Commission Report and the Fact-finding committee of eminent people have endorsed this as fact.

lexicon, the purposes of all have been different. Bureaucrats, contractors, businessmen, and engineers are targeted primarily for money. They charge a commission on every project, depending on the money involved, and expect a certain proportion of the funds to go to them. The work sites are far from the town or the police stations. Private contractors or corporations publicly deny it, but the fact is that firms and these sections of people pay what is popularly known as 'protection money' (Bose, 2011). All the Madhya Pradesh Tendu contractors must pay the Maoists roughly 5 to 6 lakhs (Bose, 2011). Thus, the main reason behind targeting the engineers, contractors, and businessmen is to extort money from the development project, which they use further to buy arms and ammunition and run their ideological and subversive activities. One reason they have shifted their base to the forest areas is that they find it easier to generate resources for their activities because, in the last few decades, the government has initiated numerous developmental projects in these areas, which have been on the margin so far.

As per an estimate, the Maoists generate a considerable amount of money, roughly 400 crores, from such extortion[3] (Tikku, 2013). It is noteworthy that Maoists have not completely stopped mining or developmental projects. They have allowed the project to operate, but only after due payment to them as commission or extortion money. This is sufficient to conclude that their opposition to capitalism is not a serious business or principled tenet in practice, though they continue to articulate their rhetorical ire more often than not. The peculiarity of this extortion is that neither the corporate sector nor the Naxals accept it openly. But in private conversations, corporate officials acknowledge that they have to pay huge extortion money to the Naxals for undertaking developmental projects in these areas. And this has now been on record. It was no less than a minister of the government of India who acknowledged this fact in his replies to the members of the Rajya Sabha (The Hindu, 2016).

The political killings are mainly intended to make political statements and to send out the message to the people and the political class that they cannot afford to ignore them. Political Mobilisation by the political parties unsettles the agenda of the Naxals and hits at their support base. Naxals, therefore, challenge the legitimacy of the political class using all possible means at their disposal. That includes even violence. Political killings go with their stated position of overthrowing the present structure by crippling the leadership. But this is primarily aimed at influencing the political class and the people.

3 The statistics are quoted differently as they are just the guess or estimates by agencies and reported in media.

Maoists so far have attacked several politicians across the states. In 2003, they attacked the convoy of Chandrababu Naidu when he was travelling to Tirumala. Naidu narrowly escaped. Naidu was then emerging as a new poster boy of the capitalist mode of development and an ardent supporter of the market economy. He sought to put the state of Andhra Pradesh on the industrial map of India. In 2010, a top CPM leader from West Bengal, Ananta Mukherjee, was pulled up from a motorbike at Silda High School premises and was shot dead in broad daylight (Mandal, 2010). The Congress lost almost the entire top leadership, barring a few, when on 25th May 2013, Maoists attacked the convoy of Congress leaders at Darbha Valley in the Sukma district of Chhattisgarh and killed 25 people, including the chief of the Congress party, Nand Kumar Patel and Mahendra Singh Karma who had spearheaded the people's protest in the form of Salwa Judum against the Naxals in the Bastar district (John & Drolia, 2013). Politicians are the weakest link as far as Naxalism is concerned. Since they have to retain the social and electoral constituency, they face a difficult dilemma of whether to support or oppose the Naxals, who often have a following in remote rural areas.

However, police and armed forces are their actual targets. For them, police and paramilitary forces are the coercive instruments of the state, exploiting the poor and suppressing the revolution. Since the common people are often the target of the police's high-handedness, arbitrariness and executive excesses, attacks on them do find a silent endorsement from this social class. Maoists seem to be working on a well-thought-out strategy of exploiting the situations that emerge from apathy and negligence of the state to social and economic exploitation of the poor villagers and tribals by the rich and the affluent. In the villages, they raised the issue of daily wages, land entitlement to the tillers, and social atrocities. All these issues make them stand against the local landholding medium, small or big peasants. As the poor and deprived sections of society find few to stand against the rich farmers and landlords, they see Naxals as people who are raising their voices for themselves in the system. Maoists have emerged as protectors of their rights, social dignity, and overall saviours against class exploitation of the poor. Naxal activities in central Bihar found roots against the social atrocities and economic exploitation by the upper caste landlords. The poor and underprivileged social classes saw them as someone who was ready to take on the pride and social assertion of the upper castes. The Maoist Communist Centre (MCC) in Bihar got its foothold primarily because it came forward to resist and violently respond to the physical assertion of the upper castes. Hence, Maoist support did not swell just because of the force behind it but because the state proved to be an utter failure on many social and economic indices.

1 Maoist Affected States and Areas

Broadly speaking, Maoist-affected states and districts can be put under three major categories: first, the worst-affected states; secondly, the states and areas that were previously Maoist strongholds but have returned to normalcy; and third, the new areas and states where they have already or are trying to make inroads. The worst-affected states today are Jharkhand, Chhattisgarh, and some parts of Orissa, Maharashtra, and Bihar. On February 5, 2019, the Ministry of Home Affairs reported officially that nearly 19 out of 24 districts of Jharkhand were Naxal-affected[4] (PIB, 2019). Now, the number of districts affected has been reduced to 5 districts in the state[5] (Deccan Herald, 2024). Similarly, 16 districts were reported as Naxal-infested at that time in Bihar[6] (The Deccan Herald, 2024). In 2021, the central government declared that 6 state districts were now Naxal-free (Thakur, 2021). Now, Bihar is almost a Naxal-free state. In Chhattisgarh, 14 districts were declared Naxal-infested in 2021. This is the only state that continues to be the hub of the movement. According to the latest data as reported by the government of India, there are 38 districts that are termed as 'districts of concern', a new terminology that was used in 2015, out of which 15 come from the state of Chhattisgarh, followed by 7 in Odisha and 5 in Jharkhand, 3 in Madhya Pradesh, two each of Kerala, Telangana and Maharashtra followed by one each from Bengal and Andhra Pradesh (Times of India, 2024). These are the states where the most striking activities have been reported in recent years. These states have the biggest Naxal penetration today, and most of the violence comes from the Naxal-infested districts of these states (The Times of India, 2024). The West Bengal, Andhra Pradesh and Kerala are states where, once upon a time, the Naxal menace was at its peak. Though the Jangal Mahal in West Bengal continues to be identified as the Maoist bastion, it has lost the iconic position that it once enjoyed. It is not that the Naxalites have been rooted out completely, but it is certain that the Maoists do not continue to have the same hold over these areas that they used to have a few decades ago. The government of West Bengal, under the CPM, used a ruthless state apparatus to crush them, along with the political

4 Districts in Jharkhand that are Naxal affected: Bokaro, Chatra, Dhanbad, Dumka, East Singhbhum, Garhwa, Giridih, Gumla, Hazaribagh, Khunti, Koderma, Latehar, Lohardaga, Palamu, Ramgarh, Ranchi, Simdega, Saraikela-Kharaswan, West Singhbhum.

5 The DGP of the Jharkhand police said that the Naxal problem is now confined to only 5 Jharkhand districts.

6 The sixteen districts are as follows: Arwal, Aurangabad, Banka, East Champaran, Gaya, Jamui, Jehanabad, Kaimur, Lakhisarai, Munger, Muzaffarpur, Nalanda, Nawada, Rohtas, Vaishali, West Champaran.

attacks against the Naxals. (CPM against the CPI-ML). Though publicly, the CPM has stood by the argument of fighting the Naxals ideologically and politically through mass-Mobilisation, it applied all tactics to break the backbone of the organisation in the state. In 2009, when the central government treated it as a terrorist organisation, the CPM swiftly reacted by stating that it would love to fight the Maoists politically and ideologically (The Indian Express, 2009). This duplicity in the behaviour of the CPM is driven by the dilemma that it does not want to be seen as anti-revolutionary, but at the same time also seeks to suggest that the Maoist revolutionary approach is not correct.

The CPM government certainly slowed the recruitment drives of the Maoists in the state. In retaliation, Naxals extended their political support to the Trinamool Congress. Nandigram and Singur provided the much-awaited opportunity to the Naxals. In both Nandigram and Singur, the government had acquired land from the farmers and handed over the same to TATA, one of the leading industrial houses of India, to establish car factories. The CPM, which used to abuse the capitalists for exploitation of the industrial workers and mobilised the masses against the government, was clueless about how to handle the situation. The land acquisition of the farmers by the state for a corporate house like Tata to establish a car factory discredited the image of the Left Front in Bengal. It lost the moral edge that it once enjoyed in the state. And the Supreme Court judgment endorsed the stand of the people. The state and corporate alliance at the cost of the poor farmers and the people at the margin emboldened the Maoists to attack the CPM government. The people's growing disenchantment with the government eroded the strong support base of the party, which had not previously found any political challenge in the state. The masses turned against the CPM and its government, and it was finally defeated in the assembly elections of 2011. The role of the Maoists was crucial in the election because they could neutralise the violent acts of the CPM cadres. It is not hidden that CPM, during its rule in the state, had thoroughly derailed the social forces through the intervention of its cadres in the social and political life of the state. While these forces are important and need to be used for the transformation of the society and economy by channeling their energies for positive gains, they were armed and used by the political elites in the state to continue their political dominance in their constituencies. The West Bengal provides examples and evidence of people being coerced to vote for and support the CPM government in the state. Maoists used this opportunity to neutralise the coercive politics of the CPM.

The Maoists initially supported the Trinamool, hoping that she would not be as ruthless as the CPM. However, the initial undeclared bonhomie between the two did not last long. Mamata Banerjee used force to clear the Jangal Mahal, and she could take pride in saying that while all the Naxal-infested states, including Andhra Pradesh, belong to the same group of states. There was a time when the Naxal movement was confined to West Bengal and Andhra Pradesh. The Naxalbari in West Bengal and the Telangana region in Andhra Pradesh were the major centers from which Naxal activities were directed. In the course of time, the Adilabad, Khammam, East Godavari, Warangal, and Vishakhapatnam districts became the hub of the Maoists' activities. This is why most of the Maoist leadership came from West Bengal and Andhra Pradesh in the initial years of the movement. The dossier posted by the home ministry listing the 'most wanted Naxals' lists the names of those who mostly come from Andhra Pradesh. This indicates that once upon a time, this belt was a major nursery of Naxal activities. When the state turned the heat on them, Naxal cadres fanned out to different states in India. No wonder cadres from Andhra Pradesh and West Bengal continue leading the movement even in other states.

The Naxal movement in India is traced back to the pre-independent Telangana movement. Telangana, which has now become a separate state, craved for this status even in pre-independent India, wherein it witnessed massive peasant and workers' risings. This laid the foundation of a revolting populace against the existing system. It is argued that most of the people who are part of the Naxal movement are people who once were part of the Radical Student Union (RSU) and the Telangana Sangharsh Samitis (TSS). They were demanding the creation of a separate state. The movement, however, was quelled ferociously.

It is also argued that the second stage of the movement resurfaced during the protests against the atrocities of the Nizam of Hyderabad. There was a massive participation of the people in the movement. But the ouster of the Nizam rule did not change the fate of the people in the region for the better. Some of the people who became part of the protest took to the red route, which appeared to them more appealing than the parliamentary path to eliminate poverty, atrocities, and emancipation from the appalling Zamindari system. Though the government of India abolished the Zamindari system soon after independence, it worked only on paper, and the reality on the ground continued to prevail.

However, the real shape of the modern-day Naxal movement took its form in the early 70s when the ideological divide within the CPI led to the formation of the CPM and further splits within the CPM and the formation of the CPI (ML). It is worth noting that the Andhra faction of the Communist leadership did not believe in 'complete annihilation of the class enemies'. Thus, they differed from the Ranadiv faction, which was for the complete annihilation of the class enemies. These two states demonstrated two different ideological streams within the Naxal movement. They had the same goal but different approaches and orientations. The Telangana movement had actually thrown a major ideological discourse within the communist movement. While a section of the Communists led by Ranadiv advocated the Russian experience under Stalin and was highly critical of Mao and Tito, the Andhra secretariat of the Communists preferred the Chinese methods. In the period subsequent to the post-Charu Mazumdar period, the Naxal movement in the state received major splits. After the split of the CPI (M), the Naxal faction made inroads in the state of Andhra Pradesh. However, the movement remained, by and large, peaceful in the initial years largely because of a lack of funds, sufficient infrastructural and human resources, and the incapacity to mobilise the masses on a large scale. Things, however, changed from the 90s, when the Naxalites started using force to run their writs. The state retaliated successfully with all physical might at its command. And today, Andhra does not make headlines on account of Maoist violence any more. The aggressive dose of development and judicious application of the armed forces broke the backbone of the Naxals in the state. It would not be wrong to delineate the fact that the Naxal movement sought its migration towards the other states and started shifting its base when the ruthless state power convincingly decimated them in the gun battle. It is estimated that between 1990 and 2009, nearly 2000 Naxal cadres were killed in the state. Hundreds of them were made to surrender, and more than that are still languishing in jails.

The third category of states are the states that, over the years, are in the process of emerging as terror centers. Garhchiroli in Maharashtra and certain areas of Uttar Pradesh and Bihar can be placed in those categories. In Bihar, the Naxal movement made a major inroad but could not sustain its vigor for long. Again, the movement reached its pinnacle in the state when the Congress party was at the helm of affairs in the state. It also flourished during the Lalu Prasad Yadav regime. Lalu selectively used the Naxal movement for political gains. However, after Nitish Kumar came to power in 2005, the movement started losing its steam. The clear direction from the political executive to eliminate the Maoist bases enabled the administration to make effective interventions. Maoists are present in several districts of the state, but their striking power has declined significantly in Bihar. Once upon a time, the Maoist Communist Centre and Party Unity were dreaded organisations in rural Bihar. But they lost their social base and revolutionary activities during the Nitish government.

If we look at the Maoist movement, it makes it amply clear that its base has shifted from Jangal Mahal in West Bengal and Khammam and Vishakhapatnam in Andhra Pradesh to Palamu and Garhwa in Jharkhand and Bastar, Bijapur, Dantewada, and Sukma in Chhattisgarh. The shift in the base area is really interesting, as it provides insights into the nature of the struggle. As discussed above, the major states that remained in the news in the last two decades for the Naxal activities were Jharkhand and Chhattisgarh. Bihar was primarily an agricultural economy when the Naxal movement was at its peak. But now, they are concentrated in areas with mines, mineral resources, and dense forests. Jharkhand and Chhattisgarh are small states rich with natural resources and account for nearly 40 percent of India's iron ore and other minerals. There are 26 highly Maoist-affected districts in the country, of which 20 come from these two states (Hindustan Times, 2013). In West Bengal, only West Midnapur is placed in the category of 'worst affected' district. In Bihar, only three districts, Gaya, Aurangabad, and Jamui, are the worst affected. Even in these three districts, the Naxals are grounded and on the receiving end. In Orissa also, there are three districts that are badly hit by the Maoist presence and their violence. They are Malkangiri, Koraput, and Bolangir. Garhchiroli is the only district in Maharashtra that falls under this category. A careful look at the districts makes three points very clear. Most of these districts under Maoist influence have rich deposits of different mineral items, where development activities have been undertaken by multinationals in recent years. Second, most of these districts have either thick forest cover or hilly tracts in or in the adjoining areas. Third, over the last two decades, these areas have been exposed to industrial activities through multinational companies excavating or mining the natural resources for commercial purposes. This has resulted in huge population displacement in and around the adjoining areas. The alienation of the people from the ancestral land causes them sentimental and emotional loss. Maoists have used this as a root in their footprints in these areas. Jal, Jangal, and Jamin have become the mobilizing issues against corporations in these areas. Dantewada, Bijapur, and Bastar have rich iron ore deposits. Apart from the National Mining Development Corporation, Tata Steel and Essar Steel are two giant players involved in extracting iron ore. Given the ideology, the Maoists' whole purpose is to overthrow the existing political system, and therefore, nothing short of complete rejection of the present system and replacing it with a new one is acceptable to them. Violence becomes an important component of their activity, which includes abduction, looting, and extortion of money.

2 Organisation, Arms and Weapons, Leadership, Janata Darbar, Jan Adalat

Maoists have certainly exploited inequality, injustice and exploitation to seek support and expand their base. The issues have, therefore, been different in different regions, besides some common factors. For example, in Bihar, they exploited the social tensions and agrarian disputes on wages and property of commons, which the upper castes had been using without any entitlement, better known as *Gairmajaruah* lands. In the state, adequate wages also became an important issue for the Naxal to mobilize the masses against the upper castes, besides the social fabric in which people belonging to the lower castes were treated badly by the upper castes. Protecting the dignity of the lower castes, which were humiliated at the hands of the upper castes in Bihar, provided fertile ground for the Naxalites to build their social support base in rural Bihar. However, the same factor did not work in all the states in the Naxalite uprisings. In Andhra, the agrarian uprisings also helped cultivate the social base of the party. In 1976, Nagabhushan Patnaik seized the hoarded grains from the house of landlords in Parvatipuram and destroyed the loan records, which were one of the major instruments of exploitation of Adivasis (Swami, 2013). In Jharkhand and Chhattisgarh, Maoists claim to be fighting for the rights of Adivasis whose lands and homes are under threat because of the entry of corporate giants in the areas for executing the mining projects. What is common across the states is that Naxals stood for the dignified rights and lives of a section of society that was socially and economically deprived and dehumanised. Therefore, when the Naxalites raised the banner of revolt against the upper castes and class dominance, the people coming from the lower rungs of society saw in them the image of emancipators.

3 Fighting against the Indian State

The Maoists' fight is against the Indian state, which, according to them, represents imperialist, feudal and comprador bourgeoisie. The instrument of the state and the forces that support it become the enemy of the Maoists. The war against these forces is to be fought tactically, and there should be a clear strategic doctrine behind it. Maoists hold that since they have to encounter the state, which is militarily far more Organised, trained with superior firepower and concentrated in the cities and urban centres, the revolutionary war has to start from the weak link, and that is the rural areas where there is discontent among the peasantry, which will be eager for revolution. Peasantry, therefore, can be an important ally in the revolution. Secondly, given the weak military power, it would not have been possible to defeat the Indian state quickly. Thirdly, the masses need to be mindful of and prepared for war. And therefore, it has to be a protracted war. But they are sure that it is possible to defeat the Indian state. It does not matter how powerful it is. A direct fight against the state is not possible. And therefore, they prescribe guerrilla warfare. A tactical use of the guerrilla forces against the state can make victory possible. It says "by applying the best part of our army against different single parts of the enemy forces and following the policy and tactics of sudden attack and annihilation, it is possible to defeat the enemy forces .... and defeat the enemy decisively".[7] The military line is very clear; "you fight your way, and we will fight us. We fight when we win, we retreat when we cannot."[8]

Maoists hold that in India, the revolutionary base should be in rural areas where the enemy (the Indian) is relatively weak. They can easily be defeated through guerrilla warfare in such areas. Once the enemy is defeated in such areas, they would be declared as liberated areas, which subsequently will act as a base from which the people's war in the country to seize political power would be coordinated. Base areas would be used to develop guerrilla zones accordingly. Maoists believe that the rural, forest and hilly areas are best suited for this purpose in India. Maoists have chosen the hilly tracts with dense forests very consciously because they consider that in these areas, the enemy is relatively weak. The hilly tracts have a huge population and territory spread over thousands of square kilometres. Along with that, they have huge economic resources. Mere forests will give them nothing, and therefore, they are conscious of the fact that development projects would enable them to extort huge amounts of money, which they would use for the purchase of weapons and other logistics in the war against the enemy. They call them strategic areas, which are favourable for building and 'manoeuvres of the people' army. It is not surprising that these are the areas that became the strongholds of the Naxal movements in the peak times. They trained the cadres in the war against the Indian state and fortified them to an extent that they made it difficult even for the armed forces to enter those areas without risk. When the forces sought to dominate these areas, they had to face the wrath of the Naxalites.

Why do Naxalites support all the fissiparous and divisive activities in India? The answer comes from reading their document. It is not out of the blue but a result of conscious thinking. They hold that instability and engagement of the Indian state in dealing with such situations, including war, will weaken the Indian state, and accordingly, it will be favourable for the party to successfully execute the plan of liberating the areas from the control of the Indian state. This also provides the answer to the question of why Naxal opposes arms procurement by the Indian state and its defence preparedness. The weaker the Indian state is, the more vulnerable it is to revolution. Their concern is not at

7 Legal document submitted by the Government of India in the Supreme Court in 2013, pp. 97–98.

8 Legal document submitted by the Government of India in the Supreme Court in 2013, p. 170.

all for human rights. Had this been at the core of their thinking and operations, they would not have used terror to coerce innocent children into their military squads. This is a proven fact that they use even women and children in their fight against the Indian state. Had human rights been a serious and sensitive issue for them, they would not have resorted to the mass killing of the innocents to create a psychology of fear in the common men and women. They would rather inflict violence against the poor and helpless so that they could come to their fold against the Indian state.

Their whole objective is to weaken the Indian state. That is precisely the reason that they do not want a nuclear India. Most of the communist comrades in India have been opposed to India becoming a nuclear power. They have a problem with it. But they have no problem with the Chinese bomb. They have rarely been seen to hit the streets against the human rights violations in China. They also had no problem with tanks rolling over the unarmed protesting students at Tiananmen Square in China for silencing the freedom of expression. The Chinese government had justified the violence against the students, terming their acts 'counter-revolutionary rebellion'. And what were the demands of the students? Just to introduce democracy and pro-people reforms, freedom of expression. They were silenced by bullets. The radical left in India and its subsidiaries spoke on the same line. For them, the students in the protests were 'CIA lackeys, juvenile delinquents, and bourgeois reactionaries. This is how the students' wings of the CPI (M) had reacted to the Tiananmen Square massacre. Maoists could never be seen taking sides with the women and weaker sections of Hindu society who had migrated to settle in Jammu and Kashmir after the partition of the country. They were denied some of the basic rights in the state. But Naxals, who always sided with separatism and demands for autonomy in the state, never mustered the courage to criticise the violence by Islamic extremists in the valley to the extent of compelling the Hindus to leave the valley in existential fear, humiliation and disgrace.

Maoists wish to forge an alliance of the masses of four classes—the working class, the peasantry, the urban petty bourgeoisie and the nationalist bourgeoisie and turn them into revolutionary organisations under the control of the revolutionary party (CPI-Maoist). This kind of united front is to be developed at all levels, starting from the village, but it should essentially be led by the revolutionary party and the party of the proletariat. They call it the New Democratic Front (NDF). The purpose of the front, which they also call the Revolutionary United Front (RUF), is to 'mobilize the masses politically to capture the state power'.[9] They would 'politically arouse masses, arm the masses

9 Legal document submitted by the Government of India in the Supreme Court in 2013, p. 172.

and lead them to defend the political power and the other political gains made'.[10] It goes to say that since the people belonging to these four classes are presently under the influence of 'comprador-feudal political parties, revisionist parties' and 'reformist and petty bourgeoisie organisations', they need to be brought under the leadership of the revolutionary party in the form of a united front. For that matter, the party should build 'tactical United Fronts at various levels, with diverse class forces with different aims'[11] without losing sight of the revolutionary path and objective.

Without roping the masses into the revolutionary struggle, it is difficult to have a successful revolution. Building mass organisations and organizing them for revolution, therefore, is a must. But they are also to subserve the cause of revolution. After the war against the state is declared, they all should be coordinated directly or indirectly to overthrow the state machine, as Mao said. They recognize that the objective conditions of China and India are different[12] but the underlying principles concerning the mass struggle and the armed struggle remain the same.[13] Both the mass struggle and the armed struggle complement each other. Mass organisations and mass struggles on revolutionary lines also become the recruitment source for the party's armed militia. The party consists of three kinds of mass organisations, namely underground revolutionary, open or semi-revolutionary and thirdly, mass organisations not directly linked to the party. The underground revolutionary mass organisations secretly conduct and propagate the party line among the masses and prepare them for revolutionary struggle. They are the ones who give an open call to the people to participate in the armed struggle against the state. They can be through youth organisations, cultural organisations etc.

The open or semi-open mass organisations are also linked to the party and openly work among the youth, writers, women, students and other sections of society. They term their activities as intended to propagate a 'New Democratic Revolution'. But in reality, they prepare them for the armed struggle. These organisations use the legal system to carry on revolutionary propaganda. Those urban organisations that fight the case of the Naxals in the urban areas can be placed in that category. The literary organisations, cultural organisations of

---

10 Ibid.

11 Legal document submitted by the Government of India in the Supreme Court in 2013, p. 173.

12 Legal document submitted by the Government of India in the Supreme Court in 2013, p. 179.

13 Legal document submitted by the Government of India in the Supreme Court in 2013, p. 179.

the radical left do this job for the party. The third set of mass organisations is not directly linked to the party. They are the broad-based organisations in the sense that they are not directly involved in the propagation of armed struggle against the Indian state. However, they try to unite non-party forces on a common programme' (Malik, 2013). Independent citizen initiatives fall under that category. Such organisations are important even in normal situations, but they become important when the state becomes very repressive and does not allow the open propagation of ideology. They subdivide the third category of organisations further into three groups, namely, fractional, cover organisations, and legal democratic organisations (Agnihotri, 2017). The first category of organisations represents the traditional mass organisations like Bhajan Mandali, women organisations, students' organisations, youth organisations etc. The cadres of the party penetrate these organisations without revealing their identity and links with the party. They work indirectly to draw members of these organisations into revolution and also provide cover to the party and its activities when the state goes repressive. Secondly, the party must form cover organisations which work as per the party without exposing themselves as integral to the party. They consider such organisations important in conditions where the radical left organisations are not allowed to work openly. The third category of organisations that the party must raise is the legal democratic organisations. Such organisations should be raised from the village and block levels to international organisations. They should aim at mobilizing the masses on broader issues like Hindutva, globalization, anti-capitalism, etc. The party directives to the cadres who work in these organisations are that they should work openly without revealing their connections with the party in all conditions. If their identity is disclosed or known to the public, they should shift to other activities or go underground. Interestingly, the documents speak nothing against Islamic or Christian theological imperialism.

The Maoists also design to rope in the members of different sections of society, such as Dalits, Adivasis, Women and minorities, by connecting with their problems and demands. They understand that they cannot be brought into class struggle directly; therefore, their conditioning of mind through aligning with their causes and concerns can deliver the desired ends. They advocate that the Naxal leaders should focus on the special problems that they face in order to bring them into the struggle. They should subsequently be educated on how their problems are 'essentially class questions' and how their liberation is linked to the class struggle. These groups and sections of society should then be taught how they should join the war against the common enemy, which for them is feudalism, imperialism, and comprador bureaucratic capitalism. Their documents suggest that the party must act with the organisations already working in these areas, even though the petty bourgeois are leading them.[14] No wonder the radical left-leaning intellectuals are the harbinger of most of the new social movements, be they about the environment, farmers, women or land issues.

The document also suggests to mobilize the vast masses against social evils like caste atrocities, untouchability and the atrocities of the upper caste Hindus on Dalits. They support the Adivasi's rights over the forest land. For them, the tribal regions are important strategic places for 'the Indian revolution from a military viewpoint due to their favourable terrain that facilitates the establishment of base areas'. Surprisingly, they also look at the population in a binary of majority-minority and Hindu-Muslims. They seek to mobilise the minorities into the class struggle. They accuse the Hindu organisations are engaged in bashing the Muslims. Interestingly, they endorse the narrative that 'Muslims are being specially targeted in recent times'.[15] The most surprising part is that they ignore the social evils, social atrocities and ills within the Muslim society but go very tough against the evils within the Hindu society. Further, they have no position on Muslims' obscurantism and sectarian radicalism driven by their theology, though they say that Naxalites should expose the fundamentalism of other religions as well.[16] But on the ground, they have never been seen as going against Islamic fundamentalism. Nowhere in the world has Islamic society been a fertile terrain for the ideology of Naxalism because Islamic society is essentially anti-democratic and anti-secular. But the Naxalites in India hardly speak on the issue. For seven decades, the women in Kashmir were denied even the right to marry the boy of their choice if he was residing outside Kashmir without losing their rights to property. The Scheduled caste members who migrated to the state after partition were denied the citizens' rights. However, the Naxals supported the radical Muslim demands for secession of the valley from India.

To them, India is not a single nation but a multinational country,[17] i.e., a conglomeration of several nationalities. Naxals borrowed the idea of national and nationality questions from the writings of Stalin and Mao. Stalin had argued in favour of the right of the nationalities to exist as independent states. Northeast

14 Legal document submitted by the Government of India in the Supreme Court in 2013, p. 187.

15 Legal document submitted by the Government of India in the Supreme Court in 2013, p. 191.

16 Legal document submitted by the Government of India in the Supreme Court in 2013, p. 191.

17 Legal document submitted by the Government of India in the Supreme Court in 2013, p. 196.

and Kashmir for them were annexed into India by the British imperial power, and their occupation is continued by the Indian state; therefore, the Naxalites must support their demands of secession.[18] However, for the other nationalities, they speak of uniting them and discouraging the secessionist appeals of regional comprador-feudal parties[19] but if the entire people of that nationality insist on secession, Naxals should not oppose it[20] Naxals consider the ethnic communities as nationalities and therefore recommend opposing the Bengali oppression of the Assamese and Assamese oppression of or lording over the Bodos, Karbis, Mishings, etc. Needless to say, their understanding of India in terms of linguistic or ethnic communities and understanding of inter-ethnic tensions in terms of dominance and dominated, oppressor and oppressed is less integrative and more divisive.

4 Naxals and Urban Areas

Though the Naxal activities are reported primarily from the rural and remote forest areas, the urban centres are not less important in their people's liberation protracted war against the Indian state. The deprivation of the villagers of modern amenities, caste and class exploitation, and denial of a dignified life for a large multitude of populations provide a fertile ground for the Naxals to reach out to people and rope them into the revolutionary struggle. To them, it is the weak link where the enemy, the state, is weak, and therefore, they can be developed as liberated areas and bases from which the revolutionary activities could further be launched.[21] They want to develop it as a major base area. However, they consider the urban areas very important in their revolutionary war because they house a big chunk of the working-class industrial workforce. They hold that 'in the absence of a strong revolutionary urban movement, their revolutionary struggle will face a lot of difficulty and challenges.

For them, the urban movement is important for cadre building, technology and information inputs, supplies and support to the revolutionary movement. The job of the Naxals in the cities and towns is mainly to 'organize the working class as well as other classes and sections like the semi-proletariat, students, middle class employees, doctors, engineers, students, professors and intellectuals, with the help of whom the masses will be politicised and roped into the

18 Legal document submitted by the Government of India in the Supreme Court in 2013, p. 194.
19 Ibid.
20 Ibid.
21 Ibid.

revolutionary struggle. The second task in the urban cities is to build a united front of the working class and other classes in the cities. The urban activities are important because it is here that the cadres to the rural areas and other activities which complement the rural armed struggle are possible. The students, professors, intellectuals, doctors, and engineers, who are now depicted as Urban Naxals, perform the same activities.[22] Naxals admit that they have developed secret party units in the urban areas under different names, which work for the Naxal movement in the cities and towns, from academic institutions to industry. Thus, the People's Liberation Army performs military work in rural areas, but these urban organisations also perform complementary military functions. They must infiltrate the military, academics, administration, and industry and pass on the information to the organisation to prepare it to resist the challenges that may come from the Indian state. The urban work of the organisation has to remain defensive in nature till the final period of the revolution. This is also because the enemy's strength, i.e., the strength of the Indian state, is in the urban areas. Therefore, they must work secretly but act as 'strong recruiting centres for the revolutionary party'. It is not difficult to understand how a bunch of intellectuals and lawyers stood all of a sudden when the state started the 'Operation Green Hunt' or Salwa Judum with the support of the locals against the Naxals.

In the last ten years, the Modi government has not only focused on the rural areas to militarily outdo the Naxals but has also worked towards controlling the urban Naxals by initiating effective measures against them. Over the years, many universities have developed as nurseries for the Naxal movement. The government has tightened their noose, and that effectively seems to be working. And this seems to be working. There is hardly any demonstration or student protest on the campuses of India in favour of the Naxals. The barrage of propaganda campaigns in favour of the Naxal movement has nearly stopped in the major universities of India, barring a few exceptions. Similarly, eulogising the Naxal activities in the media and academia as a symbol of progressiveness has seen a sharp decline. In the terror field, the government worked on multiple fronts, ranging from establishing the writ of the state in areas that hitherto were dominated by the Naxalites to developing infrastructure in the Naxal-infested areas. According to the Home Ministry data, in 2014, there were 330 police stations where Naxal incidents occurred, but now this number has reduced to 104. Similarly, earlier Naxal-affected areas have declined from 18,000 square kilometres to 4,200 square kilometres. Between 2014 and 2024, there has been a 53 percent decrease in Naxalite activities (PIB, 2025).

22 Legal document submitted by the Government of India in the Supreme Court in 2013, p. 198.

CHAPTER 3

Political Economy of the Naxal Movement

Naxals might be fighting for the poor, but their organisation is not poor. They have huge resources at their disposal. And that comes from a variety of activities ranging from membership fees to donations to levied taxes and penalties imposed on individuals to extortion and confiscation of property and wealth from class enemies and the state (Party Constitution CPI (M), 2004). Recent revelations have argued that people and members support the cause of Naxals in various ways. First, through membership fees. However, this is a minuscule contribution to their overall budget. Second, people contribute through donations. For instance, NGOs funded by foreign countries that sympathise with the cause of the movement and corporate houses or traders who donate to them, but not out of love or sympathy for the ideology, but to ensure that their business interests are not harmed by the Maoists (Prakash, 2015:902–904). This is thus also coerced and unaccounted money, though it comes in the form of a donation. Third, another category involves the money that is, in a true sense, the extorted revenue that comes through 'tax, levy, and penalty' imposed on individuals, government officials, corporate houses, etc. This includes pure extortion as well as money generated from the robbery of banks, kidnapping of people, etc. Naxals' collection of money comes from nearly 223 out of 636 districts in the country (Singh & Diwan, 2010).

Among the sources, as explained above, what in recent years has come out as the big source of revenue to the Naxals is the extortion money collected from factory owners to mine owners, landlords to the traders, contractors to government servants and small shopkeepers to bus operators[1] (Singh & Diwan, 2024). In fact, there is hardly any domain of economic activities which today is untouched by their extortion enterprise. The reason is simple. Naxals know well that they cannot sustain against the state for long if they are not well equipped in all respects. They know that the war against the state is not going to be so simple. It must be a protracted one. For that, they need a cadre and arms, propaganda machinery, food items, clothes and medicines. For all this money is required. The membership fee cannot be sufficient to do the cause. Adoption of illegal means thus becomes imperative to generate revenue. They

1 Vishwa Ranjan who served as the Director General of Police in Chhattisgarh on 29 November 2009 had claimed that Maoist extort money worth 20 billion annually across India.

 | HTTPS://DOI.ORG/10.1163/9789004765054-005

have rationalised justification for this, too. And the argument is that the capitalists have become capitalists through the exploitation of the poor, hence there is no wrong if the poor come out to confiscate the property amassed by the capitalists.

An estimate suggests that Naxals generate an amount somewhere between 1600 crores and 2000 crores annually from extortion alone[2] (D'Souza & Routray, 2013; Mahadevan, 2012:205; Prakash, 2015: 902–904). Out of the total, nearly 300 crores come from the state of Chhattisgarh alone (Kumar, 2009). Actually, the business of extortion is directly proportional to two factors: first, the economic resources and magnitude of trade and commercial activities in the area and secondly, the proportion of Naxals' influence in the region. Thus, the more economic activities mean more opportunity for extortion, provided the influence of the Naxals in terms of fear runs large in the region. This is amply clear from the fact that even in places where their influence is high but the economic activities are poor or the region is not industrialised, there is poor resource generation. For example, once some of the districts of Central Bihar were the nerve centre of the Maoist activities. But they were not the regions of rich mining or industrial activities. In such regions, the Naxals have used the areas to create their base line from where they could encircle the towns and cities. They are not the areas important for the Naxals for economic resource generation. Such areas are helpful in building cadres and instilling in them the courage and instincts of revolution. Similarly, there are several pockets of the country where economic resources are in abundance, but the influence of the Naxals is not too effective. Such areas do not produce a revenue heaven for the Naxals. Chhattisgarh and Jharkhand are not without reason so productive for the Naxals, as these two states contribute the most to their treasury. These states seem to be pushing back against states like West Bengal

2 According to figures provided by the Union Ministry of Home Affairs (MHA), it is Rs 1,400 crore annually. Chhattisgarh Chief Minister Raman Singh recently said that it is between Rs 1,000 and Rs 1,200 crore per year. The Director General of Police in Chhattisgarh, in November 2009, however, had said that the figure was as high as Rs 2,000 crore. All this has been a guess work. But one thing is sure; there is huge collection of funds through the extortion.

Earlier, documents and hard disks seized from Misir Mishra, a central committee member of the CPI-Maoist, who was arrested in Jharkhand in March 2008, had revealed that the CPI-Maoist collected over Rs1,000 crore in 2007 through their state committees and had set a target of Rs1,125 crore for 2008. Documents also revealed that there has been a target set for all the state committees. The collection of the revenue has shifted with the shift in the influence of the Naxal movement. Minister of State for Home Affairs, RPN Singh however reported the Rajya Sabha on 12 February 2014 that the CPI (Maoist) party has been collecting not less than 140 crores annually from a variety of sources.

and Andhra Pradesh in terms of the collection of money. This is also indicative of the fact that the base of the Naxal movement is changing. A few years ago, Andhra Pradesh and West Bengal were the epicentres of the Naxal movement. Now, Jharkhand, Chhattisgarh, Odisha have emerged as the prime pockets of the Naxal movement.

But that does not mean that the funds flow only from the above areas alone. Even those areas that generally do not make news and are not very well-known for the Naxal activities also contribute significantly to the coffers of the Naxal movement. For example, Maharashtra, Karnataka and the state of Tamil Nadu are relatively unknown places for the Naxal activities. But these states also contribute significantly to the Naxals. In 2007, these states raised 100, 78 and 35 crores, respectively (Singh & Diwan, 2024). Documents seized from some of the Naxal leaders suggest that every year they set a target in advance (Kujur, 2009). All the state committees are told in advance not only about the sum total that is expected from them but also the possible sources to work upon. Thus, which private sector company or which project of the government or the private company is to be targeted in the impending year is clear to the Naxal cadres who are tasked with executing it. The provincial committee gives the funds to the central military commission and the central committee, apart from funding the activities of the local units that the cadre represents. But the common denominator of all is the fact that the greatest portion of revenue generated comes from extortion.

The extortion business promoted by them is all over the patches in the region where Naxals dominate or their influence is very strong. The extortion activities in Chhattisgarh run from the Southern tip of Bastar to the Northern Surguja. Bastar region, which is treated as one of the nerve centres of the Maoist movement in India, as a maximum number of Maoist violence cases come from the Bastar region. Sukma Valley falls in Southern Bastar, wherein the deadliest ambush was executed by the Maoists, in which 75 CRPF lost their lives in 2010 when they were suddenly attacked (Mishra, 2017; Hindustan Times, 2017). This area produces high-quality Tendu leaves, which are used to make Biddis. Similarly, the Surguja region has the most coal-rich areas of the country. The highest profit-making subsidiary of Coal India Limited, Southern Eastern Coalfield Limited, is located in this area. This region also produces nearly 20 percent of India's total iron ore. The biggest and most precious iron ore mines, popularly known as the Baladilla mines, are located in the Dantewada district in the state of Chhattisgarh. The National Mining Development Corporation and the Essar Steel Group mine iron ore from the Baladilla mines and transport it to the Vishakhapatnam port in Andhra Pradesh.

It would be worth noting that the Naxal movements are more entrenched in the areas where rich mines of different kinds are located. 80 percent of the coal comes from the Naxal-infested areas of Bengal, Odisha, Chhattisgarh, Jharkhand and Andhra Pradesh. Most of our electricity-generating stations are thermal-based, and the continual digging of mines is essential to meet the requirements of these thermal stations. The same applies to other minerals as well. Maoists are effective in the Bauxite mining areas of Jharkhand. Naxals demand a heavy levy from the mining projects, beat the employees and prevent the workers from loading the materials. The terror of the Maoists runs high. The people and workers in the areas, as well as the owners of the mining projects, have more faith in the capacity of the Maoists than the state.

Many of these mines are located in thick forest zones or non-agricultural zones. The terrain serves two purposes: first, it is convenient for the Naxals to operate their extremist activities, and second, they are cash-rich area due to mines, though the benefit travels to very few. Several big companies like Tata, Essar, Jindal Steel, etc. are engaged in mining activities in these areas. Their field operations are in these areas, but the corporate offices are located in big cities. Since their mining activities sometimes lead to the displacement of the tribals from their native places, they provide ground for emotional exploitation of the tribals by the Naxals. On the one hand, they mobilise the tribals, raising their genuine concerns pertaining to their displacement and sentimental loss, compensation and jobs of tribals in the commercial activities. On the other hand, they extort these business companies to pay before they start their work in the area. It is no longer a secret that the Naxalites take money from the corporates. Displacement of tribals or farmers for industrial activities generates anger, which provides fertile ground for the Maoists to exploit them. Bringing thousands of the aggrieved onto the streets is not a daunting task for the Maoists (Denyer, 2007).

Also, the big corporations are easy targets that provide a huge sum to the Naxals. Therefore, in recent years, Naxalites have focused on corporate India, which is engaged in commercial and business ventures in the tribal areas. Tata, Essar and Jindal groups are their primary targets as they primarily are involved in coal, bauxite and iron ore mining (Phadnis, 2013). The strong presence of the Naxals in the rich states of the mines makes it easier for them. Naxals know very well that collections from the individuals in the form of membership or donation are not going to be sufficient to sustain the protracted war against the Indian state. They need a huge amount of money for this. And therefore, they use their presence to threaten them to make them realise that they cannot do mining or other industrial activities in such places without the support of the Naxalites. There is a concerted and well-calculated plan in this respect. On March 25, 2007, the Asian Age from Delhi published a detailed report on the basis of documents procured from the Central Military Commission of the Maoists. The documents make it clear that the Naxals propose to exploit the situation emerging from the local discontents due to increased mining in the areas, the displacement of the people, and poor compensation to the evacuated people. The document of the Naxals revealed that they have a comprehensive scheme to tax the corporate giants like Tata, Essar, Jindal, Pasco, Mittal groups, as these have big commercial stakes in the mine-rich areas of Jharkhand, Orissa and Chhattisgarh (Phadnis, 2013).

It has been found that major corporate groups that have a commercial interest in the areas of Naxal dominance make regular payments to the Naxals, though they officially do not admit it; hence, the quantum of extortion money is difficult to document. A major steel company is reported to have been making regular payments to the Naxals, though recently the Naxals attacked it and torched their vehicles when they refused to ferry arms on their planes. Ravi Sharma, a Naxal leader arrested from Bihar in October 2009, confirmed that corporate houses make regular payments to the Naxals (Singh & Diwan, 2024; Chakraborty, 2009). Ravi Sharma revealed the names of several corporate houses that have interests in mining, steel, coal and other commercial activities in the states of Bihar and Jharkhand (Chakraborty, 2009). According to a confessional statement, "the Naxals are extorting Rs. 2 crores from the NMDC every year" (Chakraborty, 2009). This is not something uncommon or a new trend in making at all. Corporate houses have also earlier been found funding extremist groups like ULFA (United Liberation Front of Assam) and Bodo extremists in Assam. Decades back, the Assam DGP had briefed the press that the TATA Tea company had paid medical bills of top ULFA leaders and other benefits. The company's senior executive, Bolin Bordoloi, was kidnapped by Bodo militants and they were kept hostage for 11 months in 1993 (Business Standard, 1997). ULFA also had kidnapped two tea garden managers of the company in 1995. They demand a levy from the coal, bauxite and iron ore projects, beat the employees and prevent the workers from loading the materials. The terror of the Maoists amongst the employees also runs large.

A few years back, a report appeared in the newspaper quoting the CEO of the Abhijeet Group responding to allegations of making payments to the Naxals, holding that their company works for the underprivileged in the areas, and this matches the ideology of the Maoists (Murty, 2010). Abhijeet Group, along with 'Rungta Mines, Usha Martin, Torian Iron and Steel, is alleged to have paid Rs. 2.5 million each to the Maoists in 2007–08, as per the intelligence sources (Anoop, 2011). The intelligence reports corroborate the versions of local villagers that the company pays a huge amount to the Maoists (Dungdung, 2015). It would be worth noting that the Maoists had attacked the Abhijeet group power plant in April 2009 and had killed four security staff. It is learnt that it was done so because the group had refused to pay money to the Naxals then.

The Abhijeet group, along with Hindalco and Essars, are those groups that are running their projects in the state smoothly. The Corporate Power Limited, a unit of Abhijeet Infrastructure Pvt Ltd, is establishing a major thermal power plant at Chakala village under Chandava Block in the Latehar district of Jharkhand. The company is supposed to invest 6080 crores in the project, which is likely to generate 1215-megawatt electricity. The company has been allotted a 'captive coal block for the purpose' and has also acquired a 'No Objection Certificate' from the state pollution control board. Such a no-objection certificate is generally given after the public hearing and after seeking the grievances of the affected party (Dungdung, 2015). Maoists play a prominent role in such cases. They assure these business houses of smooth sailing, provided these corporations dole out handsome amounts of money to them. The corporates have just to make a few commitments like giving jobs to the locals, good compensation, giving appointments to the people on the recommendations of the Maoists, etc. It is difficult to prove such payments because they are part of cash dealings and therefore also cannot be deciphered from the bank details. Abhijeet Group is not the only such company. There are numerous others. According to Mr. S.K. Satpathy, the Maoists blocked nearly 21 road construction projects under the Prime Minister's Gram Sadak Yojana in Jharkhand when the contractors showed their inability to make the payment that the Naxals wanted from them (Anoop, 2011). Many a time, it is not just the money but even the amount of money that becomes the bone of contention, and Naxals make a mathematical calculation of the total projects and thereafter set the demand.

The Naxal movement surely has become a flourishing source of income for the police as well. All the Naxal-infested states have been pumping money to seek people's help in the collection of information about the Naxals. These amounts are unaccounted money, and there have been cases of siphoning off the amount without giving a statement of expenditure by the senior police officials. A case in Jharkhand is a classic to know about. The report of the Jharkhand government Accountant General 2005–06 and 2007–08 reveals that both the Director General and Deputy Director General of Police withdrew Rs. 8 crores from the secret fund but did not submit the statement of expenditure (Chakravorti, 2013).

The Naxalites, in fact, tax and extort everyone who is capable of contributing to their treasury. That includes a variety of people ranging from common sympathisers to wage earners to businessmen, landlords and traders who are engaged in the business of forest and mines of the areas, contractors engaged in infrastructural developments in the area and corrupt government officials. The government officials, industrialists and contractors give the money to the Maoists because they know that they cannot survive in the area and run their business or related works if the Naxals are not obliged. They do not leave out even the pro-poor developmental projects at work in the Naxal-infested area. NREGA schemes and the Golden Quadrilateral projects had turned out to be a boon for the Naxals. It has been widely noted that there had been rampant corruption at the local level in MNREGA (Mahatma Gandhi National Rural Employment Guarantee Act) before the arrival of the direct benefits transfer facility. The infrastructural projects required a huge chunk of takeover of the farm and forest land by the state and putting in lots of investment and engagement of workers, officials, managers and engineers. It is not easy for them to initiate work in these areas without having an informal understanding with corporate dealers. Such instances are numerous, coming from the Maoist areas, most of which are part of the oral grapevine, whereas many of them also became part of the news items in electronic and print media.

For each of them, however, there is a separate logic for tax imposition and extortion. Common wage earners are asked to contribute because, first, they are told that the Naxals are fighting for their higher wages and saving them from exploitation by the contractors and the corrupt officials. Secondly, they try to convince them that they are not fighting for their personal gains but for the deprived and the poor people, taking risks with their lives, and therefore everyone should contribute his or her might from their class for which they are fighting. This is also meant to indicate and engage the participation of the common man in the movement. The government officials are to pay because it is implied that they mint money by encouraging wrongful exploitation of the forest reserves, or from the commission they get from the contractors. Contractors are charged because they earn from the infrastructural projects. And the corporates are asked to pay a charge because their activities are at the cost of trampling the rights of tribals and the poor. They are also to pay because they earn and multiply disproportionate profit from the exploitation of the local resources, both man-made and material. Many a time, these actions of the Naxals are appreciated by the common man because of poor dealings of government officials and misgovernance, which annoy the common man who harbours a trust deficit with the state. Since they are seen as the representatives of the state in the area against whom their battle is aimed, the Naxalites' actions against these officials bring delight to the poor and deprived.

Practically speaking, Naxals do not have a problem with the capitalists till the latter provide them with capital, which could be used for running the revolutionary activities. It is useful to know that they allow mining or other business activities in the area. They have rarely taken the position not to allow such activities at all. The theoretical position is that a protracted armed struggle against the state requires both manpower and material resources. Until and unless the movement is patronised and funded from outside, the struggle cannot be sustained. Thus, the collection of money and financial resources from society is essential. And there is no harm in making tactical and temporary compromises as long as the core idea of the revolution remains undiluted. And that is why they return favour and patronage to the builders, mine-owners and mafias in the tribal localities in exchange for money. There are scores of examples based on studies and reports which suggest that builders and mine-owners support the cause and activities of Naxals through backing them financially.

They consider it a tactical and short-lived compromise that has been part of all the revolutionary struggles, including the Russian Bolsheviks, who succeeded with the historic socialist revolution in 1917. Certainly, no ideology worth a mass movement works in puritan forms, and certain ideological and strategic dilutions do take place. Sometimes it comes at the top leadership also, but more frequently it is at the local levels where ideologically committed and enlightened cadres are missing or fewer in number. But the point is that in the case of the Naxal movement, the extortion business is not meant for resource generation, but it has turned out to be a big racket in the Naxal-infested areas, and the local goons have found it a suitable business to carry out their means of living.

These extortions are charged normally annually as well as on a monthly basis. It all depends on what kind of work is involved. The leadership in this regard formally issues the guidelines to its cadres, mentioning the rates according to which the money has to be collected from different stakeholders in the area. Naxals also sometimes use the local criminals to achieve this end. According to an extortion rate card as circulated by the Naxal leadership, Rs. 8000 has to be extorted annually from quarries employing manual crushers, Rs. 15000 from brick-kiln owners, Rs. 25000 from petrol pump owners, and Rs. 70000 from coal sidings (Kujur, 2009). The same applies to Bus and truck operators. Truck owners and bus operators pay through their associations. They are doubly taxed in their business. On the one hand, it is the Naxals who levy a monthly fee on them somewhere between Rupees 1000 and 5000, depending on the number of buses and the income involved; on the other hand, the police also charge them monthly for running their business. If they refuse to do so, their trucks will explode, or people will be abducted (Satapathy et al., 2010). A transporter in the Piparwar area of Jharkhand held that in 2010 itself, nearly 'twenty trucks carrying coal and bauxite were set ablaze' (Satapathy et al., 2010).

Any civil construction in the Naxalite-hit area cannot go on without making a payment to the Maoists. 'Every contractor has to cough up money when it is demanded by the Naxals.' There is no refusal. The negotiation is done only if there is a reduction in the amount. Naxals force the contractors to pay a part of the total sanctioned amount, which roughly ranges between five and 15 percent. In fact, some of the studies of think-tanks that track the Naxalite movement also hold that there is a proper rate list against all ranges of work in the areas of their dominance (Naik, 2019). This gives them a huge amount. Naxals justify this levy on the ground that the corrupt contractors who make money out of such projects also pay a huge amount to the corrupt officials. The nexus between the contractors and the corrupt officials also loots the people's money. Hence, the extortion from such people is not something unethical.

Many times, the nexus between the Naxals and the contractors in the area has also been reported, where both are serving each other's interests. What happens is that the Naxals are approached by these contractors to damage the constructions so that their quality could not be assessed by the higher officials, and they could again get the money sanctioned for further works? This arrangement of understanding benefits both the contractors and the Naxals. It has also been found that the contractors, on their own, have used explosives to destroy the constructions so that the quality of the work could not be evaluated and assessed.

Even government officials in some of the Naxal-infested areas are made to make payments to the Naxals. Each one has a quota to meet. How they would do it is left to them. This applies normally in regard to the works related to infrastructural developments; be that related to school building, road constructions, irrigation projects, etc. A part of the Government fund channelled into the remote rural areas under different development programmes and welfare schemes also contributes to the treasury of the Naxalites. Shanthie Mariet D'Souza and Bibhu Prasad Routray, in their study, found that BDOs give bribes to their seniors for the posting in these Naxal areas, as these areas are a heaven for minting unaccountable money. In fact, there is a nexus between the bureaucracy, politicians, contractors and the Naxals. And all benefit from this symbiotic arrangement. Politicians more often patronise the Naxals as they have to contest the elections in the Naxal-hit areas. Corrupt officials find such areas as a safe haven as they get unaccounted money. It is true that Naxals are very harsh to the corrupt officials, but there are also instances of both benefiting from the corrupt regime.

1 Naxals Targeting Schools and Welfare Schemes

The Naxals have also been taxing the government projects like NREGA and the Golden Quadrilateral, and whenever they got the power, they have stopped the work and allowed it to resume after receiving extortion money. In Bihar, work on several hundred km of the Golden Quadrilateral could not be made just because the Naxals wanted their share of the cut money. They do not leave even the schools which are meant for educating the tribals and preparing them to excel in their lives. Thus, in July 2009, in Latehar in Jharkhand, the Naxalites demanded that the school administration pay Rs 50000. It was communicated with a warning that if the demand is not met, the school administration will face dire consequences (SATP). Interestingly, this amount was taken out of the grant received by the school from the government. And the school met the demand. It was not without reason. In 2009, nearly six schools that refused to meet the demands of the Naxals were destroyed by the latter (SATP).

The Naxals, however, argue that they have exploded the schools in the remote areas only when and where there were instances that they had been used as camps for the policemen in the areas. It can be true in some cases, but it is not valid for all[3] (HRW, 2009). In 2009, a few other schools in the same district of Latehar were destroyed in the middle of the night. It was a polling centre for the impending assembly elections, and a portion of it was given to the police deputed for the elections. But then, even a day before the election, the classes were organised. This school catered to the needs of the 400–450 students coming from poor backgrounds. They became without school overnight. This raises several questions linked to the Naxals' commitment to the cause. It has now been made public that children of many of the top-ranking comrades have been getting an education in the urban areas in premier and elite technical and business schools of the country. If they are so committed to the cause of revolution, why don't they bring their children into the movement too? Further, when they understand the importance of education, why do they destroy the educational institutions working in the

3 Dantar Middle School, in Chatra district, blasted on or around June 22, 2008. Chak Middle School, in Palamu district, blasted on or around September 28, 2008. Satbahni Primary School, in Chatra district, blasted on October 2, 2008. Nitar Primary School, in Palamu district, blasted March 21, 2009. Saryu Primary School, in Latehar district, blasted on March 31, 2009. Banlaat village school, in Gumla district, blasted on March 31, 2009. Kiukra (Khukhra) Middle School, in Giridih district, blasted on April 18, 2009. Narayanpur village school, in Chatra district, blasted on April 21, 2009. These schools were not the schools which were occupied by the police.

remote rural areas? After all, these schools are not meant for propagating the capitalist cause. Nor are they there to promote the children of the upper caste or upper-class people. They are there to educate the poor, deprived and underprivileged people. These questions are pertinent, and no satisfactory answer has been provided by the Naxals or their academic and intellectual supporters so far. There have been instances of destruction of school buildings in different states, as well as killing of the school staff, which consequently multiplied the miseries of the rural population, as their children could not go to school in the absence of buildings and teachers. All this, however, does not make the charge of the Naxals hollow about police occupying the schools' buildings and using them as base stations for launching an offensive against the Maoists (HRW, 2009).

Fear is an important factor in the whole scheme of cultivating extortion money. Naxals pose a threat through notices pasted on the walls or other ways, which clearly outline that if their demands are not met, then the person targeted will face dire consequences. They set such examples and try to instil fear in the minds of the common people. In such situations, it becomes difficult for the common traders, businessmen or contractors to resist the Naxals as they know that they would have to pay the price for their acts of defiance. In the absence of the dominance of the state, these sections choose to surrender to the will of the Naxals. In fact, most of the businessmen pay them without making noise due to fear of retaliation from the Naxals and the economic interests involved in the area. They find it rather easier to ensure their security and unhindered conduct of their business activities. When a businessman dares to stop doing it or refuses to increase the amount in due course of time, abduction of people and destruction of property become common to them. Thus, a few years ago, the guest house of a multinational company in the Malkangiri district in Odisha was set on fire for the refusal of payment by the company.

The fear in the area runs its writ so large that these people who make the payment to the Naxals do not talk about it in the open. When it happens, those who attempt to do it are punished for the acts, and sometimes the punishment includes even a death sentence. Thus, those who make the payments also avoid talking about it. They talk, but always off the record. Interestingly, Naxals too do not harm the business houses and their interests till the latter keep meeting their extortion demands. Refusal to do so, however, proves fatal. In Bihar in 2009, approaching the Chhath (a very popular festival of Bihar dedicated to the God Sun) festivals, the Maoists slapped a ban on the traders and shopkeepers of Devaria market in Aurangabad district on opening the market for 15 days as a token of punishment because they earlier had violated the 48 hours shutdown calls of the Maoists a week ago (SATP). And the impact was total. Not a single shop opened despite the heavy deployment of the police and the assurance of the administration to provide all protections to the traders and shopkeepers. Traders not only apologised for their past mistakes but also promised not to do it again.

This was not an isolated incident. In 2007 also, Tandwa Bajar of Aurangabad district in Bihar wore a deserted look for over two weeks after the threats of the Naxals. This pattern has been witnessed not in one or two states but normally everywhere where the Naxals have a substantial impact. No one dares to contest them and their activities, however illegal they are, causing discomfort to the common man. A few years back, in Chhattisgarh, "public transport went off the roads and movement of iron ore from Dantewada district's Bailadila hills to Visakhapatnam in Andhra Pradesh was halted. Maoists blocked interior pockets of Bastar, Bijapur, Narayanpur, Dantewada and Kanker districts by placing wooden logs on the roads. But no one dared to clear the road by removing the artificial wooden log. The fear factor is crucial to their success. Contractors know it well that the price of non-payment is heavier than the value of the payment they make to the Naxals. The stoppage of the work means a loss in the business, which they can afford only at their own peril. In 2009, the MCC, a powerful Maoist group operating in Bihar, asked a contractor, Putu Kumar, in Jehanabad to pay Rs.3.5 million. On refusal to do so, two J.C.B. vehicles and tractors engaged in road construction were burnt to ashes in Narayana Mushari village under Pali police station, stopping the construction work. Such events pose a challenge to any businessman who works in the area (Kumar, 2008).

2 Emergence of Fake Naxals

The success of the extortion has resulted in a peculiar kind of business flourishing at the local level in which local goons are employed by the Naxals to do the collection for them. At the same time, it has also given rise to a new kind of extortion racket in which locals have started extorting money by posing as the Naxals. It is estimated that such extortion also runs into crores (Kumar, 2008; Business Standard, 2013). It was estimated that nearly 220 million were extorted by the fake Naxals in the year 2007 from the state of Chhattisgarh alone, of which 90 percent came from a few districts and pockets like Bastar, Dantewada, Kanker, Bijapur and Narayanpur. The problem with such extortion is that they are just a matter of guesswork based on informal reports. Because those who pay the money to the Naxalite outfits do not concede that they do so. They do not reveal it to anyone. Once the people get the letter from the

Naxals, they just do not question the demand but move to make attempts to meet it without delay. More importantly, this makes the exhortation business highly motivational for the young people, as it does not reveal the identity of the payers or the paid ones. This has significantly increased the cases of the emergence of fake Naxals extorting money from the people and traders. It is also interesting to note that in some cases, it has been found that the people who are engaged in such activities are not from the tribal belts but are outsiders.

Though the Maoists claim to be fighting against the class enemies and working for the poor, the statistics reveal otherwise. The number of deaths that have come up in counting from the Naxal violence suggests that poor, Dalits and tribals account for 80 percent of the total. Secondly, their claims of fighting a principled war also have few takers. The fact is that the top leadership of the Maoists also comes from the upper castes, as was the case with the CPI (Ramana, 2014). A major chunk of the cadres and leaders used to be from the educated rich middle class, and despite ideological trainings, they could not work against the upper castes in Bihar.

3 NGOs Funding the Naxals

One more astonishing aspect of the Naxal funding that has come to light is the NGOs working in the social welfare sectors, dissipating a portion of their revenues to the Naxals. Twenty-two such NGOs were found in the Gaya district alone, which, of course, was a major centre of Naxal activities in central Bihar. These NGOs, which run their activities partly from the government coffers and partly, or sometimes fully, from foreign funding, have been found to be employing the children and relatives of the Naxals on the one hand and making payments to the Maoists on the other. A few years ago, the government of Bihar listed out such NGOs and found out that in the majority of the cases, they were funded by international donors or visiting tourists who lend support to the Naxals directly or indirectly in the name of social welfare. These donations are very often in cash, and they run not in lakhs but in crores (Singh & Diwan, 2024). Interestingly, some of the NGOs were even run by the Naxal cadres only. For example, Dwarko Sundrani, who runs an NGO called 'Samanvaya Ashram' in Bodhgaya, was found to have links with the Maoists (Singh & Diwan, 2024).

These are not isolated incidents at all. Maharashtra police too identified some 50 NGOs which raised funds and transferred the same for the Naxals for the revolutionary cause (Kanate & Singh, 2013). The problem for the police is that they cannot act against them, as there is no law that provides for action against those who sympathise with their rule. Many of these NGOs are based in Nagpur, Pune and Mumbai. These NGOs are run by educated people under the umbrella of fronts like the Tactical United Front and the All-India People's Resistance Forum (Kanate & Singh, 2013). They, of course, are not the Naxals but extend help to the Naxals. In Jharkhand, too, several NGOs were found working in the remote forest areas, actually extending their help to the Naxals. There are NGOs that are funded by the state as well as foreign countries. In some cases, even the missionaries have been found to be party to it. Missionaries help the Naxals because the absence of a state makes it possible for them to engineer the conversion of the tribal people into Christianity (Sheshank, 2003). On June 2, 2010, Ahmadabad, father of Cedric Prakash, who himself runs an NGO, Prashant, which receives foreign funding, held a Press conference against the state government, which had arrested one person, Shrinivas, from the local NGO Darshan, for involvement in Naxal activities (DeshGujarat, 2010). The biggest worry is that these funds are unaccounted resources, and there is no audit of the same by the government agencies. Where this money goes, in fact, no one knows. A major portion of it is invested in the purchase of arms and ammunition.

Many a time, these NGOs' people work as interlocutors between the government and the Naxals. The government finds it difficult to prevent the influx of such money. In fact, there is a well-planned chain of networks that works across the country, in which some of the NGOs are in the category of sympathisers, whereas some of them directly work for their cause. The recent decisions of the government to exercise strict vigilance on the funds coming from outside the country also have to do with the concern of checking the inflow of funds to the organisations engaged in anti-national activities. The government has also come out with a plan to work out a database and to maintain it in regard to terror funding, transactions of their resources, etc. The data is likely to be created by the Financial Intelligence Unit of the government in the Finance Ministry (SATP, 2010). But all this is yet to materialise, and the terror funding from outside as well as from inside sources continues to flourish without effective checks. No government has dared to work against such NGOs and many others which were involved in nefarious work through non-voluntary organisations. The Modi government has either deregistered or derecognised thousands of such fake NGOs.

4 Maoist Directly into Business

Maoists' enterprise now goes beyond donations received or coerced. They are directly into business. They are the ones who are now investing money in Hawala and the real estate market, apart from promoting opium and (cannabis) cultivation in order to generate and rapidly multiply the revenue. And in this game of money-making, which they claim to be for the party cause, it is not that the lower cadres or middle cadres are involved in, but the high-ranking comrades are deeply engaged in this exercise. A few years ago, a Maoist leader, Parmod Mishra, was arrested by Dhanbad police. Later on, on interrogation, it came to light that he had a wide range of properties in Patna, Gaya, Kolkata, Ranchi and even in Delhi. He also had invested in the real estate market of the country (Kumar, 2008). Parmod Mishra is not an exception. There have been numerous such instances of lower-rung leaders from the Naxalite groups engaged in a money-making venture. And top leadership is not untouched by it.

Poppy cultivation is also a good source of revenue for them. Interestingly, they oppose liquor. They get a certain amount as commission for the sale of poppies. They assure the local cultivators of support in case the police come to harass them. One finds hundreds of acres of land where poppies are cultivated in Orissa, particularly near Balimela reservoir in Malkangiri area, and in the Ghaghara area of Gumala district in Jharkhand. In Bihar, Kishanganj and Purnia have come out to be the major pockets of poppy cultivation. Naxals are deeply engaged in this business to raise funds. They do a survey of the possible fields and ensure the security of the crops. The annual report of the Finance Ministry for the financial year (2013–2014) noted that the Central Bureau of Narcotics altogether destroyed 2732 hectares of illegal poppy cultivation in 2014 (NCB Annual Report, 2014:19). Poppy fields are normally not open but are covered with other crops like Maize, etc., so that they cannot be traced easily. Murshidabad and Nadia districts along the Bangladesh border have also come out to be the main pockets of opium production in Bengal. From there, it is sent to the international market via Nepal and Bangladesh. It is worth noting that opium is cultivated in India under the strict licensing procedures, mainly in Rajasthan, Madhya Pradesh and Uttar Pradesh. Production is made primarily for pharmaceutical use, and the government not only purchases the entire product but also processes it in its factory so that it does not go into the wrong hands. Naxals, however, have managed to get it grown by the farmers and sell it through the agents in the international market. They perhaps have taken the cue from their contacts with the terrorists' organisations like the Taliban, which too is engaged in the cultivation of poppies and selling of the same in the European and American markets, wherefrom they earn a huge amount of money (Singh, 1995).

Ganja (cannabis) has also been one of the major sources of revenue generation. Justice P.K. Mohanty Commission of Inquiry in Odisha in 2008 categorically mentioned the promotion of cannabis cultivation by the Maoists and their supported organisations like Chasi Mulia Samiti in the hilly tracts of the state, particularly in the districts like Ganjam, Gajapati and Malkangiri (Business Standard, 2015). The report found that at least 3000–4000 hectares of land in these areas were being used for the cultivation of cannabis in the state. Bargarh district has emerged as the major centre of trade in the state. The central government, too, is in possession of this fact and has supplied the specific information to the states in the form of satellite pictures of specific locations of cannabis cultivation.

Tendu leaves business again is a great source of extortion money for the Maoists. Tendu leaves are used more to make Biddis (leaf-rolled cigarettes). The Maoists levy a heavy tax on the traders of the Tendu leaves. They also extort money from the workers engaged in this trade on the grounds of managing better wages for the workers and stopping their exploitation by the traders. In fact, in the forest where they matter, they tax everyone from people engaged in the Biddi business to cutting and selling of forest woods like Saal, bamboo, etc., to poachers, liquor makers and smugglers. They are also engaged in huge money-making by engaging in illegal mining of the resources and thus promoting their commercial interests on the one hand and the advancement of capitalism in these areas on the other. But it has been found that Naxals themselves are involved in this enterprise for the sake of money. One of the Naxals, Mannu Baitha, arrested from the district of Giridih in 2010, confessed recently that money extorted by them is also invested in illegal coal mining and money lending business (Bhaskar, 2010; NDTV, 2010).

5 Foreign Funding

Though the government of India has not publicly confessed to the foreign funding of the Naxal movement, it has also not completely ruled out the possibility. The Minister of State for Home Affairs in the Union Cabinet informed the Lok Sabha on November 24, 2009, that 'there is no input' to indicate the foreign funding of the movement, but the officers tracking the movements do not deny it. Even the Prime Minister of the country accepted the 'rumours doing the rounds' on October 11, 2009, in Mumbai, though he did not confirm it. One reason behind such confusion is that a great chunk of money inflow from foreign countries comes through NGOs and in the form of arms supply. However, the Minister of State for Home Affairs, RPN Singh, informed the Rajya Sabha on 12 February that the possibility of getting foreign funds clandestinely by the front organisations of the CPI Maoist cannot be ruled out (Prakash, 2015:900). The union home minister accepted the fact that weapons are 'being smuggled from abroad through Myanmar, Bangladesh and possibly through Nepal which reaches the Maoists'. One can easily understand the fact that if the external agencies can supply weapons into the country, it is not difficult for them to pump money into the country through different channels. The government of India understands well the importance of dismantling the resource generation network of the Naxals. Accordingly, the government has frozen 18 bank accounts involved in terror financing (The Economic Times, 2010). Several NGOs working in the tribal areas have been put on the government radar. Needless to say, the success of the operation against the Naxalite menace will come to an end only when their resource generation and arms inflow are checked effectively. After coming into power, the Modi government started tightening the noose around their necks. The government banned several such NGOs whose accounts and operations were found dubious (Nanjappa, 2019).

6 Use of the Money by the Naxalites

Though there are no written documents on how they spend money collected from different sources but the officers tracking their 20 percent of the collected amount goes to the lower cadres whereas 80 percent of the amount goes to the central committee which uses it primarily for purchasing arms and ammunitions, managing and multiplying the media and other network, publication of material, managing website, legal expenditure for the cadres' fighting cases and so on (Singh & Diwan, 2024). Among the different heads of purchasing weapons, certainly tops the priority, notwithstanding the fact that purchasing dry rations and medicines are also important. Maoists have been spending billions of Rupees annually on arms purchases from clandestine dealers within the country as well as from outside. Mostly, the arms are Chinese made, but they are not directed to the Naxals by the Chinese arms dealers, but by Australian or Bangladeshi firms (Singh & Diwan, 2024). There had been a continuous rise in the expenditure on arms purchases, which included AK-47, hand grenades, rocket launchers, landmines, etc. Maoists once had better arms, ammunition, and firepower than many of our state police forces. Their links go beyond the border for this purpose, and the smugglers of arms fulfil their need, for which they pay a heavy amount. The guerrilla force, in many ways, sometimes dominates the state forces for this reason.

Secondly, a part of the extortion is also used to pay salaries to the cadres who are paid between Rs. 2500 and 3500 (The Times of India, 2010). This serves two purposes. First, it comes as a rescue to the unemployed young people in the area who are attracted towards it. Secondly, these people are then ideologically and militarily trained and mobilised to a romanticised cause of revolutionary struggle for an egalitarian society. These illiterate and poverty-stricken people do not have an idea of the law and the nation. Their whole world is limited to the Jungle. India does not figure in their imagination. And what they have ever realised of the taste of state or nation that has come out in the form of atrocities through corrupt officials and police. That conveniently drives them to the violent path. The unemployed youths find it an attractive destination as they find it convincing to die while fighting their class struggle than struggling for the basic needs like food and clothes.

7 Conclusion

Finance has never been an operational constraint for the Naxals. The revenue generation enabled the Naxals to open schools, run hospitals, apart from the spending on arms and running the organisational affairs and movement-related activities. The Naxals' revenue comes primarily from the extortion and illegal business they are involved in. As they have declared openly the war against the Indian state and believe in guerrilla tactics and armed revolution, they need a huge amount of money for arms and other operational costs. Further, they have to pay money to the cadres who work for them. They also use money on charity to win the hearts of the poor in times of medical emergencies and other needs. Underdevelopment and poverty provide blood and oxygen to the Naxals on which their ideological war thrives. The unequal distribution of resources, exploitation of resources and poverty by the big corporations and landlords, apathy of government officials and their agencies towards the people on the margins, prepare fertile grounds for the Naxals to mobilise the rural masses against the state. A great chunk of the population is deprived of the basic right to life as they have nothing to eat and no roof under which they could stretch out their legs at night. This is in sharp contrast to an India which is dazzling with corporate accounts and infrastructure matching the world-class. While the government comes out with the plan to roll out the infrastructural projects, Naxals find that this would enable the fast movement of troops and forces (ICA Report, 2006:10). And therefore, they attack infrastructural and industrial works. It is important to note that the attacks are in the regions which contribute nearly three quarters of India's gross domestic product.

CHAPTER 4

Recruitment of Cadres: Roping in Minors and Women

Since the 1967 peasant uprising in West Bengal, the Naxal movement has been at the core of national discourse. With incidents of Maoist violence against the Indian state and civilians, the debate on its rationale and response has gathered renewed attention. From academicians to the political class and the mass media, all tried to comprehend the structure and dynamics of the Naxal movement. Several NGOs, human rights watch groups, and intellectual activists in the country perceived their revolutionary calls as an attempt to bring egalitarian change. On one hand, they assumed that the state forced the people to pick up guns to seek just and fair distribution of resources in society. On the other hand, a section of society depicted it as a mindless method of violence against the innocents. Also, it is all against the canons of civilised society, constitutionalism, and the rule of law. The group has been an ardent supporter of a strong, proactive military approach to contain this menace.

The Naxal movement propagates claims to reconstruct society on egalitarian lines through structural changes in the production processes and authority structure. The claims might sound like music to the ears and invoke greater interest in Naxal tall claims; however, there is no scope for denial as far as the goal is concerned, but what bothers is the method and conduct of the Naxals. Rather than being messiahs of the downtrodden and deprived, they are actually adding to the already existing miserable conditions of the poor. Further, careful and deeper scrutiny of the acts of Naxals explains how they fail to promote and implement their egalitarian claims and the way in which developmental activities in underdeveloped areas are being affected; how their activities brought havoc to the lives of the poor; and how Naxals have ruined the prospects of a whole generation of youngsters by roping them into the world of weapons and violence.

The Naxals have left no stone unturned to effectuate their purpose. But by including minor children, both boys and girls who have no understanding of the political sentiments of Maoists, it comes across as an astonishingly mean

 | HTTPS://DOI.ORG/10.1163/9789004765054-006

way to bring about any kind of change.[1] (The Economic Times, 2010). Infants who should have been directed to a stream of education and who should have been given the platform to realise their potential to shape their fortunes for a better life ahead are, time and again, being made to fight for emancipation of the 'proletariat' class. These young minds have been made to bear the burden of bringing change by hanging guns on their shoulder and by carrying bombs in their hands for the sake of realising a future revolution. Naxals may have struggled butted in using minors in their struggle, but bringing minors within the fold of violence raises questions regarding the credibility of their conduct.

The Naxals also engage women, minor girls and boys between the ages of six and eighteen in implementing their revolutionary acts. The engagement of these sections does not come out willingly in all cases. Some join willingly, but the majority of them are forced or brainwashed into this world. Media reports from time to time have exposed this truth. One prominent case, as reported by The Times of India, underscores the strategic recruitment of adolescents into the Maoist cultural wing as an initial step, followed by systematic combat training. This progression ultimately transformed them into 'child soldiers,' thereby constructing a morally and operationally complex battlefield dynamic—pitting state security forces against minors (Times of India, 2025). Some parents give away their children willingly, some are made to give away their children forcibly"[2] (Drolia, 2021). Leading newspapers and vernaculars have also reported similar instances from time to time in other parts of India, particularly in the states of Odisha and West Bengal. It is reported that a recruitment drive has been going on in all Naxal-affected states, but Chhattisgarh, Odisha and Jharkhand have witnessed the most (Millennium Post, 2013; The Economic Times, 2013). Evidence in the form of reports from Home Ministry and various Human rights watch groups, independent NGOs, video tapes procured by television channels suggest that children have been made the runners of movement by being deployed to conduct various activities such as to keep watch on the movement of the security forces; transmitting information; transporting ammunition; money laundering; cooking and in laying out mines against the state agencies particularly against the security forces. It has also

1 In the year 2010 Minister of State of Home Affairs in written reply in Lok Sabha, mentions how children were from time to time being recruited by CPI (Maoist) in what is known 'Bal dasta' or 'Bal Sangham'.

2 In a survey conducted by Bastar Police from 2013–2021 with the surrendered Naxals, it was found out that recruitments of young children start as early as 15 and comprises 70% of their cadre.

been reported that children are systematically trained to participate in a wide spectrum of Naxalite activities, including "intelligence gathering, handling lethal weapons such as IEDs, and engaging in guerrilla warfare against the state" (The Times of India, 2025).

Both central and state governments, time and again, have confirmed such recruitments done by the Naxals. The reports and studies of various organisations confirm this view of the government about Naxals and dismiss the claims of the left liberal intelligentsia in media, academics and different spheres of civil society, where they argue that it is the state's strategy to defame the working-class revolutionary movement. Sriprakash Jaiswal, former Minister of State for Home Affairs, in a written reply to a question of a member in the Rajya Sabha said that, "Maoists have constituted special squad of minors" and in reply to a separate question he added that, "Maoists are attempting to expand their activities to northern states like Haryana, Delhi, Himachal Pradesh, Uttarakhand and Punjab, among others"[3] (SATP, 2008). He further mentioned that no instance of Maoist violence had been reported from these states during the last year (SATP, 2008). The organisations at national and international levels, like Amnesty International, Human Rights Watch Groups, media reports, and police sources, also confirm the recruitment of children by the Naxals in their fight against the Indian state. In one of the reports of Amnesty International, named 'Children in South Asia: Securing their Rights', it is confirmed that Naxals recruit children between the ages of eight and fifteen (Amnesty International Report, 1998). Another leading organisation, the International Displacement Monitoring Centre (IDMC), which monitors 'conflict-induced displacements worldwide', has also reported that young children are being recruited and trained by the Maoists to handle weapons. The report of IDMC of 2011 held that IDPs (internally displaced persons) in camps in Chhattisgarh in central India faced the risks of attacks by both government forces and government allied militia on the one hand and Naxalite insurgents on the other (Internal Displacement Monitoring Centre, 2012).

The reports from different Naxal-hit states depict similarities in the pattern of recruitment, violence, and extortion by Naxals. This is supplemented by the occasional arrests of the cadres and their confessional statements. Security officers and police engaged in anti-Naxal operations have further confirmed

3 For actions against Maoist to be stricter, the state government of Chhattisgarh also banned 'Krantikari Adivasi Balak Sang', an organisation of minor child soldiers created by the Maoists. For further information see: Chhattisgarh bans CPI (Maoist) frontal organisations. (2006, April 12). *OneIndia*. Available at: https://www.oneindia.com/2006/04/12/chhattisgarh-bans-cpimaoist-frontal-organisations-1144906108.html.

the engagement of the minors in the insurgent activities. Shri Vishwaranjan, former DGP of the state of Chhattisgarh, held that, "since the children are more prone to brainwash than the grown-ups, the Naxals have created their specialised unit of minors"[4] (Dixit, 2011). He added that, "Participation of children does not come out willingly. Most of the children are forcibly recruited. Many are even kidnapped and forced into it. The ones who engage willingly often get attracted by their ideological slogans, protest methods, cultural activities and employment of weapons" (Dixit, 2011). Official sources held that children were recruited for gathering intelligence about the movement of security forces, collecting rations and working as couriers[5] (Hindustan Times, 2012; The Indian Express, 2014). Naxals also take the children away without the consent of their parents for harsh training in many cases. They are given sophisticated and dangerous weapons not just to use them against the state but also against the ordinary, innocent children like themselves.

The Recruitment of minors is not limited to one or two states, but evidence from different Indian states underpins the Naxals' deployment of minors. Why do Naxals rope in the poor, the women and the minors into their ranks? Do they have some successful examples before them where children and women have played an important role in insurgencies? Do they want to send out the message that the state is so brutal and insensitive that even the children have taken up guns in their hands? Or is it because they are far more helpful than elderly people in the insurgencies? One argument is that it shows their desperation to raise their strength. It is reported that in the states of Jharkhand, Chhattisgarh, West Bengal, Odisha and Bihar, Naxals mobilise children in the age group of 6 to 12 into their junior wing. They indoctrinate, train and use them as informers against the administrators[6] (The Hindu, 2017; Outlook, 2017). Giridhari Nayak, Director General of Prisons of the state of Chhattisgarh, held that boys and girls were taken from poverty-stricken hamlets. They were denied any opportunity to enrol in any educational institute (Majumdar, 2008). Similarly, G.P. Singh,

4 Children of different age groups are assigned specific tasks in the movement led by Naxalites.

5 In years of Chhattisgarh, Odisha and West Bengal majority of recruitments took place, where boys were as low as 10 years of age and girls were 14–15. The girls were employed majorly for domestic purpose- cooking, cleaning for senior cadres.

6 In his annual report on Children in Armed Conflict, Mr. Guterres said: "Children continued to be affected by incidents of violence between armed groups and the government, in particular in Chhattisgarh and Jharkhand, as well as tensions in Jammu and Kashmir. The United Nations continued to receive reports of the recruitment and use of children by armed groups, including the Naxalites, in particular in Chhattisgarh and Jharkhand," he said. At least 30 schools were burned and partially destroyed by armed groups in Jammu and Kashmir according to government reports, he said.

the Deputy Inspector General of police in Chhattisgarh, also confirmed that Naxals do recruit children in the state. He held that Naxals in their employment of minors do not even spare the welfare hostels meant for the upliftment of the poor tribals. Naxals destroy the school buildings in an attempt to ensure the easy availability of illiterate children for recruitment into their cadres (Majumdar, 2008). In Andhra Pradesh, police recorded the recruitment of children in large numbers by Naxals. R.S. Praveen Kumar, the then superintendent of police in Karimnagar district, held that the People's War Group in Andhra Pradesh in 2003, with its partnership with an organisation named 'Baal Sanghathan', trained nearly 800 children for the spread of the Naxal cause (Ramana, 2013). Evidence in the form of video CDs procured by the Odisha Police also depicts the training of minors in a Maoist camp. Children in the video had weapons in their hands, and they were found to be hoisting guns with anti-government slogans in the air. This video was recovered from the Malkangiri district of Odisha, though the slogans were being raised in Hindi. The video CDs recovered from the Maoists by the Odisha Police in 2008 established further that children in the age group 8–15 were time and again dragged into the Maoists' cause for various purposes like sending messages, tracking police movements, or even being deployed for fighting the class enemies[7] (Dixit, 2011; Business Standard, 2013). Recently, the security personnel busted a Maoist camp inside a forest in Odisha's Malkangiri district after the exchange of fire. The security personnel seized several articles, including some explosive devices, solar kits and uniforms (The New Indian Express, 2021).

It is noticed that activities and pursuit of Naxals are similar to those of LTTE (Liberation Tigers of Tamil Eelam) and numerous Islamic terror agencies like Al-Qaeda, Lashkar-e-Taiba, Hezbollah and several rebel African militias. The notion and inclination of employing the children for such revolutionary causes can be traced back to the use of child corps by the Tamil insurgents in Sri Lanka (Sahay, 2005; HRW Report, 2007; Jha, 2016). Azad, a spokesman of the Naxal outfit's central committee, while addressing media persons at a remote village in Bihar's Supaul district bordering Nepal, disclosed rightly that Maoists learnt new warfare tactics from on-the-run and purged LTTE military commanders in 1986–87 (Ghose, 2018). It further became a conventional phenomenon of all the terrorist groups across the world, such as Lashkar-e-Taiba,

7 Acting on intelligence information, security personnel raided the training camp located inside the inaccessible forest near Mundaguda village under Mathili police limits on Wednesday night, Malkangiri Superintendent of Police Akhileswar Singh said. Leaflates, posters, banners and other literature relating to the red rebel ideology were seized from them.

Jaish-e-Muhammad and many other terrorist organisations working in Africa and Asia. LTTE aimed to reach out to every household and wanted them, especially the poor ones, to devote at least one of their children to the cause. There can be no rational justification for the employment of children for such violent causes. But organisations like the LTTE rationalised it in pursuit of the cause of the Tamil nation in Sri Lanka.

The LTTE used minors as a weapon against the state and took advantage of the innocuousness of children in shielding themselves in times of encounters and spying on the movements of the security forces. It did not happen in a day. The children were trained in such skills and drilled for months. The children were first given the standard training of around four months as soon as they reached the age of sixteen. This training incorporated physical exercises, weapons training, espionage, battlefield tactics, and crafts. When children should have been woken up early to get ready for school, they were woken up in the morning for ideological and combat training. These minors were part of the *Baby Brigade* of the LTTE and also served as bodyguards or assistants of top LTTE men in the assassinations of a few top political leaders. At times, minors proved to be more daring and combatant than the elder LTTE militants. It was precisely the reason that resulted in minors comprising a big portion of the losses in the combat in Sri Lanka. According to the study by Dushy Ranatunge, 'at least sixty percent of the dead LTTE fighters were underage boys and girls, between 10–16' (SATP).

Maoists too follow the same conventional strategy of the LTTE. Naxals have been making appeals to the tribals and toiling population to participate in the cause by giving away their children willingly. Such recruitments and using children for revolutionary causes are unethical and also against several international covenants signed by the nation-states at the international level in favour of children's rights. But all terrorist organisations, including the Maoists, have been doing it. These organisations are not concerned with the natural and human rights of children. On the contrary, they were employing minors deliberately. When these children are killed or hurt by the armed forces in combat operations, it becomes easier for them to internationally defame the armed forces. Naxals use this tactic to arouse popular sentiments against the state in society.

Despite the fact that the Naxal movement started off from Naxalbari in Bengal, Andhra Pradesh emerged as the main revolutionary hub of Maoist activity. The recruitment and training of minors, both boys and girls, in India first started in Andhra Pradesh only. At once, the *People's War Group*, a Naxal group working in Andhra Pradesh, had nearly 400 children trained in nearly three months as part of their children's squad known as '*Baal Sangham*' (Dixit,

2011). It was one of the big corps of minors engaged in the Naxalite cause. But it also disappeared into oblivion as soon as the Naxal movement in Andhra Pradesh was stamped out. Although the government banned the Baal Sangham as soon as it came to light, it did not disappear completely. From Andhra, it spread its roots to other adjacent states of Jharkhand, Chhattisgarh, Orissa and subsequently to other Naxal-infested areas in India. Though there is no official report or statistics on the exact number of children engaged in Naxal activities in India at the moment, it is roughly estimated to be around five to six thousand, working mostly in the six most affected states.

Baal Sangathans have been a part and parcel of the Naxal movements in India. It is the 'Special Squad of Minors' in Odisha and the '*Krantikari Adiwasi Balak Sangh*' in Chhattisgarh and Jharkhand. The group has acquired different nomenclatures from different splinter groups working in different states under different names. Although the names are different, they are all driven by the same goal. These groups are spreading their roots gradually towards the areas where Naxalite movements have not been traditionally strong. For instance, thirteen people, including six women and three children, were kidnapped by Maoists from the Dantewada district of Chhattisgarh, as reported by police (The Times of India, 2007). The same kind of instance was reported in Maharashtra and Tamil Nadu a few months after that.

Such engagement of minors is undoubtedly inhumane and not acceptable. No ideological underpinnings or rational justification can be given for the recruitment of children for such inhumane causes, as it violates the fundamental tenets of human rights. It goes against several national and international statutory or non-statutory commitments. What is unappealing and shocking to the core is the silence of various human rights organisations in India affiliated with the left ideology on this crucial issue. The same organisations are critical of state activities against the Naxals and never miss the chance of depicting the state as a felon. They regard the state's reciprocation with state-sponsored violence and terrorism. But they manage to remain silent over the recruitment of minors by Naxals for their personal causes. Organisations like the People's Union for Civil Liberties and the People's Union for Democratic Rights are key pan-Indian organisations working to promote the cause of human and democratic rights of citizens in India. The silence of these organisations is disparaging. Their bias and partial attitude towards Naxals can easily be perceived through their conspicuous silence on the merciless killings of the innocents. They condemn the state's violence but manage to remain blinded to the violence done by Maoists, the killing of innocent civilians, and the deployment of minors in revolutionary acts. Any type of violation of human rights should be subjected to criticism, but reports of PUDR and PUCL constantly highlight the violence by the state and violation of human rights by them and seldom are critical of violence by the Naxalites. They are not equally vocal about the violation of human rights by the Maoists. These organisations easily turn away from the fact that the state's violence is reactionary and responds to the violence first initiated by the Maoists. This further supplement the idea that both of the organisations are the extended ideological arms of the left movement in India.

The Naxals have a tendency to employ all means to achieve their revolutionary goals. They use techniques of 'ideological impregnation of mind in a shuttle' and force the parents to give away their children for a larger cause of revolution. They are convinced that this will benefit the downtrodden. Naxals manipulate the young, innocent minds through different cultural programmes in the remote rural areas. Cultural programmes and street plays are organised by the cultural organisation of the Maoists. This organisation is one of the most important platforms of Naxals to draw and recruit children in their spheres. Naxalites promote children above the age of twelve to the cultural wings, like Chaitanya Natya Manch. Ninety percent of the cultural outfits of the Maoist wings have children below sixteen, and they are further engaged in launching the propaganda war against the state by the Maoists. This type of propaganda war is launched through drama and plays by gathering people in the villages. The themes of these programmes are designed in a way that could propagate the revolutionary cause of the Naxals. Naxalites held that these programmes are a means to raise awareness among people about the atrocities of the state and exploitation of poor tribals by agents of the state, i.e., powerful, rich elites. But from various police reports and evidence, it is clear that apart from these activities, children are also employed in handling lethal weapons.

When Naxals fail to draw children willingly to their camp and cause, they attempt to forcibly take away minor girls and boys, and introduce them slowly to their cause. At times, they even kidnap the children and push them into the world of violence and revolution, which causes nothing but destruction. It is a very common phenomenon in tribal areas, where news of missing children is found very often. These children are not missing, indeed. Rather, they are kidnapped by the Maoists. And the tragedy is that the parents do not dare to report this to the police because they fear the wrath and retaliation from the Naxals. These parents are helpless and further get trapped in the dictates of the Naxals (Shah, 2019). The Times of India reported on a case in Dhanora village of Jagdalpur in Chhattisgarh that 'two girls were caught in the school uniform' in the encounter (John, 2007). On being caught by the police, they started crying and informed the forces that they had been picked up by the Maoists from the school. Police investigated the matter further and found that their parent knew about it but did not report it to the police because of the fear they had of

Naxals (John, 2007). In 2015, The Times of India reported that the Jharkhand High Court issued notices to the Union Home Secretary and four others in Jharkhand, including the Chief Secretary, Home Secretary, DGP and Secretary of the Department of Women, Child Development and Social Welfare, over the kidnapping of 35 children in Gumla district by the extremist outfit of the Naxals[8] (Deogharia, 2015).

There are also incidents of parents willingly giving away their children to the Naxals. But this number is minuscule compared to the number of cases where parents have been forced to send their children to Naxals. Naxals choose their agents in a very smart way. They target helpless girls or boys who either have lost their parents or whose parents are ridden by extreme poverty. Most of the tribals are poor and landless. Their economic conditions or struggle for survival force them to surrender to the Naxalite cause. But more than this, willing participation, there are a number of cases of forced induction. It is evident from the fact that whenever any dictate comes from Naxals, parents find themselves grounded and send their children away from villages. There have also been many instances when Naxals were seen dictating to the villagers to send at least one of their children from every family to support the violent cause.

Due to their socio-economic conditions and fear of Naxals, no one dares to not follow the dictates of Naxals. Villagers who somehow gather courage and try to stand against them are duly punished, or their children are forcibly taken away. Naxals also kidnap children. Instances of Naxalite groups coercing families to send at least one of their children to join the Maoist cadre have been widespread and documented on multiple occasions (Murty & Bandua, 2013; Pandey, 2013). Recruitment of children for the Naxalite cause first came to light in Chhattisgarh in 2002. Naxals visited the villagers along the Tanda and Bagh rivers and gave instructions to give away at least one child from each family to serve the Naxalite cause (Shukla, 2019). In response, villagers feared to protest and thus sent their children far away from the villages to escape from the dictates of the Naxals. Such dictates and instructions are given time and again to villagers by Maoists. It is a common phenomenon, and this pattern has been witnessed in other states too (Ramana, 2013; Shukla, 2019).

In 2008, in the state of Andhra Pradesh, it was found that Naxals targeted specially 'Pappuluru, Kapattoti, Naguluru, Chintagunnal, Kuntwada, Sanyasiguda, Nimmalpadu, Doraguda, Gassiguda and Allurukota villages located on the other side of the Sileru river near G.K. Vedhi mandal for their recruitment

8 The court observed that despite protection of the fundamental rights ensured to the citizens of the country the small innocent children are victims of the terror of the Naxalites and have been snatched away from their families.

drive' (The Times of India, 2014). Many parents took their children and fled to the neighbouring villages of Sileru, Koraput, Jaipore and Vishakhapatnam[9] (Majumdar, 2008). In 2008, it was reported that the Maoists were asking every Panchayat in the area of Malkangiri to send a minimum of ten children to the Naxal party (The Times of India, 2014). A similar instance was recorded in Jharkhand when police found out nearly 300 children were trained for handling lethal weapons. In Orissa, also, the recruitment of children to the Maoist ranks was found out in 2007. In June 2007, ten to twelve children were found engaged in distributing Maoist leaflets in Kishinda village of Sambalpur.

These instances contradict the Maoists' claim that people join their cause willingly. It is evident that most of the children are part of the Naxals revolutionary world, not because of their conviction or the consent of their parents. On the contrary, they are coerced or hypnotised into it. The state has also been at fault somewhere. The inefficiency of the state in providing security to the poor tribals in the areas where Naxals are predominant further makes the task easy for the Naxals. The recruited youths are trained comprehensively in the ideology and activities of Naxalism. They are trained to use weapons and asked to be physically fit and fine. They follow a rigid schedule where they get up early in the morning, undergo physical and weaponry training till noon, and are further brainwashed into the Naxalite ideology. Recruits are further told about the necessity of the violent movement in the emancipation of the downtrodden. They preach about violence in a way that makes them think that violence can be the means to ensure a dignified life for the exploited and underprivileged sections of society. Naxals do not thus limit their aim just to make the recruits physically competent to fight the battle against the state and class enemies. They are also trained to be mentally strong. This is to ensure that the recruits do not back out or get broken and share the secrets with the police amidst crisis and arrests. Naxals want their agents to commit themselves mentally and physically to the cause till the last breath.

1 Reasons for the Recruitment of the Children

There can be many reasons behind Naxals targeting the minors. One of the many reasons can be the cognitive faculty of children. Children are more prone to brainwashing than adults. Since their minds are clean slates and can be

9 It was reported that though increasing use of child soldiers has been reported from Chhattisgarh, Orissa and Jharkhand in the past, this is for the first time that Maoists are also recruiting tribals in the age group of 10–18 years along the Andhra-Orissa Border.

imprinted with anything with which they are unfamiliar. Children can be easily attracted through slogans of revolution. Slogans to bring change, to be the runners of that positive change or a romanticist version of ideology, attract the young minds. Since they are not much exposed to mature reasoning, they are driven by their emotional senses. The emotional elements narrated in the form of the plight of the poor and deprived go straight to their hearts. The instance of young women from the Warangal District of Andhra Pradesh authenticates the fact. When she was asked about the reason for her involvement in such activities, she responded that she was inspired by the lyrical slogans of the Maoists who visited her village (Janyala, 2009).

Second, participation in Naxal causes also gives a sense of social emancipation to poor youth who have been the witnesses of exploitation of their old parents by the landlords in the villages. When the children witness landlords toeing the dictates of Maoists, then they start regarding it as the agent of emancipation and thus move towards the path of Naxals (Ramana, 2008). Third, unemployment or no generative work is also the cause which draws young minds towards Naxals. When children, after passing out from school, find no efficient job to feed their empty stomachs, they tend to follow the fold of Naxals as they get the economic incentives out of what they do for Naxals. There have been confirmed reports that Maoists pay between Rs. 2000 and 4000 to the young cadres as their monthly remuneration apart from the share in the extortion amount (The Times of India, 2010; The Indian Express, 2010; Singh & Diwan, 2024). The unemployed youths find it attractive and prefer to get into the world of weapons rather than dying of hunger and starvation or leading a despairing life.

Apart from agenting the helpless children or children who lead a poverty-stricken life, Naxals also target the school dropouts (Singh, 2013). This is the group of children who swung to the revolutionary causes of the Naxals for mere economic incentives. Fourth, there are children who have no understanding of any 'ism'. They are also not convinced by any ideology, but the mere touch of deadly weapons enthrals the youngsters and their innocent mindset. It introduces them to the arena of violence, where they see themselves as agents of change without having any understanding of change.

Naxals' understanding of the recruitment of minors is not just based on the fact that it is easier to rope in minors in comparison to the fully grown-up people, but also on the idea that the ideological indoctrination from the beginning would certainly make them a hard nut to crack in the future. Minors will be mentally strong enough to deal with the crisis. Naxals' rigidness is evident from the fact that they force the women to deliver children only in the makeshift camps organised for the same purpose by the Krantikari Adivasi Mahila Sangh, an organisation of the Maoists designed to take the Maoists' cause into the lives of women and children. Such camps play a significant role in serving the purpose of the Maoists. There have been many instances when women have died while giving birth to a child. Poverty and lack of medical facilities in the Maoists' camps intensify the possibility of deaths. The state could have played an efficient role here, but its inability to fulfil the basic needs of the poor makes the matter more vulnerable. Naxals utilise this disadvantageous position of the state to their very advantage and provide basic facilities to the poor and project themselves as saviours of the poor and needy. On one hand, these facilities for the poor may not be of the best quality, but at least the poor are able to highlight their issues through the Naxals. On the other hand, Naxals' helping hand for the poor is influenced by their mere goals of revolution, which further works as a reminder for children that they are born to serve their revolutionary cause. Naxals' aim is not to have one more movement of revolution, but they aim to strengthen the present movement in a way that it remains relevant in the future. Thus, they want to develop an unending nursery of insurgency.

The Naxals use almost all tactics for the recruitment of the cadre. Recruitment of the cadre happens in a very systematic manner. They go for the full campaign for the recruitment drive. They spread the message through the posters and leaflets, calling upon the tribals to send their children to meetings. They openly circulate the message that those who would join their fold would be given cloth, food, medicines and the protection of their family members. They even give the details of the food and breakfast, as it is witnessed that recruits are promised fish and pork once a week (Mukherji, 2024). Naxals basically penetrate the nerves of the poor and touch the line that the state seldom intends to. Promises of Naxals attract the poverty-stricken children who find it better to devote their lives to the cause, which gives them food three times a day. Naxals also recruit children through sponsoring mobile schools. Although Naxals claim that they impart education to the children in Science, English, Mathematics, apart from ideological training, the fact is that their focus is quite clear. Their sole purpose is to teach the minors why and how to fight the state and its agents.'

Naxals do not even care about the lives of children. There are times when senior or grown-up cadres use children's cadres for their own leverage. They use children as a shield and to protect themselves when they face the wrath of the armed forces. This shows the insensitivity they hold towards children. Naxals camouflage themselves behind the innocent faces of children and put their lives in danger to save their own. Garhchiroli police witnessed during a raid in September 2007, four teenage boys and three girls aged between 17 and 20[10] (The Times of India, 2007). Police recorded that these children were first forced to join the Naxal movement, but as soon as Naxals faced an encounter with police, and when police opened fire on the camp, the minors were left to their fate (The Times of India, 2007). It is also interesting that the leadership of the Maoist movement is in non-tribal hands, who just play a role in structuring and finalising the plan. These handful of people sit comfortably at home while the poor tribals who were brought into the movement with promising words are thrown into the battlefield to face the wrath of the security forces. They are placed to ambush the security forces' camps and to conduct bloody operations. The government has no option but to flush out the Maoists through killings and eliminate the tribals. In operations like these, the Naxals push forward women and children from the tribal community and forward two messages through them. First, common tribals are key participants and are with the Naxals in their battle against the state. Second, the police and armed forces use force against the unarmed tribals, especially women and children. That is nothing but emotional extortion.

In response to Naxals and their violence on the soldiers whenever armed forces prepare themselves to retaliate, human rights activists come into play their part. These activists leave no stone unturned to tarnish the image of the armed forces. They use different cards to convey the idea that armed forces are engaged in the inhuman killings of the innocents. They turn a blind eye to the fact that the state and armed forces do not act but 'react' to the revolutionary acts of Maoists. Certainly, it is not that armed forces or police do not resort to violence or do not torture the innocent tribals, but that does not take away the fact that Naxals, who claim to act as the saviour of the poor and downtrodden, are not saviours. They are the first ones to drag the toiling masses into this mess.

Maoists do not just shield themselves behind innocent children, but they also use the minors to exert pressure on the government. There are times when minors have been used by the Naxals to wheedle the police. In July 2007, a veteran Maoist leader, Madanji, was arrested by the Patna police (Indian Vanguard, 2007). It was a big achievement of the police, and for various security reasons, his arrest was kept a secret. This was done so that Naxals do not get any information regarding his destination and that they don't get any further role to play in messing with the stability. But Naxals are very sharp-minded. They know very well how to play what cards and when. After Madanji's arrest, Naxals used their most efficient card. It was witnessed that they organised a rally of school

10 The Garhchiroli police found teenage boys and girls being trained at the Naxalite training camps.

children in Palamu district in Jharkhand (Indian Vanguard, 2007). In this rally, children were found to be raising slogans in favour of the Maoist leader and were demanding his release. These children were clearly asking about the whereabouts of the Maoist leader, Madanji. It is quite simple to understand that these little children had no understanding of what they were being asked to chant. They had no idea of who Madanji was, as on being asked about the details of Madanji, the children were quite in oblivion. Children and women have been used by the Naxals in various rallies and protests just to convey the idea that the Naxals have the backing of the common people.

It is traceable that Naxals use the economic condition of minors and women to bring them in their fold. Maoists justify the recruitment of children by claiming that with such participation of children in these revolutionary acts, they will not die of starvation. Naxals also present educational arguments. They held that the training of children for revolutionary causes gives minors a reality check. Children get to see the revolutionary activities from very close, and they further come out as the vanguard of the revolutionary movement. They become mentally and physically equipped to face any circumstantial problem in future. This depicts that Naxals use the children to breed their revolutionary movement. Recruitment of children does no good to children; rather, they become the means to supplement the legacy of the Naxalite movement. In the People's March (a mouthpiece of the CPI-M), the children's cadres were described to be the cultural ambassadors of the revolution. It is clear that Naxals convey the idea that it is better to sacrifice life in a fight for a dignified life and a better living situation for the poor than to accept their fate and exploitation by the exploiting class. They further question the sanity of educated and rich sections of civil society that, when children can do subhuman jobs in the field and industry, when they should have been enrolled in schools, then no section of civil society raises a question. Naxals question why the children cannot work for their emancipation from the exploiting classes or class enemies. For Naxals, joining the movement is the only means available to children and tribals through which they can liberate themselves from the inhumane life that they are forced to live.

Naxals claim that children get better opportunities and a better life in their fold. They are not asked to do what grown-ups do. Children are better nurtured and taught about the lines of revolution so that they develop a better personality compared to a lifestyle where they were being deprived of basic amenities. Naxals claim that people in civil society have high misconceptions about their movement and the involvement of children in their cause. They claim that the children are not given party membership till they attain the age of sixteen. Naxals think that sixteen is the age when children are sufficiently mature to understand the circumstantial changes around them. These minors did not see the life of schools, and they are forced to see the practicality of life, where they have to undergo worse and worse experiences.

There is no denial of the fact that children of tribals were deprived of better and dignified lives by the state apparatus, but the claim of Naxals that 'children are not asked to do what grown-ups do' does not depict the reality. Evidence through various reports, including videos of training camps, statements of surrendered and caught-up children, proves the fact that Naxals engage the children in the most daring and wrathful tasks. Minors are forced to confront the security forces with weapons. It depicts that there is no conformity between what Naxals claim and what they do. The claim that Naxals provide better living conditions to poor tribals is not justified, as they too are not giving them a better life at all. In their normal lives, they were merely deprived of resources and did not face the risk of death every minute. With recruitment for Naxalite causes, poor tribals are brought into a world where there is no confirmation of safety or whether they will see the next morning. What they are taught after recruitment in order to develop the mental and cognitive faculties is nothing but direct sloganeering and rhetoric of revolution.

No justification can be regarded to what Naxals do to the lives of children. They snatch away their childhood, the days of innocence, by dragging them into the fold of weapons. It is also seen that the militancy has affected the nature of primary and secondary education in the Naxalite-affected states of Jharkhand and Chhattisgarh. Government sources reveal that Naxals have blown up around 250 buildings and forced the government either to close the schools or shift these schools closer to the police stations or Salwa Judum camps (PTI, 2011). The Maoists justify the blowing up of schools on the grounds that these buildings are not being used for imparting education but for the purpose of launching operations by security forces against the Naxals. At times, the government has accepted that in a few cases school buildings were used by the forces to launch an operation against the Naxals, but it was applied to the areas where alternative arrangements were not present for the camping of security forces. To argue that all the schools are used for security forces camping is highly misplaced and aimed at tarnishing the image of the state. There are approximately 2500 schools run by the Scheduled Tribe Development Department of the Chhattisgarh government in the Naxal-affected area of Dantewada, Bastar and Kanker. The impact on regular sections of schools can also be seen. In 2007, nearly 11000 students from 246 schools were promoted from class 1 to class IV and class VI to VII without any annual examination because of the closure of schools in the wake of the Naxalite threat (Refworld, 2010). Something like this happened in Odisha, too. In fact, this is the story of every area affected by Naxals cause. According to government sources, 234 centres under the Educational Guarantee Scheme were closed in the Sambalpur district of Odisha, and almost 219 centres out of 276 in the district of Deogarh were closed down within a few months (Indian Vanguard, 2007). Not just students, but teachers are too scared of their lives, and no one wants to enter these areas. What are children going to do with money if they cannot lead a safe life? The first and foremost priority should indeed be a safe and healthy life.

2 Position of Women Cadre

The position and condition of women are no different from that of minors. In fact, minors are given the forefront position, but women have always been given an inferior position in the movement' (Ajitha, 1999). Women are not just tortured and exploited on a daily basis but also treated as 'sexual commodities' in the Naxalite fold. Ajitha, daughter of late comrade Mandakini Narayanan, the forefront leader in the revolutionary struggle of the late 1960s in Kerala, confessed that women are not treated as equals even in the revolutionary causes of Naxals, but they are treated as some 'sexual commodity' (Ajitha, 1999). Most of the time, the women are given the side roles. For instance, in working for the cultural organisation of the party, awakening the poor about the cause of revolution or mobilising tribals towards the movement, etc. Their capacity, skills and emotions are never recognised. Naxals take an attractive stand on the question of women for mere saying. They claim that 'there can be no revolution without women' and that 'women and working-class emancipation from the bourgeoisie fold go together'.

This idea can be traced to Lenin's notion that women's emancipation emanates from the working-class revolution. In fact, this notion runs along the lines of the whole Marxist interpretation of society, where they claim that discrimination against women is a part of the superstructure which is directly linked with the base of society. Thus, according to Marxist interpretation, the mode of production lies in the base, which is inefficient in nature. It can only be rectified through a successful proletarian revolution. This revolutionary notion to bring change or to understand the roots of exploitation in Indian society does not consider patriarchy, caste and religion as core agents of exploitation. According to them, Indian society is neo-colonial and semi-feudal. They neglect the exploitation of women and regard their suffering as trivial and as bourgeois techniques of division in society.

When we see the trajectory of the Naxals movement, we can witness that women are missing from the leadership roles in the party. Patriarchy is in the bloodline of the party, and the safety of women is in danger as it is outside the party. Women cadres are even suggested by Naxals not to engage themselves in the institution of marriage. Terms like 'Veermata' and 'Veerpatni' are very prevalent amongst Naxals. These are sexist adjectives that glorify the reproductive labour of women and her motherhood on one end, and in contrast, these terms idealise her superficial virtues and relational subordination in society. Thus, it is very evident that gender bias is inherent in the organisation as neither women nor their condition is taken into consideration when a crucial decision is taken.

Women's exploitation is not limited to considering them inferior, but there are also complaints of sexual abuse of women by the senior cadres in the organisation. What could have been worse than this? Deepti was a young Naxal who voluntarily surrendered before the police in November 2007 at Sambalpur. She held that 'she was allured by the Naxals in their fold by offering her a job when she was in the VIII standard in a rural school' (Mishra, 2008). Another story of Ramshita Nayak, who also joined the Naxal movement for money, is the same. She mentioned about the torture done by the police and the sexual exploitation by the Naxals. She stated that she too got into the movement when she was in her class VI in a village school of the district Deogarh in Odisha (Mishra, 2008). Solastica from the district of Deogarh had a starry opinion about the Naxal movement, but soon she realised the reality of the movement when she saw that cadres were engaged in the killings of the poor and the innocent. She also narrated that women comrades were made to sing and dance at the party function for entertainment purposes (Mishra, 2008). These narratives clearly depict that women are not just tortured but also exploited by the Naxals.

Sabita Munda, who surrendered before the Keojhar police in Orissa in April 2010, also narrates a similar storyline. She worked under the Naxals for the Maoist cause. She came into their fold in 2005, and she was subjected to sexual exploitation by the senior comrades (Hindustan Times, 2010). She repeatedly pleaded for her freedom, but that did not ring a bell in the seniors' ears. They continued her sexual exploitation. Later, she surrendered before the Odisha police (Hindustan Times, 2010). Geeta Murmu and Anju Murmu, the two female Maoists who were arrested by the Banka police in Bihar, also stated that sexual exploitation is very much prevalent in the Naxal movement (Hindustan Times, 2010). Geeta was also subjected to sexual assault, and later she decided to be the mistress of one of the seniors, Chirag Da. It was also noticed that she had undergone an abortion twice, as the female cadres are not allowed to be pregnant and bear children in the Naxalite fold. Both Geeta and Anju admitted that hundreds of girls and women cadre witness sexual exploitation at the hands of their male counterparts.

These stories are not some isolated incidents. These stories depict a common line that women in Naxal's fold are not subjected to equal treatment and witness the wrath of their male counterparts through sexual exploitation. These are the common happenings that run in the fold of Naxals. These happenings are claimed by several women activists who left the movement or decided to surrender. It is also regarded by many women that 'they face sexual harassment in the camp at night' (Ajitha, 1999). Maoists, in response, deny any such claim or activities in the camp. Maoists, on the other hand, claim it is the tactic of the police and armed forces to defame the Naxal movement. They posit that police make up the stories to create a feeling of distrust among tribals for Maoists. It has been reported that, at times, police use such tactics. But one cannot deny the harsh reality of women going through sexual exploitation in the camp. A report by The Times of India about the details of Shobha Mahto Alias Uma, a former Maoist who served the Maoist cause for around ten years and decided to leave the movement later, is an eye-opener. What happened to her is something that destroys peace of mind. When she left the movement, she was the commander of 25–30 Naxals placed in Jhargram in Jharkhand. She was raped for the first time when she was only 17. Disgusted by what happened with her, she tried to complain to her seniors, including Kishanjee, but got no response or support in return (Chakrabarty, 2010). Instead of protecting her dignity, she was left alone and was given threats, time and again, of dire consequences if she decided to open her mouth (Chakrabarty, 2010). When various women cadre witness the mental and physical exploitation, they try to get a grip on it and start regarding it as a common phenomenon in the camp. They further relate it to fate and start adjusting to it. Moreover, there is also another face of this exploitation. Women cadres know very well that they cannot be held highly in the camp if they do not get patronage from the senior male counterparts of the organisation. All of it encourages them to go closer to seniors and maintain a close relationship with them. It is also seen that various senior women cadres maintain multiple sexual relations in the camp.

There are several children and women in the organisation who have been in the fold of the organisation for years, and still, they want to come out of the shackles of the organisation. They wish to look for a better course of life. They wish to lead a life like a normal man or woman. But they are highly centred around by the cadres who never allow these people to reveal any aspect of revolutionary activities to the security agencies. Naxals have no doubt a very rigid mindset, but they are even harsh with the people who wish to desert them after working in their fold for years. Naxals are very well aware of the fatal consequences that such people will bring to the organisation if they decide to open their mouths. Naxals do not like people leaving the movement and further retaliate in harsh ways. Kokila, one of the cadres in Jharkhand, was inducted into the Naxal fold by another cadre named Kavita. Kokila was abducted, beaten up and raped by the Naxals. She was engaged in the cultural activities of the Naxals. She used to sing revolutionary poems, slogans and songs to mobilise the people towards the Naxalite fold. After sacrificing so many years for the Naxals, she decided to lead a normal life. Her wish to lead a normal life was not welcomed by the Naxals. She did not pay any attention to the dislikes or advice of Naxals and decided to leave the movement. This resulted in an assault on her femininity by the same people she worked with for years. So, it is very clear, once one comes into the fold of Naxals, it becomes very complicated for him or her to come out of the fold, as anyone who decides to leave the movement faces the threat of death or harassment.

As per the claims of Naxals, the Police also engage children in their war against the Naxals. There are reports of minor boys and girls being engaged as Special Police Officers (SPOs). Asian Centre of Human Rights visited Bangapal relief camp and interviewed nine minor girls, who were recruited as SPOs (William, 2007). These girls reportedly told the team they were being trained in fighting tactics (William, 2007). The Government, although, denies such allegations, cannot overwrite the findings of several independent NGOs and human rights activists. These allegations against the state are not completely baseless.

If one tries to locate the reasons, one can come down to the fact that socio-economic or pathetic financial conditions of the tribals and downtrodden due to the inefficiency or non-implementation of various states' measures in the areas where the poor are denied of basic necessities and opportunities is one of the major causes of Naxals menace in India. Naxals are prevalent in areas where poor people are displaced from their ancestral land due to mining or industrial activities of the state. Such development in the name of modernity further frustrates the poor. All these notions drive the understanding of children and the poor and push them against the state. Exploitation by the landlords, social inequities present in the system, lack of opportunities, lack of parental care or failure of parents to meet the basic needs of children, work hand in hand and give the Naxal an upper hand in alluring the downtrodden. One of the most important factors amongst these is the inadequacy of the state to reach out to the poor and to understand their needs. Thus, the government should wake up and further take steps in this regard. Mere policies won't work now; efficient implementation of the policies and adequate care or nurturing of the toiling masses should be the twin objectives of the state in this regard. The state has to work a lot to check this inundation, whether forced or voluntary. There is also a need for democratic awareness in regions and the emergence of genuine community leadership that could work and understand the peculiarity of the situation.

In conclusion, it becomes imperative to recognise that women and children are especially vulnerable to Naxal recruitment because they frequently come from marginalised communities with limited access to education and other opportunities. Naxals provide this section with a feeling of belonging and purpose, promising a better life and the opportunity to fight injustice and inequity. However, the reality is far from what they are promised. Women and children who join the Naxal ranks risk inhumane treatment. They are frequently subjected to harsh training, forced to live in deplorable conditions, and made to perform menial chores. Women are sexually molested and exploited by their male counterparts. Thus, Naxalism fosters a cycle of violence and instability, making it difficult for women and children to exit the system once they come in. Recruitment of women and children by Naxals is a severe problem that needs to be addressed. To reduce the appeal of extremist ideology, the government and civic society must collaborate to provide education and opportunities to marginalised people. Furthermore, actions must be taken to safeguard vulnerable sections from Naxalites' exploitation and abuse.

CHAPTER 5

Missionaries and the Naxal Movement in India: Is There Any Nexus between Them?

Has there been an understanding between the Maoists and missionaries in India? Do missionaries lend tactical support to the Maoists and vice versa? Is there any pattern of funding of the Naxal movement via missionary organisations working in the remote tribal areas of India? Do the NGOs which have been working in the tribal areas for the sick, illiterate and the poor actually also lend a helping hand to the Maoists and their cause? Does the Western world, which is so hostile towards Islamic extremism and highly critical of communism, ignore the left extremism at work in India? Do they silently encourage and provide strength by funding the Naxalites through funding the non-governmental organisations (NGOs) working in the remote forest areas? And do they do so consciously because Maoists have been very generous to the Christian Missionaries, whose welfare and charitable activities, as well as the evangelical programmes, are primarily located in the tribal belts. These are some questions and many more, which have been subjects of debate for a long time in India. While the right-wing organisations have been accusing the missionaries and Maoists of having both covert and overt linkages, depending on the situation, Christian organisations reject such premises and attribute them to a conspired campaign designed to denigrate their charitable works.[1]

The issue became the central point of discussion when Swami Lakshmanananda Saraswati, a Hindu social and religious worker, was killed along with four of his associates by 30-odd assailants on the evening of August 23, 2009, in Kandhamal in Odisha. The newspapers widely covered it, in which the Vishwa Hindu Parishad (VHP) had openly accused the missionaries of being behind it (The Organiser, 2024). The charge sheet filed in the case revealed that this was a meticulously planned killing in which nearly 150 people were involved. The charge-sheet also unravelled that local as well as outsiders participated in accomplishing this task. The CID Inspector General of Police, Arun Ray, endorsed it by saying that the murder was a highly 'professional job' in which 'the initial plan was hatched by someone else'. The group

1 They accuse that the RSS and its organisations are after these organisations.

 | HTTPS://DOI.ORG/10.1163/9789004765054-007

which did the planning for his murder was different from "the one which trained the killers. And the one group did not know what the other group was doing" (Hinduism Today, 2008; Mohanty, 2008).

Swami was a highly respected person in the area, especially among the poor and tribals. He was engaged in several charitable activities for them, such as providing medical facilities, schooling and other utility centres for the sick and poor in the region. And he was doing all this in the region for several decades. By caste, he belonged to the Dalit category. More importantly, he was an ardent advocate of the protection of tribal rights on their land and their culture. And thus, there was no reason for any animosity against him, except for the fact that Swami was a crusader against the conversion of the tribals to Christianity. He considered conversion as an assault on the cultural values and the belief system of the locals. And therefore, he always stood against the religious conversion of tribals into Christianity. He strongly supported and executed reconversion to Hinduism for those who had deserted the religion and converted to Christianity (The Organiser, 2022).

Needless to say, Swami Lakshmanananda was the target for the missionaries who found him a big obstacle in their conversion design. This became evident when, a few days later, Sabyasachi Panda, alias Sunil, Secretary of the CPI (Maoists), Odisha, told the journalists that the Swami was killed by the Maoists, as the Swami was engaged in a hate campaign against the other religious denominations, mainly against the Christians (Ahmed, 2008). Panda, in a way, admitted that Maoists killed him for the venom that Swami spewed against the Christians. One could have understood had the charges been that the Swami was acting against the interests of the Maoists. But this was not the reason that was issued by the Naxals. Panda also announced that many more such murders would multiply in times to come if the Sangh Parivar organisations do not desist from anti-missionary activities in remote tribal areas. He specifically named Lal Krishna Advani, Ashok Singhal and Praveen Togadia as being on the 'hit list' of the Maoists (Ahmed, 2008). Realising the fact that such statements would be damaging the credentials of the Maoists, other leaders of the organisation issued statements of denial. But the fact by then had tumbled out and was known to all. It was by now clear that though Maoists executed the task of murdering the Swami and his associates, the murder was planned somewhere else.

In fact, right from the beginning, the Sangh Pariwar (Rashtriya Swayamsevak Sangh (RSS) affiliates) suspected that missionaries were the hidden mind and force behind the killings of Swami Lakshmanananda. VHP openly alleged that the plot to kill the Swami was "hatched in the presence of RK Nayak, a former bureaucrat and a Christian leader from the Congress party in the state" (Ahmed, 2008). He was also the Chief Patron of the Pan-Christian community in the state.[2] A member of the Congress party in the Rajya Sabha, *Nayak* was also a Dalit Christian face of the party in the state. Though he claims to be a socialist, he has actually been at the forefront of mobilising the Dalit Christians for the party in the state. It is important to note that it is the *pana-Christians* who constitute the dominant proportion of the Maoist cadre in the Kandhamal district. The church, whose influence was almost negligible in the state of Orissa, found the Maoists helpful in countering the Hindu organisations. The Maoists' claim of annihilating Swami Lakshmanananda thus might have been a big surprise for the media and the secular establishment in India, but it was certainly not for the Hindu organisations like VHP, Vanvasi Kalyan Ashram and the RSS, for they have been on the target list of the missionaries from the beginning.

In fact, there are several common issues on which both the Maoists and the missionaries find it necessary to come together and act against the Hindu nationalists. They both hate the ideology of Hindutva and its idea of the Indian nation as conceived by the latter. However, the reasons are different for both. For the Christian missionaries, the ideology of Hindutva is antithetical to pluralism. For them, the ideology of Sangh Pariwar aims at Hinduization and homogenization of the nation and asserting the Hindu hegemony. This conclusion is derived from the assertion of the Hindu nationalists who make a claim that India is a Hindu nation and its Hinduness is the cementing force of the nation. Those elements should not be weakened by reducing the numerical strength of the Hindus in the area.

Interestingly, the right-wing organisations return the same accusations and charges against the Christian Missionaries. For them, the proselytisation is a scheme of homogenization by increasing the numerical strength of Christianity. It is a political design to reduce the social, cultural, religious and political dominance of Hindus in the country. Right-wing organisations, especially the constituents of the RSS, have been giving tough times to the missionaries in converting the tribal population into Christianity, which enjoyed free hand in the 18th and 19th centuries in India.

Both Maoists and Missionaries see the call for united Hindutva as a threat to their mission and activities. A divided Hindu society is fertile terrain for both to propagate their ideology and the mission. United with Hindu identity despite diversity and differences, which the ideology of Hindutva seeks to create, makes it difficult for the missionaries to use the divide within the Hindu society to convert the population. Hence, the missionaries have always

2 Pana Christians are the members of Pana Community which converted to Christianity.

focused their attention on the diversity and differences within the Hindu society, whereas right-wing organisations have been making appeals and working towards creating a united Hindu consciousness against Islam and Christianity, depicting them as 'others'. Naxalism also thrives on the divides within the Hindu society. Religious consolidation of Hindus works as an antidote to both. The Hindu nationalists treat Hinduism and Hindu culture as the core of the Indian nation and the cornerstone of Hindu civilisation. Further, they also consider it the cementing force of India. This is what irks both the Maoists and Missionaries alike. Consolidation of Hindu identity has the potential to act against both the Maoists and the Missionaries. It is easier for the Maoists as well to exploit the divide within the Hindu society to their ends.

Maoists are dismissive of religion as a false consciousness and find it a construct of the bourgeoisie to conceal class differences. It is aimed at exploiting the poor by diverting them from the real issues of economic deprivation. And therefore, Maoists discourage the population they work with from remaining distant from religious rituals and practices. Religious faith, for them, is unscientific and dilutes the revolutionary spirit. They, therefore, oppose any polarisation on that ground. No wonder, they are highly critical of the right-wing organisations who promote and nurture such consciousness with the aim to consolidate the Hindu masses. Maoists also criticise several practices within Hinduism on the grounds of reason and logic, and abhor superstitions. But surprisingly, they don't condemn Christianity, applying the same parameters. They seldom question the superstitions and rituals of the Christian community, and this makes them vulnerable to criticism of resorting to bias towards the missionaries by the right-wing organisations.

Interestingly, both Maoists and the right-wing organisations converge on critiquing the West. But while the Maoists criticise it on the grounds that it promotes an exploitative society through promoting capitalism and capitalist structure, the right-wing organisations also include the cultural and religious imperialism of the West for scrutiny. That is the reason that the right-wing organisations are so opposed to the evangelical networks operating in India. Further, the different world views bring them against each other on the very idea of the nation and handling the national issues. The right-wing nationalism is a staunch votary of a powerful centralised state capable of dismantling any kind of fissiparous tendencies, whereas the class internationalism, though a fanciful idea not yet practised by any country that applied Marxism at home, brings the Maoists to oppose it. They also oppose it because they think that the powerful centralised state would turn out to be repressive to their ideas and activities.

The right-wing organisations put out the argument that the nation must come first. They are therefore opposed to any such activities and arguments that have divisive potential. Hence, they criticise both the Maoists and the missionaries. While they acknowledge the social and economic deprivation of the people and accept the need for the improvement of their living conditions and meeting their political aspirations, they want the state to display its will and physical might to crush the violent and disruptive activities of the Naxalites. It considers that Maoism is not just an alien ideology but also works in India with the support of foreign powers who are hell bent on destroying the social and cultural fabric of India. Further, right-wing ideology is also very averse to the communist framework, including the Maoists, regarding managing economic activities in society. While the Maoists advocate for the eradication of the private capital of all shades and accord no role for it in society, the Hindu nationalists consider that such attempts would amount to strangulating the creative potential of the private entrepreneurs. Though the Hindu nationalists also support state ownership, they do not discount the productive capacity of the liberal market system. Hence, the communists consider them part of the bourgeoisie.

But what brings them completely at odds is their position on the national questions. While the Hindu nationalists make an uncompromising stand on the national security and territorial integrity of India, these issues do not matter much to the Maoists, though they, too, cry foul when the government leans towards the Americans and the West. Take, for example, the issue of Kashmir and separatist activities going on in different parts of the country. Hindu Nationalists have been uncompromising on the territorial integrity of India and have always wanted to use hard power against the separatists. On the other hand, the Maoists prefer and support the self-determination campaign of the separatists. While the BJP and all other right-wing organisations have always supported the abrogation of Article 370 and thereby full integration of the state like any other state of India with the Indian union, Naxals support the terrorists and separatist activities in the valley and talk almost the same language that the terrorists use against the Indian government. No wonder that people like Gautam Navlakha and Arundhati Roy keep on saying publicly that India has kept Kashmir as a colonised land which deserves freedom in all respects (Roy & Navlakha, 2010). Missionaries also have been very kind to such propositions.

What brings the missionaries closer to the Marxists and the Maoists in India is the denunciation of Hindutva as a backward conservative ideology, which suits the missionaries very well in their campaign against the native religions and fits into the scheme and rationale behind converting the indigenous population into Christianity. It is interesting to see that while the Maoists have been quite vocal against the Hindu nationalists on the religious and cultural issues, they are silent and mute spectators on the aggressive agenda of cultural and religious homogenization of Christian missionaries practised through large-scale religious conversion of other sects into Christianity. Missionaries' aversion to the ideology of Hindutva is not without meaning. In fact, in the last two decades, Hindutva have challenged the ideology and activities of the missionaries, particularly on the issue of the conversion of poor Hindus in the remote rural areas and the tribals in the forests. They have accused the missionaries of being engaged in changing the religious demography of India in remote rural and forest areas to increase their numerical strength and subsequently influencing the political and cultural milieu of the area. Hindu nationalists have been arguing that the relative decline in the demographic strength of the Hindus would also lead to the balkanization of the country. This argument has been at the core of the Hindu Nationalist ideology, which seeks the preponderance and dominance of Hinduism both in numerical and other forms. And they bring in Vivekanand, Gandhi, and Savarkar to denounce the missionaries' works in India. Vivekananda argued that going out of one Hindu from its fold means the addition of one more enemy to the Hindu society (Vivekananda, 1899).

RSS and its sister organisations have been opposing the conversion because they hold that it would give rise to de-Hinduization of the nation.[3] It will consequently also lead to the decline of the Hindu civilisation in the wake of the increased political strength of the non-native religious denominations. They use the example of Kashmir and the North-East states, where Hindu demography declined, and the political narrative changed with a change in the cultural and religious milieu of these states. For example, Nagaland was once a land of a predominantly tribal area. The consistent religious conversion has brought the Christian population from 7 percent in 1931 to nearly 89 percent in 2001 in the state. This has also resulted in the dominating influence of the Church in the polity and society, and the latter has started blackmailing the political system for several concessions for the Christians.

The same is the situation in some other states of India, like Kerala and Meghalaya. Meghalaya today has over 80 percent Christian population. This percentage has come at the cost of native tribes who were encouraged, allured and aggressively convinced to convert to Christianity. Missionaries always would claim that 'low caste Hindus willingly convert to Christianity to escape the stratified, oppressive caste system in Hindu society'. But the fact of the matter is that they are allured, bribed and sometimes even brought to the Christian fold by deceit. They use all tactics to multiply their numerical strength. The

3 De-hinduisation means Denationalization as per the RSS.

charitable institutions and their activities are one of the few but most important instruments in the mission. Needless to say, conversion has created a great fissure in the indigenous society. This has been purely a religio-cultural design of the missionaries for political dominance. And once they achieve the stage of numerical preponderance, they are seen to be forcing the state to bend to their cultural and political interests. The role of the Church in these states has been found very powerful indeed. It is argued that the Baptist Church is the main force behind the unrest in the North-East region in India.

The National Liberation Front of Tripura is fully backed by the Baptist Church, which is headquartered in the USA (BBC, 2000). This was admitted by none but the then chief minister of the state (BBC, 200). Nagmanlal Halam, Secretary of Noapara Baptist Church, was arrested with a huge number of explosives. Noapara Baptist Church is a very fanatic Christian group which aims to convert every inhabitant of Tripura to Christianity. It would also be worth noting that the Baptist Church in Tripura was established by the missionaries from New Zealand almost 70 years ago! Baptist Church in Nagaland spews venom against the Hindus, RSS and the BJP. Nagaland Baptist Church Council called upon the voters of the state to make a choice between 'Trisul' and the 'Cross' (Desk, 2018). It also called upon the voters to uphold 'Christian principles' and vote against 'Hindu forces', unmindful of development and other concerns (Desk, 2018). It considered the penetration of the BJP into Nagaland as 'intrusion' into the 'Christian' land. This is by and large the story of most of the Christian-dominated regions in the Northeast. Even the conflicts in Manipur between the Kukis and Meiteis also had this dimension to an extent.

By the late 50s, the RSS realised that the Sangh won't be able to stop the desertion of the poor tribals to the Christian faith unless the basic needs of underprivileged Hindus are fulfilled and their cultural and economic rights are protected against the possible onslaught from outside. The major strength of the Church was the education, health and food facility, which was possible because of the huge amount of money coming in from the Christian World in the West for charitable and evangelical purposes. RSS realised that it was essential to reach out to the forest and tribal belts and work for these communities, if at all, it intends to stop the further vivisection of Hindu society. RSS encouraged the Hindus to come out with an organised network of workers dedicated to working in the tribal areas.

Vanvasi Kalyan Ashram was constituted in the heart of Jashpur Nagar, presently in Chhattisgarh. Vanvasi Kalyan Ashram reached out to people in cities to collect funds and used the resources for charitable and welfare works in the tribal areas. It highlighted the menace of the missionaries' activities and convinced the Hindus in cities of the importance of minimising the missionaries' influence in the region. It appealed to the Hindus to donate funds for running a school, a hostel for the children, and medical facilities in order to protect the rights and cultural wealth of the tribal people, which was under assault from Christianity. It succeeded in its mission in several states where missionaries were already at work.

Vanvasi Kalyan Ashram not only opened educational and health centres but also came out openly for their property rights and identity issues. It stood in support of their cultural and religious rights and identity. The Kalyan Ashram challenged the work of the missionaries. This pace changed after the 90s when the Hindutva movement caught the national discourse. It successfully exposed the bogus working of the secular premise, which, on the one hand, allowed the Christian and Muslim minorities to go along with their politico-religious agenda, whereas the same political and religious consolidation of the Hindus was looked at with an element of contempt and criticism. Though the Ayodhya movement intended to build a temple at the place of the controversial structure, it also contained the ideological framework. The opposition to the missionaries' activities increased as Hindutva asserted against the political agenda of the missionaries to deplete the numerical preponderance of the Hindu society in tribal areas. Needless to say, Vanvasi Kalyan Ashram, RSS and its other bodies became the prime target of the missionaries. Missionaries soon realised that it should be part of their strategy to damage the RSS and its ancillary organisations. They chose to wage a propaganda war in order to discredit and defame them in the region. They increased their criticism of the Sangh Parivar. The unchallenged work of missionaries among the poor, illiterate and unexposed tribals in the remote rural areas and deep forest was now before all to see how Christianity was silently engaged in changing the political, religious and cultural landscape of the country. They were harvesting the faith for centuries. Now, there was a political Hindutva openly challenging and countering the political Christianity in their home turf. During the freedom movement, even Gandhi opposed conversion and those engaged in it[4] (Gandhi, 1928; Gandhi, 1936; Gandhi, 1937). Now the RSS and its ancillary organisations consistently took on their conversion activities. This has led to the extent of animosity of the magnitude that Graham Steins was killed with his children for converting Hindus in Orissa, and the Church has also been found arousing people against the RSS in the areas of its preponderance.

4 Gandhi has condemned the proselytization by the Christian Missionaries.

1 Maoist Not Targeting Missionaries

The Maoists-Missionaries link also comes under scanner because despite being at poles apart on ideological plain, it is rare to see the conflict between the two. Maoists claim to have been opposed to the conservative ideology and pro-market stand of the BJP. But they stand with the missionaries' conservatism and their pro-market stance. Christian missionaries who have been downright supporters of the same forces. The money that comes for the missionaries is the money from the capitalist governments of the West. Missionaries are not supporters of non-market ideology. The missionaries are also the ideological wings of capitalist countries, which often come to their rescue when they end up in trouble. These liberal democracies, which are essentially capitalist economies, interfere in the discourse in the name of religious freedom. Ideally, the Maoists should have opposed the missionaries on the grounds that they were the extended hands of Western capitalism. But they don't do so because they are also the beneficiaries of the funds pumped in by Western countries. Secondly, as mentioned earlier, Christianity too is invested with tonnes of taboos and superstitions which have no relevance for a scientific society of today. Religious conversion on a mass scale engineered and doctored by the Church is not at all a practice intended to spiritual emancipation of the individual soul. It is a political design to increase the numerical strength of the religious population. It is not a hidden secret now that the Church has a worldwide network to this effect, and they pump in millions of dollars to execute it. Thus, the whole exercise of religious conversion is an exclusivist doctrine threatening religious and social harmony in the country. Maoists claim to oppose such ideology in principle. They also do it and leave no occasion to attack the Hindu organisations, but when it comes to missionaries, they look the other way.

No wonder one does not find any clash between the Maoists and the Missionaries. RSS always puts this question: why the Church and the Christian community in remote forest areas are not targeted by the Maoists (Hindustan Times, 2015). When Alex Paul Menon, the district collector of Sukma in Chhattisgarh, was kidnapped by the Maoists, a former IB chief predicted that the Maoists won't kill him or hurt him because he is a Christian (Bhatt, 2012). He held that in the tribal area, lots of young tribals are converting to Christianity in the hope of help from missionaries in their personal and family growth, and the Maoists won't like to annoy their primary constituency in the tribal belts. This came true as the said IAS officer was released by the Maoists after 13 days of his capture. And when the matter came for hearing in the court, the IAS officer declined to identify the kidnappers. In this incident, the two gunmen of the collector were killed by the Maoists. Surprisingly, the Christian world does not approve of this variant of Marxism in their lands, but do not come out against it as aggressively against left extremism because they themselves are not victim of it. They had the same attitude against Islamic terrorism until they experienced a series of bombings in Europe and the most devastating one on 9/11 in the USA. These countries ignore the larger conspiracy theory and hold that the expansion of the Naxal movement is primarily due to the failure of the Indian state, which is true as well, but partly only, on the socio-economic fronts.

Despite the fact that the missionaries are against the native culture and religion and are engaged in cultural aggression for political purposes, the Maoists do not turn their guns on them. On the contrary, they are very harsh towards the Vanvasi Kalyan Ashram activists who work in the forest areas for the tribals. Earlier, Puri Shankaracharya Swami Nishchalanand Sarswati was also served with a threatening letter from the Maoists on the grounds that he was spreading the message of communalism and dividing society. An FIR was registered with the Sea Beach Police Station by the disciples of the Swami. Swami Nishchalanand has also been against the conversion of Hindus in the country, and he always took a bold stand against the missionaries (The Hindu, 2015). Christian Missionaries, on the other hand, argue that Naxal-missionaries commingling is alleged because both have been working for the poor and sick, illiterate and deserted ones in the remote areas. They say that the missionaries' objective is not very different from what the Maoists want; an exploitation-free society in which the tribals could enjoy their social, economic, political and other rights. In an interview to a Catholic Weekly, Sathyadeepam, published from Kochi, in May 2009, Bishop Soreng held that 'the Maoists are sympathetic to the Church' and have been supporting the missionary activities in the area (Haindava Keralam, 2010). Another Bishop from Hazaribagh, Charles Soreng, held that both Maoists and the church are waging battle against the same social evils (Haindava Keralam, 2010). He held that the Maoists are good and honest people, and they are fighting for the rights of the sections of society which is deprived and not in a position to get even the minimum required for a dignified human life. To him, Maoists are fighting against the greed and the corruption that pervades the entire tribal area, besides the government's apathy towards these people. He held that the Naxals are honest people and are fighting for justice for the poor and outcaste people. This is the argument that the Maoists advance in response to the question of why they are engaged in violence. In fact, it is rare to find the missionary related organisations that have come forward to condemn the violence perpetrated by the Maoists in the tribal areas despite the fact that the Maoists, on occasions have also raided the church for the sake of money.

2 Missionaries at Work in Other Countries: Fuelling Fire and Conflicts

All this leads to an important question, i.e., do missionaries fuel divisive tendencies in the host societies to weaken the native society to advance their agenda of proselytisation? Do their support to the Maoists ideologically and through money are largely in tune with the accomplishment of this goal? Have the missionary used violence in different countries to defame the native religion, and then fishing in the troubled water? Some examples lead to a definite pattern. Both in Sri Lanka and Burma, missionaries worked to weaken the native society to take advantage of the situation in the form of converting the people. *Karen rebels* in Burma and Tamil Tigers were also supported by the Church. The Karen rebels are mainly Christians who have been resisting against the majoritarian rule in Burma and resorting to armed rebellion for self-rule in the country. During the British occupation, they were supported by the colonial government, and the Church had been inflaming them after Burmese independence from Britain. Tamil Tigers also received support from the Church. During the Sri Lankan ethnic conflicts, the stories of the Tamil Tigers never attacking the Church always remained a point of discussion, in which the needle of suspicion rested towards the Catholic Church. It was alleged that the Catholic Church acted as an ally of the Tamil Tigers (Sri Lanka Guardian, 2009). Sri Lankan Singhalese alleged that the Church was doing in Sri Lanka what it had already done in South America and the Philippines.

Both Maoism and Missionaries find the troubled and divided societies as the fertile ground for their activities, though their missions and ultimate objectives are different. Social and economic deprivations of communities' work to their advantage as they find it easier to create fissures in society and arouse the masses against the system. However, while the missionaries' objective is to convert them into a new religion, i.e. Christianity, by depicting the native religion as atrocious and backwards, the Maoists' objective is to capture state power by mobilising them against the current state of affairs. Both of them, therefore, think it prudent to enforce each other.

It is no longer a secret that the missionaries, apart from China, played a crucial role in empowering the Maoists in Nepal. The UPA-I government, under pressure from the native comrades, allowed the power to be transferred from the pro-India Nepali Congress to the anti-India Maoists led by Prachanda. Pushpa Raj Pradhan, a journalist and editor of 'Peoples Review', wrote that the missionaries fund the FM radio to propagate the Christian views as they want to transform a Hindu state of Nepal into a Christian state. Nepal was declared a 'secular state' in 2007 after the United Communist Party-Maoists, which had waged armed struggle against the state, joined the political mainstream. It is not the people who wanted it. People by 2015 in fact largely favour replacing the word 'secular 'with 'Hindu' (Arora, 2015). The Church had been asking for the change of the Hindu state into a secular state for a long time on the basis of equal opportunity for all religions. K.B. Rokaya of the Regional Council of Churches in Nepal welcomed the decision when the Nepalese parliament decided for the same. He did not conceal the fact that the Churches have been fighting for secular and religious freedom in Nepal for a long time (The New York Times, 2006). Interestingly, the Communist government in China restricted the working of the Christian missionaries on its soil, but the Communist Party in Nepal enabled the missionaries to swell up the numerical strength from 42000 in 2007 to 32 lakhs in 2024. 24000 churches have come up in Nepal, and they have very good relations with the Maoist leader in the country.

Given the strong roots of Hinduism pervading the Nepalese society, it was common for both the Maoists and the missionaries to declare Nepal a secular state. While the monarchy was the target of the Maoists behind this campaign, for missionaries, it was altogether a religio-political design for the future because the Monarchy was very much against the work of the Christian missionaries in the country. In Nepal, the European agencies pumped in around 10–15 billion dollars every year for the promotion of Christianity in the country. In 2022, Nepal had 7758 small and big churches, and the Christian population swelling up to nearly 683261 Lakhs according to the data released by the National Christian Community Survey. In 2002, the Christian population was just 0.1 percent, but by 2020 it increased to 4.3 percent. Christian Aid, an organisation, influenced a ministry in the Nepalese government and reached out to the Magars Community, members of which are primarily engaged in basket weaving and blacksmith, and convinced the Maoists how their activities were good for the community and finally used the money for the conversion into Christianity.

Nepal, though, has been a Hindu nation, but its constitution did not contain a provision that could discriminate against any religion. The transition to the constitutional monarchy that materialised in 1990, though it declared Nepal a Hindu Kingdom, did not proclaim Hinduism as the state religion and also ensured religious freedom to all. Of course, it banned the religious conversion, a provision which has been consciously at work since 50s. The US Department of State's report on religious freedom, broadly titled as 'International Religious Freedom Report 2007', expressed clearly that in Nepal, there had been religious tolerance and no religious community was deprived of its right to religious freedom (US Department of State, 2007). But this was not sufficient for the missionaries, who wanted an open field for evangelical activities. As secularism provides a necessary cushion to their missionary acts, they worked with the Maoists to declare Nepal a secular country. Prachanda, the leader of the Maoists, openly declared a massive gathering of Christians at the Open Theatre that those 'who would oppose secularism would be kidnapped'. Prachanda himself is a Christian (Sri Lanka Guardian, 2011).

It is not without reason that Christianization has been described as the third force of colonialism, the other two being capital and military strength. J. Goonetilleke, a Buddhist intellectual from Sri Lanka, argued this point and noted that all the aristocratic family in Britain had a lord, a Bishop, a businessman in the city and a landed proprietor. The church had a deeper penetration among the aristocracy, and it had also financial interests in the colonies. No wonder the missionaries supported the British government against the independence movement in India. Jomo Kenyatta, a late Kenyan leader, depicted it very precisely how the fate of Kenya changed due to conversion and a massive evangelical campaign. He said, "When the white man came, he had the bible, and we had the land. Then he said, 'Let us close our eyes and pray. By the time we opened our eyes, we found the Bible in our hands and land in their hands."

3 How Missionaries Support the Ultras?

In India also, the missionaries have been found to be behind several unrests in the tribal India from the North-East to the tribal belts of Central and Eastern India. There are two important ways which Missionaries use to help and support the Maoists. First, there have been instances of Churches directly funding the Maoists. A percentage of the money that comes from the outside for missionary purposes goes to the Maoists. Missionaries do it due to a possible threat from the Maoists as well as due to the realisation that they are helpful in their cause in the long run. Secondly, there are hundreds of NGOs that work in the tribal areas. They are funded from outside, especially from the Christian countries in the West. These NGOs are engaged in charitable activities in the tribal belts. But at the same time, their charitable activities also became a source of support to the Naxals. In case of casualties, Naxals find them a reliable destination for medical treatment. Their medical and mobile vans provide treatment to the injured Naxals. Recently, Chhattisgarh police confirmed that International NGOs have been supporting the Maoists. The police authorities of the state accused Doctors Without Borders (MSF) and the Red Cross (ICRC) of supporting Maoists in the guise of humanitarian aid. The district SP of Dantewada claimed that the doctors of these two international organisations were engaged in treating the Maoists without informing the police. The police came to know of it when two Maoists were arrested from a pharmacy with medicines worth 6000 dollars. It is these arrested people who revealed that the doctors of MSF and ICRC were treating the Maoists (Sethi, 2016; BBC, 2016).

MSF India's head held that the organisation is not involved in political ideology and its works are limited to providing medical treatment to any sick person, but that speaks of just the half-truth. The MSF entered the state of Chhattisgarh in 2006, and since then, it has been engaged in providing medical care to the people living in remote areas. It has mobile clinics equipped with medicines and doctors who provide treatments to the needy people. But at the same time, it is also one of those organisations that are very sympathetic to the Naxals and have been rendering medical services to the Naxals in case of injury, particularly when they do not find it safe to approach any government or private hospitals. So, the war zone assistance is provided by such organisations that claim to be working only on humanitarian grounds.

In fact, it is difficult for the police and administration to nail them because they are part of the society in which the Naxals operate. And therefore, each time such activists are arrested by the police, the latter are charged with violating human rights and working against the basic tenets of humanity. There are over 2 lakh NGOs working in India, and there is no sound mechanism of tracking their working and financial transactions at the end of the state government or the central government. There are hundreds of NGOs that are working in the Naxal-infested tribal areas. Many of them are fake. In Chhattisgarh alone, a few years back, 300 NGOs were found illegally working without the Knowledge of the state. And most certainly, many of these NGOs have direct links with the Maoists. They just have not only a soft corner for them but also come out in 'open support of the guerrillas' (Naxal Terror Watch, 2007; Khan, 2011; Deccan Herald, 2013; Chaudhary, 2013; Vyas, 2013). In case of a security forces offensive against the Naxals, they organise protest rallies and mobilise public opinion.

As per an estimate, nearly Rs. 10000 crore is invested by the missionary organisations and their associated NGOs working under different names and for different purposes in the tribal areas of central India (Thamizhchelvan, 2011). This money comes from the West, and it is certainly mobilised by the evangelical organisations in the European countries. Both the government and the state are parties to this exercise.

So is the case with not all but most of the civil rights groups working in the tribal areas. These groups defend the violent uprisings in the tribal belts by advancing the argument of hunger and poverty and the inhuman conditions of the tribal people. This gives them the mask to defend their Naxal proximity. Binayak Sen was certainly one of those who were working in the areas. Binayak Sen certainly was engaged in charitable services to the poor and deprived.

No wonder Christian missionaries have a very soft attitude towards the Maoists. In April 2010, Father Xavier Manjooran, a member of the 'Adivasi Maha Sabha' of Gujarat, accused the government of treating tribals as terrorists even though they are just demanding their legal rights in the system. Father Xavier's reference was to the attitude of the Gujarat government, which came out heavily on the Maoists' activities in the state. Adivasi Maha Sabha is an organisation which works for the tribals and is controlled by the missionaries. Hence, their political commitment and affiliation have been obvious. The clue to this also came from the Maoist Information Bulletin itself. In its December 2009 edition, the news bulletin carried a letter on page 30, which read that the government of India wanted to take action against some of the organisations working in 10 different states. Gujarat Adivasi Maha Sabha was one of them. This directly indicted the missionaries' links with the Naxals. The information bulletin also mentioned the support that the Maoists were getting from the Philippines-based organisation, Cordillera People's Alliance. This organisation is a Christian organisation and though it claims to be working for the rights of the indigenous people, it is a part of the Episcopal Church in that country.

There are several such instances in the past when people from the Church have been arrested for possible links between the Maoists and the Missionaries. A pastor, Roshan, from Jehanabad in Bihar, was arrested by the state police for his linkages with the Maoists. Surprisingly, this news was available with *Gospel for Asia*, an evangelical mission organisation based in Carrollton, Texas, which claims to be involved in teaching the message of Jesus in South Asia, much before it could reach the Indian intelligentsia. After 17 months in Jail he was acquitted by the court. On 24th August 2012, eight persons were convicted by a district court in Paralakhemundi in Odisha. They were awarded rigorous imprisonment for 7 years. They were Jaccob Raita, Harshamandal, Bairagi Sabara, Surya Gamang, Gajingaraita, EshaMandal, Bhima Gamango and Alokmani. They were all arrested in September 2006, from a church in their village, Anugura, under the Udayagiri police station (The Times of India, 2012). In April 2012, nine French tourists were arrested by the Bihar Police for allegedly working with the Unity Forum, a front organisation of the Maoists predominant in central Bihar, especially in areas like Nawada, Bihar Sharif, and Aurangabad districts of Bihar (India Today, 2012). These tourists had violated their VISA conditions. The tourists' visa rules prohibit the travelling foreigners from indulging in any socio-political activities.

Arun Thomas Ferreira, a Christian activist was arrested by the Maharashtra police in 2007 (Maitra, 2012). He was an activist of Navjawan Bharat Sabha, an NGO. The moment he was arrested, the Church went on street to oppose the arrest. He was declared innocent before trial, and the Maharashtra police were accused of victimising all such persons who stand for the poor in the tribal belts.

All this does not augur well for the missionaries. It would be wrong to draw a linear equation between the Maoists link with the Christian Missionaries. Not all the missionaries are involved in the Maoists' activities. But scores of examples suggest that the missionaries have been lending indirect support to the Maoists in the forest areas through funding the NGOs which work in such areas in garb of working for the illiterate and poor tribals and defending their rights on the lands and surroundings. There are instances in the recent past and the pattern of violence which do suggest that while the Maoists are harsh and violent towards the Hindu nationalists and the organisations associated with them in the remote forest areas, they are soft towards the Christian Missionaries. And this soft attitude is read as consciously crafted to mutual advantage.

CHAPTER 6

Salwa Judum: People's Movement against Naxals?

Salwa Judum started in 2005. It was a vigilante movement, mainly supported by the Chhattisgarh and Central governments, to fight against Maoists. But following the direction of the Supreme Court of India in 2011, the state government of Chhattisgarh dismantled it. The former Chief Minister of the state, Dr Raman Singh, had formally declared that the state government was committed to the vacation of buildings and makeshift structures developed as Salwa Judum Camps. The detractors of the movement, however, had no trust in the government assurances, and they further approached the court to ensure that the network of Judum was dismantled completely. The Raman Singh government, in the meantime, decided to accommodate all the Special Police Officers (SPOs) within the police system by regularising their services under a new pay structure below the existing grades and pay scale for the police. As the declaration of closing down Salwa Judum did not stop Naxalite attacks, a huge section of the tribal people and officers engaged in the counter-insurgency combat operations questioned the wisdom of the court in passing an order for dismantling the Salwa Judum. They also criticised the human rights groups of their partisan role. Their grudge was that while these human rights groups go all out against the state, they keep conspiratorial silence on the violence of the Naxals. They seldom come out to criticise Naxals for their violence and convince them not to kill civilians and forcibly drag the innocent and unwilling people into conflict? They do not even murmur about the foreign nexus of the Maoists and their arms procurement from outside the country. In their eyes, these human rights groups are the ones who are part of the Maoists movement, who lend intellectual support to the same in the media and establishments of power. And thus, the debate continues amidst allegations and counter-allegations ever since the inception of Salwa Judum as a strategy of the government to take on the Naxals. While the government claims it to be a spontaneous self-grown and self-evolved anti-Naxal people movement, human rights activists, organisations and intelligentsia particularly close to the left-wing ideology consider it illegal arming of common people[1] who in name of fighting the Naxals have

1 Justice SriKrishna called it 'private militia' and did not approve of this way of arming the people to counter the internal insurgency. Ramchandra Guha has also been using the same term against it. But surprisingly, none of them highlighted the accommodation of the people in counterinsurgency operations in J&K, North-East and Punjab.

 | HTTPS://DOI.ORG/10.1163/9789004765054-008

turned out to be the street goons harassing and harming the innocent tribals and the poor.

'Salwa Judum' is a Gondi dialect which means 'Peace March' or a fight for peace. Some people also translate it to mean 'purification hunt', which Marxists and Maoists pollinate to describe as 'group hunting' against the Naxals, who have initiated 'people's movement' in the forest areas aimed at promoting the cause of poor and exploited tribals. Not surprisingly, human rights activists closer to the Maoists have depicted the whole movement as 'Salwa Juroom'[2] as it intends to argue the continuing exploitation of the poor tribals.

1 Origin of Salwa Judum

There are multiple stories about how the Salwa Judum started. It is difficult to pinpoint the exact date when it started for the first time. One story is that the people of some villages were very upset with the directives of the Maoists to the villagers not to collect Tendu Leaves. It adversely affected their livelihood, and therefore, they decided to protest and rise against the Maoists. They gathered and decided to proceed towards the villages, which were known as strongholds of the Maoists. As per the police account, which has been documented by the team members comprising the fact-finding Committee, they saw the people gathered for this in Matavada village and marching towards Kotarapal village for the first time. The second narrative is that it all started with the beating and handing over of the local Maoists who had assembled in a village, Ambeli, in the Kutra/Kurtu Police station. These Maoists wanted to forcibly disperse the gatherings. And the villagers, under the leadership of Mahendra Karma, caught them and handed them over to the police. The third version is that the Maoists fell into the trap laid for them by the villagers on the instructions of the CRPF, whose seven jawans were killed a few days ago by the Maoists.

However, a predominant view that flows from the oral narratives and common talking points is that it started sometime in June 2005 in the Bastar district of Chhattisgarh, which has emerged as the epicentre of the Naxal movement for the last several years in the country (India Today, 2011). The initial thrust to this effect was given by a school master from the village of Kurtu, who motivated the students to protest and resist the injustices and atrocities of the Naxals perpetrated on the common poor tribals. He was upset with

2 Dr. Vinayak Sen, General Secretary, PUCL, who has been a doctor by profession and working in the tribal areas, but at the same time is alleged to be a sympathiser of the Naxal movement and working for them, used this term to malign the movement.

the Naxals frequently visiting the tribal villages, forcing the villagers to serve food and cough up money and beating them for denying these services. There were instances of women being sexually abused and children being forcefully dragged into the movement. Their peril did not just end here. In fact, the tribals were sandwiched between the Naxals on the one hand and the police on the other. When the Naxals left their homes, the police stepped in for interrogation about their links with the Naxals. Passing information to the police was retaliated by beating and even killing by the Naxals, whereas denial of the information to the police resulted in harassment by the latter. The frequent and continuous exposure to such atrocities had already infuriated the local tribals, who wanted to come out of it. The schoolteacher from Kutru just gave a voice to this frustration (Asian Centre for Human Rights Report, 2006:15).

Salwa Judum, thus, was a local mobilisation. Even the PUDR and PUCL document, which quotes Prabhat, a newsletter of the CPI (Maoists of Dandakaranya Special Zonal Committee), also endorse it. But at the same time, their version is that it started because Maoists had conducted land distribution to the landless in 25 villages. Such exercise was also done by the Maoists in central Bihar in 1966–67. While those who gained from the distribution wished to join the Dandakaranya Kishan Mazdoor Sangathan, this was unacceptable to the headmen of some of the villages, who invited these people for a talk, and when they appeared, they were beaten up and handed over to the Kutru police (PUDR, 2006:15–22). The first organised protest against the Naxals, however, was initiated by late Mahendra Karma. Karma was a tribal leader from Dantewada constituency. He was a tribal face of the Congress party in the state who also served as the leader of the opposition in the state assembly. Despite being in opposition, Karma always supported the anti-Naxal stand of the government and its initiatives to neutralise the combat power of the Naxals in the region. One reason why he was against the Naxals was probably the fact that he belonged to the affluent section of the tribal community. Given the lead he had taken to take on the Naxals, he was always on the hit list of the Naxals. He was killed in a blast in May 2013 along with several of his supporters and many Congress leaders in the state, including former Chief Minister VC Shukla (Bagchi, 2021). In fact, the Salwa Judum is much connected to his name than any other individual personality in the state. He not only gave nomenclature to the movement but also appealed to the state government to come forward and take up the responsibility of supporting the people's movement against the Naxals. Mahendra Karma earlier also had taken up the cause of resistance against the presence of Naxals in Dantewada district and their harassment activities. He was the one who had started Jan Jagran Abhiyan in the 90s to tackle the Naxal terror. But that did not succeed. June 5, 2005, turned out to be an important date in the struggle against the Naxals in Chhattisgarh, as the

Naxals were caught and overpowered by the villagers. This certainly emboldened the tribal people as they could realise that the Naxals could be tackled with the collective capacity of the people.

The nomenclature Salwa Judum came in late June 2005. Mahendra Karma, while speaking in a meeting of tribals on 25th June 2005, finally termed this anti-Naxal campaign as 'Salwa Judum'. It was a meeting of the tribals in Bijapur, which was attended by senior officials of the district administration, like the SP and Collector of Dantewada, the SP of Bijapur district, and the IG police, apart from the BJP MLA and minister. The point of discussion was, of course, the menace of the Naxal movement in the tribal areas of Chhattisgarh. Naxal leadership and its supporters criticised this meeting and depicted it as government sponsored. On the other hand, detractors of the Naxal movement claim that it was a citizen initiative on whose request the police officials participated. The truth falls somewhere between these adverse arguments. But undoubtedly, it was organised against the violence by the Naxals and both the government and a section of the tribals and their leaders were on the same page.

Given the fact that Mahendra Karma belonged to the Congress Party, his call had a reasonable and apolitical appeal. The government of the state responded to this call positively. The only dilemma was how to engage and how to take the fight into the camps of the Naxals with the support of the people. This also signifies that the much-alleged Salwa Judum, contrary to the Naxals' claim, was an idea that emerged from within the tribal people rather than one that came from the government and was imposed thereafter. The government realised that tackling the Naxal movement was not possible without the support of the locals. The harassment of the locals by the Naxals gave the government an opportunity to rope in the tribal people in its fight against the Naxals. Thus, a journalist and Maoist sympathiser, Shubhranshu Chaudhary, admits as under: "It is just as true that the villages harboured a great deal of anger against the Naxals and the initial anti-Naxals meetings held in June had been spontaneous. But parties with vested interests, who had long been preparing a counter-offensive against the Maoists, swiftly hijacked the people's rebellion" (Choudhary, 2012:156).

In the meantime, Mahendra Karma organised several rallies against the Naxalites. The response was tremendous. Many villagers, including those who were working for the Naxals so far, left the organisation and joined Sangham.[3] On August 27, 2005, thirty members of Sangham joined Judum in its rally at Bhairamgarh. Similarly, on September 11, 2005, 26 Sangham members joined the Salwa Judum rally, which started from 'Kodoli Village'. The same followed

3 Sangham refers to the organisation which subsequently marked the protest against the Naxal Movement.

in the rally, which ended at Gangalur. Nearly 189 Naxalites joined the movement in this rally (NHRC Report, 2008:14). It is important to note that Karma calls for peace, not only encouraged the locals to rise to the occasion to resist the Naxals for peace, but it equally worked on those who had already joined the violent movement and were working for it for quite some years.

The growing popularity of Salwa Judum became a threat to the Naxalite strength and their penetration in the region. They therefore retaliated with ferocious violence. Several villages were targeted in which several people, young as well as children, lost their lives. For example, on June 14, 2005, Naxals attacked the people of the village Kotrapal in Bhairamgarh, in which eight people lost their lives (Asian Centre for Human Rights Report, 2006:15). In other villages of Dantewada too, Naxals attacked to terrorise the people so that they could desist from the anti-Naxal activities. In one such meeting at Talmendra, which was attended by a nearly 10000-strong crowd assembled from several surrounding villages, the crowd was attacked by the Naxals, in which several tribals lost their lives (Asian Centre for Human Rights Report, 2006:15). Such violent activities, however, could not break the courage and the resolve of the locals to fight the Naxals. The relatives of the victims and the people in the villages were up in arms over these ghastly killings by the Naxals. They made a request to the government to support them in their battle against the Naxals. With time, the government also realised that it was not possible for it to provide security cover to all the scattered villages in the forest terrain at night. For Naxals, villagers were easy targets at night. It was therefore important for the government to encourage the villagers to leave their villages at night and take shelter in makeshift camps.

This was also necessitated by the fact that, in light of the Naxals' ferocious attacks on the Salwa Judum members and their kith and kin, several families had left the villages. They fled to the nearby police stations for security and shelter. The government had no option but to provide safer shelter to them, which could not be very far from their villages, and also protect them against possible attacks from the Naxals. Accordingly, it created camps near the police stations or the armed forces camps. This is the reason that most of the Salwa Judum camps appeared on the outskirts of villages and closer to the security forces' camps.

The government, in fact, came out with a formal declaration only on August 15, 2005, that it would go all out to support the people's resistance campaign against the Naxal movement. Government subsequently set up a committee under the leadership of then Chief Secretary of state government A.K. Vijayvargiya to look after the needed support to the people, such as money, arms, food, clothes, management and security of the camps, etc. (Asian

Centre for Human Rights Report, 2006:16). The committee suggested that the government meet the needs of the dwellers in the camps and provide them with all necessary help and protection to prevent them from becoming the foot soldiers of the Naxals. The government of the state worked swiftly on the idea as it found a kind of political consensus on the issue and also an opportunity to take the bull by the horns. It realised that it would also give the opportunity to the government to reach out closer to the tribal people and read into their mindset.

Salwa Judum became famous overnight, and the idea spread like wildfire. In subsequent months, several villages agreed to such a campaign. To begin with, as a pilot project, the government adopted two blocks, namely Bijapur and Bairamgarh, comprising 240 villages in the Dantewada district for Salwa Judum. Village defence committees, Gram Raksha Samitis, were formed in 130 villages (Asian Centre for Human Rights Report, 2006:16). With more and more people coming in, this strength went on swelling with the passage of time. By the beginning of March 2006, 644 villages of the Dantewada district were brought under Salwa Judum. It needs to be understood that while the innocent tribals were at the receiving end due to state apathy and frequent harassments by the forest and state officials in many ways and therefore unhappy with the state but at the same time they were also not happy with the Naxalites who had started coming in to their villages, disturbing their peace and more importantly intruding and interfering in their faiths and cultural beliefs systems. Naxals' approach of using force to silence the dissent also pricked them, and they all appreciated the move of bringing together village people for a collective defence against outsiders. If the state was an outsider, so were the Naxals to them. Many Naxals who had joined the Naxal movement because of fear of the Maoists returned to the villages and came forward to contribute to the cause. Such people became important components of the Judum as they could guide the police and para-military forces more specifically because of their first-hand experiences with the movement. A fact in this regard makes the point clearer. Salwa Judum very soon became visible in all ten districts of the state with nearly 300 camps comprising over 3800 trained and untrained young and underage people (Asian Centre for Human Rights Report, 2006:16).

2 Salwa Judum Camps

Salwa Judum camps are mostly located at the outskirts of the villages and closer to the police or security forces camps. This is primarily because the people who left the village, fearing the assault of the Naxals, went to the nearby police and armed forces camps so that they could get protection from them. This was also good for the police, who do not have to send additional forces for the protection of the individual villages. There was no standard size of the camps. It all depended on the number of people coming to the camps from villages. However, normally that number ranged somewhere between 100 to 300 families spread over in different camps. Women were not generally a part of the Salwa Judum in a true technical sense, but since their husbands and family members were part of it, they used to stay in the camps. Both men and women go out of the camps to visit and work in their fields, but come back by evening to their camps. The structure of the camps also varies from tin sheds to existing school buildings to tents provided by the government. The government provides the camp dwellers free rations (rice, dal, oil, potato, onion, etc.), health facilities and also educational facilities to the children. These facilities, though, are not very adequate, as has also been alleged by the human rights organisations. It is also not as bad as compared to the prevailing general economic conditions of the tribals, most of whom are not just below the poverty line but striving to get even the minimum basics. The detractors of Salwa Judum accuse of the absence of proper food, water, health and other basic amenities. Charges are also that since these camps are placed in the schools' buildings, the state is deliberately depriving them of education. Similarly, other facilities are also not up to the mark. In sum, the conditions in which the people are placed in these camps are horrific, and they are not worth living in at all. Also, the people do not want to live in these camps, but are made to do so by the police. It is true that there are instances of erratic supply of rations. Similarly, drinking water facilities and toilets are not in good shape (The Indian Express, 2010). Doctors also do not visit the camps daily, but as and when they are called for. Thus, all that is said against the camps is not false and erroneous, but they reflect the half-truth and that too judged from the urban perspectives of living standards. If we look at it from the urban perspective of living, it will seem not to be a very good living condition, but when it is seen in the context of what they used to get in the villages, they appear to be better placed. These facilities provided to them are better compared to what they had in their villages. NHRC too did not find the condition too bad in the camps, though Naxals, human rights groups, and other NGOs working in the areas do not find it up to mark.

The trouble in recent times has increased, however, because the government, which used to provide them free rations, have now started implementing the scheme of rations against work. The government defends this on the grounds that the existing arrangement was making people not just dependent but also completely parasitic, which was not good for the people either. But this has also resulted in more and more people leaving the camps for their villages (The Indian Express, 2010).

3 Who Joined Salwa Judum and Why?

Who are the people who joined the Judum? In other words, why and who are the people behind the anti-Naxal movement? Contrary to the anti-Judum campaigners who attribute this campaign to be government-manufactured tribal voice, well designed to weaken the emerging social support base of the Naxals in the tribal dominated areas, Salwa Judum was a people's movement which, in subsequent years, found all support from the government in the state. Thus, initially, it was not the government that conceived and allowed it to be operated and led by the common people. On the contrary, the government intervention is a case of late arrival in the venture; it emerged as a token of reaction from the tribals on their own, which subsequently found mammoth support amongst the common tribals, who were tired of the Naxals. The government, too, found it a good instrument to deal with the Naxals, as the anti-Naxal rising had the potential of cutting the social support base of the Naxals. And therefore, when the Naxals retaliated to such protests and resistance from the common people, the state came forward to support and sustain the movement.

The NHRC report, which closely investigated the activities of Salwa Judum, is worth reading in this regard. The commission, which was assigned the task by the Supreme Court to investigate a wide range of issues and incidents, clearly mentions at several places that the movement was a spontaneous and conscious reaction of the tribals against the atrocities of the Naxalites (NHRC Report, 2008:28). In its report, the commission noted that the investigating team of the commission came across several atrocities and activities which factored into the Salwa Judum. The commission, after having the field visit to different villages and camps, noted that the tribals of the "South Bastar suffered at the hands of the Naxalites not only due to the violence perpetrated by them, but also due to the constant interference in their day-to-day activities. Many village Sarpanches and Patels were humiliated, beaten up, and sometimes even killed in the Jan Adalats held in the villages by the Naxalites. Similarly, in order to create a fear psychosis among the tribals, many villagers were also brutally murdered in Jan Adalats after accusing them of being police informers" (NHRC Report, 2008:9–10). Naxalites did not stop just here. They started interfering in the village economy. They forced the villagers to part with their forest and land produce to the Naxals. They also started redistributing 'the land and the livestock amongst the villagers as per their own will'. More importantly, they shifted the 'traditional Haats' to more interior areas, causing a lot of inconvenience to many tribals (NHRC Report, 2008:10). Their activities stopped the developmental activities in the villages. School children who had even gone out of the village to study in the nearby towns were recalled, and the parents were forced to send them to join the rank and file for the Naxal movement. There were several instances of sexual abuse of the girls to the extent of making them pregnant and taking them to a revolution after delivery of the child (NHRC Report, 2008:11). The villagers were always used as a shield during the police operations in which several tribals lost their lives. They were often used to cut trees and block the access of the security forces. Naxals did not spare even the religious domain of the tribals' lives. Governed and guided by their informed atheist ideology, many Pujaris who used to perform rituals for the tribals were killed by the Naxal. There were hardly any development activities that were not taxed or halted by the Naxals. It was the cumulative impact of all this that forced the tribals to stand against the Naxalites. NHRC in its report even quoted one of the petitioners who had admitted before the court that Salwa Judum resulted from the atrocities of the Naxals on the village tribals (NHRC Report, 2008:11). Obviously, people were just looking for articulation of their anger against the Naxals, and the moment they got that opportunity, they did so. It is also worth noting that they voted for the BJP in the parliamentary and assembly elections and refused to buy the election boycott calls given by the Naxal outfits in several elections.

In fact, Salwa Judum comprises three sets of people. There are the ones who do not handle arms against the Naxals, but they do mobilise the masses against the Naxals by organising rallies and meetings of the people from village to village. They also encourage the youth and common tribal men to fight against the menace of the Naxal movement. They convince the common man of how and why it is essential for them and their interests to do so. It helps in building cadres to counter the Naxal insurgency. There is a second set of people who actually are the sympathisers and become part of the rally or campaign. They are not self-activated cadres and do not take arms to counter the violence of the Naxals. The third set of people is the Special Protection officers, popularly known as SPOs. These SPOs are generally young people from villages. NHRC makes a distinction between the Salwa Judum and the SPOs. For the NHRC, Salwa Judum in fact consists of the first two sets of people. SPOs are the ones who are recruited by the state government under the provisions of the State Armed Forces Act. However, the Supreme Court questioned the appointments of SPOs on the grounds that the state cannot appoint and send people to the war zone. The state government, on the other hand, argued that they were not forced to be part of it but willingly joined the people's movement, and the state limited its role to enable them to receive effective training to protect the people against the Naxalite forceful coercion of the people to stand with their revolutionary movement.

There is no one reason or factor that motivates people to join the Salwa Judum campaign. Broadly speaking, there were four categories of people who joined the Judum camp. First, there were people who were attracted to the promises given to them by the government. Apart from the food, clothes, shelter, education for the children and medical support, what attracted them the most was the monthly salary and the possibility of becoming permanent employees in the state police. After all, the regular salary was also one of the primary reasons that the Naxals managed to attract a lot of youths in the tribal belts to their side. Naxals promised to pay a sum of Rs. 3000 to 4000 to each one of them. This was sufficient for the youth who was uneducated and unemployed and had no secure means of meeting the needs of livelihood. The government thus picked a leaf from the Naxals and approached the village youths. A large number of the young boys and girls joined the Salwa Judum because they saw a possibility of getting a government job in return for serving as SPOs. This is not without reason. The government used to make such promises through their officials to entice them to join the people's campaign against the Naxals. Thus, the government worked on a strategy to blunt the recruitment drive of the Naxals by approaching the young unemployed and uneducated in villages. It used the same means and mechanisms that the Naxals use in their recruitment. A villager from the Bastar district who thus joined the Salwa Judum camp held that it was better to join the movement than to be forced to be part of the Naxals and then wander from one corner of the state to another corner of the state to protect their lives from police bullets. Given the absence of industrial activities and agricultural employment, it was not a very comforting choice, but it was relatively better, which could change their future, too.

There were also many who were convinced of the fact that Naxals were a threat to their livelihood as their crusade against the development projects had forced the companies to halt their work, leading to unemployment. Naxalites set the terms and conditions for the industrialists, the contractors, and the businessmen, which are difficult to meet. The controversy on rates of payment often leads to the termination of business and trade activities, which adversely impact the livelihood of the tribals. This applied even in the case of a traditional occupation, such as the collection of Tendu leaves from the forests. Controversy on the rates of Tendu leaves between the tribals and the contractors finally led to a non-conciliatory point. The rates agreed between them have always been seen as exploitative by the Naxalites. But the rate that the Naxals wish to force upon the contractors is so high that they make it impossible for any contractor to negotiate. What has happened in the tussle between the Naxals and the contractors on the price of Tendu Leaves is that the tribals lost the market for the same, which significantly contributed to their resources. Collecting Tendu leaves gave them a livelihood, which ceased due to non-negotiation on prices.

People falling in the second category were those who or whose family members had been victims of the Naxals in some way or another. There were many who had suffered the dictates issued by Jan Adalats of Naxals, also termed as Kangaroo courts. Ultimately, it was the poor tribals. Naxals called it Jan Adalat, but they were actually meant to instil terror in the minds of the villagers and aimed at those who were supposed or likely to be police informers (NHRC Report, 2008:10). It is very common in the Naxalite-affected area that the Naxals frequently make visits to the villages and ask several kinds of favours from the villagers who unwillingly have to fulfil them. The demands fall between asking for food and shelter and giving away one family member for the revolution. Denial of the same leads to severe punishment, which sometimes includes even a death sentence. For example, once the whole family of a village in Dantewada was killed because they refused to follow the dictates of the Maoists. Thus, a villager from a government-maintained camp in Chhattisgarh expressed as follows: "*We often wonder what sins we committed to be born at this time. Our lives are impossible. Naxalites come and threaten us. They demand food and ask us to help them with information about police movements*" (Human Rights Watch, 2008:2). Further, forced recruitment of children from families of poor and marginalised segments of society by the Maoists has also come to notice. In order to instil a sense of fear in their areas of dominance, the Naxals also kill civilians after branding them as police informers. Out of 5811 civilians killed by the Maoists since 2001, the overwhelming majority are tribals (PIB, 2013). Such people and their relatives see the Judum as a platform providing the opportunity to take revenge against the Maoists with armed support from the government.

The people in the third category were the people who worked with the Naxals but subsequently decided to join the Salwa Judum. There were two sets of people within this group. First, there were people who had been consciously planted by the Naxals to act as informers. They were expected to win the confidence of the police and the Judum members and, thereafter, could provide information to Naxals about the movements of the security personnel. The other kind of people from this category were those whose experience was bitter, and those who found the dreams of socialism in Marxian terms an impossible romanticism. There was yet another category of people who did not wish to join but were nearly coerced and cornered to do so.

There were actually three components of the Salwa Judum. There were the common people who became part of the rallies, which were organised from village to village. In these rallies, people were told what was wrong with the Naxal movement and why they, the common people, should oppose the Naxals. These rallies were led by people who were committed to the anti-Naxal cause. Such rallies were actually a social campaign aimed at mobilising the masses. It was from these rallies that the youths came forward to actively resist the Naxals by joining the Judum members. The second category of people was those who were actively involved in leading these rallies. People associated with this role were generally people who came from a rich background within the tribal community. This included people like Mahendra Karma.

The third category of people was those who were trained in arms by the security forces. They were called Special Protection Officers. They lived in the camps adjoining the security camps. These SPOs helped the security forces in their combat operation against the Naxals in several ways; from guiding the security forces in unknown and inhospitable dense forest terrain, and the Naxal hideouts in some cases, as some of them who had joined as SPOs were also the ex-Naxalites to handling the arms, as well as they were trained by the security forces for these purposes. They also guarded the tribal villages against the possible Naxal retaliation. SPOs were paid in cash as well as in kind. They were given an honorarium of nearly Rs. 3300/-per month apart from free oil and food grains at much subsidised rates. Interestingly, this expenditure is shared between the state government and the central government.

Though the government denied the charges of the recruitment of children as Salwa Judum members, particularly as SPOs, such denials were a denial of truth. This is hard, but crude facts that several SPOs had been underage, and from all angles of legality, they should have been discouraged from operating deadly weapons. Even the National Human Rights Commission acknowledged that there had been instances of children being recruited by the government as SPOs. But at the same time, the NHRC did not buy the arguments that the Salwa Judum was flooded with such recruitments (NHRC Report, 2008:36). NHRC also did not approve of the idea that supporting Salwa Judum was legally wrong. On the contrary, it held that the government was within its rights to constitute such an instrument in order to tackle crime and violence. It is worth noting that there is a provision for the appointment of people as police officers if the need arises for it, as per the Chhattisgarh Armed Forces Act (NHRC Report, 2008:13).

4 Salwa Judum: A Short-Lived Euphoria?

It was witnessed that the initial euphoria about the Salwa Judum did continue for a long. It lost momentum with the passage of time, and it became evident as the recruitment of people and the number of camps came down sharply. It was reduced to just 23 camps in 2008 (NHRC Report, 2008:34). Several factors contributed to this decline. First, the people who joined initially, not because of a deep commitment, returned to their normal lives with the passage of time. This happens with all social movements, with popular uprisings in the beginning. Secondly, there were people who joined it but later thought that it was not worth sacrificing their whole lives for the cause. The failure of the state to prevent the Naxal violence convinced many that it was not good for them to make the Naxals hostile to them and their family members. It would be worth noting that there were and are many tribals who decided to side with the Naxals because they found that the state had failed to give them assured security against the possible Naxal assault. They were not convinced by the purpose and methods of the Naxals, yet they joined them because the Maoists were successful in creating fear in the minds of the people. The concerted, well-organised campaign by the Naxals in the media and social domains and in the judiciary against the Salwa Judum also weakened the enthusiasm and strategy of the government. The Judiciary was always harsh against it as it considered arming the common man against the trained violent groups.

5 Campaign against Salwa Judum

In fact, the movement of Salwa Judum created a great problem for the Naxals. Primarily, it restricted their reach to the villages and hampered their recruitment drive. So far, the young unemployed youths who were readily convinced to take up arms in their hands found it better to fight on the side of the government. It was important for the Naxals to counter the movement, and as it has been a tested weapon for them, they worked first on maligning the movement on several scores. They raised the bogey of violation of human rights. But this did not work in the wake of Maoists' attacks on innocent civilians to terrorise them with the purpose of deterring them from joining the government side. They also put several houses on fire and propagated that it was done by the Salwa Judum people. Nearly fourteen houses in the village were allegedly burnt by the Salwa Judum members. But on investigation, it was found that they were the handiwork of the Naxals. Similarly, Naxals were conducted targeted attacks on SPOs and police (Bose, 2015). All these were found deftly crafted to arouse anger in people against the Salwa Judum. There was a visible pattern in this campaign. While these activists would express disapproval of violence by the Naxals, they would immediately argue that the state should look into the causes of violence. In other words, the intellectuals siding with the Naxal uprisings criticised the violence by them in public but always hyphenated it with the logic of their social and economic exploitation. No doubt that the state needs to look into the social and economic factors that cause elements of deprivation and exploitation in the minds of people and take them to the extent of picking up arms against it, but this is not as linear and simple as it seems at first glance. But those who stand by the cause of Naxals hide the fact that there is a well-calibrated design behind it, and such statements are indeed clever indirect shield to the misdeeds of the Naxals. On the other hand, when the state indulges in counter-insurgency measures, such intellectuals and their eco-system would leap and bound and release all their latent potential to the extent of a propaganda war to demonise the state. It is no longer a secret that the intellectual sympathisers of the Naxal movement have created a system of such propaganda-cum-defence machine that the moment the state goes for a massive hunt and operation against the Naxals, they put in place that mechanism and force the government to go overboard to defend itself. And it includes mobilising even the foreign intellectuals who have little idea and understanding about India and the ongoing Naxalite movement in the country. Yet, they are roped in to give a picture as if the whole of the intellectual world across the seven seas is up in arms and agitated over the worst human rights violation in the state. The campaign in favour of Binayak Sen, allegedly working for the Naxals, is worth noticing.

In April 2009, several UK-based academicians wrote to the editor of The Guardian, London, to publish their appeal for the release of Dr. Binayak Sen, who had been languishing in one of the Jails in Chhattisgarh. Interestingly, most of the signatories were British, and very few of them had any idea of the Naxal movement and the anti-insurgency people's movement in the state. The request involved the content that 'he has been a political prisoner', and there is no credible evidence against him, who has been one of the most noted champions of social justice' (Ramanan, 2008).

Dr. Binayak Sen was given the Jonathan Mann Award in 2008 for Global Health and Human Rights. Dr. Sen had been working in the tribal areas for the last 20 years in the field of health and protection of the human rights of these distressed people. But at the same time, it is also a fact that he was a PUCL activist and had been clandestinely working for the Naxals. Those who know the PUCL know it well that this is the organisation that has been highly biased in favour of the leftwing activism and has been ignoring the violence and violation of human rights by the leftwing organisations, whereas it has been very harsh in its presentation when it comes to writing reports in which right-wing organisations are involved in conflict. It is rare to find any report in which PUCL has been fair in its assessment. People know in advance what the PUCL is going to write about. This applies in the case of Maoist violence as well. They have been using all adjectives against the state but are almost silent on the violation of human rights, abuse of human dignity, killing of innocents, including children and women, by the Maoists. PUCL reports, thus, are completely partisan, and one does not require special expertise to identify such bias. To them, human and democratic rights are precious, but unfortunately, they do not give those rights to the tribals to keep them away from the Naxalite thought system.

The supporters of Dr. Sen held that he was arrested for publicly criticising the state government, which had brutally evacuated nearly three lakhs and fifty thousand tribals from their homes in Dantewada and Bijapur districts of the state between 2005 and 2006 for initiating Salwa Judum against the Naxals. But this alone is far from the complete truth. In fact, Dr Sen was acting for the Naxals while working for the poor and the needy people in the region. Dr. Sen was arrested on the charge of 'abetting terrorism' in the state by meeting Narayan Sanyal, a Naxal in Raipur Jail and handing over to him a letter from a businessman close to the jailed Naxals (Punwani, 2010:21–23).

A massive campaign was launched against the state in favour of Dr. Sen, and none other than a very reputed senior justice of the Supreme Court of India, Justice V.R. Krishna Aiyyar, wrote to the Prime Minister Manmohan Singh to ensure the release of Dr. Sen, then languishing in the Chhattisgarh jail. He termed the internment of Dr. Sen a grave injustice and a matter of shame on the Indian State.

In fact, ever since the Salwa Judum was launched, the Naxals and their cultural and academic organisations and people, be that in the media or running NGOs, came out against it. One finds two strategies which they worked upon; first, demonise the anti-Naxal movement, and secondly, drag the government to court to stall the operation. The demonisation involves, as mentioned above, bringing out excesses by the Judum activists, appointments of the minors as SPOs, human rights violations by the police and the SPOs and so on. There have been massive campaigns to this effect. Several NGOs have come out to narrate the story of the victims of Salwa Judum. These NGOs, many of which are funded from outside and which very much support the Naxals for their supportive role in the region, have been the ones which have been at the forefront in attacking the government for anti-Naxal state offensives. It is not that all that they complain about the state is spurious and fake, but, in many cases, they deliberately lay out the design for this. All this has been intended to defame the Salwa Judum in the public's eyes and prove it anti-people and anti-poor. This was done deliberately and in spite of the fact that nearly four decades back, the government of Bihar also had issued arms licenses to the villagers to counter the increasing Naxal extremism in some of the districts of Bihar, like Patna and Bhojpur (The Indian Express, 2015). This was a version of Salwa Judum. What the other governments had been doing was done by the state of Chhattisgarh in institutionalised form.

This propaganda war is fought in the media through the Naxal sympathisers in academic institutions and the media. It is not a hidden truth that the social sciences and liberal arts in Indian universities have been primarily dominated by the left intelligentsia. Nehruvian accommodation of the left and patronising them to counter the right-wing ideology allowed the left-wing to overshadow the whole academic discourse. And they have cleverly used the state institutions to propagate their worldview. An ideological brainwash has been going on in the academic world for the last several decades, which has produced a predominant intellectual class both on campus and outside in the media, which has a closer affinity with left ideology. They are the ones who have been launching the campaign against Salwa Judum in the cities and fighting court cases for the Naxals. Sometimes, they rope in even the non-Naxal people of public repute who have been highly critical of the right-wing ideology to make their representation credible. They project their initiatives as 'independent initiatives', representing the whole of India's civil society, but a closer look at their ideological activism and background does leave little doubt that they are the Naxal sympathisers who provide a shield to the Naxal activities in the name of human rights and state atrocities. The petition that was filed in the court against the Salwa Judum is a case to the point. The case was filed by Nandini Sunder, a Professor of Sociology at the University of Delhi, Ramchandra Guha, Arundhati Roy, Swami Agnivesh, Kartam Joga and others. While Ramchandra Guha has been a bitter critic of the BJP, who does not see any merit in the party and hates its ideology, Nandani Sunder is a known Naxal sympathiser on campus[4] (Sundar, 1999:16). Arundhati Roy's positions in favour of separatists in Kashmir and on Naxals are also well known. She has always been vocal and supportive of these movements because it all benefits her international credentials, particularly in the Western world. The independent initiatives are not as independent as they are projected to be, but a tactical cover to the Naxals,

4 Nandani's acknowledgment in her prologue of her book is a great admission. She writes "I was quite ready to put my research at the service of struggling masses, represented by Naxalites or some other movements".

in which even some liberals who are against the BJP ideology join hands. The so-called civil society is the society primarily comprised of the left-liberal intelligentsia, which is heterogeneous and amorphous from within, but they speak in unison against the BJP government. They spoke against the recruitment of SPOs in Chhattisgarh but have been silent over similar recruitments in J&K, Kerala and other states of India. The NGOs working in the forests are primarily those ones which are close to the Naxals. They get funding from outside. And the more they become critical of the Indian state and project the exploitation of the people and the repressive conduct of the government, they fit into the colonial design to get more funds. It is also because the organisations that are working in the deep forests are bound to play out to the tunes of the Naxals; otherwise, they cannot work at all in the region. No wonder human rights groups used all tricks to force the government to ban the Salwa Judum. They knew that the success of the Salwa Judum could break their backbone by drying up both their recruitments and coerced support in the villages. The petition charged that the government was abetting crime by assigning money and arms to private individuals to tackle the Naxals.

The bench of the Supreme Court, which heard the case, comprised even the Chief Justice of India, KG Balakrishnan, apart from Justice P. Sathasivam and Justice JM Panchal. They held that the state was free to deploy as many policemen as it wanted to tackle the crime, but assigning this task to private individuals and assisting them through monetary incentives and arms is not justified at all. Later on, the case was heard by a bench of Justice Reddy and Justice Nirjhar, who passed the judgment in August 2011 that Salwa Judum was unconstitutional and it should be banned with immediate effect. The court also declared the appointment of SPOs unconstitutional and a violation of the right to equality and the right to life and liberty (The Hindu, 2021).

There is no doubt that the children were also appointed as SPOs. Many of them were between the ages of 12 to 16. This certainly violated the constitution and laws which prohibit the employment of children below the maturity age to any such activities which involve the wielding of guns. Also, there is no doubt that the SPOs committed crimes and misused their new incarnation. They, too, like the errant Naxal cadres, indulged in gagging the dissenting voice, and cases of extortion have also been found. The admission of the Chhattisgarh police DGP was worth noticeable. He admitted in an interview with The Pioneer that '3250 SPOs were discharged on various grounds of indiscipline' (Ramanan, 2008). But that does not mean that the whole idea of Salwa Judum was wrong.

The Naxal violence had led to the displacement of over 1 million people from nearly 644 tribal villages in Bastar and Dantewada. These people had fled to the camps for security. The Naxals accused these people had been forcefully taken to these camps for two reasons. First, it aimed at discrediting the

Naxal movement by depicting it as anti-tribal. They claimed that those who did not wish to go to the camps were threatened and tortured by the police and the Judum activists. Naxals and their organisations came out with several such video-clippings of the people imported from the internet in which people were shown saying that they did not want to go to the camps, but they were forced by the police to do so.

Such clippings, however, seem to be taken with the supporters' audience and therefore lack credentials in respect of neutrality. Many of them seemed to be tutored ones. Naxals also argue that such evacuations were intended to capture the lands of the tribals. There was a design behind all this. The government wanted to give land to the corporate giants for mining purposes. These lands belonged to the tribals, who were very much emotionally attached to them and therefore did not want to vacate the place at any cost. Thus, one activist of the Maoists argues that it is remarkable to note that the Salwa Judum started in the same month of the year 2005 when Tata signed a memorandum of understanding with the Chhattisgarh government for its Steel project. The people, in fact, are picked up from villages and are placed in the relief camps. But such stories may be true in some cases, but not true for all. There were several people who took shelter in the relief camps because their lives were threatened due to their stand against the Naxal violence. There were several camps that housed the people who had lost their parents. They were killed mercilessly in front of their children by the Naxals for being soft on the government.

The fact is that the movement of Salwa Judum polarized the society between the pro and anti-Naxals or pro and anti-Judum. Those villages and the people who did not come to the relief camps (internally displaced camps) were considered to be Naxal sympathisers or pro-Naxals. Naxals also charged that such villages were subject to discrimination by the state government as they were denied 'all health, education and other facilities, including access to the markets.' The NHRC team in its investigation did not find such discrimination, and the petitioners who had charged the government of practising such thing also could not cite concrete evidence in this regard. However, the tribals are sandwiched between the Naxals and the state. There is a violence and coercion from both sides to win the loyalty of the common tribals. The Naxals' credentials on this count are poorer compared to the Judum activists as the former are more engaged in merciless violence to win people over to their side. Though the Judum activists are also not blotless they are not as much indulged in violence as the Naxals. There are scores of such videos on different sites that suggest that Salwa Judum alone caused violence and destruction in tribal lands, and Naxals were not responsible for it. But that was not the correct portrayal of reality.

Naxals do not recognise the Salwa Judum as the 'peaceful and self-initiated people movement' against the Maoists atrocities. Far from being a 'Peace campaign', it is a 'state-sponsored violent counterinsurgency programme for them' (Asian Centre for Human Rights Report, 2006:15). The PUDR fact-finding report of 2005 depicted it as 'a war on its own people'. It calls Salwa Judum a 'state-sponsored violent campaign to crush the voices of dissent and democracy'. Human Rights Forum on 6 December 2006, in its report, depicted it as an instrument of the state aimed at the unwanted militarisation of society (Human Rights Forum Report, 2006:13).

Their argument flows from the fact that the 'Salwa Judum activists were lashed with guns, lathis, axes, bows and arrows'. Secondly, SPOs who were also very much part of the Judum were trained, recruited and paid by the government. To say that SPOs were different from Salwa Judum was not correct. They were picked up from the groups which are anti-Naxals. Thirdly, all the Salwa Judum rallies are given due protection by the police and district administration, whereas the same is denied to anti-Judum rallies. Fourthly, on several occasions, meetings of the Salwa Judum were seen being addressed by the district administration (Guha et al., 2006: 47–61). The Government defended that the SPOs were appointed as per the law. Chhattisgarh Police regulations allowed such an appointment as well as the payment to such appointees. Also, the government came to support when it was asked to do so. Fifth, camps were essential in order to provide basic amenities like shelter, food and health facilities to the displaced people. Of course, the Salwa Judum activists carried lathis, bows and arrows, but these are the arms which tribals more often carry for their safety. And more importantly, they did so not to kill someone but to protect themselves against the possible Naxal attacks. Detractors of Salwa Judum also questioned its efficacy. Their argument is that Salwa Judum turned the social life into a warzone, and yet it failed to contain the Naxal violence, which, contrary to decreasing, has increased over the years. Nalini Sunder also made the same argument that the retaliatory violence of the Naxals has increased ever since Salwa Judum came into operation. And therefore, they suggest that Salwa Judum should therefore be abandoned.

There is no doubt that Salwa Judum created a big polarisation in the society. Certainly, 'a cycle of retribution and revenge was set into motion' due to both Maoists and the Salwa Judum activists targeting each other and their supposed sympathisers. But for this, the Naxals were more responsible than anyone. They were the ones who forced the people to take sides or face the consequences. Secondly, the increased Naxal violence did not indicate the failure of the Salwa Judum. On the contrary, it indicated that the violence was the result of the desperation of the Naxals, who wanted to prove that their hold on the areas remains intact, which is not. There are miles of land where the security forces used to think twice before walking through. Now they are no more liberated zones at all in Maoist terms, and the writ of the government has been retrieved. Nearly 644 out of 1354 villages i.e. 47 percent were involved in Salwa Judum (Menon & Das, 2007). Such a large-scale mobilisation is not possible at all just because the state wants. It is possible only when the people at large are convinced to align with the cause.

After all, the tribals are very much intimately linked to their lands and forest surroundings, not only in territorial terms but also in emotional and spiritual contexts. Their gods and goddesses are not very far, and so are their ancestors. Notwithstanding this, if they decide to leave their native abode and go to the relief camps, the answer lies not in force applied from the government but the torturous experience at the hands of the Naxals. They feel threatened that if they don't adhere to the dictates of the Naxals, they will be punished to death by them. This fear brings them to the camp. After all, no independent agency has come out so far with the premise that the Naxals are just the propagators of the ideology and they are not at all engaged in methods and mechanisms of extortion, torture, destruction of property and lives of the people to comply with their directives.

It is argued that the people in camps wanted to come back, but the government did not allow them to do so. In the majority of the cases, it was true. But the reason did not lie in the charges levelled by the pro-Naxal activists that the government did not allow the tribals to do so because it wanted migration of the tribals from the land so that the same could be transferred to the big corporate houses for industrial and mining purposes. This was a part of the political narrative that the Naxalites used to garner the support of the locals and intellectuals in the urban areas who were sensitive to the rights of the tribals on their land. There was no reality behind it.

After all, the tribals went to the villages in the daytime to undertake economic activities. The government fear emanated from the fact that villagers' lives would be in danger if they went back to their villages before the Maoists were neutralised effectively in the areas. The forces could not provide security to each and every village. Given the firepower and striking capacity of the Naxals, it was certain that the people on their own could not resist the Naxals. Moreover, tribals wanted to go back to the villages, not because they were not scared of the Naxals, but more so because they feared their lands and houses would be grabbed by the outsiders from adjoining areas. As it happens with every individual, it is natural for them to be nostalgic about their homes. It would be wrong to draw the conclusion that people did not feel threatened by Naxals in the areas, or they liked or did not mind the presence and interference of the latter in their lives and justified their activities. On the contrary, the Naxals to them were as outsiders as the state, and one reason why the people rose against the Naxals is that the Naxals had started bringing more trouble to their lives compared to what they had prior to the arrival and entrenchment of the Naxalite movements. Secondly, relief camps did provide security cover to their lives, but did not provide the psychological, social, and cultural space and freedom which they are accustomed to. Life in the relief camp certainly does not enthuse them, and they really wish to return to their homes. It all depends on the security cover that the society and state ensure for them. PUDR reports have always been articulating the premise that Salwa Judum activities are supported by the non-tribals in the tribal lands (PUDR, 2006). But this logic applies to the Naxal movement as well. People fighting in the Chhattisgarh and other Naxal areas are not totally manned by local cadres. They too are supported by the cadres drawn from intellectuals from different parts of the country and even outside. For Salwa Judum activists, Naxals are outsiders. Though after the Supreme Court order, Salwa Judum was disbanded, but the son of Mahendra Karma, Chhavindra Karma, continued with the mission in the name of Vikash Sangharsh Samiti. Even the killing of his father did not deter his will to raise the popular masses against the Naxal movement in the state of Chhattisgarh.

CHAPTER 7

Intellectuals' Support of the Maoist Movement in India

The former Home Minister of the country, Shivraj Singh Patil, once stated in the Parliament on December 5, 2006, "Like the forests provide safe hideouts to the Naxalites in the tribal areas, the cities also provide them the cover" (Chakravarti, 2008:18). Actually, Patil was referring to the intelligentsia and the NGOs who lend support to the Naxalites in the cities. The Naxal movement is often identified with its support base in remote rural areas and the forests. They have been the real base from where it seeks to expand. But we ignore the support that it receives from the educated urban class, popularly known as urban intellectuals, now pejoratively depicted as Urban Naxals. These people are those who provide intellectual rationale and ammunition to the activities and missions of the Naxals. They comprise journalists, students and academicians. There are some campuses of Indian universities that have earned the famed distinction of being in the headlines for the same. Interestingly, these people also stand in support of the Muslims, even though the latter are radicalised and speak the language of intolerance.

10 February 2016 took the entire nation by surprise and shock when the 24×7 news channels broke the story of anti-India slogans raised in the Jawaharlal Nehru University (JNU) campus on the occasion of the anniversary of the hanging of Afzal Guru, a Kashmiri terrorist who was given a death sentence by the Supreme Court of India in parliament attack case (Sebastian, 2016). The slogans that ranted the air were '*Bharat Tere Tukade Honge, Tukde Honge, Insa Allah, Insa Allah … Bharat kee Barbadi Tak, Jang Rahegi, Jang rahegi, …. then … Tum Kitne Afzal Maroge, Ghar Ghar se Afzal Nikalega, Tum Kitane Maqbool Maroge, Ghar Ghar se Maqbool Nikalega ……* (*India will meet the fate of split, we will fight till the destruction of India ….. how many Afzal will you kill ….. every household will produce an Afzal …. how many Maqbool are you going to kill ….. every household is going to give birth to a Maqbool ….. and so on*).

These anti-state, anti-India slogans were outrageous for the nation at large. However, the left-liberal intellectuals, as expected, did not find it inciting and culpable. On the contrary, they defended the same in the name of freedom of expression, university autonomy and the right to dissent. They brought in incongruent and dissimilar examples from the West to prove the point that India is going haywire under the present dispensation led by Narendra Modi.

 HTTPS://DOI.ORG/10.1163/9789004765054-009

A parallel was drawn from America that the Americans had criticised their own government for the role it had in the Vietnam War, and Cambridge students discussed further division of the country! Surprisingly, these precious words of praise by the left intellectuals were for the American democracy, which they often are critical of. They had no examples from totalitarian states like China, where the state used tanks and modern, sophisticated weapons at Tiananmen Square in 1989 to quell the students' protests, which sought basic democratic rights: the right to expression! A whole division of the army was put in place to crush the protesting voice of the students.[1] Political parties opposed to the BJP, including the centrist Congress, surprisingly sided with sloganeering students.

This was not the first time that the campus of JNU witnessed such slogans. It has groomed and matured with such slogans over the decades because of its ideological overleaning towards the left. Jindabad and Murdabad are the most familiar sounds on the campus. It is taken both seriously and non-seriously depending on which side of the ideological continuum a faculty and student place themselves. There are numerous for whom these slogans do not carry any meaning. They are accustomed to such assemblages and slogans and don't consider them worth reacting to. There are a few who are opposed to such slogans on the campus. They consider it highly objectionable as these things should not be encouraged on the campus. For them, university is a place for breeding ideas and not ideology-centric activism. This section represents the right-wing nationalist voice. And yet there are those who inhibit missionary zeal and are committed to revolutionary ideology. They are more than convinced that a successful revolution is not very far away, and what is required at the moment is to give it a kick to it. Almost all the pamphlets of radical left student groups on the campus foresee an impending revolution not very far off.

Understandably, those who have spent some time on the campus did not find anything unusual or uneasy even this time. But it shocked the people at large across the nation when they saw the campus resonating with the same slogans which the terrorists and separatists rant in the Kashmir valley or in the public meetings of Hafiz Syed in Pakistan. People are aware of the fact that JNU is a citadel of the left of all shades, and the ideological osmosis touches the mind and heart of everyone who comes here for study. But they were not conscious of the fact that the university has travelled so far in pursuit of ideological moorings that the students and teachers would reverberate with the

1 China used tanks against the student's protests. It had butchered over a million of its citizens in the name of cultural revolution. But Communists in India never took to the streets to criticise human cannibalism in the name of protecting ideology. One rarely finds scholarly articles on the protest movements with critical insights.

idea of breaking the country. They were not ready to accept the fact that the students would sing the rhyme, and would sympathise with the terrorists and would commit to fulfilling the desires of Afzal. (Afzal Ham Sharminda Hain, Tere Katil Jinda Hain. … Afzal Tere Armanon ko Ham Pura Karenge!). And what was the aim of Afzal? To break India! V.K.V Rao quoted that the founder of the JNU had envisioned to develop it as a centre of academic excellence with the core value of imparting 'principles and sentiments of national solidarity and national integration' (Batabyal, 2014:32). Critics, on the contrary, argue that contrary to integration, the campus cultivates the ambience and recipe of national disintegration! People's perception that JNU opens up to everyone who joins the campus and broadens the critical faculty of students, better prepares them for an objective understanding of the issue in question, was marred by this ideological fiasco indeed.

What happened in JNU might have been new to the nation and its people at large, but such incidents, including slogan shouting of this nature, have been going on for decades on campus. Anti-Indian forces have been finding it a stable place to operate their campaign blitz in the name of human and democratic rights. Way back in 1996, a professor of linguistics had written a letter with detailed accounts that the Commemoration of the day of the hanging of Afzal Guru has been held since 2014. JNU also attracted national attention when, in 2010, 76 CRPF Jawans were killed by the Naxals in Dantewada, Chhattisgarh (Gohain, 2010). Accordingly, two of the army officers were roughed up when they objected to anti-India articulations aired in a Mushaira organised at the campus. What was new this time was that a student group, with the help of 24/7 channels, made it known to the world and forced it to become an issue of larger public discourse.

Anti-statism is the moving ideology at JNU which breeds, nurtures and patronizes left world view in the campus with the active support of the faculty, course structure, learning modules and reading materials. This anti-statism stretches beyond just rational and scholarly theoretical critiquing of the state and its institutions on a merit basis, but has degenerated into legitimate political semantics. Displeased with the Bourgeoisie and the capitalist system, long live the proletariat revolution, down with fascism are favourite buzzwords and very familiar phrases all across the campus. These are settled vocabularies which peep through all the posters and pamphlets in classrooms and academic chaupals around Ganga Dhaba over cups of tea or snacks for hours and hours. There is a strong interlinking of political ideology and teaching and learning, which imparts a solid ideological grounding for the political left on campus. It inculcates a fine argumentative mind, but that is often loaded with more semantics than facts. However, the campus charms every young boy and girl, and the students who pass out and join other walks of life seldom shed off the intellectual legacy they inherit. As JNU, being a leading institution, has also given faculty to other institutions, it has helped the left in evolving a strong intellectual network which surpasses even the state boundaries. No wonder, when the controversy broke at JNU, they all joined the signature campaign.

Never in the past has the media been so divided and so polarised on such an issue. It was to the extent that channels and their anchors openly crossed swords against each other. While channels like Times Now, Zee TV, India News, etc., accused NDTV especially of diverting the issue and thereby lending support to such anti-national activities, NDTV reacted with the accusation that some channels were setting aside the core issues of freedom of speech and the right to dissent. The battle of journalists went to the personal level when NDTV questioned the media ethics pursued by some of the journalists for allegedly showing doctored video and preferring noise over discussions. It had indirectly referred to the prime time of Arnab Goswami, who had taken the matter most vigorously, and Deepak Chaurasia's show on India News. NDTV satirically blacked out the screen, and only text and voice appeared in order to convey the message that TV channels have brought noise and darkness to debate. Zee TV also opened front against NDTV. It wanted to settle the score with those channels that had questioned the media ethics of Zee TV in the Navin Jindal case. The prime-time anchor Sudhir Chaudhary coined a new term, 'Afzal Premi Gang', to mark the disdain against the media channels and left-leaning intellectuals who were supporting Kanhaiya and other students (Pande, 2016). This barb trended on social media. NDTV and other channels that were pushing the stories of doctored video, however, fell flat when the forensic lab of the CBI declared the tape genuine (Times of India, 2016). In a reaction, left student groups of both the JNU and Delhi University took to the streets, and the issue was twisted so much so that the real issue got sidelined.

What was lost in the din were the core issues that emerged from organising and patronising such events and ideological activism on campus in the name of academic freedom. Freedom of speech was not the issue at all. The intellectuals and channels that were raising concerns on this ground were just providing the intellectual cover fire to the event, so that what had happened would not tarnish the face of the extreme left in the country. They also knew that no constitution, including the Indian constitution, provides an unfettered, absolute right of expression. They come with limits; otherwise, there will be chaos. They also knew that this was also not a question of university autonomy at all, as the government never interfere in the working and teaching learning of the campus. It did not stop any seminar or act against the organisers of such seminars, which were intentionally organised to incite venom against the Indian state (Hindustan Times, 2016). The crackdown of the government was criticised on the grounds that it was intended to strangle the ideas. It was projected as if the government was against the JNU. The government was neither against the JNU nor against its students. It was merely handling a case in which some students had been using the campus for political activism, which promoted a separatist cult among the students. It was not an interplay of ideas against which the state acted. Instead, it acted to save the democratic values on campus.

The actual narrative of the event was not as complicated as it was presented to be and then projected in the media. The programme was organised by the Democratic Student Union (DSU), a student group that propagates Maoist ideology, in conjunction with Kashmiri Muslim students. Since DSU has been supporting the cause of self-determination and the freedom movement of the separatists in Kashmir, Kashmiri Muslim students have a greater affinity with the organisation. They had together organised the programme to commemorate the hanging of Afzal Guru, a terrorist who was given the death penalty by the highest court of the country and was hanged on 9 February 2013. But the separatists and left activists in academia continue to hold the position that it was a case of judicial murder, as he was not given a fair trial. Members of both these constituents raised slogans against India. When the members of ABVP opposed, as usual, they were shouted down.

But this time, instead of making just notional protests, members of the ABVP recorded the event and reported the same to the JNU administration. When the police arrested the students involved in sloganeering and organisation of the event, the political parties found an opportunity to attack the Modi government. As expected, non-NDA political parties and forums came in support of the students and politicisation of the issue took a new flight. From Sitaram Yechury of the CPM to Rahul Gandhi from the Indian National Congress to Delhi CM Kejriwal, all took to Twitter to condemn the arrests of the students and projected the arrest as a government design to suppress 'the right of dissent and protest' (The Indian Express, 2016). Sitaram Yechury reached the campus and addressed the students. Even the Congress joined the chorus, keeping in mind the impending electoral alliance with the CPM in the West Bengal assembly elections of 2016. All the non-NDA political formations came out united in support of the students (India Today, 2016).

Both the Maoists and supporters of separatists of Kashmir have been working together at the JNU campus since long. Both have been using the phrase 'democratic and human rights violations' to justify their acts. Surprisingly, for both, human rights do not matter at all as both are driven purely by their separate political ends. There are no common converging ideological grounds between the two. In other words, they happen to be the strange bedfellows in the campus fighting against the Indian state, though the purposes are different. Since Maoists do not accept India as a singular nation but a set of sub-nationalities, they support the separatists' demands for self-determination for the people of Kashmir.

More importantly, it is a one-way relationship. Separatists do not endorse the ideological premise of the Maoists at all. Separatists of Kashmir are driven by the ideology of Pan-Islamism, and religious obscurantism lies at its roots. They are not for the toiling masses. Their fight against the Indian state is religious in substance. They were not in favour of J&K being part of India because it is a Muslim-dominated state. Nothing else guides them, and yet the Maoists come to their support. This looks not just an oxymoron but hypocrisy at best. Maoists claim to be against religious fundamentalism and obscurantism. But in practice, they represent a definite and visible hypocrisy. While they are very critical of obscurantism within the Hindu society and venom against the Brahminical social order, they seldom use similar hard barbs against the Ulemmas and their Fatwa system, let alone talk against Islam. Kashmiri Brahmins faced the worst kind of atrocities, including the mass exodus from their ancestral land due to Islamic obscurantism in the valley. But Maoists never opposed such atrocities.

Unlike earlier, this time the rival student organisation Akhil Bhartiya Vidyarthi Parishad (ABVP), was prepared in advance to capture the whole event on camera and expose the Naxalite supporting students' group. The event and the slogan were recorded by news channels. Students at the campus also used their smartphones and shared the clippings with the news channels. When the news channels broke the story, both the central government and the Delhi police woke up from slumber. The students were booked under sedition charges and put behind bars. This triggered a national debate on sedition and freedom of speech, which lost direction in the polarised political stance of the parties and intellectuals. For the first time, news channels openly crossed swords against and publicly ridiculed each other (Calamur, 2016).

JNU issue, however, highlighted the fact that some of the premier universities of the country have been driven away from their core purpose of promoting academic excellence and true scholarship to nurturing young and innocent minds on ideological lines to manufacture cadres. The way some teachers came out to protect the students strengthened all the more the perception that, in the guise of freedom of expression and the right to dissent, JNU, over the years, has emerged as the nursery of generating leaders who commit to liberation movements as espoused by the Maoists. This was further endorsed by the pressure tactics that the faculty members exercised on the university administration to sabotage the investigation.

It was shocking for all to know that the students who raised slogans against the country were hiding under the roof of the teachers' quarters on the campus. This was denied by the faculty members, but the self-confession by a student leader before the media punctured the lies. While talking to *Hindustan Times*, one of the members of *All India Students Association* (AISA) said, "We were around but just did not come out in public because of the prevailing atmosphere. There is mob-lynching and witch-hunting going on, but now we have decided to go out in public" (Hindustan Times, 2016).

There are no differing views across the political spectrum that universities must be the playground for the exchange of ideas. But what about those universities where faculty commit to one set of ideology and seek to promote the same among the students? Do the universities do real service to the discipline of knowledge when they force upon the students one set of ideas as the absolute truth and do not allow alternative voices to come out at all? Scientific rigour and critical insight are very important in academic discourse. But does the scientific rigour exist when ideological precincts dominate the minds of researchers? This is where some of the best universities have failed us. Ideological rigidity confines the ideas and limits the discourses. Every ideology has its own vocabulary, conceptual framework and methodology which do not allow 'others' to intrude into the mind. There is a fine distinction between the academic brainstorming exercise and political activism, which seeks to mobilise students and teachers to engage in and support an armed liberation movement. While the former marks a journey of ideas, the latter seeks to promote mindless militancy.

Ideology breeds passion and obscurantism. It does not allow space for what we call alternative views or ideas. What has happened to JNU that, in order to emerge as the citadel of the left, it has silenced the alternative voices? There is discourse within the left, but it does not hold any dialogue with the ideas which think differently. Second, the penetration of the left in the system is far deeper than it looks from the outside. Third, though its core support base is not very large, but it receives strength from other factions of the left when the ideological battle line is sharply defined between the left and the right. There is certainly an ideological divide within the left on numerous issues, and they condemn each other, but they group up and align together despite internal differences when they are pitted against or are at odds with the BJP. Fourth, their support base on the campus is not one that has come up in a day or a few months but has grown over decades. A systematic plantation of ideas through course structure and teaching learning module has been at the core of this historical edge of the left on the campus.

In post-colonial India, they were not a powerful political force, but they slipped into the system and have come up as the most powerful talent pool influencing the national discourses. This took decades, but the left consciously perfected this niche after independence with the support of the Congress. Nehru's impulsive fascination for socialism on the one hand and inability to counter the right-wing ideologically gave space to the left to have cosy and close relations with the Congress and capture the education system and academic institutes of higher learning. Several universities and research centres of the country came under the control of the left and, over a period of time, became their ideological forte. JNU, Delhi University, Hyderabad University, and Aligarh Muslim University became the harbinger of the left ideology. These institutions were systematically and consciously packed by people with left-leaning intellectuals sprinkled with Nehruvian socialists. The emergence of JNU as the bastion of the left provides a clue to the network that has become so wide and dominant today.

Jawaharlal Nehru University was conceived to emerge as the centre of higher learning of world repute. It was not destined to be the hub of political activism or, for that matter, a machine for producing the academic and political left in India. But somehow it happened. With the split in the Congress in 1967, Mrs Gandhi became dependent on the Communist Party of India, which was close to the Soviet Union. Congress left the ideological space for the left and focused more on its political survival. The communists used this opportunity to enter the premier universities and research bodies of the country. Nurul Hasan, who was the education minister, used his clout in the PMO. D.P. Dhar, P.N. Haskar, and Mohan Kumar Mangalam, who were close to Mrs Indira Gandhi, had a soft corner for the left. No wonder that when the JNU was established, the majority of the appointments in the mid-60s and 70s were from the left ideology (Batabyal, 2014:130).

Even several members of the communist party of India entered the world of university, though they were not very well known for any scholarship. Rakesh Batabyal mentioned in his book that, "several members of the communist Party of India found their way into the university in the early phase" (Batabyal, 2014:130). The first appointment was of Moonish Raza, who was not a distinguished scholar from any angle. He was teaching in a non-distinct engineering college in Kashmir. He got his appointment purely because of his left-leaning views and connection with the Aligarh Muslim school of thought. The second set of appointments was made in the 'Institute of Russian Studies'. Here, also left-leaning intellectuals such as Ramadhikari Kumar, S.K. Mathur and Kumari Preeti Kaul were appointed (Batabyal, 2014:125). The history department was filled with personalities like Romila Thapar, Satish Chandra and then

Vipin Chandra, who were emerging Marxist historians. Some liberals also got lucky to join the university, but even they belonged to the 'socialist tradition' (Batabyal, 2014:130).

All these appointments were basically nominations by the Vice-Chancellor, who himself was a journalist. These eminent historians and social scientists developed their clout in the system so much so that the award of scholarships, research grants, and appointments in other universities came under their influence and control, as they happened to be on the selection committee. Funding agencies like the Indian Council for Social Science Research and the Indian Council of Historical Research, for all practical purposes, came under their control, physically as well as in terms of scholarship. It needs to be noted that the left scholarship did not flourish in the state universities, where appointments were not based on merely an open interview but on a different system which involved a written examination and an interview.

NCERT came under control, wherefrom the history written by the left academicians became the most authentic and universally acceptable premise and was pushed down the throats of the small, innocent children. This was done in the name of promoting an indigenous historiography in place of colonial ones, as well as the promotion of non-communal history (Batabyal, 2014:134). Aryan Invasion theory, which was a colonial construct to legitimise the British occupation of India and was intended largely to debunk the theory of nativity, was propagated as the most objective, scientific interpretation of India. Communists had already taken the cue from the Soviet Union to float the idea of multiple nationalities and their rights to decide whether they wanted to be part of India or not.

The invasion theory had no historical facts behind it, and subsequently, when it was put to scrutiny, it was reframed as the Aryan migration theory. The territorial idea of India was questioned. The left scholarship picked exceptions to trace a trend and neglected the prevalent dominant stream. All this was done deliberately as it suited the Congress, the left and the Islamists. History texts book deliberately and rightly ignored the medieval Islamic vandalism, which resulted in the destruction of temples. A politically correct history rather than an objective history was served purposefully. The idea of a golden past, or for that matter, a rich civilizational past, always generates pride in the people of the land. It would have given ammunition to the Hindu nationalists against the Islamic forces. Similarly, the medieval Islamic vandalism was deliberately constructed to contain the possibility of Hindu vengeance against the Muslims. This historiography suited both the left and the Islamists, and no wonder they became co-sharers and co-sponsors of thoughts in the academic domain.

The right-wing intellectuals were seen with disdain and contempt. They were discriminated against all over, and there was no space for them. On the economic issues, both the left and the Congress criticised each other, but they converged on most of the issues which were central to the ideology of the right-wing organisations like the BJP. In 1966, Mrs Gandhi's government issued an executive order that amounted to the prohibition of people of the RSS from joining government jobs (Puniyani, 2016). This was a continuation of what the colonial government had done to the RSS way back in 1932, when the central province's chief minister issued an order that declared the RSS a communal and political organisation and restricted its members from entering the central government services. This was further extended to local bodies in 1933. In the budget session in 1934, there was a comprehensive discussion on this issue, and the government of the day was struggling for a convincing reply. The policy of the colonial government towards the indigenous knowledge system continued even after independence.

This had an overall reflection on the ideological bent of the university students who joined different professions later, be it academics, media, or bureaucracy. The Left became a symbol of progressive ideology, which allowed abundant freedom and thoughts on egalitarianism. Emancipation from poverty and atrocities from the rich and landlord peasantry and Zamindars and caste atrocities legitimately and sanely attracted the educated class, and the left ideology became the academic voice and discourse in the campuses across India.

Talking of the language of the poor and deprived synced with the ideology and mission of the post-colonial state. Therefore, it received wider acceptability in academic discourse and became the icon of progressiveness and forward thinking. Absence of indigenous structure of education and course content related to the glorious past became the symbol of obscurantism and repressiveness. This propelled as well as attracted the young mind who joined the portal of higher education.

This multiplied manifold with the left coming into power in West Bengal and Kerala. The growth of the intellectual left also flourished with the growth of the political left. The communist party government of these states knew the importance of the role of education and its use in shaping the ideological discourse. The left started packing the institutions of higher learning with people who were loyal to its ideology. No wonder universities in Bengal and Kerala over the years became the hub of left intellectuals. A book by Santosh Bhattacharya, himself a CPI cardholder, titled 'Red Hammer on Calcutta University' explains through comprehensive documentation of incidents, activities and intervention from the left during his five-year tenure in Calcutta University. This book entails how "the CPM in West Bengal imposes its ideological and political hegemony, giving way to rules and statutes, through the packing of academic institutions with intellectuals who owe loyalty to it (Bhattacharya, 2009). The CPM and its cadres, both in teaching and among the students, became intolerant not only to the right-wing and the centrist student organisations but also to non-conforming other left-leaning intellectuals.

The change in the intellectual left on the scale of moderate on the one hand and radicals on the other found expression with the change in the political left. When the split in the CPI took place, CPM emerged as a far more radical political formation. As a result, in 1967, a commensurate change in positioning was also seen in the intellectuals of the left. While traditionalists supported the CPI, far more radical people moved towards the CPM. Accordingly, the student wings of the left also witnessed a split across campuses. But that did not stop there. A section within the CPM did not like the parliamentary path, and when the Naxalbari uprisings surfaced, it openly declared to support it against the wishes of the CPM and declared itself as the genuine follower of the revolutionary path and thus came up with the Maoists. Naxalbari uprisings became very popular among youths in West Bengal, and thousands of students who were dissatisfied with the parliamentary politics of the CPM came out openly to support the movement. They protested against the CPM, which, a few years ago, had come up after a split in the CPI on radical revolutionary grounds. In the Naxalbari uprisings, the state power represented and tried to suppress it with all its might.

The split in the political left also led to a split in the intellectual left. While those who decided to live with the power structure slipped towards the CPM, the radical left moved towards the Maoist brand of revolutionary struggle. Thousands of young students sacrificed their professional individual careers and opted for revolutionary struggle to realise the dream of a just and equitable society. The youth of prestigious academic institutions in Calcutta moved towards the radical left. Some of the best minds of the elite Presidency College of Calcutta joined the new radical movement emerging from Naxalbari, which subsequently proliferated to many campuses of universities and colleges across the country, including even JNU, Delhi University, Hyderabad, Patna University, etc. In the seventies, Elphinstone College, Mumbai, once emerged as a hub of Naxalites in Maharashtra. Many social activists turned to left extremism and contributed to the causes of the Naxal movement. Sridhar Srinivasan, Anuradha became the backbone of the Maoist movement in Maharashtra. Sridhar, who passed away in 2015, led the biggest student movement in Mumbai University, which involved all the colleges (Haygunde, 2015). This had paralysed the functioning of the university. He was also the founder member of Vidyarthi Pragati Sangathana and initiated 'go to the village campaigns.' This attracted the youth of the university. Today, Gadchiroli is one of the bastions of the Naxal movement in Maharashtra. Sridhar played a crucial role in spreading the Maoist activities in this area and Gondali and Balaghat of Madhya Pradesh.

It was essentially an urban phenomenon where young youths had dreams of realising an egalitarian society free from exploitation, who thought that it was better to work for social and political transformation than to work for material and other gains. One after another, institutions in Bengal, especially the colleges and universities, plunged into left politics. Surprisingly, it was the upper caste intellectuals coming from a rich economic background that moved towards the new radical liberation movement. It fought the moderates and those who sought to realise the goal of social, political and economic transformation through the parliamentary route. Needless to say, the Naxalbari movement attracted the youth and the Bhadralok of Bengal immensely and therefore the movement spread like wildfire there (Gupta, 2009).

This radical left not only rejected the parliamentary left but also took a political line different from the rest of the left parties in India. A careful peep into the academic, social and economic background of the leaders of the radical left speaks volumes that it was a movement of the educated elite upper class who got trained into the liberation movement through reading of Marxism. Most of them were from the affluent rich class and the upper caste in the social strata. They were not the victim of capitalism or the agrarian system but were beneficiaries of the same. Charu Mazumdar, whose essays became the guiding principles of the Naxal movement, was born in a rich landlord family in Siliguri, adjacent to Darjeeling. Kanu Sanyal also belonged to a very rich class. Jangal Santhal was the only exception to it. Some big names of the second-generation leaders of the Naxal movement also come from a decent social and academic background. Kobad Ghandy, who died recently, was mainly entrusted with the job of running propaganda in the urban areas. He was well educated and was given the job to rope in the urban middle class and intellectuals in the Naxal movement in Central and Northern India.

The split in the political left not only split the faculty but also the students on the campuses across the country. They appeared under several names, but some of them, such as AISA and DSU, made a categorical distance from the parliamentary left and openly supported the ideological lines of the Maoists. A DSU pamphlet in the university provides some light in this regard. The summary of the pamphlet is that 'India is not a nation but a country or the sub-continent'. Second, 'it is a prison house of nationalities like Kashmiris, Tamils, Nagas, Assamese, etc.' Third, these nationalities are forcibly occupied and annexed. They are not integral to the country. Their annexation is not because of any mutual agreement or understanding. It happened because the British transferred the control of these nationalities to the Indian elites, who are now engaged in a hegemonic agenda and destroying the multiple cultures within India. Fourth, these are 'oppressed nationalities, and they have the right to secede' (Singh, 2016). And therefore, there is nothing wrong with lending support to the cause of self-determination demands of Kashmir and working for the same. Interestingly, the whole idea of sub-nationality was a British construct, and the Marxist intellectuals have largely borrowed it from the same. Interestingly, comrades at home do not question the forcible occupation of several nationalities in China on similar grounds of diversity.

What flows from this argument is that it would have been all right had these nationalities been made part of India as a result of mutual understanding or agreement. But they fail to answer with whom the Indian state should have entered into an agreement, the Government of the day of these nationalities or the people of these nationalities? Is there any such glorious example in human history where such a mutual understanding-based amalgamation of territories has taken place at all? They, however, again fail to suggest who these Kashmiris are. Do the Kashmiri nationalities not include the people who belong to Hindu or other religious sects? Is the demand for Azadi not triggered by and driven by the idea of Islamic fundamentalism? Is there only one culture in Kashmir? Who should be treated as the real representative of the will of the people? Social and cultural solidarity erected on the sediments and sentiments of religious gospels, do articulate the real will of the people? Are comrades ready to accept this premise? If they do, they will be doing a great disservice to Marx's understanding of the functioning of society. But these arguments do not matter for those who believe in the utopian world of a classless and exploitation-free stateless society of their own meaning. It is equally interesting to observe that Patel is also a villain for them. One does not find any appreciation for his works of territorial integration of the country. For DSU, Patel is the biggest people killer. DSU brought out a pamphlet dated nil in which it condemned AISA, which had argued for 'critical appreciation' of the role of Patel in the national movement and building of India. DSU condemned Patel on the grounds that it was he who opposed the Hindu Code Bill. It was Patel who destroyed the possibility of a captured Kashmir and forcibly occupied several nationalities in India. He was also instrumental in changing the demography of Jammu through the killings of over 200000 Muslims.

These pamphlets, however, serve the purpose of radicalisation of youths in political ideology, and they become the ideological instrument of the Maoists in the field and garner intellectual support for them on campus. It is difficult to give a correct numerical account of how many students are involved in different forms of lending support to the Maoists, but they certainly are not minuscule. A few years back, a student doing a bachelor's degree in Chinese studies at JNU, Hem Mishra, was arrested by Maharashtra Police sometime in 2013 on the grounds of acting as a 'prominent Naxal Courier' to the media. He was then a known cultural activist associated with the left-wing organisations. This brought boil on the campus, which led to the police being accused of arresting a student on 'fictitious and surreptitious ground'. The then JNUSU general secretary Shakeel Anjum described the police action as 'state terror' (Sanhati, 2013). Professors also joined the chorus, and many of them found it a part of the design of 'defaming the JNU'. To them, this was an act of 'state terrorism'. Many teachers and student groups associated with the left came forward to express their solidarity with the students and criticised the government. Despite being at odds with each other, organisations like AISA, SFI, AISF, SIO (Students Islamic Organisation), Naga Study Forum, United Dalit Students Forum, Untouchable India, Krantikari Nawjawan Sabha, and cultural organisations like RCF, Bahroop, IPTA, JSM, etc., poured in their attacks on the government (Sanhati, 2013). The student organisations were denied permission to make demonstrations before the Maharashtra Sadan. The government of the day was declared as fascist, a popular phrase in the Marxian political armourer, which appears very lofty and dear but does not carry any meaning and substance. They alleged that the government was against those students and teachers who cherish the idea and ideals of 'progressive and revolutionary transformation of the society'. Their arguments were also that anyone who has different views and beliefs cannot be arrested for the same. Fortunately, unlike this time, it was the Congress government at the centre and the state government was also run by the Congress. BJP supported the government and did not choose to fish for political capital from the campus.

A Professor at the University of Delhi was arrested by the Maharashtra police for supporting and acting for the Naxals. Both the Maharashtra police and the Delhi police had also tried earlier to take him into custody. But it could not be possible because every time before, the police could approach the alleged professor, the teachers at the university were up in arms. A chorus of allegations that the state was transgressing its limit, and the Vice-chancellor was colluding, conspiring and scheming against the professor to settle his personal vendetta ranted in the air. There was no role of the Vice-Chancellor in inviting the police, yet the former was accused of it. For the police, it was a simple case of conspiring against the Indian state and violating the country's rules. For the professor, it was blatant misuse of the law by the ruling establishment. Finally, the police arrested him and sent him to jail. The charges against the professor were that he had been acting for the Maoists. The counter-narrative is that he has been subject to harassment and is a victim of state power. He charged that he was being punished for opposing the oppressive state power and seeking justice for the poor and the deprived. The name of the professor had not fallen from heaven. It was revealed by the people arrested from the JNU campus (Chowdhury, 2013). The people arrested by the police had claimed that the aforesaid professor worked for the Maoists and helped their organisation in recruiting the young. The professor is a member of the Revolutionary Democratic Front (RDTF), a small group on the campus known for its radical political ideology of the left.

The intellectual groups and organisations pertaining to the left expressed not only their displeasure over the entire issue but also charged the government of falsely framing the young cultural activist who dared to criticise the government. Interestingly, the Democratic Student Union called Hem 'Comrade' and a 'political and cultural activist'. Just because someone holds an ideology which is different from the ideology of the ruling party does not entitle the state to arrest him or her. The state normally does not do so unless there is a political score to be settled. How could a student be the target of the police, and why would the police implicate him? There are lakhs of students studying in Delhi. Why was Hem alone picked for the trial or questioning? Police otherwise also are very sensitive when it comes to arresting a student. Normally, it does not act unless there is a substantial lead in the case. He was arrested by Gadchiroli police in Maharashtra. Surrounded by thick teakwood forest and bamboo, Gadchiroli, over the years, has emerged as an upcoming bastion of Naxal activities in Maharashtra.

As usual, the intellectuals belonging to the left liberal class gathered and denounced the state and police with all the vocabulary and intellectual ammunition they had in semantic form. Family members were interviewed who denied the charges and declared that the state was 'shamelessly implicating their son'. Friends on campus denied the charges of Hem being involved in Naxal activities. To them, he was a very sensitive student who had the courage to raise his voice against injustice to the poor and Dalits. And the government of the day was insensitive to such a conscious call for justice. They held that he had gone to Gadchiroli to meet Dr Prakash Amte, whose works impressed him as well as possibly for the medication, as despite two surgeries, he was not feeling well (Sanhati, 2013). Even if all these explanations are accepted as true, this does not rule out the charges against him of sympathising with the Naxals and acting for them. He was kept in police custody by the Metropolitan magistrate, who finally sent him to jail.

One does not want to repeat it, but we have already explained how the arrest of Vinayak Sen was opposed by a section of the intelligentsia in India and abroad. A campaign against the government was launched, which was signed by even those who had no idea of India and who had been sitting thousands of miles away and were unaware of its geography and social dynamics. There were many foreigners who seldom or never visited India at all, but they were signatories on the campaign, which condemned the government of India and the state government for violating human rights and imprisoning a person without a fair trial. If one looks at the names in the list of intellectuals, one does not have to labour hard to find that the majority of them are common signatories on campaigns against the right-wing organisations. Their protest against the right-wing organisations does not emerge from an objective assessment of their activities but from the ideological position that they hold. Be it post–Godhra riots in Gujarat or demonstrations on Salwa Judum. They were critical of the Indian state without knowing about it. Needless to say, there is a group of intellectuals trained in the Marxist ideology that is present in India and abroad. Many of them have earned distinction and repute in their field, and therefore, they are recognised faces. They have different positions on a host of issues, but they stand united when it comes to American and European capitalism.

The intellectual support to the Naxal movement has come from different organisations and in different forms. Apart from university and college campuses, there are over three dozen national and state-level literary and cultural forums across the country which moderately or completely lend their support to the Naxal ideology, and they contribute to the movement in many ways, such as street plays, dramas and folk music. Dramatics in colleges have played a crucial role in tapping the young, creative minds towards their ideology. Such forums organise street plays and raise egalitarian and humanitarian questions, which certainly attract the young mind.

All this makes a powerful ideological network of the Maoists across the country. Broadly speaking, there are three sets of educated people within the Maoist movement. First, there are those who left their academic and professional careers and moved to the forest to lead the movement from the field. The second set of people is those who are closely and organically linked to the Maoist movements but are settled in urban and semi-urban areas. They are the ones who write for and run the publicity for the movement in the urban centres to create awareness and counter the negative campaigns against the movement. The artists, students and teachers fall in this category. And yet there are some people who are not closely linked to the Naxals, but they share the concerns of the Naxals. They defend the cause, but they do not defend the violence perpetrated by Naxals. They often participate in candle marches or signature campaigns against the state because this gives them respect as members of civil society who care and value human rights and civil liberties. In fact, most of the civil rights and human rights forums have effectively come under the control and influence of left-leaning intellectuals who often use the forum against the ideology of the right-wing political and social organisation. The account of fact-finding committee reports of People's Union for Civil Liberties (PUCL) and People's Union for Democratic Rights (PUDR), Human Rights Watch explains their bias.

1 Fact-Finding Reports: Facts or Bias Documents?

PUCL and PUDR were constituted during the emergency period to protect the civil rights of individuals against state tyranny. Various people joined it initially, but subsequently, these organisations have come under the control of the left-leaning intelligentsia. These organisations display selective bias in picking and reporting the events or incidents. They have rarely been seriously seen condemning the violence by the Maoists, except for shedding the rituals. PUCL and PUDR reports are always on expected lines. PUCL came in 1977 to fight for the civil liberties and democratic rights of the citizens. The Delhi region came up as the People's Union for Democratic Rights in 1981. These organisations claim to be ideologically neutral, but they are not. It is true that some right-leaning people also remained associated with the PUCL for several years, as was the case with Arun Jaitley, but over the years, the organisations have come under the definite control of the left-leaning social political activists and intellectuals, and they have effectively used this against the state as well as the political ideologies of their opponents.

The reports of these organisations through fact-finding committees are worth noting and reading. They have been highly biased in their report writing. Seldom does one come across reports wherein Maoists have been condemned. When Maoists massacre civilians, they maintain silence, but when the state retaliates in its defence and in the protection of citizens, they disproportionately flag off the issue of human rights violations. In 2005, barely had the Salwa Judum started when they came out with a fact-finding report in which they condemned it in the worst possible terms. The National Human Rights Commission report on Salwa Judum exposes the atrocities of the Naxals, who used women and children as shields in their fights against the state. This was not reflected in any of the PUCL and PUDR reports.

In January 2016, they published a report of the fact-finding committee, which contained reports on fake encounters and sexual violence in the Bijapur and Sukma districts of Chhattisgarh. When one goes through the report, it gives a picture of a carefully crafted pamphlet against the state, which comes in the form of an intellectual exercise, but that truly is a political and ideological document to draw attention and run a campaign against the state (PUDR, 2016). This is not to suggest that the armed forces and members of Salwa Judum did not show high-handedness or indulge in violence, nor does it suggest that there are no incidents of sexual abuse of women by the armed forces. While such incidents have been found, they have been over-proportionately projected through these reports. Secondly, these reports often discount the violence perpetrated by the Maoists in the village. Human rights violations by the Maoists seldom get documented in the fact-finding reports of the PUDR and PUCL fact-finding teams. 2015 Reports of the PUDR titled 'War and Lightness of being Adivasi: Security camps and Villages in Bijapur Chhattisgarh' provides a glimpse of oft-repeated known phrases which contain themes that there is terror in the minds of the civilians because of the excessive presence of the armed forces who make frequent raids and rape the women which leads to heavy displacement of the tribal population from their land (PUDR, 2015). And all this is done to hand over the land to the big corporation for the purpose of mining! It reads as under:

"The operation combines strategies of raids, encounter killings, forced surrender of civilians passed off as Maoists and rampant sexual violence of the civilian Adivasi population to achieve its objectives the heavy militarization, killings and rapes have been tactics to compel mass displacement of tribes from their settlements so that the land can be made available to the corporations for the mining activities" (PUDR, 2016). These are the running vocabulary of all the reports that the PUCL and PUDR generate. This is akin to the Maoist positions, which justify even violence on this ground. Varavara Rao, a retired college teacher who spent eight years in jail due to a Maoist connection, echoed what the Maoists have been thinking about. He said the fight is for justice, justice for the marginalised people. And therefore, means can be ignored. He, with his left clubs, justified the Naxals' revolutionary act under the notion of people's war (OpIndia, 2020). For them, the need is to focus on the goal.

The National Human Rights Commission also documented a fact sheet on the presence of the army personnel and members of the Salwa Judum, but they are more balanced and objective. They do not go to criticise the state in totality but expose the areas that they find wrong. They exposed the terror and forced creation of cadres, sexual abuse of Adivasi women by the Maoists in villages, forced extortion, recruitment of underage children and women in the battle against the state. Needless to say, the PUCL and PUDR Reports are biased because these organisations are not independent institutions free from ideological bias and prejudices. They are under the control of the left cadres, and they sing the ideological tune and rhetoric of the Maoists in their reports. These documents are often used by foreign agencies to castigate the Indian state on the issue of human rights.

In 2006, once again, a team of intellectuals visited some districts of Chhattisgarh to find out the facts on Salwa Judum. The team claimed that it was an independent initiative on the part of some citizens concerned about the reports of Naxal violence and counter-violence from Salwa Judum Naxal areas. However, the composition of the team revealed that it was not as independent as it was claimed. The ideological position and activism of one of the members in favour of the Naxals are well known. She has consistently been defending the Maoists' cause, despite their violence in her writings and condemning the role of the state. Another member has often expressed his despise for the BJP in his writings. The document notes that several people in the Konta and Bhairamgarh/Bijapur area showed their displeasure over Maoists pressuring the villagers not to pluck the Tendu leaves, which caused them serious cash loss during the season. Maoists justify that it is meant to pressurise the Tendu traders to double the wages, and, therefore, they are intended to benefit the tribals who are not getting their due. The villagers also reported that they are asked to prepare food for the Maoists when they stay overnight in the village, take away their cattle, declare them in possession, force them to till the land, attend the meetings of the Maoists in the villages, and do not allow road building in the area. The meetings are organised by the Maoists in the villages where they force their opinion on the rest. No one is allowed to express their opinion. It is not the voice of the village people but the voice of the Naxals that prevails (HRF, 2006:13). In the next paragraph, there are counter viewpoints that argue that Naxalites do not kill innocent civilians but target only those who are involved in the denial of justice to the poor tribals. The contractors and police officials, therefore, are their targets. However, the report does not present any counter viewpoints against the terrorising of the people by the Maoists, forcing them to join their squads and prepare food for the Maoists (HRF, 2006:13).

The committee appealed to both the Maoists and the government to shun the violence and engage in dialogue. They questioned the Maoists on several incidents of violence, the appointment of young people and throwing them into war against the state, as well as the destruction of schools and hospitals and obstruction of infrastructure facilities. But they were harsher in condemning the state. More importantly, they were asking for what the Maoists were asking, i.e., disbanding Salwa Judum. Maoists knew that the success of Salwa

Judum would be fatal to them, and therefore, they ran a campaign against the same. All these intellectuals knew very well that the Maoists who had declared war against the state were not going to be satisfied with the infrastructure and living conditions. Their objective is to overthrow the present economic and political system and put in place a new one which is far more radical and equitable. Violence is their creed through which they want to achieve it, as they have no faith in the parliamentary process and democratic set-up which emerges from the non-socialistic structure.

The fact-finding team has concluded that Salwa Judum is not at all a spontaneous rising against the Maoists' atrocities. That may be valid, that the government might have encouraged the locals to come out and fight against the high-handedness of the Maoists. It is true that the government is providing the logistic support to the people. But to suggest that there was no support to Salwa Judum and no anguish against the Maoists among the villagers and Adivasis would be a gross lie.

Under the subheadings, the committee notes that the administration has gagged the press. But the fact of the matter is that it is not possible for the press person to report anything that goes against the Naxals. It is easier for them to criticise the government, as the government cannot retaliate against the press even if the reports are untrue or incorrect. But the same does not apply to the Maoists. They go ruthlessly against all those who write against them. Reporters of all newspapers express this on condition of anonymity, as it is not possible for the local journalists to write anything against the Maoists, as they suffer from the threat of abduction and killing. The threats to the journalists come in the form of advice to them to do 'the correct reporting' (Mishra, 2021).

The above-mentioned report of the Independent Citizens' Initiative says that the start of Salwa Judum has deeply divided the village society and has injected the elements of civil war in the village communities, with both the pro and anti-Maoist camps suspecting and targeting each other. The report does not deny that people are against the Maoists. On the contrary, they openly speak their mind that they have no option but to support Salwa Judum because Maoists put pressure on them to hand over the lands and cattle to those who are little financially better off. The committee notes several such cases. The fact-finding committee notes the version of the people of Belnar village, where it finds a sharp vertical division between pro and anti-Naxalites (HRF, 2006:13). And those who spoke in favour of Salwa Judum did not do so under the shadow of the power of the state, yet the burden of fissures within the villages has been attributed to Salwa Judum. The committee notes, "The creation and support of Salwa Judum has divided entire villages and families, perhaps irreversibly" (HRF, 2006:13). Does this mean that the people who were opposed to the Maoists should not speak their minds and that they are not entitled to self-defence? It would be naïve to argue that there were no fissures within the village society despite the fact that Maoists were forcing one section of the society to transfer a part of their land and cattle wealth in favour of other members of the same village who had openly come out in their support. A vertical division in the villages could be possible because people who were under Maoists' duress found a platform to resist the Naxalites. Salwa Judum empowered those who were fearful of the Maoists and had not mustered the courage to speak out against them till now.

There is another report from the Coordination of Democratic Rights Organisation, which also reached the same conclusion. The report came in April 2016 with the title, 'State of Siege'. Again, the members were from CDRO, West Bengal; Civil Liberties Committee from Andhra, Telangana; PUDR, Delhi; Committee for Protection of Democratic Rights (CPDR), Tamil Nadu; Women against Sexual Violence and State Repression. All the members of the team came from left-leaning civil rights movements. The team endorsed that there is heavy militarisation, killings and rapes of Adivasis, which force them to leave their lands and villages. There is a huge displacement of the Adivasi population, and this is being done consciously to ensure the mining of the lands by the corporate giants like Tata and Essar, with which the government has entered into a contract. The government has scant respect for the Forest Rights Act 2006. The interesting part is the conclusion, which reads: The people of Chhattisgarh are living in a state of siege. Frequent combing operations by the security forces, sexual assault on women, fake surrenders, fake encounters, and disruption of everyday activities have become the order of the day. In the end, the report asks for the withdrawal of paramilitary forces from the state. It asks for the ban on state-sponsored and state-supported vigilante groups or organisations, it talks of the abduction and killing of Adivasis, but nowhere does it document the atrocities and excesses of the Maoists, abduction and killing by the Naxalites, forcing women and children to join its ranks and equally important abuse of modesty of women and young girls by its cadres and members of its armed squads (PUDR, 2016). PUDR came out with another report in 2015 with a title 'War and the Lightness of Being Adivasi: Security Camps and Villages in Bijapur'. And again, the blame was squarely on the state.

All the committees and fact-finding reports have some common points. First, the Maoists are fighting against the injustice done to the tribal population and in pursuit of their basic rights. It is the poverty and denial of dignified human living that is the reason behind the spread of Maoism. Therefore, the issues that they are raising are not insignificant. Salwa Judum has been conceived and supported by the state. It is intended to use a section of the tribal population against another section of the tribal population. Members of Salwa Judum are engaged in the rape of women, extortion of money, threatening and killing of villagers who refuse to join its squad and so on. All the reports carry names to substantiate the charges. However, it isn't easy to ascertain them in many cases. Further, it is also difficult to suggest who has executed it. It has also been found that Maoists did this to provoke popular anger against the state. Secondly, it has also been noticed that while all the reports are highly critical of the methods adopted by the state, there is an element of rationality in the presentation of violence perpetrated by the Maoists. Third, several forums and organisations claim to be working dispassionately and objectively about the facts in Chhattisgarh, but that does not happen in a true sense. All the organisations have their ideological affinity and are politically connected. They do not report unbiased at all. Therefore, fact-finding reports have no value as they present one side of the story and ignore the other. Most of the human rights watch groups and NGOs fall in this category. They hold the banner of objectivity, but they are not. Look at the Report of Independent Citizens' Initiatives. First, if one goes by the list of members of this citizen group, one can see that it amply speaks of their political and ideological affiliations.

What comes to mind is strong intellectual support for this movement in a section of the intelligentsia, particularly in some universities that have become a nursery of the ideology over the last few decades. In the university and college system, it again dominates in liberal arts and humanities. It is not equally powerful and popular in science and professional courses, where they are either completely missing or stand to be insignificant forces. Some professional and technical universities are exceptions to it and are mainly located in Bengal, Kerala, and Andhra Pradesh, which once upon a time had emerged as the epicentres of the radical left movement in India. With the spread of the market system, professional courses and private institutions have mushroomed phenomenally in the country. In all such institutions, there is no presence of left radicalism. The supporters of the radical movement, however, have no answer to the question of why the idea of an egalitarian and equitable society they aspired to could not be realised despite 37 years of ruthless rule in Bengal. The double speech of the supporters of the Naxal movement within the left is quite manifest. They opposed the state's use of force and power in Chhattisgarh and Madhya Pradesh but justified the same in Bengal. Look at how the CPI (M) reacted to the Maoist Violence in 2006. In a reply to the press, CPI (M) said, 'How will we have dialogue with those who do not believe in democracy and carry arms? If they give up arms and strengthen the democracy, then talks should happen' (Hindustan Times, 2009).

CHAPTER 8

Maoists, Courts, and Salwa Judum

The campaign against Salwa Judum started ever since it was introduced in Chhattisgarh. The intellectuals and organisations associated and sympathised with the Naxals, and their cause did not recognise Salwa Judum as a 'self-grown grass-roots' people's resistance against the Naxals.[1] To them, it was a deliberately and consciously created band of people encouraged and patronised by the state to counter the expanding influence of the Naxals in remote rural areas of the state. They found the new strategy of the state very damaging as it involved arming the locals, who were not very happy with the high-handedness of the Naxals, who forced their instructions of dos and don'ts on the villagers. Travelling through the remote areas of Bastar makes it clear that not all tribals are involved in the Naxals and their activities. There is a clear pro and anti-Naxal divide among the forest dwellers. Naxalites operated in a difficult terrain, and it is always a herculean task for the police to operate in such unknown terrain. The locals' involvement in the counter-insurgency strategy and operations amounted to breaking the social support of the Naxals. They realised that if the Salwa Judum movement were allowed to work, that would not only neutralise the striking capacity of the Naxals but would also weaken their social base. Their ideologues, sitting in cosmopolitan cities, found the revolution and revolutionary narratives not taking ground. Sensing a great loss to the revolutionary movement, they unleashed a barrage of campaigns against the Salwa Judum movement on social media, apart from print and electronic.

Fact-finding reports with selective instances and selective videos were put into the campaign to demonise the Salwa Judum. The left-liberal intelligentsia spearheaded this campaign. Even non-Marxist liberals and Gandhians joined the campaign and took it to the Supreme Court of India. Nandini Sundar, a professor of sociology at the University of Delhi, along with a few other human rights activists such as Swami Agnivesh and Ramchandra Guha, filed a writ

1 Nandani Sundar and Others vs State of Chhattisgarh. Nandani Sundar is a Professor of Sociology at Delhi School of Economics, University of Delhi. She talks about the legal and human rights of tribals in the forest. But at the same time, she has been an ardent supporter of the Naxal Movement, though She refuses the charge that she supports the violence perpetrated by the Naxals. For the right-wing groups and intellectuals and the state establishment, she falls in the category of Urban Naxals.

 HTTPS://DOI.ORG/10.1163/9789004765054-010

petition in the Supreme Court in 2007 in which they pleaded to direct the state to dismantle the Salwa Judum. They argued that Salwa Judum was a private militia created, funded and supported by the state to tackle the Maoist menace. And therefore, it was against the spirit of the Constitution. The court gave its verdict in July 2011, declaring the scheme of Salwa Judum illegal and unconstitutional. The court's decision was based on the fact that the appointment of the SPOs was not in consonance with the law of the land. SPOs were not just immature as they did not fulfil the minimum age but also lacked the minimum degree required to join the police force (Bhatia, 2011:14–16).

Equipping such semi-illiterate, innocent and premature younger people with rifles and guns and asking them to fight against the Naxals amounted to risking their lives, which could not be permitted in any civilised society. It was just like throwing the young children in the battleground and exposing their lives to the war zones. They were not sufficiently trained to counter the Maoists. The court found merit in this argument and castigated the state for making the young ones the cannon fodder in the crossfire between the Naxals and the state. It directed the state of Chhattisgarh to disarm immediately. They should no longer be employed in any use of firepower to resist, fight against or eliminate the Naxals directly or indirectly, and the guns and arms that had been given to them, both current and former SPOs, should be taken back by the state government. The Court directed the Chhattisgarh police to "immediately cease and desist from using SPOs in any manner or form in any activities, directly or indirectly, aimed at controlling, countering, mitigating or otherwise eliminating Maoist/Naxalite activities" (Sethi, 2011).

Secondly, the court did not accept the state government's argument that Salwa Judum was a self-grown movement in self-defence. The state's role was limited to making them available arms and requisite support to fight the Naxals in their self-defence (The Hindu, 2021). The court, in turn, accepted the petitioners' charges that Salwa Judum was a band of private militia raised by the state. Augmentation of such civil militia and engaging them in counter-insurgency amounted to shifting of the responsibility of protection of law and order to a private agency, which primarily is the duty of the state. The state cannot delegate this responsibility to a private militia. And therefore, Salwa Judum was illegal and lacked constitutional propriety. The Supreme Court thereby reiterated its earlier position when a bench of judges headed by Chief Justice K.G. Balakrishnan, which included Justice P. Sathasivam and J. Panchal, made similar observations in 2008. The then Chief Justice of the Supreme Court had remarked, "When somebody (Salwa Judum) is given arms, he claims to be a pseudo police. Once he is given arms, he will commit an offence though he has no right to do any such act" (The Hindu, 2008). This bench also observed: "… large tracts of the State of Chhattisgarh have been affected by Maoist activities, which is widely known. It has also been widely reported that the people living in those regions of Chhattisgarh have suffered grievously on account of both the Maoist insurgency activities and the counter-insurgency unleashed by the State. The situation in Chhattisgarh is undoubtedly deeply distressing to any reasonable person. What was doubly dismaying to us was the repeated insistence, by the respondents, that the only option for the State was to rule with an iron fist, establish a social order in which every person is to be treated as suspect" (The Hindu, 2008). Further, the court noted that anyone who questioned the constitutional limitations of the state and spoke about the human rights of the people was 'deemed a suspect' and a Maoist. It went on to say in the same flow that Nandani Sundar, Swami Agnivesh, former bureaucrat E.A.S. Sarma, and Ramchandra Guha were all called Maoists or the supporters of the Maoists.

The premise that the state wanted to establish a social order in which everyone was to be suspected was the court's conclusion. Neither the state's reply nor its counsel even verbally had said so. The court also accepted that the state had suffered because of the Maoist insurgency. However, it concluded that it resulted from the 'amoral political economy that the state endorses'[2] (Nandini Sundar & Ors vs. State of Chhattisgarh). And it did not ask the petitioners why they maintained silence on the human rights violations by the insurgents despite being in constant touch with the Maoists. Those innocents who were roped into the movement were, after all, illiterate, innocent and poor people. They were made cannon fodder by the Maoists, who engaged even the small children and women in the movement. But the court maintained a stoic silence. There are scores of examples before all of us that the Maoists targeted the armed forces because they were agents of the state. Several schools, roads and hospitals have been torched and blasted by the Naxals. However, the court did not care about it and said nothing about how to deal with this terrorist act. Do we accept that the armed forces who are on duty to protect the citizens are not entitled to basic human rights? Further, there was no point in the court castigating the state for questioning the credentials and intentions of the petitioners. They are known social activists who hold left-leaning ideologies, and it is known that these intellectuals were in touch with the Maoists. Questioning the state activities on the grounds of law and the constitutional premises was valid and justified. However, the state was within its rights to question the credentials of these people as Maoist sympathisers, and there was no need to

2 Nandani Sundar and Others vs State of Chhattisgarh Para 5 of the Supreme Court Judgement on SPOs appointment in the state of Chhattisgarh.

lampoon the state on this ground. This allowed the non-left political organisations and academia to criticise the court and question its neutrality.

They charged that the court was not neutral and unbiased in approach. The state had questioned the petitioners' credentials because some had consistently supported the Naxal movement's ideology and larger objectives. The point that the state wanted to convey was that the petitioners were not impartial in raising the bogey of human rights, as they had not been critical of human rights violations by the Naxals. They raise the human rights issue to obstruct the operation and weaken the counter-insurgency move of the state. In other words, raising the issue of human rights is a mechanism for lending tactical intellectual support to the Naxals. The evidence produced by the petitioners was selective and fabricated to malign the counter-insurgency. It argued that the court must assess the workings of Salwa Judum in the larger framework of the state's endeavour to contain the extremists. However, the court, on the other hand, observed a rationalisation of taking up arms to secure justice. The court said, "People do not take up arms, in an organised fashion, against the might of the State, or human beings without rhyme or reason. Guided by an instinct for survival and, according to Thomas Hobbes, a fear of lawlessness that is echoed in our conscience, we seek order. However, when that order comes with the price of dehumanisation, of manifest injustices of all forms perpetrated against the weak, the poor and the deprived, people revolt" (Nandini Sundar & Ors vs. State of Chhattisgarh). This indirectly justified the Naxal movement and its violent activities.

The question following this is whether the judiciary should also look into the policy analysis and analyse the reasons for poverty and unemployment. Arun Jaitley, the BJP leader and one of the finest legal minds of India, raised exactly the same question when he said "'Why Maoism took root, how it should be tackled. These things, the Judiciary cannot tell the Executive. It is for the Executive to decide ... The Judiciary cannot tell the government" (DNA India, 2011). While participating in a debate in the parliament on the removal of a judge of the Calcutta High Court, Saumitra Sen, Jaitley reiterated the argument that "policy decisions do not fall within the judicial space. How terror is to be fought is in the executive domain" (Hindustan Times, 2011). Jaitley also referred to the language and pronouncements by the judges in respect of the Salwa Judum in the Court and took this opportunity to criticise the ideologically motivated judges and judiciary for appropriating the power of appointment of judges.

The language of the court indeed sent out a message that the court favoured the ideological premise of the left. Therefore, the judgment invited sharp reactions from non-left liberal intelligentsia. They questioned the proverbs and literature the honourable court used to write the judgment. It is true that Nandani Sunder and Ramchandra Guha are intellectuals of great repute, but that does not obliterate them from the charges that they harbour prejudice in favour of a particular ideology. Intellectuals are entitled to have their ideological positions, and they are within their right to question the intent and content of the state's actions and inactions. Similarly, the state too has the right to question its credentials when it finds that the conduct and activities of the individuals do not violate the defined tenets of law and constitution. Moreover, it would be wrong to assume that intellectuals of great strength and repute do not commit mistakes. In other words, intellectuals are human beings and therefore fallible. After all, many of the terrorists have been found intellectuals of great repute. The people who bombed the Twin Towers in America were educated people, but at the same time, they were also ideologically driven fanatics. To suggest that the state has no right to question them just because they are known intellectuals would be a wrong premise to work on judicial verdicts. There are thousands of scholars who have been supportive of the Naxal cause. Does that mean the state should not question their credence?

What led to furious criticism at large was due to the selective quotes made from a politically and ideologically loaded book by the learned judges. The court made a very harsh comment on the privatisation policy. It endorsed almost the left-wing criticism of the political economy, the system of privatisation, and the free market economy. The court compared the political economy of Chhattisgarh to the state of Congo between 1890 and 1910. Drawing heavily from the book 'The Dark Side of Globalisation,'[3] The court held that the state of Chhattisgarh marked 'the state of horror' due to the 'vilest scramble for loot'.[4] It further concluded that the Naxal problem emanated from the over-exploitation and appropriation of resources by a few. As happened in Congo, when the civil war erupted due to the exploitation of the resources, the state of Chhattisgarh also witnessed the same. The learned judges quoted extensively

3 'The Dark Side of Globalization' is a book edited by Jorge Heine and Ramesh Chandra Thakur that got published in 2011 under the aegis of the United Nations. The court while quoting the book remarked "set against the backdrop of resource-rich darkness of the African tropical forests, the brutal ivory trade sought to be expanded by the imperialist-capitalist expansionary policy of European powers, Joseph Conard describes the grisly and the macabre states of mind and justifications advanced by men, who secure and wield force without reason, sans humanity, and any sense of balance".

4 The Judges observed, "Thus the same set of issues, particularly those related to land, continue to fuel protest politics, violent agitator politics, as well as armed rebellion ... Are governments and political parties in India able to grasp the socio-economic dynamics encouraging these politics, or are they struck with a security-oriented approach that further fuels them?"

from one set of literature and appeared to be siding with one set of subjective policy arguments. By doing this, they allowed the criticism to pour in. The experts in public policy and economics questioned the expertise of the judges, who had expertise in law but certainly not good training in economics, public finance or public policy. Their intervention in policy is limited to examining legal aspects to examine whether they violate any principles of law or constitutional provisions.

Even the commentators and editors who otherwise solidly supported the legal finesse of the judgment accepted that the court walked a 'considerable distance', and instead of setting the question of law, it entered into the domain of public policy and set out on a course of deciding the question of ideology. The metaphors and tones of the judgement showed as if the judges were personally very hurt at the pace of globalisation and were against the policy of privatisation, resource management and distribution in a free market economy. The question is: are judges there to judge the policy and apply their personal likes and dislikes towards a policy to be the basis of supporting and dismissing a case? The judgment certainly raised this question, which reflected most of the editorial comments.[5] They all questioned the proverbs and metaphors used and criticised them for their ideological bias. Why did the court quote only one source reflecting the left world view on the subject in the discussion? Will the court apply socio-economic interpretations and conclude as per the worldview that the judges ideologically hold in future? A commentator on the judgment used very harsh words, and the whole judgment gave a replica of proverbs used in the pamphlets prepared by the media wing of the communist party. The words like evils of 'predatory capitalism', 'danger of neo-liberal policies of the state' resemble the communists' ideology, and they do not go with the language of law at all (Rao, 2011).

Except for the left-liberal intelligentsia and left political and intellectual outfits, the media reacted sharply against the judgment. They criticised the judgment and described it more as a lecture on political economy than jurisprudence. The Indian Express expressed its anguish over the 'value-driven judgment' at the bottom, which was the criticism of the government's neo-liberal policy. Instead of interpreting the law in light of the statutes, the judges stretched beyond their jurisdiction, and in doing so, they looked more focused on delivering a judgmental decision driven by populism and self-image (The Indian Express, 2011). The paper went on venting its criticism. Shekhar Gupta,

5 By and large, the majority of the Editorials next morning questioned the Supreme Court's judgement on Salwa Judum. They questioned the judiciary for entering into ideological narratives rather than restricting itself to the question of law and constitutionality.

editor-in-chief of the daily, questioned the wisdom of the judgment and raised questions about the role of judges. Should the judges comment on policies, whether they are good or not, or are they there to decide the question of law? Shekhar also criticised the judges for drawing a linear conclusion from diverse cases of a specific nature, such as corruption in telecom licenses, land acquisition, etc. All these cases are different, and suggesting the conclusion that they all are the result of neo-liberal policies adopted by the government is an over-simplification of the cases.

Chandan Mitra, the editor of Pioneer, an English daily from Delhi, too, came down heavily on the judgment. Mitra wrote, "It is not my intention to suggest that their Lordships acted out of ignorance in declaring this mass movement 'unconstitutional'" and harangued the State Government for converting innocent tribals into armed vigilantes, but I do wish the judges had travelled to Bastar to acquaint themselves with the ground reality before passing this draconian order. Mitra found that this judgment would do great harm to the ongoing operation against the armed Naxals. The Economic Times wrote, "It is unfortunate that the Court chose to pass facile judgment on economic paradigms and development strategies ..." (The Economic Times, 2011). It criticised the judgment for judges commenting on the development paradigm and economic reforms. It questioned the wisdom of judges, whether they realise that if the government can spend huge amounts of money on popular welfare schemes today, it is all because of the market-driven economic reforms that enabled the state to finance these schemes. Therefore, the outright condemnation of the privatisation and market-led reforms was unwarranted. It observed that the court failed 'to distinguish between economic reforms and the unreformed, degenerate politics that abort much of the emancipatory potential of economic reforms.' The Times of India found that the court intruded into others' domains and thereby exposed itself to criticism (Times of India, 2011). It was a case of 'judicial overreach'. A columnist in The Hindustan Times wrote that judges behaved like the JNU postgraduate students commenting on post-colonial studies (The Hindustan Times, 2011). Another columnist wrote in the Times of India, in which he criticised the judgement that it provided 'intellectual legitimacy' to the Naxal movement (Times of India, 2011).

Among the national dailies published in English, the Hindu was the only exception, and this was not a surprise to anyone, given the editorial and ideological line that the paper holds. It described the judgment as 'a landmark judgment' in saving the lives of the tribal youths who, under the compulsions, had become 'cannon fodder' of the state. It endorsed the court observations that linked the neo-liberal market economy and the rise of Naxal activities and asked both the central and state governments not to seek a review of the judgment but 'immediately implement' the 'splendid expression of judicial wisdom' (The Hindu, 2011). The paper also gave enough space to the stories, news items, and articles critical of Salwa Judum and favoured the Supreme Court's judgment. Thus, Madhav Khosla, writing on 23 July 2011 in the Hindu, admitted that the court travelled a considerable distance in interpreting the political economy, 'rhetorical narratives and ideological framing of the judgment', but he appreciated the judgment on the ground that the standing of the court on the central issue was based on legal facts. The centrality of the question that was scrutinised was whether the vigilante group created by the state of Chhattisgarh was constitutional. He argued that the ideological narratives were not required, yet the judgment was based on the legal merit of the case. It was not judgmental at all, as commentators at large reacted to it. He argued that the court found that the appointment of SPOs was illegal. It also violated human rights and the right to life as they were asked to do the job of police officers without proper training in arms and counter-insurgency, risking the lives of innocent tribals.

The left-leaning newspapers, monthly and journals unleashed a barrage of attacks against the state government. The Economic and Political Weekly, a very prestigious monthly known for its left-leaning views, published a series of articles that demonised Salwa Judum and appreciated the judgment of the Supreme Court. Sanhati, another journal that over-leaned towards the left ideology and has often been very critical of the Supreme Court Judgement on the Bangladeshi infiltrations, which also exposed the anti-national and communal politics of the left, observed: … "The recent Supreme Court order in the Salwa Judum case bolsters our confidence in the judiciary" (Bhatia, 2011).

A full reading of the judgment, the author goes on to say, warms up to the extent of feeling being in the company of like-minded. The People's Union of Democratic Rights (PUDR), in its press release, demanded the implementation of the court's verdict. It asked the government to 'immediately stop using SPOs, recall the firearms distributed to them and file FIRs against the members of the SPOs. As expected, the PUDR appreciated and endorsed the courts' observation that the Naxal violence was a result of the shameless culture of greed and rabid exploitation of resources that the neo-economic ideology has promoted (Sanhati, 2011). Amnesty International, whose voice lacks credibility in the absence of impartiality, also appreciated the judgment. Sam Zarifi, the International Director of Amnesty International for Asia and the Pacific, held that the state must comply with the court's decision and initiate investigations into serious human rights violations by the Koya Commandos or the members of the Salwa Judum (Amnesty International, 2011). Interestingly, Amnesty International talked about the violence and the number of deaths in violence, but it did not speak a word against the human rights violations by the Naxals. That endorses the perception that Amnesty International is basically a tool of the Western powers who use it to exercise pressure on third-world countries under the pretext of violation of human rights. More importantly, the director of the organisation depicted it as a conflict between the Indian state and the local and indigenous Adivasis. Far more surprising were the facts that none of the left-leaning educationists, intellectuals, or their mouthpieces condemned the Naxals for appointing the children and women in the Naxal movement and for sexual abuse of the girls and women by the comrades, even though the NHRC report explicitly noted such acts.[6]

Some editorials welcomed the judgment but feared it would trigger demands in other states where states have used the people against counter-insurgency. More importantly, they found that the judgment of the Supreme Court would have ramifications on the counter-insurgency operations of the police and the armed forces in the other states. The Deccan Herald thus wrote: "The Supreme Court's declaration as illegal the recruiting of tribals into anti-Maoist militias in Chhattisgarh will have ramifications not only for the anti-Maoist operations in the state but for India's counter-insurgency operations in other parts of the country" (Deccan Herald, 2011). The editorial accepted that such counter-insurgency operations and mechanisms were at work in other parts of the country as well, such as in the North East and the state of J&K. The editorial thus concluded that the court had done well to disband it. It was apprehended that the Maoists would now target these SPOs; therefore, it was incumbent for the state to provide them protection! Commentators and editorials who have been gracious to the movements in the Northeast and Kashmir took the cue and kicked off the debate in their states. The Kashmir Times wrote: "Salwa Judum is to (mainly) BJP-ruled states what the so-called Special Operation Group (SOG) is to this state" (The Kashmir Times, 2011). The paper went on to lament further, "What the apex court detailed judgment says in justification for banning Salwa Judum applies in letter and spirit to the SOG." It went on to describe the Salwa Judum as a brainchild of communal ideology fed upon public money and loot, and a licensed crime against society. The creation of Ikhwanis and the recruitment and training of the converted militants to counter the insurgency in Kashmir were similar to what Salwa Judum was all about in Chhattisgarh. They, too, were inducted into the regular police after the public outcry in the state. Thus, a section of the media that has developed inherent hate against the BJP saw it as a big slap on the face of the BJP; others read it as a morale booster for the Naxalites (Deccan Herald, 2011). But by and large, the

6 See the NHRC Reports on sexual abuse of women by the Naxal leaders.

Hindi dailies, except for Jansatta, criticised the judgment for the ideological overtones that it carried along. So was the case with most of the news channels. Barring a few, most of the national channels questioned the ideological underpinnings of the judgment. Social media resonated with fierce arguments and counterarguments on the subject.

There were five major observations in brief. First, the court overreached and transgressed its boundaries. Instead of limiting itself to the interpretation of the law, it moved on to comment on the ongoing economic reforms, which were not required at all. It also amounted to judging the developmental model adopted by the Indian government, which does not fall in the domain of the judiciary. Second, the tone and tenor of the judgment have provided legitimacy to the ongoing Naxal insurgency on the one hand and the campaign against the state on the other. This was remarkably different from the NHRC report, which had accused both the state and Naxals of the recruitment of children and women and of making them suffer in the crossfire. Third, the 'ideology of the author of the judgement prevailed over constitutionalism' (Jaitley, 2018). Fourth, the court openly sided with the rationale of violence argued by the Naxals. It said, "People do not take up arms, in an organised fashion, against the might of the State, or against human beings without rhyme or reason. Guided by an instinct for survival and, according to Thomas Hobbes, a fear of lawlessness that is echoed in our conscience, we seek order. However, when that order comes with the price of dehumanisation, of manifest injustices of all forms perpetrated against the weak, the poor and the deprived, people revolt" (Nandini Sunder vs. State of Chhattisgarh, para. 52). Further: "Many of these tribal youngsters, on account of the violence perpetrated against them, or their kith and kin and others in the society in which they live, have already been dehumanized. To have feelings of deep rage and hatred and to suffer from the same is a continuation of the condition of dehumanisation. The role of a responsible society and those who claim to be concerned about their welfare, which the State is expected to under our Constitution, ought to be one of creating circumstances in which they could come back or at least tread the path towards normalcy and mitigation of their rage, hurt, and desires for vengeance" (Nandini Sunder vs. State of Chhattisgarh).

Fifth, the court's judgment would unsettle the ongoing counter-insurgency in the states. The community help and arming them against the Naxals were proving successful, and that is why the Naxals had unleashed so much powerful a campaign against it. The division within the community gave the state an edge in tracking the movement and tackling it accordingly. Many counter-insurgency operations could be successful because of the community cooperation and help. There was no harm in raising the awareness of the people to desist from the Naxals and preparing them to defend themselves against the armed Naxals. The court was swayed to the Naxals' campaign spearheaded by the intellectuals in cities who sympathised with them. Democracy, human rights, egalitarianism and similar conceptions and rhetoric worked to their advantage. On the whole, the judgment was ideologically leaned. It also endangered the lives of the SPOs, who now would be the target of the Naxals. In the absence of the arms, it will be easier for the Naxals to target the SPOs and bring the territories under the influence of the red zones.

The state's argument was that the state used the members of the Salwa Judum for intelligence inputs and guidance, and they were not at all doing the police's job. The state arguments were not something unusual. There have been times when police use such means to tackle organised crime. They were given the firearms for self-defence only. This has been done in the past by state governments as well. The state of Bihar, way back in 1975, decided to provide a licence to the villagers to keep arms for self-defence in the Naxal areas of Bhojpur, Patna. Also, the Police Act of 1861 provides for such appointment, and various states have passed such legislation into effect. It was also argued that in Jammu and Kashmir, SPOs work in the area of insurgency to protect the village people. They are part of the village protection committees. The same mechanism was developed in Punjab during the times of insurgency, keeping in mind that the state cannot deploy police forces in each and every village where there is apprehension of breach of peace or the possibility of violence.

The court, however, did not accept the arguments of the state. It concluded that the state was recruiting, training and using the SPOs in the combat operations against the Naxals. The court also rejected the arguments of livelihood that the SPOs would likely be deprived of if Salwa Judum were dismantled. The court held that the appointment of SPOs and payment to them for supporting the counter-insurgency operations cannot be under the 'rubric of livelihood' is unacceptable. The court accepted the petitioners' arguments that the state was using the SPOs to perform the duties of the police officers without proper training and thus risking their lives. Accordingly, it struck down the appointment of SPOs and directed the central and state governments not to fund such projects. As far as the legal issues are concerned, the court was within its right to adjudge the legality of the appointment, training, and use of the SPOs for counter-insurgency purposes by the state. However, the court's several observations have validly raised many questions. Is there any essential link between the neo-liberal market economy and Maoist movements? If that is true, as the court explicitly held, why have neo-liberal pro-market economies not triggered such movements in the developed world? Why did the state-driven economies of the communist and socialist countries return to the pro-market economies?

Questions also become pertinent as to why the Naxals, who are so often seen to be critiquing the capitalist system, do not come out to criticise the Chinese model, which has returned to capitalism after experimenting with state socialism for several decades.

Some states in India, such as Gujarat, Rajasthan, Maharashtra, etc., are far ahead of Bihar and Bengal in terms of a neo-liberal market economy. These states also resorted to land acquisition policies to industrialise the state. Why have the Naxals not got their footprints well entrenched over there? Why is this mainly in the agriculture-based economies and not in India's far more industrialised states? More importantly, why is this phenomenon largely visible in the states where mines are located? Is this because of the local communities' displacement factor, which could provide an opportunity and fertile ground for the Maoists to settle there and exploit the people for the movement? Or is it because these areas allow them to extort and mobilise ample money to sustain the movement? These questions need to be looked at carefully when assessing the Naxal movement. No one denies that the farm unrest and government policies might have led to social unrest among the masses, and the Naxals exploited them to their advantage. But why could there be no possibility of manufacturing discontent among the masses by the activists and ideologues that adhere to the ideology of Maoism? After all, some areas are far more underdeveloped and poverty-ridden and yet they are not under the influence of the Maoists. There is no doubt that these issues are important, and in free democracies, they need to be put to scrutiny through discourse in the public domain, but the courts are not the place to do this. Such ideologically leaned judgments are sure to enamour the Maoists on the one hand and discourage the armed forces who are battling against all odds to contain the organised rebellion against the Indian state. Dilip has raised some important questions pertaining to the appointment of SPOs. Is it only the government of Chhattisgarh that has made such appointments to meet the challenge of counter-insurgency? It is worth noting that there are several states in which it is in practice, and Chhattisgarh is not alone. Jammu and Kashmir continue to use this. When terrorism was at its peak in Punjab, the police in the state also employed the youths to counter the insurgency, and the model and objectives were the same. Terrorists used the young unemployed youths to recruit their cadres. The success of any insurgency lies in the appeal it holds for the people from whom it draws its strength. Unemployed youths fell victim to their prey very easily. Hence, the government employed the young youths in a big way to collect intelligence information. Even today, in the Northeast, the government has been using the SPOs to tackle crime. Hence, what Chhattisgarh employed was not something that was unique in design and structure.

The critics of the judgment have rightly questioned the essential linkages between poverty and terrorism. The fact is that Naxals are located in areas that are minefields of resources, and they extort annually nearly 2700 crores from this, which they use to run the organisation and purchase arms. If we look at the political economy of the Naxal movement, it is obvious that they have shifted their activities to areas where industrial activities are abundant. They are less concentrated in central Bihar, where the conflicts between the landlords and wage earners remain a serious question. Still, the Naxal movement has lost its initial steam in these areas. They shifted their base to Jharkhand primarily because the state is rich in mineral resources, and industrial activities are mainly located in these areas. Naxals do not face a cash crunch here.

The court seems to have been influenced by the ideological campaign that the Maoists unleashed through the left-liberal media and academicians on the campus. This left-liberal intelligentsia, which once happened to be the proponents of left extremism and ideological radicalism, has found that the radical left has no future at all. They, therefore, have resorted to the same bourgeois expressions that they once celebrated to criticise. The issue of human rights violations concerns everyone. No one seems to be standing with those who decide to violate it. It is a powerful tool to beat the government despite all precautions by the latter. Judges should not be carried away, but often fall into such logic. On the Maoist issue, it was not happening for the first time. It reminds me of a case in the Andhra Pradesh High Court, which heard the case of Appa Rao, an alleged Maoist who was under trial in the murder of an inspector general of the state, Mr K.S. Vyas, in 1996. The judges of the court, M. Rao and S. Nayak, concluded that the violence and counter-violence between the police and the Maoists were of no use. They could not bring lasting peace in the areas, and therefore, what was needed was to constitute a peace commission to instil confidence in all sections of society. The court took a lenient view and set Appa Rao free as the then Director General of Police, Mr. Dinesh Singh, who was having a morning walk with the killed inspector general, failed to identify him as a witness! The same Appa Rao was found to be the mastermind of the attack on Chandra Babu Naidu in 2003, and finally, the police killed him deep inside the forest in 2010. It was the terror of Rao that had made the DGP to be a witness. Subsequently, it was only the ruthless state action that stamped out the terror that had emerged from the left extremism in Andhra Pradesh. The state had refused to follow the armed chair preaching of the court, and the state refused to have peace committees to solve the Naxal problems.

It is difficult to suggest that the Kerala High Court Judge Muhamed Mustaque took a cue from the Supreme Court Judgment, but it declared that being Maoist is not a crime (Shyam Balakrishnan vs. State of Kerala, 2010; Times of

India, 2019). In other words, the propagation of the ideology of Naxalism is not a crime. The honourable judge made the point that the person cannot be detained unless the law of the land is broken. Therefore, the court directed the state to pay compensation to the detainee Shyam Balakrishnan on suspicion of his links with the Maoists. The court also directed the government to pay compensation of Rs. one lakh to the petitioner, which was challenged in the division bench of the same court comprising Chief Justice Hrishikesh Roy and Justice A.K. Jaysankaran Nambiyar, who declined to undo the single bench judgment. One can argue that how a speech of hate is a crime. After all, the person only speaks of, incites, but does not commit the crime. Balakrishnan was arrested by the special force, Thunderbolt commandos, based on local intelligence inputs. The single-judge bench decision was challenged because section 13 of the Prevention of Unlawful Activities Act held that even advocating and abetting such activities are unlawful. The state thus was not convinced as it found that if that criterion is applied, then it will be difficult to catch hold of those who, through pamphlets, propagate the hate campaign. The state argued that nobody, after the arrest, claimed that he had been working for the Maoists. The Maoists openly advocated for armed rebellion and the overthrow of the established governments. The learned judge had gone on to say that though Maoism and its political system are not recognised by the constitution, Maoism as an ideology is not a crime to believe in. The observation was not illegal, and merely believing in an ideology does not make one an accomplice in the act of crime. But the propagation of that ideology, which incites and makes violence an integral weapon to accomplish its ideological goals, cannot be treated as 'just belief in an ideology'. That amounts to advancing the logic of violence and giving credence to the same. One can further ask the question that if an ideology is not illegal, how come its practice and propagation be described as illegal?

This was clearly different from the Single bench judgement of the Chhattisgarh High Court on December 16, 2011, in a matter of Asit Sen Kumar Gupta vs State of Chhattisgarh. Justice Prashant Kumar Mishra had upheld the judgment of the trial court, which had declared the punishment to ASK Gupta for his association with, and acting for, the Naxalite networks (Asit Kumar Sen Gupta vs. State of Chhattisgarh). The charges were that Mr Sen Gupta stayed in a rented house at Gobrapara in Raipur, where he conspired with the members of the Communist Party of India (Maoist) and used to 'spread hatred and contempt' and excited /attempted to incite against a government established by law through speaking and writing against the government. The court observed that Mr Sengupta was supporting the banned organisation in conjunction with the Maoists, and as per the prosecution side, he indulged in unlawful activities as per the Act of 1967, as amended by the Act of 2004 (Asit Kumar Sen

Gupta vs. State of Chhattisgarh). Further, the suspected people used to visit him. The charges were that he helped the Maoists. The High Court interpreted Section 124 A of the IPC that deals with sedition, and for this, it referred to Kedar Nath Singh v. State of Bihar {AIR 1962 Supreme Court 955}.

Kedar Nath Singh was convicted by the trial Magistrate under Section 124-A of IPC for criticising the then government and had called upon the people to 'throw out the Government managed by the Capitalists, Zamindars'. He also equated the act of the Congress Party with the Britishers and gave a call to reduce it to ashes. He called Vinoba Bhave an agent of the Congress Party. The trial court accepted the charge of sedition, and the High Court upheld it. The accused filed a Special Leave Petition (SLP) and challenged both the conviction and the constitutional validity of Section 124-A of the IPC. While deciding the constitutional validity, the Hon'ble Supreme Court extensively deliberated upon the fundamental rights of freedom of expression and upheld the sedition charges against the petitioner. The Chhattisgarh High Court also relied upon the Supreme Court Judgement in a matter of Raghuvir Singh and the State of Bihar reported in 1986, in which the court observed that for sedition, it is not essential that the person in question is the author of the material. It observed that "distribution or circulation of seditious material may also be sufficient on the facts and circumstances of a case." To act as a courier is sometimes enough in a case of conspiracy. It is also not necessary that a person should be a participant in a conspiracy from start to finish. Conspirators may appear and disappear from stage to stage in a conspiracy. Needless to say, the observation of the Kerala High Court on Maoism and also the Supreme Court's leaning into the domain of public policy while dealing with SPO appointments did not augur well with the constitution experts who found the observations crossing the limits of constitutionality.

Arun Jaitley, who was a legal luminary, while raising the question against the judgment, observed that a legitimate question is whether the courts enforce the constitution or enforce ideologies. The Maoists are no reformers. Their principal objective is to destroy India's parliamentary democracy and establish a Communist dictatorship in India. The Maoists wish to dismantle every established democratic institution. If the Maoists were to take over India, the author of the judgment and other well-meaning judges like him would not be manning the Supreme Court. The court would be controlled by the ideology and ideological objects of the Maoists. The judgment itself makes an interesting reading. He went on to conclude that the judgment justified the Maoist violence and their acts of revolution on the one hand, and the denunciation of those who were involved in dismantling the Maoist activities in India. This court invited this criticism because it sought to justify the Maoist violence in a way.

The perception over the years has got traction that the courts have overlooked the security threats that Naxals pose to the internal security of India and have preferred the false humanitarian and democratic cry of the pro-Naxal intellectual echo system. The preferential treatment given to Gautam Navlakha and others associated with acts of actively supporting the cause of violence is a case to the point. Navlakha has been charged with inciting the Bhima Koregaon violence in Maharashtra in 2018. His association with the Naxal movement is something that is known to everyone. He has been in prison, technically, since April 2020. But he was not in jail. He was under house arrest at the direction of the court. The Bombay High Court had given him bail, but the NIA had appealed against this order in the Supreme Court. Navlakha appealed to the Supreme Court not to send him to jail, given his age and health condition. The court accepted his plea and directed for his house arrest in Mumbai. Interestingly, the house he lived in was on the first floor of the library building of the CPI (Marxist). The NIA did not want this. It was also of the view that Mr. Navlakha had suppressed the truth. And therefore, he should be sent back to Taloja Jail. But the bench of Justice K.M. Joseph and B.V. Nagarathna dismissed the petition because Mr Navlakha was too old and suffering from multiple ailments (The Wire, 2022). This again raised the question that the court was not looking into the law but other aspects besides the law in granting him bail. There is a section of society that thinks that the court has been lenient to the Maoists and their ideology. In contrast, Maoists welcomed it because, by doing so, the court protected the right of the citizens to dissent against the state. In the matter of Salwa Judum, the court had said that the Salwa Judum was intended against 'alleged Maoist extremists' (Nandini Sunder vs. State of Chhattisgarh). In the same order, the Court quoted a novel, "Heart of Darkness", by Joseph Conrad, in which the author argued how the colonial powers exploited the resources of the Africans who were struggling for life in the forest, whereas the colonial power was trying hard to expand its resources. This certainly smacked the ideological bias reflected in the judgment as it pushed ahead Naxal's premise that the violent armed struggle was aimed at bringing an egalitarian society. Do the Indian courts not know that the Chinese have been the mind behind fomenting the Naxal movement as well as the insurgency in the Northeast by funding the intellectuals and supplying funds and arms for the same? Their intent is simple: to make India bleed through such insurgent and violent acts. The kind of sophisticated arms that the Naxals handle and use against the state speaks volumes, besides the Chinese inspiration behind the Naxal movement in India. Tons of literature with primary sources are in the public domain today. This mindset is gradually on a downward slide with the coming of the Modi government in power, which has decided to use hard power to crush the Naxal movement in India.

CHAPTER 9

National Human Rights Commission and Salwa Judum

The introduction of Salwa Judum in the fight against the Maoists drew heavy criticism from left-liberal intelligentsia in India. It was demonised in public intellectual discourse in news media and academic campuses, in the courtrooms of the country. A slanderous campaign was launched, with the key points being that Salwa Judum employed women and children in the fight against the Maoists. And therefore, this violated the human rights of the minors. Secondly, instead of the state fighting the Naxals, it has raised a private militia and is lending support with arms and ammunition to fight against the Naxals. Third, the members of Salwa Judum have turned out to be extortionists and exploitative under the patronage of the state. Interestingly, nearly all such allegations were and are made against the Maoists, except that they are fighting with the patronage of the Indian state. The matter reached the highest court of India, which asked the National Human Rights Commission to look into the matter and submit the report before the Court. The National Human Rights Commission submitted its report in 2010, which appreciated as well as criticised Salwa Judum. But it was projected again in such a fashion that it appeared that Salwa Judum was outrightly condemned by the NHRC. The selective paragraphs were picked up from the Report, and it was made part of the narrative, into which even the Supreme Court of India got embroiled.

First, who were the people who led the campaign against Salwa Judum? Needless to say, they were the public intellectuals who were either working closely as activists or sympathisers in the urban areas. They are now depicted as 'Urban Naxals' by the right-wing intellectuals, which has now become a popular vocabulary. Even the Prime Minister of India, Narendra Modi, used the term in many of his political speeches and cautioned the people against their nefarious anti-India design. He said that Naxalism is getting uprooted from the Jungles but getting roots in urban centres (The Hindu, 2025). Many public intellectuals whose writings amply demonstrate that they have throughout stood with the Maoists' movement led the intellectual campaign against Salwa Judum.

The second category of people is the left-leaning human rights activists who, by nature, sound like liberals, but their true face is that they have largely leaned towards the left. They, too, are part of the first, but they are not the

 | HTTPS://DOI.ORG/10.1163/9789004765054-011

direct activists of Maoism. Some professional human rights groups, NGOs, and human rights and democratic and civil liberty rights watch groups, such as PUCL, PUDR, etc., are the ones that fall in this category. Their names resound like the organisations and institutions which are genuinely concerned and committed to the human rights violations and violations of civil rights and basic democratic freedoms of Individuals, but in reality, they preconceived agenda and ideological predisposition. These organisations, by and large, sing to the tunes of the political left, though occasionally a sharp divide is seen there also. For example, on the matter of Singur in West Bengal, Maoists were critical of CPI and CPM politics as much as the position of the Indian right on corporations. However, the right-wing ideology is their common enemy. Maoists were critical of the CPM government of West Bengal and Kerala for their highhandedness, use of repressive state apparatus and human rights violations. But the same CPI and CPM engaged in double speak when the BJP government used force to crush the Maoist movement. It is a harsh reality that the Naxals violate human rights, use violence to spread terror and fear in the minds of the people, and kill innocent civilians, but these organisations have seldom brought comprehensive reports on the barbarous acts of the Maoists. They would rather prefer to maintain stoic silence. The third category of people is the liberals who distance themselves from the left and claim to be Nehruvites and Gandhians. They are genuinely upset with the violence and death in the Naxal-infested areas. They never justified the violence of either the Naxals or the Salwa Judumists. Make no mistake that the Gandhians are largely critical of the Maoists' movement and their use of violence to create elements of terror in the minds of people to win or expand their support base.

There is yet another category of people who are depicted as anti-national by the right-wing organisations, as they are the ones who even prescribe secessionism of sub-nationalities. For example, Arundhati Roy, who carries a lot of goodwill among the Maoists because she is a harsh critic of the Indian state and goes on to the extent of defending the rights of secessionism of Kashmiri separatists if they do not wish to stay with India. These people have scant faith in the Indian democracy, and they hardly have regard for anything that is India. They receive funds and publicity for accusing India and its cultural heritage. That gives her the space in the media and an invitation to speak within the country as well as outside by those people and organisations who really pilot the vivisection agenda of India. A few years ago, Arundhati Roy exhorted that India needs 'Azadi from Kashmir as much as Kashmir needs Azadi from India'. According to her, there has not been a complete accession of the state of J&K in India, and the state, in fact, has been kept colonised by the Indian state. It is not difficult to understand why such people also constitute one of the important groups against the Salwa Judum. She ridicules the Indian democracy by calling it the biggest scam, the biggest PR myth.

Those who genuinely are concerned about the human rights violation want to see peace prevail in the tribal land, and there is no further bloodshed. Such people are Gandhian activists, and some apolitical NGOs working in the remote rural areas, etc. They seriously want the warring factions to denounce the violence and resolve the problems in context and totality. Such people have little political baggage and a closed, convoluted mind on the issue. But such groups and people are not very dominant, and they are at most confined to being part of the signature campaign of the other initiatives. There are several humanists who are working in the remote tribal areas despite receiving threats from the Naxals, as they are non-partisan and their activities are constructive to help out the poor and deprived.

A closer examination of the incidents, media coverage, and articles in the newspapers suggests that a well-organised and calibrated campaign was launched to demonise the Salwa Judum. When the campaign was launched, the signatories were also from different parts of the world, and the names included those who perhaps had no idea about Salwa Judum at all. The intellectual left has a list of such scholars across the globe who come on board and become part of the signature campaign to exercise pressure on a host of issues ranging from protests against building the Narmada Dam and compensation and rehabilitation of displaced people to civil nuclear installations in the South to communal issues in India. Now that the people have come to know that a network works in such cases, they do not lend too much credence to such voices. In the case of Salwa Judum, a well-known campaign was launched, but it did not succeed on the ground. And finally, Nandini Sundar, a well-known professor in the Department of Sociology, raised all the questions of murder, extortion and engagement of the minors and women by the state to tackle the menace of Naxalism. It had charges of rape and murder of poor tribals by the security forces and members of Salwa Judum. The gist of the whole exercise was that Salwa Judum was illegal and indulged in inhuman activities. The writ petition no.119/7- Kartam Joga and others vs. State of Chhattisgarh also contained the list of such 500 victims. The writ petition also contained details of how inhuman conditions prevailed in the Judum camps.

The left liberal intellectuals opened a barrage of a campaign based on the report of the NHRC, picking the selective pages and paragraphs. It was projected as if the report of NHRC outrightly rejected Salwa Judum as illegal and accepted that it was engaged in inhuman acts against the poor tribals. A careful reading of the report suggests that the NHRC report was highly balanced, and it described in detail the good as well as the bad parts of the Salwa

Judum activities. In other words, Salwa Judum was not villainised the way the left-liberal intellectual echo-system projected it as such in the media and the public discourse. It was presented in the same manner in the Supreme Court of India.

Contrary to the popular perception created by the media, the NHRC report nails down, in fact, most of the allegations against the Salwa Judum. The report of the National Human Rights Commission is an eye-opener to all those who so far believed that the government of Chhattisgarh is really engaged in atrocities on the poor tribals by erecting, supporting and sustaining the Salwa Judum movement in the state. Findings of the NHRC nail the lies and the manufactured malicious campaign against the Salwa Judum movement. Turning the table on the Naxals, the team of the National Human Rights Commission which visited the state and talked directly to the people in the camps and the villages found that the Naxals were the real culprits and it is they who are actually involved in atrocities and extortion, destruction of public property and deliberately destroying the schools and health centres, roads and other means of development as all these provide them the safe, secured and fertile terrain to propagate the ideology.

1 Salwa Judum under Scrutiny: NHRC's Observations

The first and foremost charges against the Salwa Judum were that it was created, funded and sustained by the government. The detractors accused the government of organising a private militia to take on the Naxals, and the Salwa Judum movement is not at all a movement of the common tribals against the Naxalite movement, but one that is designed and made to work by the government. The government of Chhattisgarh consistently refused these charges and held the position that the state was not the mind behind the movement at all. But certainly, it has backed the movement of the people who were willing to come out openly to oppose the Naxalites. The NHRC investigation approved the government's stand and maintained it at several places in the report, where it dismissed the human rights groups' contention that the movement was created and sustained by the government directly. The NHRC team, which went into details of the events, noted that the movement was not created by the government and thus it was and is certainly a movement of the tribals against the Naxals' atrocities, extortion and more importantly, their interfering with the local economy, taboos and religious rituals. The report categorically reiterates it at several places that the Salwa Judum movement started as 'a spontaneous revolt of the tribals against years of atrocities and harassment suffered by them at the hands of the Naxalites' (NHRC Report, 2009:32). The role of the government came later when the Naxals started retaliating against such resistance to maintain their dominance in the region (NHRC Report, 2009:15). The report states that the Salwa Judum camps came into existence when people felt helplessness and insecurity against the Naxals' onslaughts. Such attacks became frequent after the launch of Jan Jagaran Abhiyan, aimed at educating the people against the Naxalite movement and encouraging and persuading them to join the front, which intends to do so.

It is a case to point that Shri Bhuneshwar Singh Thakur was kidnapped from a Jan Jagaran meeting held in Kotrapal village in Bijapur district. He was later on killed by the Naxals on 27th July 2005. The leaflet left with the dead body contained a stern warning to the villagers to participate in any such people's programme aimed against the Maoists. Nearly a week later, on 7th July, Vijay Giri, a member of the district Panchayat, was kidnapped and killed by the Naxals (NHRC Report, 2009:13). Such incidents were sufficient to weaken the resolve of the villagers to come out openly against the Naxals. Villagers had no option but to flee to the nearby police stations for their safety. Police, on the other hand, had insufficient staff and resources to meet their security and other needs. They had no food or shelter. What could have been done except making an alternative arrangement and encouraging them to fight out the battle against the Maoists? It was in this context that the Salwa Judum camps came up. People approached the police for their safety, and the latter came forward to support them, and also arranged food, clothes and other basic needs. The state found an opportunity in it to mobilise the tribal populations and the common masses against the Maoists. As the police were instrumental in lending support to the Salwa Judum camps, most of these camps came up close to the police. This also endorses the point that people joined the Judum camps out of fear of the Naxals.

It is true that all those who joined the camps did so not willingly. The government and its agencies played a crucial role in persuading and convincing them. The nature and magnitude of the fear that the Maoists had created made it difficult for the police to galvanise that much manpower to cover the security of all villages, which are sparsely scattered in the tribal belts. The government convinced them that their stay in the Judum camps was important for both the villagers and the police. However, most of them joined on their own out of fear of the Naxals. This is evident from the fact that the number of tribals living in Salwa Judum camps reduced from 60000 to 40000 with the passage of time, when people realised that the threat was minimised. These forty thousand people were closely linked to the activism of Judum, such as SPOs or their family members, as they fear their lives could be in danger in case they go back home to live. It was also found that thousands of people who went back home, leaving the Judum camps, found it difficult to handle their lands and properties and manage their crops. Thousands of members of Salwa Judum also preferred to go back to the villages during the day and came back at night to stay in the Judum camps. This was precisely because they had no confidence in secure living in the villages. Such people were also receiving positive feelings from the Naxals, as they were not directly connected to the Judum activities. Yet they did not muster the courage to stay in their villages.

The second important question that the petition raised was that people were being forced to join the Salwa Judum Movement. The NHRC report contested this. Contrary to the claims of the human rights activists who said that the Salwa Judum activists are engaged in terrorising the innocent tribals to join the movement against the Naxals, the commission found that it was the Naxals who actually are and were engaged in the forceful employment of children and women in the Naxalite cause. The Human Rights Commission noted that the Naxals forced 'the tribal families to send their minor children to work for the Naxal movement'. There have been instances of Naxals forcing the students to withdraw from the schools so that they could be commissioned into the corps of comradeship. Several organisations working in the field of watching human rights violations, including the National Human Rights Commission, have noted it in several pages in their report, have categorically pointed out that there has been forced induction of the people in the Naxal movement.

NHRC also rebutted the charge that the Salwa Judum members harass the commuters by illegally checking their vehicles and extorting money from such commuters. Critics of Salwa Judum alleged that check posts created in all the disturbed areas in order to check the fleeing of the criminals were used by the SPOs to extort money. This was found as a wild allegation. It was true that SPOs of the Judum were certainly involved in it. However, it must be put forward that when the SPOs discharged such activities, police and Paramilitary or security forces were also there. The allegation that at such check points Salwa Judum activists were engaged in extortion of money was also unfound by the National Human Rights commission (NHRC Report, 2009:31). The NHRC investigative team did not came across 'any complain of Salwa Judum carrying out illegal checking of vehicles, levying illegal taxes on occupants of vehicles and indulging in looting the occupants of vehicles when they refuse to pay the illegal taxes' (NHRC Report, 2009:100).

2 Ignoring Development

The sympathisers of the Naxals always blame the state for ignoring the development of the region and hold the non-reach of the state to these areas to be one of the primary reasons behind the rise of the Naxal movement. They use the logic of underdevelopment for the justification of violence in the region. They claim to have non-negotiable faith in non-violence, but by equating the underdevelopment with violence, they seem to be tactically supporting the violence. Anyway, they are hardly seen condemning the anti-development and destructive activities of the Naxals. NHRC found that Naxals discourage education and encourage the children, often forcing them to join Bal Sangham (NHRC Report, 2009:25). Several children left their schools because of the fear of the Naxals. The NHRC report also noted that most of the school buildings were destroyed by the Naxals in the villages. It is not only the schools but also health and other services were disrupted by the Naxals. Naxals deliberately target road constructions and bridges on rivers because they facilitate the early reach of the security forces in the Naxal-hit areas. They 'dig up and blow up' the roads in the area of dominance to restrict the security forces. Moreover, whoever takes the contract is subjected to heavy extortion of money. As a result, the private contractors do not wish to come to take up a job in the Naxal-infested areas. The government has been forced to employ organisations like 'Border Road Organisation' to construct the national Highways in such areas (NHRC Report, 2009:24).

Not only do they disrupt the developmental activities, but they are also involved in merciless killings of the poor tribals to inject fear in their minds so that they could not muster the courage to resist the Naxalites. More importantly, the method and the manner in which they use violence are not only heinous and atrocious but also barbarous in nature. They do so by injecting fear and terror into the minds of the people so that they cannot muster the courage to ignore or resist the dictates of the Naxals. Slitting the neck and hanging the dead body on the road so that every passerby could see it are some of the most common murders that the Naxals inflict on those who refuse to follow their dictates or work against them. They hold Jan Adalats to pronounce the death sentence or other kinds of punishment. The NHRC report extensively notes the heinous crimes in which the Naxalites are involved. Writing about the merciless killings of the tribals, it notes, 'Naxalites sometimes chose to kill the detractors or police informers.' The killings in the Jan Adalat organised by the Naxals demonstrate the worst form of heinousness. The people in such Adalats, in many cases, are not killed in one go. The Naxalites start beating the person and chopping off various parts of the body, making sure that he does not die quickly. Sometimes the beating and chopping of the body parts continue for hours so that the person suffers the maximum pain (NHRC Report, 2009:23). Sometimes they would slit the neck of a person and hang them on a tree on the road so that every passerby could see the death. All this is done to terrorise the locals to the extent that they could not raise a voice against them and easily submit to their dictates. There have been instances of 'indiscriminate killings of tribals' by the Naxals. The Darbhagudda, Errabore and Manikonta massacres were executed by the Naxals, in which several tribals lost their lives.

The NHRC report makes it clearly evident that there had been a well-calculated design to defame the Salwa Judum campaign so that it could be stopped. And the biggest in the series came in the form of several fake charges of serious nature, such as rape, extortion, and merciless killings of innocent tribals by the Salwa Judum activists. But except for the few, the majority of the charges turned out to be fake and forged. For example, Shri Kartam Yoga, one of the petitioners in the Writ Petition no. 119/07, stated that he was so badly beaten up by the activists of Salwa Judum that he had to undergo an operation. But the NHRC team found that, actually, it was his hernia, which was long overdue, that was operated upon (NHRC Report, 2009:38). And in no way did this operation result from the beating of the person by Salwa Judum activists at all. Similarly, one petitioner had charged that in the village Pakela on Sukma Jagdalpur Road, an old lady had died of thirst, and another, Korsa Bukka, had starved to death after the village was burnt down by the security forces and Salwa Judum activists. But this was found to be fake by the NHRC team. It found that 'no old lady in the village had died in the village due to thirst'. The villagers also told the team that there was no one by the name of 'Korsa Bukka' in the village at all, and thus the name mentioned in the petition was found to be fake. The petitioners had also mentioned the names like Korsha Budhram, Gudyula Kanna, Korsa Mallaiah, Wodyulo Vimaiya, Nilkand Kanna, Korsa Bandhu, Korsa Dharmaiya, Korsa Maiya and Chinu Pujari. These names were faked as none of them were the residents of the said village (NHRC Report, 2009:71–72).

There were also instances of violence and killings by the Naxals, which were attributed to the police, security forces and the Salwa Judum activists to discredit them among the tribal people. Even the accidental deaths of the Naxalites in the villages were credited to the Salwa Judum activists. For example, Madvi Bonda alias Vijja of village Keshkutal under Bhairamgarh police station was killed while he was trying to plant a bomb, which exploded, in the Salwa Judum rally. He was a known Naxalite. But when he lost his life in the accidental explosion of the bomb, the killing was attributed to the security forces. It was propagated that Salwa Judum activists had executed the explosion to kill him.

In one of the petitions, the petitioners had claimed that in the village of Gangalur, a woman named Yenki had been killed, and three houses were burnt down by the Salwa Judum activists. This also turned out to be fake after an enquiry. The NHRC report rather indicated that it was the Naxalites who had actually burnt the said houses. Interestingly, it was also found that no person in the name of Yenki and Madvi Sanku was killed at any point in time. Their names were not even on the voter rolls. They were found to be fake names. On the contrary, the Naxals killed several people in the village between 2005 and 2008. The NHRC report lists out the names of the person and the case diary, which gives a total of 32. But the petitioners' document did not mention the name of any of these. And this was deliberate, as these thirty-two people were, as villagers informed the NHRC team, killed by the Naxals (NHRC Report, 2009:48–49). The story of the village of Hariyal Cherali was also not very different. The names of the 11 people allegedly killed by the Salwa Judum activists and the security forces were actually kidnapped and taken to the Okenara hills to make them participate in the Naxalite meet. Later on, all of them were found killed, though only 9 bodies were recovered. Prior to this incident, earlier too, Mangu Kadti & Budhram and Bhimsen (NHRC Report, 2009:52–53) from the same village had been killed by the Naxals. These were the people from the same family and had always been the target of the Naxalites.

In the writ petition of Kartam Joga and Others vs State of Chhattisgarh, a long list of 537 people was given to have been killed by the Salwa Judum activists. The inquiry team of the NHRC went into 168 representative cases extensively to unravel the truth. What it found was really startling. It noted that many of these allegations were 'based on hearsay' (NHRC Report, 2009:101). In many cases, the people listed as having been killed by the Salwa Judum activists turned out to have been killed by the Naxalites to defame the anti-Naxal uprisings. Many of the people listed in the killed category were also the Naxals who belonged to this or that village, killed by the police in an encounter. They were not killed by the Salwa Judum activists (NHRC Report, 2009:102). In order to thicken the list of the killed and enhance the magnitude of the crime, even the people who met a natural death were attributed to the Salwa Judum activists. Also, the people who were listed as 'deceased' were found alive in the village (NHRC Report, 2009:103). All this goes to suggest that Naxalites and their echo-system in cities structured the design to deliberately malign the Salwa Judum because it was damaging the Naxal movement significantly, as people were coming and joining the movement against the Naxalites.

3 Cases of Rape against Salwa Judum Activists

The petitioners had complained of several rape cases against Salwa Judum activists. The commission, however, did not find it true at all. The petition had categorically listed out the names of the victims. And the petitioner, Nalini Sundar, had made it categorically clear that these names were enlisted on the basis of a meeting she had with the victims. As the charges were serious in nature, the members of the NHRC decided to meet the victims in person in order to establish the truth. They expressed their desire and informed the petitioners of the same almost ten days in advance in order to ensure the presence of the victims. But to the surprise of the members, not even a single victim turned up for cross-examination. Instead of presenting the victims before the Commission, the Petitioners came with the statements of the victims. The Commission did not find them convincing on cross-examination. The fact was that many of the allegations were charged without even bothering to verify them (NHRC Report, 2009:36). And this fact was admitted by none other than one of the petitioners, Ms. Manish Kunjam, before the commission.

It is not a hidden fact that Naxals have been forcing the tribals to send their children to work for them. Organisations that watch out for Naxal activities know it and have been reported several times in the news media. It is difficult to believe that a fact which is so well-known in the public domain is unknown to these Human Rights organisations. However, in their petition, they selectively targeted the Salwa Judum movement for using young children and women in their fight against the Naxals. Thousands of such stories have come up so far in the media, where it has been found that Naxals used women and children during encounters with the police to escape. That should not be used to suggest that Salwa Judum members did not engage young children and women. Even the NHRC admitted that all those who joined the Judum camps or the movement did not do it based on their allegiance to the cause. There were several who resisted it. There were many who saw opportunity in it, and many people were either allured to join or were forced to join. But then this also applied to the people who joined the Naxalite movement. Many houses were asked emphatically to donate a young boy or girl for the revolutionary activities in order to fight against the discriminatory and repressive regimes.

No doubt, there were several people who were initially reluctant to join the Salwa Judum and the Naxal movement. In both cases, people were uncertain of their security. Initially, people were reluctant to join Salwa Judum. But this reluctance emanated from the element of insecurity. They were not sure that the state will be able to provide enough security against the violence of the Maoists. Similarly, those who joined the Naxal movement did the mathematics how it was going to benefit them. There are plenty of instances which suggest that people were forced to join the Naxal movement. So was the case with Salwa Judum. There were instances of Salwa Judum activists forcing the villagers to join their rallies and processions (NHRC Report, 2009:27). That started a competition between the leaders of the Salwa Judum and the Naxals, resulting in pro-Naxal and pro-Salwa Judum polarisation. There was another set of people who were not on either side but were dragged into the battle. On the days of rallies organised by the Salwa Judum leaders, villagers used to leave their villages. But all those who left the villages were not the sympathisers of the Naxals, but they bore the brunt of the Judum activists (NHRC Report, 2009:27). Such an atmosphere of conflict has resulted in major people displacement in the areas where both the Naxals and the Salwa Judum activists are active.

Apart from these serious allegations, the human rights activists who petitioned before the court also cited the subhuman conditions prevailing in the Salwa Judum camps, which were one of the reasons why they wanted to ban the Salwa Judum campaign, adding a human and economic aspect to their campaign. It was argued that these camps do not provide the basic needs of life, such as education, proper food, etc. It was argued in the petition that such camps have deplorable conditions, and by displacing the tribals to such camps, it was, in fact, placing the tribals in more pathetic conditions. First, most of those who joined the camps came on their own. And they came because most of them either had lost their kith and kin at the hands of Naxals or were feeling the threats from the Naxals. But more than that, the NHRC team did not find such allegations correct at all. It found that the camps were better managed. One argument forwarded by the petitioners was that the children in the camps were not getting educational facilities, and thus, the government was playing with the future of the children. But such allegations fall flat, especially in the light of the fact that Naxals were the ones who were responsible for destroying the existing school buildings and forcing the children to join their ranks.

The NHRC report did not find in its investigation any discrimination by the police and administration towards the villagers who did not support Salwa Judum. Though such charges were there in the petition, the people who charged did not name any specific village where 'district administration had deliberately withdrawn any services or development work' just because the people of the village did not support the anti-naxal operations (NHRC Report, 2009:70). The NHRC team specifically asked Nandini Sunder if she had any idea of it at all so that the NHRC team could verify it, but the former showed ignorance of it. Thus, she was proved false by the NHRC team in her claim that she had mentioned in her petition.

All this is not to suggest that everything associated with Salwa Judum was fine, and allegations made against it were completely wrong and baseless. There were elements of truth in charges made against the Judum. And this was acknowledged by the NHRC as well. The NHRC accepted that there were instances of high-handedness by the Salwa Judum activists, even the burning of houses belonging to the Naxals was found to be true, but these were exceptional. So was the case with indiscriminate killings by the members of Salwa Judum. There were some encounters that raised questions and suspicion. The NHRC report clearly spelt out a few such cases, such as the encounter in Santoshpur under Bijapur police station on 31-03-2007, wherein three villagers were killed in Hirapuram under Basguda police station. The NHRC could single out only one instance in which it was found that the Salwa Judum activists were found behind the killing of a person. This, however, was not registered at the police station. NHRC also came across the false FIR against the tribals supposedly to be pro-Naxals, as it happened in the case of the Matwada camp incident (NHRC Report, 2009:102).

The NHRC held that there were several Acts that were applied by the police and armed forces along with the SPOs, which were all attributed to the Salwa Judum movement, which was not correct. The NHRC report repeatedly made a distinction between the Salwa Judum activists and the SPOs. SPOs, according to the Commission, were justified under the Chhattisgarh Police Acts, and they were different from the Salwa Judum activists. SPOs were employed by the state to help the state armed forces in their combat operations against the Naxals. SPOs were the people who had been appointed by the government from the tribal villages themselves to protect the people living in the Salwa Judum camps. SPOs' help was crucial for the police because the former were aware of the terrain and therefore much useful for tracking the Naxals. SPOs, thus, according to the NHRC, were the police officers recruited under Section 17 of the Police Act, 1861 and Section 9 of the Chhattisgarh Police Act 2000 (NHRC Report, 2009:27).

On the other hand, Salwa Judum activists were relatively non-violent activists who were engaged in mobilising the masses against the Naxalites by invoking consciousness among the tribals through village meetings, holding big rallies and people's programmes in which they educated the poor tribals why they should not support the Naxals and openly should come out to oppose them. Therefore, they were the ones who were mainly involved in the advocacy programme of the Salwa Judum. Their job was to convince the people why to join the Salwa Judum movement and why to oppose and renounce the path of revolution and violence, as espoused by the Naxals. For this, they used to hold rallies from one village to another, asking the young and the women to fight the menace of the Naxal violence in the area. This overlapping interpretation and failure to make the distinction between the SPOs and the leaders of the Salwa Judum have resulted in a wrong conclusion, in which even the operations by the SPOs and the Security forces against the Naxals have been attributed to Salwa Judum (NHRC Report, 2009:27). The truth lay in the fact that Salwa Judum activists were not saints, and they too indulged in bad activities like beating people and extortion of money. But this was found in a few cases and not a new normal at all. The charges that the cases against them were not registered in the police station are squarely balanced by the fact that the Naxal violence went unreported in the area of their dominance because of fear. Many cases were exaggerated, for example, nearly 50 tribals lost their lives in the remote Konta block in the Southern tip of Dantewada. They all were subjected to the merciless killings by the Maoists. Some of whom had been killed in Jan Adalats in full public view in the most gruesome manner, such as beheading or gunning down, but no one from their families mustered the courage to report to the police. This was not the story of one part of the state, but everywhere where the guns of the Naxals dominate.

Interestingly, contrary to the perception built through news narratives, detractors of the Salwa Judum prescribed banning the Salwa Judum. But this was false and fabricated. Rather, the NHRC strongly supported the continuity of the Salwa Judum. It held that disbanding of the Salwa Judum means 'putting all those who are in camps' at the moment at the 'mercy of the Naxalites' (NHRC Report, 2009:20). The NHRC appreciated the role of the SPOs in containing the Naxal movement. It further noted that it could be possible because the SPOs were appointed from the locals. They were well aware of the terrain and the people, and therefore comparatively better placed to identify the people useful for the police and the local administration. Many of the SPOs are also ex-members of the Sangham, hence they knew very well the modus operandi of the Maoists. There were several villages that were earlier under the control of the Naxals, popularly known as 'liberated zones. They could be liberated with the active support of the Salwa Judum. If they are now under the control of the paramilitary forces, the credit goes to Salwa Judum activists as well. The Commission, therefore, strongly supported Salwa Judum and made it clear that it was not at all irrelevant (NHRC Report, 2009:35). The petitioners also held the position that the Naxalite violence has increased due to Salwa Judum, and therefore, it should be discontinued. NHRC did not buy this argument precisely because it found the argument tilted deliberately to favour what is being carried on in the tribal areas by the Naxalites. It indirectly supported the subjugation of the tribals by the Naxalites.

In fact, the Salwa Judum badly broke the spine of the Naxal movement. This was also admitted by the National Human Rights Commission. As a result, the Naxals were working overnight to get it stopped at any cost. They understood that the continued success of the Salwa Judum would make it difficult for them to continue their dominance in the region of their influence. Naxals were engaged in all sorts of brutal activities ranging from merciless killings to kidnapping of people and men in business for extortion, and so on. Their support base rested not on convincing the people about their purpose and application of means, but on a reign of terror in the minds of the people. Salwa Judum, despite all its weaknesses, was a kind of people's resistance movement raised by the police or spontaneously evolved, but certainly driven by the spirit of confronting the Maoists in the same language that the Maoists were using to spread terror and establish their dominance in the region. Gradually, it started costing the Naxals dear, and therefore, they used their extended comrades and their ecosystem in the cities to launch a slanderous campaign raising the question of legality, human rights violations, and so on. The NHRC nailed their lies, but the media carried the stories that supported the campaign of the Maoists. The urban elites wrote articles in newspapers, picking up selective paragraphs. Editors had no time to read through the entire pages of the NHRC Report on Salwa Judum. The people from the government side also had no time to read through the report in its entirety. It could have saved Salwa Judum had they taken the time to read it and feed the people in the Supreme Court.

CHAPTER 10

State and Political Response to the Maoists

On July 8, 2011, all the newspapers carried the story with varied headlines, but the content was almost the same. The central government has not taken the judgment of the Supreme Court as a positive decision at all, and it was all set to file a review petition against the decision[1] (The Economic Times, 2011). It was reported that the former Prime Minister was briefed by the former Home Minister P. Chidambaram on the decision of the court on Salwa Judum, and the minister portrayed very grim consequences of this decision of disbanding and disarming the SPOs (The Economic Times, 2011). While the state government was worried that the Naxals would escalate the attack in times to come in the absence of SPOs, the central government worries were driven by the fact that it will have an adverse impact on the practice of appointment of the SPOs in many states of the North East, Jammu and Kashmir and also in Kerala (The Economic Times, 2011).

Though the judgment of the Supreme Court had made it clear that its judgment was restricted to the state of Chhattisgarh only, but the central government was not very convinced, and it realised that sooner or later, the demand for withdrawal of appointment of SPOs in this state would also come out. The apprehension and fear were writ large that it would be extremely difficult for the party and the government to neutralise such a campaign. The government was also worried about the security consequences in the states hit by militancy and left extremism. The Central Government, as was reported in the press, conveyed by the Solicitor General of India that the review petition can be filed (The Economic Times, 2011; FirstPost, 2011). It was also reported that the state government also was thinking of filing the review petition. But all this did not happen.

The judgment came in August 2011, and the state was to go for assembly elections in November 2013. The Congress government at the centre preferred to look at the political dividends in future and decided to observe silence instead of swiftly arguing against the judgment. The State government also did not file the review petition in view of centre's reluctance. It assessed the situation and drew the conclusion that in the absence of the concurrence of the central government, it was difficult to win the case. Accordingly, the DGP of

1 Union Home Minister P. Chidambaram briefed the then Prime Minister Manmohan Singh on Supreme Court's controversial verdict for disbanding and disarming Special Police Officers.

 | HTTPS://DOI.ORG/10.1163/9789004765054-012

the state made a statement to the effect that the government would comply with the judgment of the Supreme Court[2] (The Economic Times, 2012). The state thus lost a major battle against the Naxals by agreeing to dismantle the village vigilante groups across the state, which it had enabled to counter the insurgency in the state.

1 Government Going Soft on Naxals: UPA I and UPA II

The decision of the political class on Naxals has been, by and large, governed by the ideological position and political convenience. What suits the politics is far more important than the security concerns. Their stands have varied with time accordingly. The BJP and Shiv Sena have been the only exceptions to this fact. It is because their political positions converge with their ideological positions, whereas they stand in dichotomy in the case of other political formations in India. The glaring example is the rehabilitation of Vinayak Sen in the power structure of the central government after release from jail (The Hindu, 2011). The left organisations went all out to get him released. There was an intellectual echo system which was round the clock to get him released. His arrest was depicted as India's war on a man of peace (Sharma, 2010). Vinayak Sen was imprisoned on the order of the session court of Raipur, which had sentenced him to life imprisonment. The charge against Vinayak Sen was that while he worked for the poor and tribals in the remote forest areas, he also worked for the Naxals. The then government of Chhattisgarh charged him under various sections of the Indian Penal Code (IPC) as well as other provisions[3] (Global Freedom Expression, 2021). But once he was released from jail, he was readily accommodated in the government. The government of India, led by Congress, placed him on the advisory board of one of the committees of the Planning Commission (The Hindu, 2011). Though the claim was that

2 Though contempt notice was served to the state government for not complying with its order. Nalani Sundar and Ramchandra Guha had approached the court against the decision of the state government to regularise the services of the SPOs by augmenting them into State Police Force.

3 Binayak Sen was charged of Sedition in 2010 for possessing the Maoists documents and supporting the movement by acting as 'Naxalite Daakiya'. His bail application was rejected by the Chhattisgarh High Court which said that the right to freedom does not stretch up to preaching and exciting disloyalty to the state. Initially the Supreme Court also rejected his bail application but when he moved second time he was granted bail with direction to the trial court to set the terms. It was unprecedented that the Supreme Court did not give any reason for granting him the bail.

it was done to benefit from his wide experiences in the tribal belts, in reality, it was a tactical political ploy of the Congress government to subject the state government of Chhattisgarh to criticism and win over the Naxal-supported tribals to their side. This is not the singular incident which demonstrates the directionless approach of the government. In fact, there was a wide difference between what it said for public consumption and what it actually did on the ground. A careful look at the changing stances and tone and tenor of public speeches throws some pattern to decipher.

2 Government under UPA I

Salwa Judum was started in 2005 by a Congress leader, Mahendra Karma. He was not under the influence of the state government of the BJP, but it was a result of his personal conviction. The involvement of the poor people in the Naxal movement, destruction of the rural economy, abuse and extortion of money, derailment of development activities, and killing of innocent civilians drew him to conclude that what the Naxals were doing was not the right path to the empowerment of people and their emancipation from deprivation. But the Congress Party neither at the state nor at the centre level approved it. The politics prevailed over, and the state unit of the Congress Party found that it amounted to strengthening the hands of the BJP government. Mahendra Karma was accused by his own party members of doing harm to the party's interests by hobnobbing with the BJP regime for his personal interests.

The former central government, led by Congress, too, did not miss any chance to discredit the then government in the state. The impact of the left parties which were supporting the UPA-I was clearly visible. Though the CPM in Bengal and Kerala dealt ruthlessly with the Naxal movement and forced them to flee to other states to have their bases, the party lent full support to the Maoists by raising their victimisation at the hands of the armed forces. Other allies of the CPM thereafter followed suit. They pressurised the central government to deal with the case more humanely instead of using the might of the state to suppress it. This was contrary to the administrative understanding and long-drawn conviction of the former central government, which favoured the use of measured but decisive force to control the Maoists' activities. But the central government of the UPA during that time succumbed to the political pressure of the left.

This dichotomy and dualism of the mainstream left in dealing with the Naxal movement is not very difficult to discern. The CPM did not want Maoists to have their footprint in the states where they were in power. But their position in regard to other states has not been the same. They publicly dissociate, disapprove and even condemn the Maoists' violence. But they do not approve of the state actions, which for them are an example of state repression. They make a distinction between the violence by the state and the Naxals. When the state retaliates, their outcry is audible enough, but when the Naxals kill the armed forces and civilians, their criticism is either soft or conditional. When armed forces were blown out, the condemnation was soft with a rider, but it is louder on the jailing of Vinayak Sen.

The support of the CPM to the Maoists and the groups leading the movement against Salwa Judum is also because of the work of a number of Non-Governmental Organisations (NGOs) in the remote areas. The majority of the NGOs are funded from outside. They are largely critical of the state on issues of violation of human rights, environmental degradation, and the displacement of people due to development projects. These left parties earlier were sceptical of these NGOs as they ate into what could be their potential social support base. Many of the new social movements emerged in these areas, which were actively supported by the left intellectuals as they were against the state. The left parties, however, gradually started forging alliances with these NGOs and the new social movements. Be it the Narmada movement under the leadership of Medha Patekar or the Jungle Bachao Andolan (JBA) of the eighties.

Their own position on the human rights issue has been pathetically dismal. They made a number of political killings in Bengal and Kerala, where they ruled for decades (Chathukulam & Manasi, 2022; Jacob, 2022). They were ruthless on the Maoists when they were in power in Bengal and often accused Mamta Banerjee of having been hobnobbing with the Naxals to enlarge the party's support base. When Trinamool Congress organised a Lalgarh rally, CPM members raised the issue in the parliament and charged and questioned the silence of the former central government, as the state unit of the Congress party was also supportive of it (The Economic Times, 2010).

As the left intelligentsia and the NGOs were up against Salwa Judum, the left parties exercised their influence and forced the central government not to support Salwa Judum. This also became far more obvious during the UPA II regime, in which the Left was no longer a constituent and started cooperating with the state government on the issue of Salwa Judum, both in armed solutions and in the Supreme Court. There was a vertical divide within Congress on this issue at the state level. A faction of the state unit of the Congress party in Chhattisgarh, led by Ajit Yogi, also opposed Salwa Judum. This group tried to convince the Central Leadership that supporting the state government on the issue would further shrink the party's social base and seal the political fortune of the party forever. The central leadership of the Congress Party saw merit in the argument. As a result, the then central government recoiled and made a retreat on its earlier stand. It fell to the political mathematics of electoral losses and gains in the state. The government of the time had earlier adopted the policy of 'clear, hold and develop' (The Hindu, 2013). That means, to defeat the Naxals, maintain the dominance, and develop the region economically so that the Naxals could not get ground for their acts in future. But soon the government retreated from the aggressive plan it had desired to embark upon.

And none other but Rahul Gandhi and Sonia Gandhi sent out political messages to this effect when they talked about the human touch to solve the Naxal problem. Then Congress Vice-president who visited the state of Jharkhand gave a political speech to woo the Naxals (Tiwari, 2008). This must have come at that time from the local party unit, which was facing a tough political battle in the state to regain its displaced foothold. This also resulted from the kind of image that the advisors of Rahul wanted for him. Rahul was carving out the image of a young, upright leader who is down-to-earth and is concerned about the poor and deprived. He visited the house of Kalawati in UP and stayed overnight with the poor family. This was widely publicised in the media. Media advisors of Rahul Gandhi sought to craft a new image that he was not elitist, as is projected in mainstream media. It is learnt that Rahul was advised that he should not endorse the statist approach to handle the Naxal problem as it would send out a wrong message of him being anti-poor, anti-Dalit because Naxals social support comes from these sections of society, which had gone against the Congress and whose support the party was trying hard to retrieve in its favour to brighten its political fortunes. Two things emerged from it. First, it was a calculated electoral stand, and secondly, it was driven by the endeavour to create a pro-poor political image of Rahul Gandhi. This had an immediate bearing on the government's response. When the Naxals created a lot of hue and cry across the country and also filed a case to stop Salwa Judum, the central government's attitude at that time was not found very encouraging at all. Its replies filed on the subject in the Supreme Court were not that encouraging.

The same happened in 2010 when the Supreme Court asked the former Central government to file a reply on Salwa Judum. The central government informed the court in writing that it did not support Salwa Judum. The then Solicitor General Gopal Subrahmanayam, who appeared in the court representing the central government, told the court that, "We have instructed the state government not to extend any support to Salwa Judum activists or to any private armed group" (The Hindu, 2010). The affidavit of the central government that was filed in 2009 was reversed in 2010. In 2009, it said that it was not averse to Salwa Judum, whereas in 2010 it reported to the Supreme Court that it did not favour lending support to any private militia to counter left-wing terrorism (The Hindu, 2010).

The affidavit of the state government made it clear that the state government was not behind the creation of Salwa Judum. It was a people's initiative in their self-protection, and it was the duty of the state to stand by those who were rising to the occasion against perpetrators of violence and terror in society. It had a duty to protect and enable those to ensure their self-protection who were willing to resist and defend themselves against the Naxals' plan to maintain dominance in the region. In other words, the state was merely providing security to those who were fighting against the forces which were against the state. It appeared that, having come out of the left influence under UPA I, the then government of India must be taking a tough and conscious decision on how to tackle Naxalites. The initial jerks also gave hope when the government was reported to have committed to supporting Salwa Judum (Times of India, 2009). But soon the government returned to the old position adopted during UPA-I.

It would be worth noting here that the Administrative Reforms Commission under Veerappa Moily and an expert committee on Naxalism constituted by the Planning Commission also came out against the Salwa Judum (Second Administrative Reform Commission 8th Report, 2008). Needless to say, the report was an eyewash, and it was a ploy of the Congress Party to hide behind the report of what it wanted as a politically correct move. This committee was constituted to give a recommendation on the political lines of the Congress. And it did not disappoint the party. As expected, the committee recommended the disbanding of Salwa Judum. The committee put the whole blame on the state government for the vigilante and declared it unconstitutional and against the spirit of democratic politics (Second Administrative Reform Commission 8th Report, 2008). The committee also noted that counter-insurgency movements were the handiwork of the state government. And more astonishing, it was a law-and-order problem, and the state cannot delegate the same to an extra-constitutional authority (Second Administrative Reform Commission 8th Report, 2008). Needless to say, this report was more a political document aimed at two purposes. On the one hand, it wanted to keep the left faction of the UPA in good humour, on the other, it intended to embarrass the then state government. It also had another dimension that the CPM government in Bengal, which used all repressive measures to eliminate the Naxals, and which forced the extremists to shift their operational base towards Jharkhand and Chhattisgarh, and which was well aware of the Naxals menace, was most vocal among the coalition partners against Salwa Judum.

The same political pronouncements were made by the party after the gruesome ambush in Satara district of Chhattisgarh in which 15 armed forces and a civilian were killed. The CPI in its press statement condemned the death of armed forces at the hands of the Naxals, but at the same time blamed the state government for not responding to the alerts sent to the state by the centre (CPI (M) Press Release, 2014). The party changed the explanation and said that the Naxal question is a political question, and it should be dealt with ideologically and politically (The Hindu, 2011). In other words, police and military solutions to the problem were inept and disproportionate. This was diametrically opposite to what the CPI-CPM government did to Naxals in West Bengal. The CPI also opposed the initial decision of the central government to file the review petition in the court, in which the court had asked to dismantle Salwa Judum. D Raja, a senior left leader, condemned the formation of the vigilante group, Salwa Judum, for tackling the Naxalite movement[4] (The Hindu, 2011). He termed such a force a threat to democratic politics. D Raja was not the only Left leader to articulate the opposition on the grounds of violation of human rights. But they failed to explain why the then Bengal government under the CPM endorsed all the military measures to tackle the Maoist extremism.

Before the coming to power of the Narendra Modi government at the centre, the central government's response to the Maoists' questions had been highly incongruous and innocuous. The dilemma has been on the question of the nature and magnitude of the response. Not only is there a divide across the parties, but also between the parties and the government. Therefore, the responses were inconsistent, blowing both hot and cold at the same time. During the UPA regime, there seemed to be a divide within the Congress Party on methods of approaching the problem. One section within the Congress, led by the Home Minister P. Chidambaram, was highly critical of the Maoists and wanted a military and police solution to the problem. He was of the view that the first thing which was required was to establish the dominance of the state. Maoists cannot be won through development (The Economic Times 2010). They would oppose all development activities in the region. The development activities should follow thereafter.

Another section of the Congress represented by Digvijay Singh and Mani Shankar Ayyer endorsed the development route to tackle the Maoists menace. Jairam Ramesh, another vocal minister of the cabinet in Manmohan Singh's government and known as the advisor of Rahul Gandhi on social issues, had

4 D Raja the CPI leader opposed Review Petition against Salwa Judum.

a double mind on the subject (PIB, 2011). Ramesh termed Maoists as terrorists and condemned all those who romanticise it in the form of a progressive ideology of social and economic transformation, but for most of them, the best way to tackle the Naxal menace is to enable and empower the tribals in the area. This was also the view which came from the National Advisory Council, chaired by Sonia Gandhi (Singh, 2010).

That is the reason that the UPA government could not decisively work in the direction in which it wanted to sail. Former Prime Minister Manmohan Singh described the Maoists and left extremism as the biggest threat to the internal security of the country. He held that it was obstructing the growth of the country, and it needs to be tackled squarely, on which there is broad agreement among the chief ministers of the Naxalite-infected states (PMO, 2006; The Hindu, 2009; The Hindu, 2011). He repeated it on several occasions. So was the case with Chidambaram when he took over charge of the Home Minister. Chidambaram openly supported Salwa Judum on several occasions. His views were not congruent with the views of the Moily committee at all. Chidambaram, contrary to the Moily committee, publicly accepted that the appointment of the SPOs by the state of Chhattisgarh was justified and that "the special police officers (SPOs) have played a useful role and should be appointed wherever required" (Times of India, 2009). He was the one who initiated and favoured the much-publicised Operation Green Hunt. Even in the meeting of the Chief Ministers of the seven Naxal-infested states, he piloted the idea of joint operations against the Naxals (The Times of India, 2009). But all this did not work. The politics within the Congress on the issue of Naxals overshadowed all other considerations, including the protection of the larger interests of tribals and the emancipation of the tribal belts from Naxalite excessiveness. And it was the politics that led to the non-filing of the review petition by the central and state governments. The travesty of dilemma within the Congress and the government could be seen in the fact that even after the killing of 25 Congressmen in the state of Chhattisgarh, the then minister in charge of tribal affairs was found to be saying that the Naxals are fighting for a political cause! And while the former Prime Minister was chairing the meeting of the Chief Ministers of Naxal infested states and the Home minister mulling for an unified command across these states and appreciating the outcome of Salwa Judum, the planning commission document and the report of a team of the central government was saying that over 350000 Adivasis were displaced due to 'death squads' of Salwa Judum which razed down or burnt the houses and huts of 640 villages so that the corporate like Tata and Essar could have foothold there and grab the minefield for their business interests! (Swami, 2013).

3 Political Parties and Naxals

Seeking political support of the Naxals in the elections has often come to the notice and public discourse, especially in the Naxal-infested areas. Whenever elections come, there is a major strike in the Naxal-infested areas. Posters of the Naxals threatening the people against participation in the election start making an appearance on the roadside and in the countryside on walls. Further, they inflict violence in different areas to terrorise the psyche of the people. A pattern is visible that they strike the civilians and armed forces in the areas where elections are to be held or are underway. The attack on the CRPF and the Congress leader in Chhattisgarh is worth examining. When the Jharkhand elections were declared in 2014, they successfully conducted several attacks. They chose to strike the armed forces in Sukma Valley in the Bastar region of Chhattisgarh when the parliamentary elections were underway.

By doing this, they reaffirm their distrust in the existing political system at work under the tutelage of the capitalist structure. They make their political statement that the true democracy does not lie in the rotation of elected representatives through election, but in equitable and just distribution of means and fruits of production, and genuine people empowerment and their participation in the decision-making process. However, the actual purpose is to demonstrate that they cannot be ignored and that they are capable of influencing the electoral outcomes. They choose the timings of violence accordingly. The political class, instead of fighting, has been found to be aligning with the Maoists clandestinely to win their support in elections. Mamta Banerjee became hard-nosed against the Maoists after winning elections, but it was clear that she did her best to allure and win the support of the Maoists before elections to dislodge the CPM in West Bengal (Sahni, 2011). Kabir Suman, a Bengali singer and a Trinamool Congress MP at the time, had composed songs in favour of the release of the Maoist Chhatradhar Mahato (Bhattacharya, 2016:101). He was very popular among the Maoist cadres.

Shibu Soren, the former Chief Minister of Jharkhand, always had a soft corner for the Naxals. He was often alleged to have an understanding with the Naxals for support in the elections. More importantly, he had been vocal on the issue and justified his stand on the grounds that both Maoists and his party fight for the common cause of the tribal people. In an interview with a correspondent, he said that Maoism is a 'people's movement' (The Economic Times, 2010; The Indian Express, 2010). His son, Hemant Soren, who subsequently became the Deputy Chief Minister in a coalition government, and is now the Chief Minister of the state, openly had asked the central government to withdraw the armed forces from the state (The Economic Times, 2010;

The Indian Express, 2010). However, he withdrew his statement as soon as criticism started pouring in from all quarters. As it happens, with politicians of all hues and cries, they attributed the blame to the media for creating confusion. Soren denied the statement which he had said in the press conference, but at the same time condemned the state government under the leadership of the CPM for the operation *Green Hunt* (The Economic Times, 2010; The Indian Express, 2010). The Health Minister of his government of the time, Hermal Murmu, went on to attack the CPM also for engaging 'Harmad Vahini', which he held was engaged in unleashing untold atrocities on tribals and minorities in the state (The Economic Times, 2010; The Indian Express, 2010).

It was widely published in the media that Soren's messenger also met Koteshwar Rao alias Kishenjee somewhere in Jharkhand and sought his help in elections (The New Indian Express, 2022). This meeting was held after Soren had taken the oath as the Chief Minister of Jharkhand. It was attributed to the political understanding between the Maoists and the Jharkhand Mukti Morcha (JMM) in the state assembly elections in which Maoists helped the party to win at least six assembly constituencies (Ranjan, 2010). The fact is that the Naxals have the capacity to influence several constituencies of Jharkhand. And it is now known to all that they support and oppose the candidates depending on political convenience. It would be wrong to judge the Naxals on the basis of what they say in public.

Ideologically, Maoists oppose parliamentary democracy. Therefore, when the dates for elections come nearer, they would often paste big posters on walls threatening the people not to participate in elections. But rarely has it been seen that the people responded favourably to their calls. It needs to be deciphered why the people, even in the Naxal-dominated area, come out openly to participate in the vote. In the 2013 assembly elections in Chhattisgarh, people came out to vote despite the Naxals' call to boycott the elections. The voter turnout was over 67 percent. People defied the boycott call. Even in the villages close to the Sukma Valley, there was a very high voter turnout (Sharma, 2013). In Bihar, people in the Jamui area defied the Maoists' call to boycott the elections despite the fact that the ultras had kidnapped three poll officials. In the second phase, 53 percent of voters turned out to vote despite threats from the Maoists. Often, it has been found that such declarations by the Maoists are tactical ways to support and oppose the candidates contesting from the constituency.

One of the reasons why Mamta could dislodge the CPM in West Bengal at that time was that the Trinamool Congress exposed the facade of the CPM on the land acquisition policy, which was pro-corporate, against which it had been talking about all these years. The biggest support in this regard, which came to the Trinamool, was the Maoists who infiltrated into the popular resistance movement called Bhumi Uchhed Pratirodh Committee (*BUPC*) and lent all support to the Party. It was also alleged that the Trinamool Congress cadres were also trained by the Maoists to attack the police and the CPM activists. In March 2010, CPM claimed to have given a document to the Home Ministry which establishes a link between the Trinamool Congress and the Maoists in West Bengal (The Indian Express, 2010). The spokesperson of the CPM in Bengal, Md. Salem charged that the CPM cadres were killed by the Maoists in Bengal (The Indian Express, 2010). The document provided by the CPM did not come out in the public domain, and therefore, it is difficult to suggest to what extent they were true, but Maoists-Trinamool relations were at best in Bengal prior to the assembly elections of 2011 in the state. In several of her election meetings, Mamta Banerjee in the area of Jangal Mahal spoke the language of the Naxalites and attributed all violence to be the handiwork of the CPI (M) to defame the anti-government movements in different parts of West Bengal (Gupta). She held that there was no presence of the Naxals in Jangal Mahal areas at all (Rediff News, 2010). It was not hidden to her who came out to support the movement. Venkatesh Reddy alias Telgu Deepak, who was arrested on 4 March 2010, revealed this to the police, which was widely published in the newspaper, that during the Nandigram agitations, Maoists trained the TMC cadres in handling arms (Sahni, 2011). Kishanji, the Maoist leader who revived the Naxalite movement in Bengal after its suppression in 1972, admitted that its cadres were supporting and monitoring both the Nandigram and Singur movements (Bhattacharya, 2016:11). This further got traction when, despite the fact that the Lalgarh movement was directly monitored and steered by Kishanji, Trinamool Congress called it a people's movement (Bhattacharya, 2016:02). And it is widely acknowledged that Maoists played a crucial role by favouring the Trinamool against the CPM in the elections. Their supporters contributed to build the movement against Nandigram and Singoor and countered the aggressive and violent methods which the CPM cadres have been using so far to establish their political dominance.

It is another thing that after winning elections, Mamta Banerjee turned the heat against the Naxals and started arguing that all have entered into an unholy alliance against her party, including the Maoists and the BJP (Sengupta, 2013). She called upon the government to stop the joint operations against the Maoists and charged that the CPM government was deliberately propagating canards against them (Rediff News, 2010).

In the run-up to the assembly elections of 2010, Mamta had very cosy relations with the Maoists. Maoists were running their writs in the area called Jangal Mahal. Whatever destructive activities they executed during this period,

Trinamool did not react against. On the contrary, when the state government accused the Naxals of being engaged in work, she often jumped to their defence. As Ajai Sahni wrote in 2009, as per the data collected by South Asia Portal, "a total of 158 fatalities connected with Maoist violence were recorded in West Bengal, including 134 civilians and 15 Security Forces (SF) personnel. By 2010, the total had risen to 425 fatalities—the highest for any State that year—including 328 civilians and 36 SF personnel. Banerjee insisted that the violence was being orchestrated by her *bête noire*, the then-ruling Communist Party of India-Marxist (CPI-M), despite the fact that the overwhelming proportion of civilians killed were CPI-M cadres. Throughout this period, the TMC did everything in its power to obfuscate the Maoist role in violence in the State and to bring SF operations in the Jangal Mahal area to an end" (Sahni, 2011). In fact, the TMC leaders approached the then President of India and submitted a memorandum demanding 'end to the joint operations by state and paramilitary forces' in the state.[5]

It is also no longer a hidden fact that the Gyaneshwari Express was derailed by the Maoists, and it took a toll of 141 lives. While the state government had pointed fingers towards the Maoists, Mamta Banerjee again came to the defence of the Naxals. Shae said that it was not the handiwork of the Naxals. She was the Union Railway Minister then and had better access to the truth than anyone. Since she wanted to discredit the CPM at any cost and seek also the support of the Maoists in the impending assembly elections, she did not utter anything against the Maoists. But the same cannot be said after the election. Critics argued that prior to the election, there was a deal between the two that after coming into power, she would release the jailed Maoists, describing them as political prisoners and charges against them being politically motivated. She declared it in her election rally, too. While addressing an election rally in Jhargram in Paschim Midnapur district, which also has been a Maoist-affected area, though not fully but partly, she accused the CPM of being responsible for the Maoists' upsurge in the Jangal Mahal area. And that the whole problem of Naxalism would come to an end once she comes into power (NDTV, 2011; The Hindu, 2011). She also said that people have been victims of CPI (M) governance. The poor and tribals are exploited in the regime. They have been falsely implicated, and once she comes into power, she will ensure the release of all those who were languishing in jail in fabricated cases (The Hindu, 2011).

5 Trinamool Congress to end joint operation of state police and paramilitary forces in the state.

But what looked to her an easy job before the election became a difficult task in government. She refused to do so, and the understanding which both the Trinamool and the Maoists had reached came to an end. She started fully cooperating with the central government. Maoists had great hope from Mamta, and they welcomed the 'peace initiatives' and development projects, but the relationship strained when the latter refused to withdraw the joint forces from Jangal Mahal and other areas (Bhattacharya, 2016:218–219). The state police also swung into action, and Kishanji was killed on 24 November 2011 in a gun battle with COBRA forces assisted by a thousand CRPF jawans and state police (Times of India, 2011). Moreover, she openly started condemning the Naxals by saying that they are more dangerous than the terrorists even. Further, she also accepted that the Maoists were the ones who were behind the Gyaneshwari Express in May 2010. More than that, she came down heavily on those intellectuals and academicians in the university who glorified Naxals with a threat that such people would be arrested (Sahni, 2011).

Needless to say, one finds a different Mamta Banerjee after getting elected and becoming the Chief Minister of the state. What she did before the election was purely a case of political opportunism. She wanted to defeat the Left by using any and every means which possibly could damage the electoral support base of the CPI (M). She did not even pause to think that aligning with such forces would be a dangerous game altogether in the long run for the state. And by the time she got the opportunity to address the election rally in the 2016 assembly elections in the state, she boasted how she freed the Jangalmahal and other areas from an atmosphere of fear and fright. While referring to the atmosphere of despair and fear in Bankura, Purulia and Mednipur, she said: "I know every morning you would wonder if armed men would come to your homes and attack. If young men and women left home for work, their mothers would worry till they returned safely. Now all that has gone. We have peace in Jangalmahal. And we have done this. … you share a border with Jharkhand. Has the BJP managed to bring peace there? Even in Chhattisgarh, they have not managed. But the Trinamool has done that in West Bengal" (Roy & Biswas, 2016). The stark reality of Bengal as of date is that the Naxal movement has died in the state, and their cadres have either shifted their base or have started acting for the Trinamool Congress Party.

4 Bihar

Though the communist movement was a powerful social and political force in the state of Bihar for a long time, it moved on the lines of Maoism seriously only in the 1980s. The first sign of it, however, was seen in the Mushhari block in Muzaffarpur in 1968. It was suppressed by 1971 with killings and arrests of Naxalites. But soon it spread out in other districts of North and South Bihar, such as Darbhanga, Munger, Jamshedpur, Bhojpur, etc. Subsequently, it engulfed other districts of the state, such as Aurangabad, Gaya, Rohtas, Singhbhum, Vaishali, etc. Rohtas and Bhojpur later on became the key centres of the Maoists' activities (Narayan, 2011:1070). Two issues played a crucial role. First, the atrocious caste relations in the villages and peasant-labourer relations in the fields. Posters for armed revolution and the capture of the land of landlords or the forcible harvest of the crops started coming up on walls in villages and towns. CPI (ML) had organised its state-level conference at Nathupur, Khudra in 1970, in which it called upon the party cadres to mobilise the people for guerrilla warfare against the class enemies (Narayan, 2011:1070). This inspired the lower caste people who defined class enemies in terms of the upper castes, the landlord or the no-landlord. The caste killing became equal to class killing. And the first case in this regard was the killing of a Rajput landlord of Ekwari, Sheopujan Singh. Communists belonging to lower castes, like Jagdish Mahto, Rameshwar Ahir, Bhikhari Kahar, Maharaj Mahto, Singhasan Charriar, were implicated. They were arrested, but the momentum of the movement towards the elimination of the class enemies did not stop. One after another incident of organised killings, particularly in the Sahar area, especially areas near the village of Ekwari, started taking place (Narayan, 2011:1070). Between February 1971 and 6 May 1973, nearly 15 such killings were executed in the Sahar Block, including Thana Singh, a Rajput landlord of Jagdishpur. The term Naxalites by now had become intimidating and fearful (Narayan, 2011:1070). But one thing was certain: there was no political patronage for such activities by the political class. Things started changing with the arrival of Lalu Prashad Yadav as Chief Minister in Bihar.

During the Lalu regime, the government patronised them because Naxals challenged the dominance of the upper castes in many districts of the state. This suited Lalu Yadav's politics as the lower castes' rise automatically strengthened his social base. It is pertinent to note that during the RJD rule in Bihar, the state witnessed several major caste clashes, particularly in Central Bihar and districts like Ara, Buxar, Rohtas, Palamu, Aurangabad, Jehanabad, Gaya, etc. "On October 7, 1986, the MCC killed 11 persons belonging to the upper caste Rajput community in Darmia village, Aurangabad district in Bihar. On May 29, 1987, the MCC massacred 42 persons belonging to an upper caste Rajput family at Dalelchak-Baghaura village in Aurangabad district, Bihar. On February 12, 1992, the MCC massacred 37 members of the landowning upper caste Bhumihar community at Bara village of Gaya district in Bihar. On March 18, 1999, the MCC massacred over 34 upper caste Bhumihars in Senari village, Jehanabad in Bihar. On November 18, 1999, the MCC killed 12 persons in Latu village, Palamu in Jharkhand. On April 14, 2001, the MCC killed 14 persons at Belpu village, Hazaribagh district in Jharkhand" (Jha, 2005). All these resulted in the evolution of Ranveer Sena, which carried out several massacres in different districts of central Bihar. On 16 June 2000, its cadres killed 34 persons at Miapur village in Aurangabad district. On 21 April 1999, 12 people were killed at Sendani village in Gaya district. On 20 February 1999, 11 persons were killed at Narayanpur village in Jehanabad district. On 25 January 1999, 23 persons were massacred in Sankarbigha village again in Jehanabad district. Again, on 1 December 1997, 58 persons were massacred at Lakshmanpur-Bathe village in Jehanabad district. On April 10, 1997, 10 people were killed at Ekbari village, Jehanabad. And on 23 March 1997, Ranvir Sena cadres killed 10 persons at Habispur village in Patna district (Jha, 2005). Ranveer Sena, though, claimed to have originated to counter the Naxalites only, but subsequently it degenerated into a caste army against the lower castes and massacred even the innocent Dalits on the pretext of being a suspected Maoist supporter. Interestingly, Lalu sought the support of both in the elections by patronising them in their area of dominance. Since the class war of the Maoists in Bihar generally turned to the caste conflicts, Maoists' presence helped in the polarisation of the lower castes, which always went in favour of the RJD. The RJD government never cracked the whip on the Naxals. On the contrary, it patronised them by giving out contracts to their cadres. Since the Maoists had a lot of clout in the areas of their dominance, political parties always looked towards them for support in the elections.

In Bihar, both the JD(U) and the RJD have been alleging each other of using Naxals for their electoral gains, and in return, patronising them (Mishra, 2020). When RJD was in power, the allegations came from the BJP and the JD(U) that RJD was deliberately very soft towards the Naxalites because they were fighting against the upper castes' landlords in Central and South Bihar, which were traditionally either the voters of the Congress or the BJP. Undoubtedly, during the Lalu regime, a number of Naxal attacks took place in different parts of Bihar (Kleinfeld & Majeed, 2016).

When Nitish Kumar took over the reins of power, he declared the policy of 'zero tolerance' towards the Naxals. Nitish did it because he had the tremendous support of the upper castes of Bhumihars, Rajputs and Brahmins, who predominantly had openly supported his leadership against Lalu Yadav, who had emerged as the representative icon of OBCs and the poor in the state. Behind the administrative commitment, it also had a political angle. It worked in the beginning as the police tightened its noose on the criminals. Some most Naxal affected areas started moving towards normalcy. However, the politicians continued to maintain their relations with the Maoists. In February 2011, the spokesperson of the RJD, Shakeel Ahmad Khan, alleged that politicians were giving patronage to the Maoists in several constituencies in Bihar, such as Sherghatti, Imamganj, etc., to ensure their support in the elections (The Bihar Times, 2011). He asked the Chief Minister to initiate a probe into the Maoists-politician nexus in Bihar. He alleged that the Naxals were being patronised by the speaker of the assembly, Mr Uday Narayan Chaudhary, in his Imamgang constituency and demanded for an independent enquiry (Bhalla, 2014). He also charged the police with harassing innocent and poor people and threatened to take the matter to the streets if it was not stopped. Needless to say, the statements were a well-crafted balancing act (Bhalla, 2014). They wanted to be seen against Naxalite violence, but sending out a message at the same time that these articulations should not be taken seriously by those against whom it has been said. The threat of movement against the police was particularly aimed at assuaging the feelings of the Naxalites.

It is not a secret that in the 2005 state assembly elections, though the CPI (Maoists) had officially declared that they would work towards the ouster of the present regime, it admitted at the same time that both the RJD and the Maoists had the same social base of support. This is true as well. The major support in the election for Lalu came from the Dalits and OBCs. Maoists have always been giving a call for a boycott of the elections. If that had occurred, Lalu would have lost the elections long back before 2005. But it never happened. Interestingly, the allegation between the Maoist Communist Centre (MCC) and the RJD was also publicly stated by the CPI (ML) Liberation, Dipankar Bhattacharya faction, which decided to participate in the assembly elections. Liberation also charged the MCC with extending support to JMM in Jharkhand (Jha, 2005:23). It also charged MCC cadres of openly canvassing for the RJD candidates in elections (Jha, 2005:23).

However, Nitish's third stint as chief minister saw a different turn. After dissociation from the BJP, Nitish Kumar moved towards forging a new social coalition. It resulted from the compulsion of compensating the social base which weakened after separation from the BJP. He not only went soft towards Lalu Prasad Yadav, whom he considered as the epitome of corruption, but also became soft on Naxals. It was the reason that during 2012–13, there was a rise in the Naxal violence in the state (Saqib, 2018:04).

5 Chhattisgarh

BJP and Congress have been the two main political parties in the state, and both have been recklessly accusing each other of having Maoist links. Thus, when the entire convoy of tall leaders of the Congress Party was attacked suddenly at Darba in Chhattisgarh by the Naxalites on 25 May 2013, the Congress Party accused the BJP of hatching a conspiracy to finish the entire leadership of the party for its political ends. Though the top national leaders of the party did not use such language of allegation, but they condemned the state government for its failure to give enough protection to the Congress leaders (Chaturvedi, 2013). On the other hand, the BJP charged the Congress leader Ajit Yogi of conspiring against the deceased leaders in connivance with Maoists. The president of Madhya Pradesh BJP, Narendra Singh Tomar, made a direct attack against Yogi while addressing a meeting of the members of the state executive (Gupta, 2013). Another MP of the BJP, Rakesh Kumar Singh, also demanded that the 'role of Ajit Yogi' needed to be investigated (Gupta, 2013).

Allegations of the BJP were based on the investigation of the NIA team, which is supposed to have reported to the Union Home Ministry that four of the Congress members were in direct linkage with the Naxalites, and the Maoists were getting all minute-to-minute information regarding the movement of Parivartan Yatra[6] (Times of India, 2013). The attackers had even idea of the changed routes of the Parivartan Yatra (Katoch, 2012). BJP leaders also questioned the absence of Ajit Yogi hours before the incident took place.

Congress, on the other hand, has been accusing the BJP government of not deliberately exercising force against the Maoists because the presence of Maoists brings a good electoral dividend for the party. Ajit Yogi, the former chief minister of the state and a prominent member of the Congress party in the state, castigated the BJP for benefiting from the conflicts between the leaders of the Naxal movement and Salwa Judum, as it has brought electoral victory to the party in elections. He apprehended that the BJP would benefit once again in the parliamentary elections of 2009[7] (Zaidi, 2007; Anand, 2013). In the Baster district, there are 12 assembly constituencies out of which the

6 Parivartan Yatra was started from 12th April 2013 by the Congress state leadership in Chhattisgarh for the assembly polls to highlight alleged corruption and other omissions and commissions of BJP Government.

7 Salwa Judum also has been in controversy because the opposition finds it a big design of the BJP to create a huge population as 'paid vote bank' as the people benefitted from the anti-Naxal movements have developed deep and cordial link with the party.

BJP won 9 in 2003, 11 in 2008 and in 2013. These consecutive wins for the BJP were possible only because of the tactical understanding between the Naxals and the BJP. It also came to light that Podium Linga, charged with the murder of the BJP Leader Shivdayal Singh Tomar, also had revealed before the CRPF and the Chhattisgarh police that he had campaigned for the party in the assembly elections of 2008 (Bhardwaj, 2020). Tomar was the Vice-president of the party in Dantewada district and also a big contractor who was involved in several construction works allotted to him by the government, and Linga allegedly killed him because he refused to give him the commission worth Rs.60000 (Bhardwaj, 2020).

6 Maharashtra

Maharashtra, over the years, has seen increased Naxal activities in the state. Gadchiroli and Gondia, two districts of Maharashtra, have lately emerged as highly Naxal-infested areas in Eastern Maharashtra. The state has succeeded in pushing the Naxals on the back foot through social awareness campaigns and initiatives like 'Gaonbandi' (no entry into villages) and tightening the noose through effective intelligence inputs and police actions. Many Dalams (a Group of Naxalites operating in the area) were closed down in the Vidarbha region also. However, politicians kept on wavering in their stand. A senior politician like Sharad Pawar can be seen doing a balancing act. He considered Naxalism a 'wrong ideology', but at the same time also said that it resulted from the exclusive growth story in which the tribals are left out (Pawar, 2013; The Indian Express, 2013). Their exclusion from the development allows the Naxals to mislead the innocent tribals and rope them into a cult of violence and arson. For him, Naxalism was not a law-and-order problem but emanated from unemployment and underdevelopment of the region, deprivation of the people and so on. And therefore, what was needed was to build roads, hospitals, educational institutions and more importantly, include them in the growth story of the country. Pawar thus held that both the strategy of force and development should go hand in hand to eliminate the Naxals' influence (NDTV, 2021). Interestingly, the same Sharad Pawar started saying that Naxals are trying to create public opinion and create hatred against the government in other parts of the state too. He held that such forces are active in Nagpur, Pune, Mumbai and in parts of the Sahyadri ranges, as far as Kerala. Interestingly, he called it 'urban naxalisation' (NDTV, 2021).

The articulations of political leaders in the state of Andhra Pradesh and other states are in no way different. People still remember that in 2005, the

Naxals had attacked the convoy of Chandra Babu Naidu, the then chief minister of the state of Andhra Pradesh. He narrowly escaped the attack. But recall 1983 when the father-in-law of Chandra Babu Naidu, Mr NT Rama Rao, the then Chief Minister of the state, had declared the Maoists as 'true patriots' who were being misunderstood by the ruling classes (Swami, 2013). BJP condemned the competition between the TDP and the Congress for wooing the Naxalites for electoral gains. In its National Executive meeting at Thiruvananthapuram from 28 to 30 September 1991, the party passed political resolutions against the Naxalite menace and accused the political parties like TDP, Congress I and Janata Dal of seeking Naxals' support in the elections (BJP Resolution, 2000:149).

The response of the regional parties is understandable as they are narrow in their vision, which is solely guided by their electoral concerns. But if the same is seen with the national parties, it does not augur well for the nation. The double-speak of Congress has patently been part of its strategy. It seems there is a deliberately crafted role division within the party in which some, like Mani Shanker Aiyyer and Digvijay Singh, sympathise with the Naxals and their cause and even go to the extent of publicly questioning their own party and the government for their highhandedness, whereas Chidambaram and Manmohan Singh considered them as the biggest threat to national security. Kishore Chandra Deo, the tribal minister in the government of India under Manmohan Singh, said that Maoists were fighting a political battle and therefore the government should take a different approach to handle them (Times of India, 2010).

Such double-speak serves the electoral purpose because the Naxals are in a position to influence the voting in some areas. Secondly, since they raise the issues which are closer to the poor and deprived sections of the society, politicians don't wish to be seen as those who are away from or do not concern themselves with their sufferings. It was one reason that when Rahul Gandhi went to Jharkhand, he was very considerate towards the Naxals, whereas the government of his party was engaged in Operation Green Hunt. It is said somebody convinced Rahul that anti-Naxalism would badly hurt his pro-poor image, which was being carved out and pushed to be sold in public. Those who look at the issue from a security perspective find that it is convenient for all to argue this line. Because the administrators have to do nothing, they can easily pass on the buck to others. police do not have to enforce the law and display their superior power, which often leads to casualties, and politicians always find them as their ally (Swami, 2013).

BJP, however, has always maintained a consistent position on tackling Maoist terrorism. It fits into its ideological discourse and masculine nationalism. Since the times of the Jan Sangh, it has been holding the position that

Naxals are a product of the imported ideology of communism, which does not go in consonance with the essence of India. Secondly, it has been anti-national in the sense that it has links with the forces outside the territorial bounds of India. Third, Naxals are essentially anti-Hindu and native culture. Therefore, irrespective of the government in power in the state or the centre, the party has always been supportive of the use of police and paramilitary forces to tackle communist, violent radicalism. The party supported the Congress government in Bengal when the latter resorted to police to contain the CPI (ML) activists in the state. When the central government, under the leadership of Manmohan Singh, designed to execute the 'Operation Green Hunt' the party lent its hand to the government.

7 Conclusion

The success of any policy measures against the Naxals depends largely on three things: firepower, people's support and the united political response or stand on the issue. But unfortunately, the response of the political class to the Maoist menace has been less than honest and more of opportunistic in character. Their conducts are governed more by the mathematics of the electoral and political gains than stoppage of violence and bringing in lasting peace. As a result, there is little congruency between what they say for public consumption and what they do in real terms. Publicly, they condemn the Naxal violence, but at the same time also wish not to annoy the Maoists. Their response to the Naxal violence, therefore, has not been a consistent and linear one. They oscillate between human touch and tough military/police actions. This also emerges from the fact that political parties and politicians have been using them as allies for electoral gains. Many politicians still don't have comprehended the magnitude and dynamics of the problem. There are many who see that the Naxals are raising and doing good to the neglected sections of society. PUDR reports of 1985 pertaining to the killing of a person by the Maoists reported that even the Member of the Parliament, Manku Ram Sodhi, belonging to the Congress Party, appreciated the good work done by the Naxals. N.T. Rama Rao found them as patriots. Way back in 2010, Rahul Gandhi shared the dais with an alleged Naxal leader when he visited Orissa.

Such proximity of the political leaders and political parties with the Naxals for political gains has not lasted long, and they were forced to act against the Naxals. Congress was alleged to have entered into an understanding with the Maoists in which the latter had agreed to support the party in the assembly elections of Andhra Pradesh against the Telugu Desam Party. The party gave space to the Naxals after winning elections, but not beyond a point. In the beginning, the government ignored the Naxal activities, and it allowed Maoists to recruit the cadres and operate their activities. But it became burdensome when the Naxals increased their violent activities. So was the case with Mamata Banerjee, who aligned with the Naxals on the Singur issue and before the assembly elections of 2011, but had to take tough decisions and use force thereafter when Naxals increased their activities. She found that tactical support to the Naxals and silent support to them would not only erode her social base but would also discredit her government.

Political parties, by and large, except for the BJP and Shiv Sena, have been wavering in their positions on the Naxals. Instead of condemning the violence outright, they have been diplomatic in their response. When the Maoists killed 15 armed forces in the Sukma district of Chhattisgarh, the CPM condemned it and asked both the central and state governments to work together to deal with the Maoist violence. It accused the government for not keeping adequate vigilance despite the central government alerts. However, in order to assuage the feelings of the Naxals, they disapproved of Salwa Judum. This is a shuttle way of defending the Maoists' activities. Even the PUCL, which is a known left leaning human rights organisation regretted the loss of lives of the soldier and appealed to both the state and the Maoists to agree to unconditional ceasefire and end the hostilities to stop the poor Trible who often fell victim to the crossfire but when it came to discussed the human rights violation it referred only to the rapes and people being killed by the security forces and members of Salwa Judum (The Hindu, 2021). Political parties are engaged in blaming each other of colluding with the Naxals. Right-wing political parties alone are an exception to it. They have been very consistent in their position on the Naxal menace. BJP not only reiterated a very tough stand in the parliament but also reaffirmed its commitment in the form of political resolutions passed in national executive meetings. It holds that until the Indian state proves its superiority through firepower and contains the Maoists forcefully, the Maoists cannot be brought to the negotiation table. Hence, a military solution alone will not bring a lasting solution to the problem. The wavering attitude of political parties would do more damage to the interests of the nation than resolving the problem forever.

CHAPTER 11

Tackling Left Extremism during Modi Regime

The trajectory of Naxalism in India is characterised by a heavy spatiotemporal unpredictability in the matter of operational intensity and ideational articulation on the one hand and durative territorial consolidation on the other. From its inception as a radical peasant movement in the late 1960s in West Bengal's Naxalbari, the movement broad-based into an insurgent-at-large primarily organised from the Communist Party of India (Maoist) across what came to be called the "Red Corridor." While the movement's attraction has waxed and waned over the decades, it is this long-standing ability to exploit systemic governance deficits, particularly in the resource-rich but development-deficient tribal hinterlands, that marks the constant. These areas usually stand in utter neglect of the state developmental and security apparatus, thus providing ample workspace for insurgent mobilisation. Here, the presence of the state is either tokenistic or perceived by local communities as coercive, extractive and insensitive to indigenous rights. Within these disputed spaces, the political will, defined as the sustained commitment of the governing elite to design and implement coherent counterinsurgency and developmental strategies, may emerge as an important variable that has determined the trajectories of this insurgency.

In the formative years of the Naxalite movement across the Indian territory, the Indian state, under the leadership of Prime Minister Indira Gandhi, could not realise the gravity and long-term implications of this radical insurgency. The Congress government's initial appraisal, as stated by then Union Home Minister Y.B. Chavan in a Lok Sabha statement on 13 June 1967, treated the Naxalbari uprisings merely as one of many expressions of localized lawlessness (LiveMint, 2007). One could assume from the existing statement that disturbances could easily be brought under control through normal law enforcement procedures, especially by dispatching local policemen. This thinking dramatically underestimated the ideological mooring and structural forces behind this people's uprising.

As the Naxalite movement grew in the late 1960s and early 1970s, criminality was certainly within the frame of reference of the government logic, but it was fast emerging that this was not all that was to be considered. Increasingly savage attacks, especially in the agrarian belts, especially by the late 1960s and early 70s, made the central leadership reconsider their position. Speaking at a Chief Ministers' conference convened by Prime Minister Indira Gandhi in

 | HTTPS://DOI.ORG/10.1163/9789004765054-013

1972, Home Minister Y.B. Chavan warned of the growing extremist activities. He famously said, "We should not allow the Green Revolution to turn into a Red Revolution" (LiveMint, 2007).

But contrary to the rhetorical shift given to the nauseating, otherwise incoherent measures, nothing decisive was achieved in counteraction to the rebellion. Ideological ambivalences existing within the Congress Party represented one of the biggest obstacles to a resolute counter-insurgency policy. Many leaders at the top held sympathies for the broad redistributive goals espoused by left-wing factions, hesitating to favour an option of sheer coercion. Further, this ideological proximity toward the left prevented the evolution of a common political strategy against the Maoist insurgents; rather, it scattered the state response. The inertia, at this decisive moment, allowed the movement to consolidate, recruit, and expand into other territories, making itself further institutionalised as an erstwhile internal security threat. This misreading of the movement in its formative years, coupled with a later realisation of its consequences have had a lingering impact on how the course of left-wing extremism went on in India even into the present times.

1 Naxalism in the 2000s—the Soft State and Silent Surge

Under the rule of UPA-I, the approach of the Indian state towards Naxalism between 2004 to 2009 was ambiguous and mostly conciliatory, which is termed in policy circles a 'soft-glove' approach. The former Prime Minister Dr. Manmohan Singh also brought Naxalism forward as the "single biggest internal security threat" of the country in the public audience; however, this did not contain any substantive, coherent or assertive policy position. The limits of state response were, however, contained in the structural constraints of coalition politics. Key left-leaning parties supported the UPA-I, such as the CPI (M), whose ideological proximity towards certain aspects of the Naxalite movement would complicate endeavours to decisively criminalise or suppress insurgent activities. Notably, Sonia Gandhi consulted CPI (M) general secretary Harkishan Singh Surjeet in Dr. Singh's appointment as Prime Minister, reflecting the ideological undercurrents that shaped the political calculus of the ruling coalition (Chatterji, 2018).

The ideological underpinnings found their institutional expression in the drafting of the Common Minimum Programme (CMP), a consensus document collaboratively drawn by Congress leaders Jairam Ramesh and Salman Khurshid and CPI (M) leaders Sitaram Yechury and Prakash Karat. On one hand, therefore, while the CMP formulated a developmental agenda, it circumscribed the government from adopting a truly robust strategy against Naxalism since overlapping ideologies associated with some groups of the UPA and the wider left movements came into play. The initiation of peace talks with representatives of the CPI (Maoist) and Janashakti in October 2004 seemed, at the outset, a constructive step toward resolving the conflict. By January 2005, however, the withdrawal of the insurgents from negotiations confirmed the timid nature of the peace process. Following this early validity, the government disengaged from the peace process, declaring the lack of one on strategic foresight and political grit, hence losing a unique opportunity for de-escalation and dialogue (GOI, 2008:60).

The UPA-I government also strove to deal with the structural roots of insurgency through rights-based legislation and welfare schemes. Among the most promising were the Scheduled Tribes and Other Traditional Forest Dwellers (Recognition of Forest Rights) Act, 2006 (FRA), and the extension of the Panchayats (Extension to Scheduled Areas) Act (PESA), which sought to empower tribal communities through the legal recognition of land and forest rights, decentralized governance, and setting up a Left Wing Extremism Division under the Ministry of Home Affairs to approach insurgency holistically. Although these steps had worthy intentions to some extent and were attuned to the grievances driving insurgent Mobilisation, they faced severe operationalisation impediments from bureaucratic inertia, fragmentation among departments, and, most crucially, an absence of continued political will across state bureaucracies to ensure compliance.

In the absence of an integrated civil-security implementation framework, which would have allowed governance, development, and law enforcement to work together, policy implementation was thus broken. Bureaucratic apathy limited political accountability, while poor coordination between the Centre and states further deepened the problem. As a result, laws passed had scant actual impact on the real lives of affected communities in conflict zones. It is this chasm between legislative vision and outcomes that stood out in the UPA-I failure of counter-Naxalism strategy-the schism between normative commitment and operational capability, highly affected by the unwillingness and incapacity to politically impose itself on a very contested and ideologically sensitive issue.

The Indo–U.S. Civil Nuclear Agreement of 2008 became a key moment of inflection in the foreign policy orientation of India and, on the other hand, transformed the very space of domestic political configuration that put clarity on the dynamics of the United Progressive Alliance (UPA)-led coalition. The decision to pursue the nuclear deal with the United States was viewed largely as a concrete manifestation of strategic alignment with liberal capitalist democracies, and this irreversibly ruptured relations between the Indian National Congress and its left allies, most significantly the CPI (M). Ideologically opposed to the deal, CPI (M) found the same standing in the ideological periphery of the liberal-capitalist paradigm so forcefully promoted by the U.S., a direct contradiction to the party's Marxist-Leninist orientation. This very ideological contradiction was exacerbated by the party's long-standing denunciation of American imperialism and neoliberal economic policies.

The Congress leadership made several efforts to placate the left bloc through intra-coalition talks and negotiations, but Prime Minister Dr. Manmohan Singh stood his ground on the agreement. He stressed that the deal was crucial to India's energy security and global stature, subtly inferring a strategic shift in India's global positioning. This resolute posture culminated into a formal political rupture when the CPI (M) under Prakash Karat withdrew support for the UPA government, but not before some internal dissent within the CPI (M) (The Economic Times, 2007). The Karat faction was adamantly opposed by other leaders such as Yechury and West Bengal lobby members, who were sceptical of the political fallout that could emanate from this decision, particularly regarding the Left Front's role in national politics. However, the Karat faction managed to stay firm on its decision, consequentially marking a split in the Congress-Left alliance.

The political disengagement of CPI (M) from the UPA coalition was, in some policy circles, interpretable as an opportunity for the Congress-led government to take a more confident and unrestrained posture against internal security challenges, notably Naxalism. Because of leftists' ideological sympathies with Maoist insurgents—who, in certain sections, are viewed not so much as security threats but as radical expressions of profound socio-economic grievances—it was thus widely presumed that CPI (M)'s exit had freed the central government from normative restraints and delivered a greener pastures advantage vis-à-vis a counterinsurgency strategy.

This orthodox logic, however, did not play itself out in any concrete or consolidated fashion. Although with the exit of the left-wing veto from the arena of national security policies, Congress's top leadership still contained some individuals in an ambivalent or sympathetic mood towards the structural grievances raised by the Naxalite movement. This ideological ambivalence was manifested in the continuation of the erstwhile, development-oriented, but poorly implemented Naxalism policy: good welfare schemes and legal reforms were prioritised above security engagement. In effect, CPI (M)'s withdrawal of support could have absolutely been a monumental non-event that would have catalysed a paradigmatic change in the operational response of the state. Rather, it laid bears to the contradictions within the Congress party: a soft corner for the Naxalites due to the left-oriented ideological underpinnings of the party's top leadership (Agnihotri, 2018).

A major turning point for the Indian state's response to the Naxalite insurgency occurred in 2009 with the UPA-II (2009–2014) government under the Indian National Congress, which achieved larger seats than in the former term of rule. During this period, a notable shift was carried out with respect to the discourse and legal status of left-wing extremism. One of the most fateful developments was the designation of CPI (M) under the UAPA as a terrorist organisation, placing it alongside Lashkar-e-Taiba and the Students Islamic Movement of India (SIMI) in the list of internationally banned organisations (LiveMint, 2009). This categorisation was not merely a symbolic act but remarked the reasserted state view of the Maoist movement, not as a socio-political deviation, but as a threat to national security requiring counter-terrorism mechanisms. Especially crucial were the timing and political context of this decision. With respect to the political atmosphere, UPA-I was severely curtailed by the ideological proximity and political leverage of these left-wing allies, while a relative loosening of these constraints was observed in the second term of the UPA.

Most visibly, the change in state posture under UPA-II was the transformation from a mainly development-centric engagement to a more overtly securitised counterinsurgency strategy. In the period of 2009–10, Chidambaram served as the home minister under whose leadership Indian counterinsurgency against Maoist insurgents was intensified through an operation later known as Operation Green Hunt. He publicly declared there was no such operation, while authorising a significant deployment of central paramilitary forces to the Red Corridor. However, within the walls of the Home Ministry under Chidambaram's leadership, things were augmented at a relative level to increase the state offensive posture and position Chidambaram at the vortex of the policy that would polarise the political and civil society as much. Central to UPA-II's anti-Naxal strategy was Operation Green Hunt—a coordinated offensive by central paramilitary forces, state police and intelligence networks. Yet it was never claimed to be a named operation by the MHA; instead, it became the de facto term used by the major Mobilisation of force in Naxal-affected areas, particularly in Chhattisgarh, Jharkhand, Odisha, and Maharashtra.

There was one other event that happened recently in Raipur, upon which the country has waited for an answer, which Chidambaram is famous for after the ugly Maoist ambush in Dantewada killing 76 people: "There is no Operation Green Hunt," said Chidambaram. Yet, the eight months of paramilitary buildup had told a different story. Security analysts like Prakash Singh later criticised the strategy as being a conventional area domination, not at all valid against the asymmetric warfare presented by guerrilla insurgents. By not naming the operation, Chidambaram seemingly calculated the exercise politically, in order not to acquiesce in a militarised approach opposed to the Congress's publicised developmental focus (Sethi, 2021).

In fact, the entire outcome then was a very extraordinary public insurrection in the Indian National Congress. Chidambaram's "wipe them out" rhetoric was criticised from within the party by Digvijay Singh, Mani Shankar Aiyar, B.K. Hariprasad, Ajit Jogi, and K. Keshav Rao. However, with the sharpest tag was Digvijay Singh, who crowed to the Home Minister: "There is not much condemnation to his call for a united front against the 'intellectual arrogance' and narrow legalistic framing on socio-political insurgency." He also remarked that "When I raised these issues with him, he said it was not his responsibility … as Home Minister, it is his responsibility to take a holistic view", indicating his resentment towards the methods opted by the Home Minister to tackle rising Naxalism.

K. Keshav Rao shared the same concerns on this issue and also cited party resolutions defining the Naxal threat as primarily related to the socio-economic level, and bemoaned Chidambaram's over-deployment of force without enough development elements attached. Under insurmountable pressure from the party, Chidambaram soon lowered his voice before he started raising the gongs and climbed the lead. Over the next few months, he graduated from a hardline to a more humanised dialect with the importance he considered to the phrase "trust deficit" in Maoist-affected areas. In an address to the Confederation of Indian Industries on May 13, he tilted the argument to saying that what was required was the winning of hearts and minds of tribals as much, if not more, necessary than the restoration of state control. Later, Rao said the tonal shift would align the Home Minister's speak closer to the Congress's general narrative.

Chidambaram also faced attacks from outside the party. Columnists from publications such as Frontline admonished accusations that the Home Ministry blurred the boundaries between dissent and terrorism. They pointed to notable cases of abuse against activists like Binayak Sen and Himanshu Kumar and condemned the state's use of "militarist dimensions" that include helicopter gunships. This critique raised fears that the manner by which Chidambaram articulated his approach could undermine constitutional norms and the democratic ethos.

The Gandhi face- Sonia and Rahul Gandhi- was also not unkind to it. Congress insiders claimed that Sonia Gandhi, the party president, had a lot of faith in Chidambaram's strategising skills, primarily in establishing sovereignty and governance over contested areas of forests. Rahul Gandhi would publicly defer to Chidambaram's expertise. Insiders recollect periodic advisories to the Home Minister to walk a fine line-combining dignity-centric engagement with disciplinary governance. Their influence was muted but critical- Chidambaram was thus empowered at the cabinet level while he mellowed his rhetoric.

There was a massive deployment of the Central Reserve Police Force with elite commando forces like the COBRA (Commando Battalion for Resolute Action) under the Operation Green Hunt. The operations were search-and-destroy, area domination, and tactical strikes against Maoists suspected of hiding. The Unified Command structure was established in several states aimed at facilitating decision-making and inter-agency coordination between state police, paramilitary forces, and intelligence agencies.

But the operational efficacy of Green Hunt is still contested. The government maintained that with more encounters, arrests, and surrenders, yet the more structural issues regarding land dispossession, forest alienation, and tribal marginalisation remained largely unaddressed. Further, there were rampant allegations about extrajudicial killings, fake encounters, and violations of human rights, raising certain ethical and legal questions concerning the security forces' conduct. The absence of tightly bound transparent oversight mechanisms increased the criticisms.

In direct contrast to the militarised approach of Operation Green Hunt, on 1 June 2010, the government simultaneously introduced the Integrated Action Plan (IAP). The objective of the IAP was to fast-track development in the 60 most severely LWE-affected districts through funding small-scale infrastructure projects little classroom blocks, health centres, rural roads, and drinking water facilities. Each district was allocated ₹25 crore per annum, with decision-making authority vested in a district-level committee comprising the District Collector, Superintendent of Police, and the District Forest Officer. While the IAP was a well-intentioned initiative, it suffered from critical implementation deficits. First, the absence of community participation and consultation rendered the projects top-down and often misaligned with local needs. Second, the funds were frequently absorbed by existing administrative bottlenecks and clientelist networks, diluting their intended impact. Third, there was no coherent linkage between IAP efforts and the broader counter-insurgency strategy, creating parallel tracks of development and security with little synergy. Again, the IAP added teeth to the proposition, then going round the world that development could be made into a counterinsurgency paradigm through which economic assistance be looked upon not as a means of empowerment but rather as the pacified outcome of violence. Such instrumentalism failed to acknowledge the deeply politicised nature of grievances beneath the insurgency and to create any real legitimacy within the state in relation to the people affected.

For all the expansion in the security apparatus, UPA-II failed to develop a sufficiently sophisticated intelligence and surveillance infrastructure to tackle the potentialities of guerrilla warfare in dense forest terrain. Human intelligence remained extremely weak due to the lack of trust between security forces and local populations. The dependence on grounded Maoists as informants, while tactically meaningful, was of doubtful reliability and gave grounds for questionable targeting. Attempts toward technological integration, such as satellite imaging, drones, and real-time communication systems, were ad hoc and inappropriately institutionalised. This technological defeat left the security forces nowhere but disadvantaged, especially in the very dense forests where the Maoist cadres knew the terrain best and could move around the most freely.

There was nothing of a long-term political vision, nor the inability to ensure rights-oriented governance, and an increasing proclivity toward securitisation without accountability has gone largely to destroy the credibility and sustainability of the counter-insurgency effort. It was neither eradication but, in reality, relocation, reconfiguration: in some areas, now is a shrinking geographical spread for Naxalism, but causation within its structure remained unresolved as a result. Therefore, the best characterisation of UPA-II's counter-Naxal legacy is not said to be resolution, but containment—frail, partial, and ultimately reversible.

2 NDA-I: Modi Government's Response to Naxalism in First Phase

When Narendra Modi took over as Prime Minister on May 2014, Left-Wing Extremism (LWE) still produced well over 1,000 violent incidents a year and remained India's gravest internal-security challenge. The new administration adopted an explicitly "whole-of-government" template: the National Policy and Action Plan to address LWE, approved in January 2015, set the doctrinal core for the next decade (PIB, 2024). parallel restructuring of fiscal instruments—the Security-Related Expenditure (SRE) scheme, the Special Infrastructure Scheme (SIS) and the Special Central Assistance (SCA) window—sought to match force projection with accelerated welfare (PIB, 2018). The Home Ministry, under the leadership of Rajnath Singh, codified an eight-pillar kinetic doctrine—Smart leadership, Aggressive strategy, Motivation, Training and so on—under the mnemonic SAMADHAN (MEA, 2025), instructing Central Armed Police Forces (CAPFs) to adopt continuous, intelligence-led "seek and destroy" missions. While addressing a function on the 2015 Foundation Day of the CRPF, Modi remarked, "Naxalism is not just a law-and-order problem, but a battle for development and trust … Our jawans are fighting not only enemies of the state but enemies of progress." Additionally, Operations such as Prahar I & II in Sukma (June 2017 and November 2017) involved joint CRPF, COBRA, District Reserve Guard and IAF air-mobility elements, eliminating at least 48 insurgents in two raids, which clearly indicated the government's stand with respect to Naxalism. Greyhounds' teams extended similar deep-forest strikes along the Andhra–Odisha border, removing several senior cadre in 2018 (The New Indian Express, 2018).

The Home Minister also portrayed active engagement and undertook frequent visits to Naxal-affected states, communicating with state police chiefs, commanders of paramilitary forces, and civil administrators. Rajnath Singh conducted regular review and coordination meetings involving the Chief Ministers and DGPs of LWE-affected states, whereby he stated in one of the meetings in May 2017, "There is no place for violence in democracy. We will neutralise the Naxal menace through a mix of strong policing, better intelligence and proactive governance." Good logistics supply, technology, and intelligence inputs fronted by an efficient command structure, resulted in NDA-I hold several noteworthy accomplishments. The efforts led to a significant change. Between 2014 and 2018, the geographical spread of Maoist violence contracted from 76 to 58 districts, while violent incidents fell by 20% and related deaths by 34% (PIB, 2025).

Besides intensifying the security operations, the Modi government undertook several developmental and connectivity levers. The 2016 Road Connectivity Project for LWE Areas authorised 5,412 km of all-weather roads across 44 worst-affected districts, linking police camps to markets and health facilities. Rehabilitation schemes such as ROSHNI and DAY-NRLM earmarked funds for 27 LWE-affected districts, linking surrendered cadres to vocational training and micro-enterprise finance. The surrender policy was overhauled in September 2014 by the government, raising monetary incentives and front-loading housing grants. The success of the policy was seen in terms of large-scale surrenders; Chhattisgarh alone reported 2,642 surrenders between 2014 and 2018. Critics, however, alleged coercive "mass surrenders", prompting civil society demands for independent verification mechanisms. Critics, however, alleged coercive "mass surrenders", prompting civil society demands for independent verification mechanisms.

The Modi regime also focused on the issue of trust deficit in Naxal-affected areas. One of the important incidents is that of when PM Modi, while speaking in Bijapur (Chhattisgarh) in April 2018, commented:

> I don't carry a bulletproof jacket … I trust the people of Bastar. This is a war not just of weapons but of development and trust.

This statement, in many people's opinion, was a charm offensive by the BJP aimed at connecting with tribal populations while giving an impression of confidence in the security apparatus.

Critics of NDA-I, however, were not wanting. The opposition leaders, civil society groups, and former civil servants questioned both the moral and sustainable aspects of the model. Congress leader Digvijay Singh, a constant critic of forceful approaches, said, "Suppressing people through force and denying their land rights will only deepen the insurgency. The BJP must realise you cannot bomb your way to peace."

Human rights groups, such as PUCL, Amnesty India, and HRW, expressed alarm over allegations of fake encounters, custodial torture, and arbitrary detention. The targeting of dissenters using UAPA provisions and labelling activists as "Urban Naxals" also drew immense condemnation. Striking down the public intellectuals Varavara Rao, Sudha Bharadwaj, and Gautam Navlakha in the Bhima-Koregaon case led to allegations of the state criminalising dissent, blurring the line between ideological sympathy and insurgent collaboration.

The BJP also ensured the publicity of these security successes, often through televised felicitation of jawans and visits to the forward areas by senior leaders. This militarised nationalism allowed the party to strike a strength while solidifying electoral support in Chhattisgarh and Jharkhand. By the end of NDA-I in 2019, it was widely accepted that the geographical and tactical influence of the Naxalite insurgency had eroded. Operationally significant areas were once again under government control, the violence had receded, and the Indian state had gained in confidence to counter the Naxalite threat.

Modi 1.0 replaced ad-hoc counterinsurgency with an integrated doctrine that combined relentless operations, targeted connectivity projects and calibrated amnesty. Violence curves bent decisively downward and several traditional strongholds—particularly in Jharkhand and parts of Odisha—transitioned from active conflict to residual risk zones. Yet episodic mass-casualty ambushes such as the April 2017 Sukma attack (26 CRPF fatalities) revealed persistent tactical gaps, underscoring the need for simultaneous improvements in local intelligence and human-rights safeguards.

3 Modi 2.0: Phase II of Eliminating Naxalism

From October 2023, the NDA-II under the Prime Minister of India, Narendra Modi, underwent a period of establishing a strategic posture against Naxalism. Building on infrastructure and operational advances made in NDA-I, the centralisation of these advances meant that NDA-II could adopt an even more security-dominant posture towards its operational aspects. Once more, the

Ministry of Home Affairs could be expected to be more aggressive under Amit Shah, Union Minister of Home Affairs, at least as indicated by its activities of sharpening intelligence, expanding liberated zones, and enhancing the legal architecture of states for counterinsurgency.

In fact, Amit Shah made behind him a much tougher, streamlined administration style. Shah announced a "zero tolerance" to left-wing extremism. In his first review meeting with Chief Ministers and the DGPs of LWE-affected states in August 2019, Shah said:

> We have reached the final phase of this battle. Now we have to make irreversible damage to the gains we have made so far.

The government focused on leadership decapitation with targeted missions removing 15 top-level CPI-Maoist leaders between 2020 and 2023, including Central Committee member Nambala Keshava Rao ("Basavaraju") in 2023 and strategist Gajarla Ravi (India Today, 2025). Three successive reviews reduced the official list of LWE-affected districts from 126 (2018) to 38 (April 2024); only six now fall in the "most affected" category. Violence incidents also fell from 509 in 2021 to 374 in 2024, and annual fatalities dropped below 150 for the first time in three decades. To ensure that legal measures also support the government's efforts in eradicating Naxalism from the soil of India, amendments were made to the Unlawful Activities (Prevention) Act. Further, tighter anti-money-laundering rules were applied, which disrupted Maoist extortion networks, coordinated police-modernisation plans, and aligned state procurement with Union intelligence grids. The Home Ministry also widened victim-compensation norms and digitised land-acquisition payments to tribal households, pre-empting grievances that insurgents traditionally exploited. While ensuring tribal development and welfare in terms of education, 178 Eklavya Model Residential Schools were set up, coupled with 46 industrial-training institutes and 49 district-level skill centres in core LWE belts. Additionally, completion of 3,970 km under RCPLWE and acceleration of the Kothagudem–Kirandul rail line (< 160 km) not only opened mineral hinterlands of Sukma, Dantewada and Bijapur, but simultaneously supports troop mobility and commercial freight (MRD, 2019:280–281).

While congratulating itself for its statistical successes, the government had a storm of dissenting voices accusing it of equating Naxalism with civil dissent. Some of the leading academics, students, and tribal rights activists were booked under sedition or UAPA charges. According to Arundhati Roy in 2021, "A war against Naxalism has become a war against the idea of justice. If you speak for the poor, you are now an enemy of the state."

Modi 2.0 translated the foundational architecture of the first term into measurable territorial and statistical gains. Steep declines in incidents, fatalities and affected districts signal strategic ascendance; simultaneously, the embedding of fibre, roads and welfare institutions in once-inaccessible forest blocks integrates these regions into the constitutional mainstream. Nonetheless, sporadic high-impact strikes and recurring allegations of excess force—especially in Bastar—demonstrate that tactical success must still be matched by steadfast adherence to human-rights and community-participation norms if Naxalism is to be uprooted from India.

4 Modi 3.0: the Final Blow

The third Narendra Modi administration framed the elimination of Left-Wing Extremism (LWE) as a non-negotiable national-security objective and assigned it an explicit deadline—31 March 2026—thereby transforming a decades-long counterinsurgency into a time-bound mission under operation Kagar (PIB, 2025). Union Home Minister Amit Shah reiterated the target during successive field visits to Chhattisgarh in June 2025, promising uninterrupted operations even through the monsoon months and urging Maoist cadres to surrender under an expanded rehabilitation package (Drolia, 2025). Annual LWE incidents fell from 1 080 in 2014 to 374 in 2024; security-force fatalities dropped from 88 to 19 over the same period, while the number of recorded Maoist deaths climbed to 2 089—a statistic security planners interpret as evidence of enhanced force dominance (PIB, 2025). The government expanded Central Armed Police Force (CAPF) deployments, integrated real-time drone imagery and precision-guided munitions, and approved "all-weather" operations that no longer pause during the monsoon (Putul, 2025). However, high-impact strikes such as the 6 January 2025 Bijapur IED attack, which killed eight District Reserve Guard personnel and a civilian driver, illustrate the residual lethality of the insurgency (Dash, 2025).

On the economic front, the Union Budget 2025–26 raised allocations for Security-Related Expenditure and the Special Infrastructure Scheme in LWE areas to ₹3 481.27 crore, a 41 percent increase over the previous year (The Economic Times, 2025). Parallel development funds flow through the Special Central Assistance programme, which has disbursed ₹3 724.95 crore since 2017 to fill "critical gaps" in public services across the most-affected districts (MHA, 2025).

The surrender policy was revised by the government in July 2024 to offer ₹500 000 for weapons laid down and accelerated housing, education and livelihood grants for former insurgents. A record 928 Maoists surrendered in 2024, and 718 more had done so by April 2025 (PIB, 2025). Nevertheless, civic-action programmes—jointly executed by CAPFs and district administrations to deliver mobile medical camps, agricultural toolkits and sports kits in remote villages focuses on "security-development continuum" (PIB, 2025), which resonates with the Modi Regime's slogan of "Sabka Sath, Sabka Vikas, Sabka Vishvas."

The government treats LWE districts as a litmus test for its "Viksit Bharat" narrative. Parliament's winter session 2024 passed amendments streamlining land-acquisition compensation in scheduled areas and tightened anti-money-laundering provisions targeting Maoist cadre finance networks (Kumar, 2024:37–40). State governments under the BJP synchronised their police-modernisation plans with the Union's 'National Policy and Action Plan', producing a unified chain of command for inter-state hot-pursuit operations, especially along the Chhattisgarh-Telangana-Maharashtra tri-junction. Official mapping now designates only six districts as "most affected", down from twelve in 2021 and thirty-eight in 2013 (Nair, 2024). The Ministry of Home Affairs further claims that 70 percent of former 'red corridor' territory has shifted to "residual influence" status. Independent datasets corroborate the downward trend in violence indicators but caution that tactical retreats often precede adaptive guerrilla resurgence (SATP, 2025). Civil-society observers also decry reports of collateral harm from drone-assisted strikes and allege under-reporting of custodial abuses, particularly in Bastar.

Modi 3.0 operationalises a dual-track doctrine: kinetic dominance sustains pressure on Maoist military capacities, while accelerated welfare spending aims to close the governance vacuum that insurgents exploit. Early data—declining incident curves, shrinking insurgent footprints and unprecedented surrender rates—suggests strategic momentum in favour of the state. Yet episodic mass-casualty attacks and human-rights concerns reveal a still-fluid conflict environment. Meeting the March 2026 deadline will require continuous intelligence-led policing, judicial oversight to uphold rights, and demonstrable improvement in socio-economic indicators across erstwhile red-corridor districts.

5 Conclusion

The Modi administration's decade-long counterinsurgency has progressed through three calibrated phases—foundational integration under Modi 1.0, accelerated consolidation under Modi 2.0, and deadline-driven finishing operations under Modi 3.0—creating a cumulative strategic momentum that now places the once-intractable Naxalite movement on the brink of strategic defeat.

Prime Minister Modi's first term supplied the institutional scaffold. The National Policy and Action Plan to address Left-Wing Extremism (LWE), approved in 2015, unified security, development and perception-management measures in a single doctrine. In 2017, the Home Ministry codified the SAMADHAN doctrine, directing Central Armed Police Forces to conduct intelligence-led, continuous and increasingly joint operations.

Modi 2.0 translated doctrine into measurable territorial gains. By March 2024, 17 589 km of strategic roads had been sanctioned for LWE belts and 14 618 km completed, shrinking guerrilla mobility corridors. Telecom Phase I–II commissioned 7 768 of the 10 505 planned mobile towers, extending 4G coverage—and along with this e-governance and digital payments—into forest interiors. A 160 km Kothagudem–Kirandul rail line, now in the final-survey stage, promises permanent logistics access to Sukma, Dantewada and Bijapur, districts once considered inaccessible red zones. Fiscal commitment matched kinetic ambition: the Union Budget 2025–26 raised Security-Related Expenditure and Special Infrastructure Scheme allocations to ₹3 481 crore, the highest ever for the LWE theatre.

The statistical impact is stark. National incident counts fell from 1 080 in 2014 to 374 in 2024, while security-force fatalities dropped from 88 to 19, and insurgent surrenders hit a record 928 in 2024, with another 718 in the first four months of 2025. The official map of LWE shrank from 126 affected districts in 2013 to just 38 in April 2024, of which only six remain in the "most affected" category.[1]

Modi 3.0 has moved to the strategic annihilation of the Maoist high command. The updated surrender policy and near-real-time drone intelligence facilitated leadership-decapitation missions such as Operation Kagar (May 2025), which eliminated CPI-Maoist general secretary Nambala Keshava Rao ("Basavaraju") and 26 other senior cadre, corroborated by independent field reportage. Earlier, deep-forest sweeps like Operation Prahar I–II in 2017 had demonstrated the viability of large-force raids in terrain once dominated by insurgents. The gruesome Sukma ambush of April 2017, which killed 26 CRPF personnel, now serves as a historical benchmark for how far the security curve has since tilted in the state's favour.

---

1 Year-wise incidents of violence, murder, explosions and counter-insurgency have been graphically depicted in **Annexure I** at the end of the book, providing a comparison between UPA and NDA regimes.

Developmental dividends are beginning to register locally: Maharashtra now records active Maoist presence in only 16 talukas, mainly in Gadchiroli, after systematic security-development drives. Analytical assessments by independent think-tanks likewise conclude that Bastar—the traditional epicentre of red insurgency—has "turned the corner" after successive clear-and-hold cycles.

Collectively, these outcomes validate the Modi regime's three-phase doctrine of doctrinal integration, territorial consolidation and final eradication. Integrated budgets, synchronised inter-state command structures and technology-enabled precision operations have closed the historical governance vacuum that insurgents exploited. With violence indicators at multi-decade lows and Maoist organisational integrity fatally compromised, the administration's target of a "Naxal-free India" by 31 March 2026 now appears attainable, provided that operational intensity, rights-compliant policing and accelerated welfare delivery persist across the residual six districts.

Conclusion

Before the 2024 general election, a journalist known for his ties to the Maoists visited our department. He was known to me and my colleagues as well. Informal discussions about Naxal activities in India began, and he quickly latched onto them. In the discussions, he expressed his wish that the Modi government should engage with the Maoists to bring them into the mainstream. He was concerned that, after resolving the Ram Janmabhoomi issue and the abrogation of Article 370, eliminating the Maoists would be on their agenda after the government formation. He was almost certain that the BJP would form the government and found no hope for the Maoists to carry forward the extremist activities in the future. I endorsed his assessment based on my tracking of government policy, which was committed to eliminating left extremism in the country. BJP, from the days of the Jansangh, has been holding the position that left ideology does not sync with the culture and civilisation of this country. It is un-Indian and deliberately implanted in Indian soil to weaken India by outside forces. Naxalism in particular, they claim, was a Chinese implant to bleed India. The ideological parent of the party, the RSS, has also been holding it as an enemy of the country, along with the other two being Christianity and Islam. Golwalkar explicitly articulated this view in his seminal work, the Bunch of Thoughts, which is a must-read for RSS cadres and Pracharaks. RSS considers them the ones who have been running academic and intellectual propaganda to demean the Indian civilisation and its history. And therefore, hold that this ideology needs to be uprooted. Unlike the Congress party, which vacillated between extremes of cold and hot, the BJP was consistent in its approach to dealing with left-wing extremism.

Therefore, when the BJP government came in power in the states of Jharkhand, Chhattisgarh, and Madhya Pradesh, a concerted attempt was made to contain the Naxal violence in the state. The Congress government at the centre in 2004 tried to carry forward the momentum against the Naxal violence, but the party leadership went into political mathematics, and the government at the centre, under the leadership of Dr Manmohan Singh, though termed it as the biggest threat to the nation, did not go with resolve to stamp it out completely. It started Operation Green Hunt, but soon retracted its efforts under pressure from the party leadership. It initially supported Salwa Judum, a people's campaign with the active support of the state government, but soon stood against it under pressure from the coalition partners, especially the left parties. Therefore, the initial success achieved by the security forces against the Maoists started to decline.

 | HTTPS://DOI.ORG/10.1163/9789004765054-014

The entire security doctrine and operations against the Naxals underwent a complete transformation with the victory of the BJP, led by Narendra Modi, and its stable mandate in 2014, marking a turning point in the fight against Maoism. It decided to adopt a comprehensive, integrated approach to tackle the Maoist menace. The state governments of the BJP in Chhattisgarh and Madhya Pradesh, which had not been receiving the required support from the centre during the UPA regime under the leadership of the Manmohan Singh government, now began receiving all support from the central government. Now, the number of killings of the security forces started declining, and the number of deaths, surrenders, or arrests of Maoists started picking up. After coming into power in 2024, the Modi government intensified the operations against the Maoists, and on 9 February 2025, the Home Minister of India, Amit Shah, declared that Naxalism would be eliminated from Indian soil by 31 March 2026. It is difficult to recall a claim of this nature being made by any government in the past. Never had such an emphatic date been predicted earlier towards wiping out any extremist movement. But soon the declaration started paving the way towards the actual on the ground. It was realised that the statements were not just any other politically motivated rhetoric, but rather a carefully crafted resolve. The government had broken the will of the Naxalites to fight any more. One after another, districts under the 'Red Corridor' started getting liberated from the Maoists by the security forces, which encircled them and mounted pressure enough either to surrender or fight against the forces.

There was a time when Naxalites used to capture the headlines for their strikes on civilian and military assets. In the Red Corridor, which was depicted as a liberated zone, the Naxalites had partial control over the area. They used to dictate terms to the civil and police officials at the local level. The situation has changed today. There is hardly any day when news related to the killing and surrender of Naxalites does not appear in the newspapers and electronic media. The government has gone all out to finish the Naxals. The CPM leader alleged that the government of India is not listening to the appeals of the Maoists for a negotiation and a ceasefire. The media is also not taking much interest in their appeals. The national narrative has changed. The intellectual support, which previously manifested in the form of rallies and demonstrations in support of Naxals under the guise of protecting human rights and criticising the state apparatus's highhandedness, is now on the margins. The courts are also less proactive on the issue than they were earlier. It looks like the entire scenario has changed.

When compared with the time when the Salwa Judum case was brought before the Supreme Court, or when Binayak Sen was arrested and jailed, or when Gautam Navlakha's bail petition was being heard in the Supreme Court of India, the media was so assertive in their favour that the BJP governments were portrayed as villains. Despite the fact that the report of the National Human Rights Commission had also highlighted the atrocities perpetrated by the Naxalites on the innocent civilians, the Judgment of the Supreme Court looked overtly biased and leaned towards the ideological left, which was widely criticised by the editors, except for a few, who wrote editorials against the observation and ideologically loaded passage of the judgment. Parliamentarians expressed their concerns. But the party in power then wanted to win the support of Naxalites despite the fact that the Central government had started 'Operation Green Hunt' and the government was on record saying that Naxals were the biggest internal threat to the security of India. Gautam Navlakha was given house arrest on the grounds of bad health and age.

The Naxal movement thrived on an emancipatory ideology, fear created by firepower, social support due to poverty, lack of basic needs of life, and an intellectual echo-system that lent support because it believed in that ideology. Over the last decade or so, this ideological ecosystem has lost its steam and strength. It was precisely because the media and university campuses that nurtured the ecosystem of left ideology did not get much support in the current political establishment. The weakening of the political left in India, as well as the decline of the Congress Party, has directly impacted this ecosystem. The left-liberal political establishment provided fertile soil for the growth of ideological left and left extremism in India. With the BJP coming to power at the centre and in several states of India, it broke the ideological dominance of the left on campuses and in the media. Market, technology, electronic gadgets, and Artificial intelligence have replaced the vocabulary of revolution, socialism, communism, proletarianism, and nuances of capitalism. The electronic media, driven by market forces, have overtaken and overshadowed the print media, especially the English media, where the left presence continues to dominate the editorial columns and news orientation. The result is visible. Naxalism is no more a fancy idea on the campuses.

There was a time when Naxalism was a progressive idea for the youth to emulate. Inroads of the market economy have dampened that zeal, and there are few takers of working towards a violent revolution to establish a classless and stateless society. Ideological discourses of communism have been replaced by the market and market morality. Electronic gadgets in hand, coffee and burger shops around, coupled with modern fashion items, they are on a new path of making life meaningful by skilling and enabling themselves for future challenges. The market not just teaches individualism but nurtures it. It presents a variety of choices and does not leave them free to consider violent revolution against the state. The market has engaged the mind and labour into its framework and broken the thought and infrastructure that recruited and nurtured the zeal and passion for violent revolution. Hence, the Naxal movement is not getting ideological traction from well-meaning people in the intelligentsia and on the ground.

The ideological hypnotisation of young minds and roping them into the movement weakens the moment youths realise that the utopian world visualised has not only failed elsewhere in the world, but there is also no possibility of making it come true here. Even the intellectuals and ideologues of the left concede that the ideal of a communist state, as visualised by Marx and Mao, has not been realised, even in lands where it was implemented under authoritarian regimes. The Soviet Union broke apart without realising the state of communism, which was embedded with elements of egalitarianism. Millions were butchered in China to realise communism, but it finally drifted towards capitalism and market expansionism. The countries that, after the Second World War, moved towards a capitalist path of development one after another. Communism as an ideology at ground failed to be realised in any part of the world, even at the cost of human lives. Needless to say, the ideology lost its communicative power in India as well, gradually.

Poverty, underdevelopment, state apathy to the poor and deprived, and lack of effective and accountable governance provide the fertile soil for the Naxals to grow and prosper. When deprived people are told that their deprivation is a result of exploitation by the rich and state apathy, they tend towards picking up guns against inequality, indignity, and injustice. When they are told that look how the corporations are exploiting the rich minerals from their habitats, destroying their forest cover, and how they are not treated with dignity and fairness by the state, they see meaning in it and rally behind the ideology and its operational design. The percolation of fruits of development carries the capacity to dilute and dissolve the revolutionary outburst to an extent. But ideological inclination is not the only factor that draws innocent people into Maoism. The fear of violence in the absence of toeing the line of the Maoists also adds to the cadre building. In other words, thousands of people were roped in by the Maoists forcefully into the fight against the Indian state. And therefore, military dominance was used to instil a sense of security among the poor and innocent and to enable their access to a dignified life. The government's social welfare schemes, combined with the construction of roads, schools, hospitals, and the expansion of the healthcare system to remote areas, as well as access to gainful employment, make the soil infertile for Naxalism to prosper.

The Naxal cadres on the ground sought to grab the headlines and their presence through acts of terror and violence. And therefore, engagement of the Naxals towards dialogue and the hope to persuade them to leave the guns and join the path of liberal democracy was impractical. This needed a military response, as was the case in Bengal, where the CPM government forced them to flee and take refuge in Andhra Pradesh, Madhya Pradesh, and Chhattisgarh.

The BJP government, therefore, decided to take on the Naxals and free the red corridor, which happened to be the liberated zones in their ideological lexicon. It created special forces to tackle the Maoists and mounted relentless operations against them. In the last ten years, almost all the top-ranking leadership of the Naxals have either been put behind bars or eliminated in police encounters. Every second day, the front page of newspapers grabs the headlines of Naxals, either killed in an encounter or arrested by the police. According to the PIB post-dated 10 April 2025, there is a drastic decline in Maoist violence in the country. The number of Left-wing affected districts is now reduced to 38 in April 2024 from 120 in 2018. West Bengal, Kerala, Bihar, and Andhra Pradesh, which once upon a time were citadels of the Naxal activities, drew either zero or a couple of scattered, minuscule, and violent incidents. The number of most affected districts got reduced from 12 to 6, four districts in Chhattisgarh, one district in Jharkhand (West Singhbhum) and one district in Maharashtra (Garhchirolli). Compared to 2010, when the total loss of civilians and defence forces was close to 1005, it has now come down to merely 150 in 2024, i.e. a total of 85 percent decline. There has also been a sharp decline in attacks on economic infrastructure from 365 in 2010 to 25 in 2024. In 2023, 380 Naxalites were killed, 1,194 were arrested, and 1,045 surrendered. And this pace has not receded. In the last 10 years, several top leaders of the Naxal movement have been eliminated by the security forces. That includes Nambla Keshav Rao alias Basavraj, the general secretary of the CPI (ML), who was killed in an encounter in Chhattisgarh in May 2025. Chhattisgarh is the only state which can be said to be the epicentre of Naxalism today because the majority of activities of the Naxals come from their areas. But there too, 85 percent of the Left-Wing Extremism has been decimated.

What worked in favour of the government and against the Naxalites is the decisive approach reflected in the form of a zero tolerance for left-wing extremism. No ideological or socio-economic pretext was acceptable to the government. It was embedded in the security doctrine specific to the Maoists that the government would not tolerate any justification for the violent activities. The message was clear; either lay down the arms and surrender or be prepared for an encounter. The government went tough on the urban Naxals, who lent intellectual and moral support to the movement. Their narrative was countered aggressively, and in certain cases, actions were taken as well. Professors from universities and intellectual activists were picked up and put behind bars for their direct or indirect support of the violent Maoist activities. The second approach was to ensure that the fruits of development reached the people without leakage or corruption. A well-thought-out National Plan with a multi-pronged strategy was applied. The government ensured that the developmental plans designed for and planned in Naxal-infested areas were completed on time. It could be possible only when there was an environment of safety and security. This could be possible only when the writ of the Naxals in those areas depicted as 'no-go zones' was liberated. And this is where the government remained firm and bold in taking on the Naxals.

The police system was modernised, equipped with modern weapons and gadgets to monitor the activities of Naxalites and overpower them in case of encounter. A series of programmes were unfolded in the area, which included special training for the police force, equipping the police stations with modern security equipment, financial security to the forces receiving death on the line of duty, expenditure on publicity material to counter the narrative of the Maoists, development of infrastructure in the areas, etc. All this changed the whole narrative in the Naxal-infested areas. Maoists lost the local support that they used to enjoy earlier, and this reflected in the massive surrender of hardcore cadres across the states. Salwa Judum, in fact, was also intended to create a local support base in the fight against the Maoists. However, it was projected as a state-sponsored creation of a private militia to counter the Maoists. The court also interpreted it as such and directed the state to disband the appointment of SPOs under the Salwa Judum scheme. The court's judgment overlooked the merits of the programme, as outlined in the report of the National Human Rights Commission, which had addressed both the positive and negative aspects of the programme. This certainly hindered operations and weakened the state's operation against the Naxal movement.

The Modi government decided to work on an integrated and comprehensive, coordinated operation against the Maoists, which included countering their ideological narratives, defeating them militarily on the ground, and building a social support base against them. The success is visible on the ground. In the last three months of August, September, and October 2025, there has been a series of thousands of dreaded Naxals surrendering across the states of Maharashtra, Jharkhand, and Chhattisgarh. In Garhchirolli in Maharashtra, 61 Maoists, including the commander Bhupathi, surrendered with weapons before the Chief Minister Devendra Fadanavis in a function. Bhupathi carried a Rs 60 million bounty on his head. On September 30, Naxals surrendered in Jharkhand, which included Ravindra Yadav and Anand Singh, the zonal and sub-zonal commander of the Maoists. On October 16, 170 Naxals again surrendered in Chhattisgarh, and the very next day, 208 more laid down their arms. When the Home Minister declared that the Maoist movement would be eliminated by the end of March 2026, it was initially held as political rhetoric. But given the pace at which Maoists have surrendered or been killed, the target is not just achievable, but seems to be coming to reality much before the deadline.

Bibliography

'Probe politicians–Maoists' nexus: RJD. (2011, February 2). *The Bihar Times*. Available (Consulted 24 October 2025) at: http://www.bihartimes.in/Newsbihar/2011/Feb/Newsbihar02Feb3.html.

'Salwa Judum case ruling against spirit of Constitution'. (2021, November 17) *The Hindu*. Available (Consulted 14 November 2024) at: https://www.thehindu.com/news/national/salwa-judum-case-ruling-against-spirit-of-constitution/article2353960.ece.

'Snake tried to occupy anthill, they will retaliate': While media calls him a 'human rights activist', Varavara Rao justified the massacre by Maoists. (2020, November 19) OpIndia. Available (consulted 23 December 2023) at: https://www.opindia.com/2020/11/watch-varavara-rao-defended-massacre-of-police-by-maoists/.

"Being neutral is our biggest crime": Government, vigilante, and Naxalite abuses in India's Chhattisgarh state. (July 2008) *Human Rights watch*. Available (Consulted 14 November 2024) at: chrome-extension://efaidnbmnnnibpcajpcglclefindmkaj/https://www.hrw.org/reports/2008/india0708/india0708_insert_web.pdf.

18 bank accounts involved in terror financing frozen: Government (2010, March 31) *The Economic Times*. Available (Consulted 19 November 2024) at: https://economictimes.indiatimes.com/news/politics-and-nation/18-bank-accounts-involved-in-terror-financing-frozen-government/articleshow/5747815.cms.

26 districts highly Naxal-hit in country—govt. (2013, April 12). *Hindustan Times*. Available (Consulted 2 September 2024) at: https://www.hindustantimes.com/delhi/26-districts-highly-naxal-hit-in-country-govt/story-qMPbnPE2IjlmkkV1AEtZ6H.html.

62 minors among 130 new Maoist recruits, says Naxal 'report' found at encounter site. (2025, March 28) *Times of India*. Available (Consulted 18 August 2024) at: https://timesofindia.indiatimes.com/city/raipur/62-minors-among-130-new-maoist-recruits-says-naxal-report-found-at-encounter-site/articleshow/119611344.cms.

8 convicted for Maoist activities. (2012, August 24) *The Times of India*. Available (Consulted 14 November 2024) at: https://timesofindia.indiatimes.com/city/bhubaneswar/8-convicted-for-Maoist-activities/articleshow/15626047.cms.

Agnihotri, V. (2017, May 4) *Urban Naxalism: Strategy and Modus Operandi—Part 1*. Swarajya Magazine. Available (Consulted 22 August 2024) at: https://swarajyamag.com/politics/urban-naxalism-strategy-and-modus-operandi-part-1.

Agnihotri, V. (2018). *Urban Naxals: The Making of Buddha in a Traffic Jam*. Garuda Prakashan. Available (Consulted 10 June 2025) at: https://www.garudabooks.com/urban-naxals.

 | HTTPS://DOI.ORG/10.1163/9789004765054-015

Ahmed, F. (2008, October 19). VHP, BJP leaders on Maoists' hit list in Orissa. *India Today*. Available (Consulted 19 April 2025) at: https://www.indiatoday.in/latest-headlines/story/vhp-bjp-leaders-on-maoists-hit-list-in-orissa-31829-2008-10-18.

Ajitha. (1999, January 12). *Interview by D. Jose & S. Jacob*. Rediff on the Net. Available (Consulted 18 August 2024) at: https://m.rediff.com/news/1999/jan/12kerala1.htm.

Amnesty International Urges India to Implement Court Ban of Anti-Maoist Militia. (2011, July 07). *Amnesty International*. Available (Consulted 30 October 2024) at: https://www.commondreams.org/newswire/2011/07/07/amnesty-international-urges-india-implement-court-ban-anti-maoist-militias.

Anand, A. (2013, November 19). *Salwa Judum sparks political slugfest*. DNA India. Available (Consulted 17 June 2025) at: https://www.dnaindia.com/india/report-salwa-judum-sparks-political-slugfest-1247318.

Anonymous (n.d.) Charu Mazumdar. Available (Consulted 18 August 2024) at: https://www.marxists.org/reference/archive/mazumdar/index.htm.

Anoop, A.J. (2011) Maoist Funding: Dimensions, Sources and Implications. Vivekananda International Foundation. Available (Consulted 09 October 2024) at: https://www.vifindia.org/article/2011/january/14/Maoist-Funding-Dimensions-Sources-and-Implications.

Apex Court Ruling on Salwa Judum. (2011, July 11). *The Economic Times*. Available (Consulted 08 September 2024) at: https://economictimes.indiatimes.com/opinion/et-editorial/apex-court-ruling-on-salwa-judum/articleshow/9179776.cms.

Army won't be used against Maoists—Chidambaram (2009, September 25). *The Indian Express*. Available (Consulted 23 September 2024) at: https://indianexpress.com/article/india/latest-news/army-won-t-be-used-against-maoists-chidamba/.

Arora, V. (2015, August 24). Should Nepal be secular? *The Diplomat*. Available (Consulted 19 April 2025) at: https://thediplomat.com/2015/08/should-nepal-be-secular/.

Arun Jaitley slams judicial over-reach. (2011, August 18). *Hindustan Times*. Available (Consulted 08 September 2024) at: https://www.hindustantimes.com/delhi/arun-jaitley-slams-judicial-over-reach/story-YbBW3dPZlNqptO5lGybAeM.html.

Arun Jaitley slams Supreme Court for declaring Salwa Judum unconstitutional. (2011, July 14). *DNA India*. Available (Consulted 2 September 2024) at: https://www.dnaindia.com/india/report-arun-jaitley-slams-supreme-court-for-declaring-salwa-judum-unconstitutional-1565815.

Asit Kumar Sen Gupta vs State of Chhattisgarh on 16 December 2011. (2011, December 16). *Indiankanoon.org*. Available (Consulted 14 November 2024) at: https://indiankanoon.org/doc/123461068/.

Assam DGP accuses Tata Tea of funding ULFA (1997, August 8) *Business Standard*. Available (Consulted 09 October 2024) at: https://www.business-standard.com/article/specials/assam-dgp-accuses-tata-tea-of-funding-ulfa-197090801265_1.html.

Batabyal, R. (2014). *JNU: The making of a university*. Gurgaon: HarperCollins Publishers.

Bhalla, A. (2014, April 23). *Bihar Assembly Speaker and Lok Sabha candidate Uday Narayan Chaudhary strikes deal with Maoists for support in polls*. India Today. Available (Consulted 17 June 2025) at: https://www.indiatoday.in/elections/highlights/story/2014-lok-sabha-polls-uday-narayan-chaudhary-maoists-bihar-187358-2014-04-03.

Bharatiya Janata Party. (2000). *BJP resolutions: Political, 1980–1999* (p. 149). BJP. Available (Consulted 23 October 2025) at: https://nla.gov.au/nla.cat-vn3012510.

Bhardwaj, A. (2020, June 16). *BJP's cozy nexus with Maoists in Chhattisgarh flourishes despite leaders' murder, arrest*. The Print. Available (Consulted 10 June 2025) at: https://theprint.in/opinion/bjps-cozy-nexus-with-maoists-in-chhattisgarh-flourishes-despite-leaders-murder-arrest/442326/.

Bhaskar, Utpal (2010) Illegal coal-mining revenue going to Naxals. *LiveMint*. Available (Consulted 19 November 2024) at: https://www.livemint.com/Companies/hbYVbMuknQEwoHBYrCwsKJ/Illegal-coal-mining-revenue-going-to-Naxals.html.

Bhatia, B. (2011) Judging the Judgment. *Economic and Political Weekly*, 46(30).

Bhattacharya, S. (2009) *Red hammer over Calcutta University*. Kolkata: Statesman.

Bhattacharya, S. (2016). *Lalgarh and the legend of Kishanji: Tales from India's Maoist movement*. Gurgaon: HarperCollins.

Bihar Police deports nine French tourists for violating visa rules. (2012, April 23) *India Today*. Available (Consulted 26 April 2025) at: https://www.indiatoday.in/india/east/story/bihar-police-deports-9-french-tourists-for-violating-visa-rules-99976-2012-04-22.

Billington, J.H. (1966) Six views of the Russian Revolution. *World Politics* 18(3): 452–73.

Binayak Sen on the Planning Commission Committee. (2011, May 11). *The Hindu*. Available (Consulted 24 October 2025) at: https://www.thehindu.com/news/national/binayak-sen-on-planning-commission-committee/article2007261.ece.

Binayak Sen v. Chhattisgarh—Global Freedom of Expression. (2021, July 6). *Columbia Global Freedom of Expression*. Available (Consulted 14 November 2024) at: https://globalfreedomofexpression.columbia.edu/cases/binayak-sen-v-chhatisgarh/.

Biswas, A. (2005) Maoism: an exercise in anarchism. *The Marxist* 21(4).

Bose, P. (2010) Maoism: a critique from the left. New Delhi: Left Word Books.

Bose, S. (2011, September 18) *Corporates paying protection money to Naxals. The Times of India*. Available (Consulted 18 October 2024) at: https://timesofindia.indiatimes.com/city/nagpur/corporates-paying-protection-money-to-naxals/articleshow/10024980.cms.

Bose, S.S. (2015, November 1). Naxals targeting SPOs throw fresh challenge to police. *The Times of India*. Available (Consulted 24 November 2024) at: https://timesofindia.indiatimes.com/City/Nagpur/Naxals-targeting-SPOs-throw-fresh-challenge-to-police/articleshow/49613156.cms.

Brinkley, G. (1998) Leninism: what it was and what it was not. *The Review of Politics* 60(1): 151–164.

Buddha, PC meet over Naxals. (2009, October 12) *Hindustan Times*. Available (consulted 23 December 2023) at: https://www.hindustantimes.com/delhi/buddha-pc-meet-over-naxals/story-gXnd4fmZ7ieND2wTpIRToL.html.

Burman (2009) Naxalite movement that was not in Naxalbari. *Mainstream* Vol. 47(25).

Calamur, K. (2016, February 18) The angry debate over sedition in India. *The Atlantic*. Available (consulted 23 December 2023) at: https://www.theatlantic.com/international/archive/2016/02/india-jnu-sedition/463131/.

Catholic Church, an ally of Tamil Tiger terrorists. (2009, April 4) *Sri Lanka Guardian*. Available (Consulted 26 April 2025) at: http://www.srilankaguardian.org/2009/04/catholic-church-ally-of-tamil-tiger.html.

Centre bans CPI Maoist, CPM strikes different note. (2009, June 22). *LiveMint*. Available (Consulted 2 September 2024) at: https://www.livemint.com/Politics/KULDarYemfjsri6R1eETuJ/Centre-bans-CPIMaoist-CPM-strikes-different-note.html.

Centre gives its tacit approval to Salwa Judum. (2009, January 8). *The Times of India*. Available (Consulted 23 October 2025) at: https://timesofindia.indiatimes.com/india/centre-gives-its-tacit-approval-to-salwa-judum/articleshow/3948503.cms.

Centre repeats: CPI-Maoist a terror outfit, CPM insists on political fight (2009, June 22). *The Indian Express*. Available (Consulted 2 September 2024) at: https://indianexpress.com/article/india/regional/centre-repeats-cpimaoist-a-terror-outfit-cpm-insists-on-political-fight.

Centre to file review petition in SC on Salwa Judum order. (2011, August 2). *Firstpost*. Available (Consulted 14 November 2024) at: https://www.firstpost.com/fwire/centre-to-file-review-petition-in-sc-on-salwa-judum-order-52921.html.

Centre's policy to combat Naxalism incongruous: BJP. (2013, June 8). *The Hindu*. Available (Consulted 27 October 2025) at: https://www.thehindu.com/news/national/centres-policy-to-combat-naxalism-incongruous-bjp/article4795191.ece.

Chakrabarty, R. (2010, August 24). Raped repeatedly, Naxal leader quits red ranks. *Times of India*. Available (Consulted 18 August 2024) at: https://timesofindia.indiatimes.com/india/raped-repeatedly-naxal-leader-quits-red-ranks/articleshow/6423200.cms.

Chakraborty, S. (2009, November 2) Naxal leader claims corporates funding rebels. *News18*. Available (Consulted 06 February 2025) at: https://www.news18.com/amp/videos/india/corporates-fund-maoists-327865.html.

Chakravarti, S. (2008) *Red Sun: Travels In Naxalite Country* (p. 18). New Delhi: Viking (Penguin Group).

Chakravorti, T. (2013, January 20) Jharkhand DGP in trouble over withdrawal of SS fund. Business Standard. Available (Consulted 15 October 2024) at: https://www

.business-standard.com/article/economy-policy/jharkhand-dgp-in-trouble-over-withdrawal-of-ss-fund-109090700075_1.html.

Chathukulam, J., & Manasi, J. (2022, April 2). *Political killings have been a phenomenon restricted to Bengal and Kerala.* Mainstream, 60(15). Available (Consulted 10 June 2025) at: https://www.mainstreamweekly.net/article12122.html.

Chatterji, S. (2018, April 22). *When CPI(M) had a 'pact' with Congress in 2004. Hindustan Times.* Available (Consulted 2 September 2024) at: https://www.hindustantimes.com/india-news/when-cpi-m-had-a-pact-with-congress-in-2004/story-bi89IR7LejwVr639m7DljP.html.

Chaturvedi, A. (2013, May 26). *Chhattisgarh Naxal attack: Top state Congress leaders among 25 killed.* NDTV. Available (Consulted 27 October 2025) at: https://www.ndtv.com/india-news/chhattisgarh-naxal-attack-top-state-congress-leaders-among-25-killed-523359.

Chaudhary, S.R. (2013, November 19). Maoists infiltrate NGOs to expand support base in Bengal. *DNA India.*

Chhattisgarh Govt says anti-Naxal group Salwa Judum infructous. (2010, October 28). *The Indian Express.* Available (Consulted 24 November 2024) at: https://indianexpress.com/article/india/regional/chhattisgarh-govt-says-antinaxal-group-salwa-judum-infructous/.

Chhattisgarh inquiry report. (2008). *National Human Rights Commission (Investigation Division).* Available (Consulted 08 November 2024) at: http://sanhati.com/wp-content/uploads/2010/10/nhrc-chattisgarh-enquiry-report.pdf.

Chhattisgarh: On the Supreme Court judgement terming appointment of SPOs as unconstitutional. (2011, July 12). *Sanhati.* Available (Consulted 30 October 2024) at: https://sanhati.com/articles/3861/.

Children in South Asia: Securing their rights. (1998, April 21). *Amnesty International.* Available (Consulted 22 August 2024) at: https://www.amnesty.org/en/documents/asa04/001/1998/en/.

Choudhary, S. (2012). *Let's call him Vasu: With the Maoists in Chhattisgarh.* Gurugram: Penguin Random House.

Chowdhury, S.R. (2013, September 26) *G N Saibaba: The revolutionary in Delhi University.* The Times of India. Available (consulted 03 January 2024) at: https://timesofindia.indiatimes.com/city/delhi/g-n-saibaba-the-revolutionary-in-delhi-university/articleshow/23104776.cms.

Christian father protests Naxal's arrest in Ahmedabad (2010, June 2) DeshGujarat. Available (Consulted 02 November 2024) at: https://deshgujarat.com/2010/06/02/christian-father-protests-naxal-suspects-arrest-in-ahmedabad.

Church backing Tripura rebels. *BBC News.* (2000, April 18). Available (Consulted 19 April 2025) at: http://news.bbc.co.uk/2/hi/south_asia/717775.stm.

Communist Party of India (Maoist) (2004) Party constitution, Central Committee (Provisional), Article 60. Available (Consulted 12 January 2025) at: https://www.satp.org/satporgtp/countries/india/maoist/documents/papers/partyconstitution.htm.

Communist Party of India (Maoist) (n.d.) Party constitution, Central Committee (Provisional). Available (Consulted 18 August 2024) at: https://www.satp.org/satporgtp/countries/india/maoist/documents/papers/partyconstitution.htm.

Communist Party of India (Marxist) (2019) On the programme of the CPI. Available (Consulted 22 August 2024) at: https://cpim.org/content/programme-cpi.

Communist Party of India (Marxist) rules out withdrawal of support to UPA government. (2007, August 16). *The Economic Times*. Available (Consulted 10 June 2025) at: https://economictimes.indiatimes.com/cpim%20rules%20out%20withdrawal%20of%20support%20to%20upa%20govt/articleshow/2285658.cms.

Communist Party of India (Marxist–Leninist) (1970) General programme and constitution adopted at the First Party Congress, May 1970. Available (Consulted 22 August 2024) at: https://www.marxists.org/subject/india/cpiml/constitution-cpml.pdf.

Communist Party of India (Marxist–Leninist) (n.d.) Political resolution of the Communist Party of India (Marxist–Leninist).

Communist Party of Italy (Maoist) (2023) Long live Marxism–Leninism–Maoism! Joint declaration on the occasion of the 130th birth anniversary of the great Marxist teacher Comrade Mao Tse-tung: Proletarians and oppressed peoples of the world—let us unite! Available (Consulted 22 August 2024) at: https://cmpa.io/en/wp-content/uploads/sites/2/2023/12/Final-text-JD-130 °-mao-Eng.pdf.

Cong MP suspected behind VHP leader's murder. Ahmed, F. (2008, October 17). *India Today*. Available (Consulted 19 April 2025) at: https://www.indiatoday.in/latest-headlines/story/cong-mp-suspected-behind-vhp-leaders-murder-31757-2008-10-17.

Congress to embark on 'Parivartan Yatra'. (2013, April 3). *The Times of India*. Available (Consulted 27 October 2025) at: https://timesofindia.indiatimes.com/city/raipur/congress-to-embark-on-parivartan-yatra/articleshow/19353296.cms.

CPI opposes review of court order on Salwa Judum. (2011, September 12). *The Hindu*. Available (Consulted 14 August 2025) at: https://www.thehindu.com/news/national/cpi-opposes-review-of-court-order-on-salwa-judum/article2445156.ece.

D'Mellow, B. (2010) What is Maoism and other essays. Kharagpur: Cornerstone Publications.

D'Souza, S.M. & Routray, B.P. (2013, January 19) Estimates of Maoist extortion vary between ₹1,200–2,000 crore annually. *Business Standard*. Available (Consulted 15 January 2025) at: https://www.business-standard.com/article/opinion/shanthie-mariet-d-souza-bibhu-prasad-routray-red-kitty-and-beyond-110052000002_1.html.

Dash, J. (2025, January 6). *Eight policemen, driver killed in Maoist attack in central India*. Reuters. Available (Consulted 2 September 2024) at: https://www.reuters

.com/world/india/ten-policemen-feared-killed-bomb-blast-central-india-tv-report-says-2025-01-06/.

Datta, S. (1974) 1 divides into 2. Communist Party of India (Marxist–Leninist) (n.d.), 419–423. Available (Consulted 2 September 2024) at: https://www.marxists.org/subject/india/cpiml/1-divides-into-2.pdf.

Deadliest Maoist attacks in the last decade. (2017, May 10) *Hindustan Times*. Available (Consulted 18 January 2025) at: https://www.hindustantimes.com/india-news/deadliest-maoist-attacks-in-the-last-decade/story-LHYc1pdoSomzXy75vq9i2L.html.

Death, Displacement and Deprivation: The War in Dantewara: A Report. (2006) *Human Rights Forum*. Available (Consulted 08 November 2024) at: http://cpjc.files.wordpress.com/2007/07/hrfdantewadareport.pdf.

Denyer, S. (2007, March 16) Indian Maoists exploit anger over land seizure. *Reuters News*. Available (Consulted 06 February 2025) at: https://www.reuters.com/article/us-india-maoists-idUSSP970520070316.

Deogharia, J. (2015, April 23). Jharkhand HC issues notice to Union Home Secretary over kidnapping of children by Naxals. *Times of India*. Available (Consulted 22 August 2024) at: https://timesofindia.indiatimes.com/city/ranchi/jharkhand-hc-issues-notice-to-union-home-secretary-over-kidnapping-of-children-by-naxals/articleshow/47030156.cms.

Desk, H. (2018, February 12). Nagaland Baptist Church Spews Anti-Hindu & Anti-India Hate, Exhorts Voters to Choose "Christian Principles over Development". *HinduPost*. Available (Consulted 07 February 2025) at: https://hindupost.in/news/nagaland-baptist-church-spews-anti-hindu-anti-india-hate-exhorts-voters-choose-christian-principles-development/.

Drolia, R. (2021, September 29). Kids snatched at 15 comprise 70% of Naxal cadre: Survey. *Times of India*. Available (Consulted 22 August 2024) at: https://timesofindia.indiatimes.com/city/raipur/kids-snatched-at-15-comprise-70-of-naxal-cadre-survey/articleshow/86593994.cms.

Drolia, R. (2025, June 23). *No respite for Maoists this monsoon in Bastar, says Amit Shah: Operations to continue without break. The Times of India*. Available (Consulted 5 August 2024) at: https://timesofindia.indiatimes.com/city/raipur/no-respite-for-maoists-this-monsoon-in-bastar-says-amit-shah-operations-to-continue-without-break/articleshow/122007316.cms.

Dungdung, G. (2015) *Mission Saranda: A War for Natural Resources in India*. Ranchi: Bir Buru Omapay Media & Entertainment LLP.

Empower tribals to fight Naxals: Pawar. (2013, May 31). *The Indian Express*. Available (Consulted 27 October 2025) at: https://indianexpress.com/article/news-archive/web/empower-tribals-to-fight-naxals-pawar/.

Fletcher, R. (1982) British radicalism and German revisionism: the case of Eduard Bernstein. *The International History Review* 4(3): 339–370.

Former IB chief: Maoists won't hurt collector. Bhatt, S. (2012, April 23). *Rediff.* Available (Consulted 07 February 2025) at: https://www.rediff.com/news/special/former-ib-chief-maoists-wont-hurt-collector/20120423.htm.

Four JNU clips found 'genuine'. (2016, May 17) *The Times of India.* Available (consulted 03 January 2024) at: https://timesofindia.indiatimes.com/city/delhi/four-jnu-clips-found-genuine/articleshow/52323421.cms.

Four Maoists killed in encounter with Greyhounds in cut-off region. (2018, May 18). *The New Indian Express.* Available (Consulted 27 November 2024) at: https://www.newindianexpress.com/states/odisha/2018/May/18/four-maoists-killed-in-encounter-with-greyhounds-in-cut-off-region-1816179.html.

Gandhi, M. (1928, 19 January). Young India 10(3). Available (Consulted 13 February 2025) at: chrome-extension://efaidnbmnnnibpcajpcglclefindmkaj/https://www.gandhipedia150.in/static/data/highlighted_pdfs_output/Sabarmati_volume35_book_364.pdf.

Gandhi, M. (1936, 18 July). Harijan 4(23). Available (Consulted 13 February 2025) at: https://archive.org/details/HindSwaraj.Harijan.vol4.

Gandhi, M. (1937, 3 April). Harijan 5(8). Available (Consulted 13 February 2025) at: https://archive.org/details/HindSwaraj.Harijan.vol5/page/n57/mode/2up.

Gandhi, M. (1937, 6 March). Harijan 5(4). Available (Consulted 22 February 2025) at: https://archive.org/details/HindSwaraj.Harijan.vol5/page/n57/mode/2up.

Gave proof of Trinamool-Maoist link: CPM. (2010, March 6). *The Indian Express.* Available (Consulted 23 October 2025) at: https://indianexpress.com/article/cities/kolkata/briefs-44/.

Ghose D. (2018, July 19). Bastar development offensive: How LTTE trained Maoists and transformed tribal youths into merciless killing machines. *Firstpost.* Available (Consulted 2 September 2024) at: https://www.firstpost.com/india/bastar-development-offensive-how-ltte-trained-maoists-and-transformed-tribal-youths-into-merciless-killing-machines-4754011.html.

Global overview 2011: People internally displaced by conflict and violence. (2012, April). *Internal Displacement Monitoring Centre.* Available (Consulted 2 September 2024) at: https://www.internal-displacement.org/sites/default/files/publications/documents/2012-global-overview-2011-global-en.pdf.

Gohain, M.P. (2010, April 11). Pitched battle over "people's war" at JNU. *The Times of India.* Available (consulted 03 January 2024) at: https://timesofindia.indiatimes.com/india/Pitched-battle-over-peoples-war-at-JNU/articleshow/5783093.cms.

Government of India, Planning Commission. (2008, April). *Development challenges in extremist affected areas: Report of an Expert Group to the Planning Commission.* Government of India.

Government of India. (2008, June). *Combatting terrorism: Protecting by righteousness* (Second Administrative Reforms Commission, 8th Report). Available (Consulted 23 October 2025) at: https://darpg.gov.in/sites/default/files/combating_terrorism8.pdf.

Govt has right to use force to tackle Maoists: Chidambaram. (2010, March 12). *The Economic Times*. Available (Consulted 14 August 2025) at: https://economictimes.indiatimes.com/news/politics-and-nation/govt-has-right-to-use-force-to-tackle-maoists-chidambaram/articleshow/5675413.cms.

Graziosi, A. (2019) A century of 1917s: ideas, representations, and interpretations of the October Revolution, 1917–2017. *Harvard Ukrainian Studies* 36(1/2): 9–44.

Grewal, P.M. (2010) Indian Maoists: flawed strategy and perverted praxis. In: Bose, P. Maoism: A critique from the left. Delhi: Left Word.

Guha, R. (2007) *Adivasis, Naxalites, and Indian Democracy. Economic and Political Weekly*. Available (Consulted 23 September 2024) at: https://ramachandraguha.in/archives/adivasis-naxalites-and-indian-democracyeconomic-and-political-weekly.html.

Guha, R., Harivansh, Naqvi, F., Sarma, E.A.S., Sundar, N., & Verghese, B.G. (2006). *Salwa Judum: War in the Heart of India: Excerpts from the Report by the Independent Citizens Initiative*. Social Scientist, 34(7/8).

Gupta, B.D. (2009) *CPM and "Third Front"*. Mainstream, Vol. XLVII, No. 20. Available (consulted 03 January 2024) at: http://mainstreamweekly.net/article1333.html.

Gupta, M. (n.d.). *Singur–Nandigram–Lalgarh: Movements that remade Mamata Banerjee*. Indian History Collective. Available (Consulted 14 August 2025) at: https://indianhistorycollective.com/singur-nandigram-lalgarh-remade-mamata-banerjee/.

Gupta, S. (2013, May 31). *BJP names Ajit Jogi as conspirator in Maoist attacks*. The Times of India. Available (Consulted 27 October 2025) at: https://timesofindia.indiatimes.com/india/bjp-names-ajit-jogi-as-conspirator-in-maoist-attack/articleshow/20358637.cms.

Haygunde, C. (2015, September 26) *Top 'urban' Maoist in Maharashtra dies of heart attack*. The Indian Express. Available (consulted 08 January 2024) at: https://indianexpress.com/article/cities/pune/top-urban-maoist-in-maharashtra-dies-of-heart-attack/.

Human Rights Forum. (2006) *Death, Displacement and Deprivation: The War in Dantewara: A Report* (p. 13). Available (consulted 08 January 2024) at: http://cpjc.files.wordpress.com/2007/07/hrfdantewadareport.pdf.

Human Rights Watch (2009, December) Sabotaged Schooling: Naxalite attacks and police occupation of schools in India's Bihar and Jharkhand states. Available (Consulted 23 October 2024) at: https://www.hrw.org/reports/india1209web.pdf.

Human Rights Watch. (2007, February 1). *Children in the ranks: The Maoists' use of child soldiers in Nepal*. Available (Consulted 2 September 2024) at: https://www.hrw.org/report/2007/02/01/children-ranks/maoists-use-child-soldiers-nepal.

I support Maoist movement: Shibu Soren. (2010, December 29). *The Indian Express*. Available (Consulted 24 October 2025) at: https://indianexpress.com/article/india/latest-news/i-support-maoist-movement-shibu-soren/.

Illegal Militias. (2011, July 08). *Deccan Herald*. Available (Consulted 14 November 2024) at: https://www.deccanherald.com/content/174779/illegal-militias.html.

Independent Citizens' Initiative (2006). *War in the heart of India: An enquiry into the ground situation in Dantewara District*.

Indian Vanguard (2007, August 9). Schoolchildren took out a rally against police act. Available (Consulted 08 September 2024) at: https://naxalresistance.wordpress.com/2007/08/09/schoolchildren-took-out-a-rally-against-police-act/.

Indian Vanguard (2007, June 02). Maoists setting up bal militia. Available (Consulted 08 September 2024) at: https://naxalresistance.wordpress.com/2007/06/02/maoists-setting-up-bal-militia/.

Jacob, J. (2022, April 18). *How political murders continue to stain Kerala*. India Today. Available (Consulted 10 June 2025) at: https://www.indiatoday.in/india-today-insight/story/how-political-murders-continue-to-stain-kerala-1938969-2022-04-18.

Jaitely, A. (2018, May 23). Supreme Court verdict on Salwa Judum—Can courts enforce ideology? *Arise Bharat*. Available (Consulted 14 November 2024) at: https://arisebharat.com/2011/07/26/supreme-court-verdict-on-salwa-judum-can-courts-enforce-ideology/.

Janyala, S. (2009, April 09). Home to Naxal Movement for 30 years, Warangal has no issue to debate now. *The Indian Express*. Available (Consulted 08 September 2024) at: https://indianexpress.com/article/news-archive/web/home-to-naxal-movement-for-30-years-warangal-has-no-issue-to-debate-now/.

Jha, P. (2016, June 13). Nepal tactics, without the strategy. *The Hindu*. Available (Consulted 08 September 2024) at: https://www.thehindu.com/opinion/op-ed/nepal-tactics-without-the-strategy/article4769758.ece.

Jha, S. (2005). *Naxalite movement in Bihar and Jharkhand*. Dialogue, 6(4). Available (Consulted 07 October 2025) at: http://www.asthabharati.org/Dia_Apr05/Sanj.htm.

Jharkhand Bishop backs Maoist cause. *Haindava Keralam*. (2010, May 27). Available (Consulted 22 February 2025) at: https://haindavakeralam.com/jharkhand-bishop-backs-maoist-hk9712.

Jharkhand Timeline 2009 (n.d.) South Asia Terrorism Portal. Available (Consulted 15 October 2024) at: https://www.satp.org/satporgtp/countries/india/maoist/timelines/2009/JHARKHAND.html.

JNU row: Sedition charges filed against Rahul Gandhi, Kejriwal, Yechury and 6 others. (2016, March 1) *India Today*. Available (consulted 08 January 2024) at: https://www.indiatoday.in/education-today/news/story/jnu-sedition-311269-2016-03-01.

John, J. & Drolia, R. (2013, May 26) *Maoists kill senior Congress leaders, VC Shukla critically injured. The Times of India.* Available (Consulted 07 October 2024) at: https://timesofindia.indiatimes.com/india/maoists-kill-senior-congress-leaders-vc-shukla-critically-injured/articleshow/20264983.cms.

John, J. William. (2007, May 29). Children at war in Insurgency Zone. *Times of India.* Available (Consulted 08 September 2024) at: https://timesofindia.indiatimes.com/india/children-at-war-in-insurgency-zone/articleshow/2081272.cms.

Kanate, G. and Singh, V. (2013, November 19) 56 NGOs raising funds, cadres for Naxals in state. DNA India. Available (Consulted 23 October 2024) at: https://www.dnaindia.com/mumbai/report-56-ngos-raising-funds-cadres-for-naxals-in-state-1156453.

Katoch, D.C. (2012, June 12). *Massacre at km 43: The unanswered questions.* Centre for Land Warfare Studies. Available (Consulted 27 October 2025) at: https://archive.claws.in/1029/massacre-at-km-43-the-unanswered-questions-maj-gen-dhruv-c-katoch.html.

Katrak, S. (1961) India's communist party split. *The China Quarterly* 7: 138–139.

KCR meets Hemant Soren, says country needs a new direction for development. (2022, March 4). *The New Indian Express.* Available (Consulted 02 August 2025) at: https://www.newindianexpress.com/states/telangana/2022/mar/05/kcr-meets-soren-says-country-needs-a-new-direction-for-devp-2426512.html.

Kejriwal writes to PM Modi: Wrong to brand JNU as a 'centre of terrorists'. (2016, February 16) *The Indian Express.* Available (consulted 19 January 2024) at: https://indianexpress.com/article/political-pulse/kejriwal-writes-to-pm-modi-wrong-to-brand-jnu-as-a-centre-of-terrorists/?ref=archive_pg.

Kerala HC says Maoism not a crime, upholds Rs 1 lakh fine on police. (2019, July 9). *The Times of India.* Available (Consulted 14 November 2024) at: https://timesofindia.indiatimes.com/city/kochi/kerala-hc-says-maoism-not-a-crime-upholds-rs1-lakh-fine-on-police/articleshow/70136872.cms.

Khan, S. (2011, September 22). Essar faces probe for funding NGO linked to Maoists. *India Today.*

Kishanji, top Maoist leader, killed in gunbattle in West Bengal. (2011, November 24). *The Times of India.* Available (Consulted 02 August 2025) at: https://timesofindia.indiatimes.com/india/kishanji-top-maoist-leader-killed-in-gunbatlle-in-west-bengal/articleshow/10858345.cms.

Kleinfeld, R., & Majeed, R. (2016, June 9). *Fighting insurgency with politics: The case of Bihar.* Carnegie Endowment for International Peace. Available (Consulted 17 June 2025) at: https://carnegieendowment.org/2016/06/09/fighting-insurgency-with-politics-case-of-bihar-pub-63769.

Kujur, K. Raju (2009, August 11) Underdevelopment and the Naxal movement. *Institute of Peace and Conflict Studies (IPCS)*. Available (Consulted 18 January 2025) at: https://www.ipcs.org/focusthemsel.php?articleNo=2937.

Kumar, A.P. (2024, July 27). *State (in)security laws. Economic and Political Weekly*, 59(30).

Kumar, S. (2008, July 1) Changing face of the Naxalites in Bihar: From homelessness to real estate. Institute of Peace and Conflict Studies. Available (Consulted 23 October 2024) at: http://www.ipcs.org/focusthemsel.php?articleNo=2608.

Kumar, S. (2009, July 4) Maoists extort ₹300 crore annually in Chhattisgarh. *The Economic Times*. Available (Consulted 12 January 2025) at: https://economictimes.indiatimes.com/dateline-india/maoists-extort-rs-300-crore-annually-in-chhattisgarh/articleshow/4739046.cms.

Left, PUCL condemn Sukma ambush. (2021, November 16). *The Hindu*. Available (Consulted 10 June 2025) at: https://www.thehindu.com/news/national/left-pucl-condemn-sukma-ambush/article5781869.ece.

Left-wing extremism-hit districts down from 72 to 58: MHA (2024, March 16). *The Times of India*. Available (Consulted 2 September 2024) at: https://timesofindia.indiatimes.com/india/left-wing-extremism-hit-districts-down-from-72-to-58-mha/articleshow/108539190.cms.

Lenin, V.I. (1920) Draft theses on national and colonial questions for the Second Congress of the Communist International. Available (Consulted 2 September 2024) at: https://www.marxists.org/archive/lenin/works/1920/jun/05.htm.

Lenin, V.I. (1957) The national liberation movement in the East. Moscow: Foreign Languages Publishing House.

Mahadevan, P. (2012, May) The Maoist insurgency in India: between crime and revolution. *Small Wars & Insurgencies*, 23(2).

Maharashtra—Statements condemning the detention of Hem Mishra and others. (2013, August 25) Sanhati. Available (consulted 19 January 2024) at: https://sanhati.com/articles/7871/.

Mahendra Karma killed, V.C. Shukla injured in Maoist attack. (2021, December 4). *The Hindu*. Available (Consulted 08 November 2024) at: https://www.thehindu.com/news/national/other-states/Mahendra-Karma-killed-V.C.-Shukla-injured-in-Maoist-attack/article12149560.ece.

Maitra, K. (1976) Lenin and Roy on national and colonial question at the Second Congress of the Third International. *Proceedings of the Indian History Congress* 37: 499–504.

Maitra, P.K. (2012, January 5). After four years, 'Naxalite' Arun Ferreira walks free. *Hindustan Times*. Available (Consulted 22 February 2025) at: https://www.hindustantimes.com/india/after-four-years-naxalite-arun-ferreira-walks-free/story-4ReVGk69KXAnBkVIrRMXFI.html.

Majumdar, B. (2008, May 22). Indian Maoists step up recruitment of child soldiers. *Livemint*. Available (Consulted 30 October 2024) at: https://www.livemint.com/Politics/NPTvtyQ6crsENoRDEd78II/Indian-Maoists-step-up-recruitment-of-child-soldiers.html.

Malik, A. (2013, October 6) *The government identifies 128 front organisations for Naxals. Mint.* Available (Consulted 22 August 2024) at: https://www.livemint.com/Politics/B9Pmu3NurDrcRdD9ttb6JP/Government-identifies-128-front-organisations-for-Naxals.html.

Mamata Banerjee addresses rally in Naxal-affected Jhargram. (2011, October 15). NDTV. Available (Consulted 02 August 2025) at: https://www.ndtv.com/india-news/mamata-banerjee-addresses-rally-in-naxal-affected-jhargram-569753.

Mamata charges CPI(M) with spreading terror in Jangal Mahal. (2011, May 7). *The Hindu*. Available (Consulted 02 August 2025) at: https://www.thehindu.com/news/national/mamata-charges-cpim-with-spreading-terror-in-jangal-mahal/article1997237.ece.

Mandal, C. (2010, September 20) *CPM leader Ananta Mukherjee shot by suspected Maoists near Jhargram, succumbs to injuries. The Times of India*. Available (Consulted 07 October 2024) at: https://timesofindia.indiatimes.com/cpm-leader-ananta-mukherjee-shot-at-by-the-suepected-maoists-near-jhargram-succumbed-to-his-injuries-he-was-on-the-way-to-jhargram-hospital-mukherjee-who-was-an-influential-cpm-leader-at-silda-belpahari-area-of-west-midnapore-was-a-member-of-belpahari-zonal-committee-armed-maoists-shot-him-from-close-range-and-also-injured-his-bodyguard-/articleshow/6591172.cms.

Manmohan: Naxalism the greatest internal threat. (2009, October 11). *The Hindu*. Available at: https://www.thehindu.com/news/national/Manmohan-naxalism-the-greatest-internal-threat/article16886121.ece.

Mao Tse Tung. Quotations from Mao Tse Tung, Chapter 33. Available (Consulted 2 September 2024) at: https://www.marxists.org/reference/archive/mao/works/red-book/ch33.htm.

Mao, Zedong (1965) On New Democracy. In: Selected works of Mao Tse-tung, VOL. III. Beijing: Foreign Languages Press.

Mao, Zedong (1965) Selected works, VOL. II. Peking: Foreign Languages Press.

Mao, Zedong (1965) The role of the Chinese Communist Party in the national war. In: Selected works of Mao Tse-tung, VOL. II, 195–210. Peking: Foreign Languages Press.

Mao, Zedong (n.d.) Quotations from Mao Tse Tung—Chapter 3. Available (Consulted 08 September 2024) at: https://www.marxists.org/reference/archive/mao.

Maoist attack derails 13 coaches of Express train, 68 dead. (2010, May 28). *The Times of India*. Available (Consulted 23 October 2025) at: https://timesofindia.indiatimes.com/india/maoist-attack-derails-13-coaches-of-express-train-68-dead/articleshow/5983218.cms.

Maoist Basavaraju killed: How 50-hour-long Op Kagar ended era of red terror. (2025, May 21). *India Today*. Available (Consulted 27 November 2024) at: https://www.indiatoday.in/india/story/nambala-keshava-rao-basavaraju-killed-chhattisgarh-naxal-encounter-red-terror-2728416-2025-05-21.

Maoist camp busted in Odisha's Malkangiri district. (2021, October 17) The New Indian Express. Available (Consulted 30 October 2024) at: https://www.newindianexpress.com/states/odisha/2021/Oct/17/maoist-camp-busted-in-odishas-malkangiri-district-2372525.html.

Maoist child-soldiers worry Nepal. (2014, April 25). *The Times of India*. Available (Consulted 30 October 2024) at: https://timesofindia.indiatimes.com/maoist-child-soldiers-worry-nepal/articleshow/34504772.cms.

Maoist killings condemned. (2014, March 12). *Communist Party of India (Marxist)* [Press release]. Available (Consulted 17 June 2025) at: https://cpim.org/pressbriefs/maoist-killings-condemned.

Maoists arrested—training camp destroyed in Odisha. (2013, February) *Business Standard*. Available (Consulted 30 October 2024) at: https://www.business-standard.com/article/pti-stories/maoists-arrested-training-cam-destroyed-in-odisha-113020100465_1.html.

Maoists attracting youths with salary, cut of extortion money (2010, March 28) *The Times of India*. Available (Consulted 19 November 2024) at: https://timesofindia.indiatimes.com/india/maoists-attracting-youths-with-salary-cut-of-extortion-money/articleshow/5734428.cms.

Maoists attracting youths with salary, cut of extortion money. (2010, March 29) *Times of India*. Available (Consulted 30 October 2024) at: https://timesofindia.indiatimes.com/india/maoists-attracting-youths-with-salary-cut-of-extortion-money/articleshow/5734428.cms.

Maoists attracting youths with salary, cut of extortion money. (2010, March 28) *The Indian Express*. Available (Consulted 31 October 2024) at: https://indianexpress.com/article/india/latest-news/maoists-attracting-youths-with-salary-cut-of-extortion-money/.

Maoists raising money through NGOs, says IB. (2013, November 24) *Deccan Herald*. Available (Consulted 25 February 2025) at: https://www.deccanherald.com/india/maoists-raising-money-through-ngos-2296337.

Maoists raising money via illegal marijuana plantations: experts (2015, March 21) *Business Standard*. Available (Consulted 02 November 2024) at: https://www.business-standard.com/article/news-ani/maoists-raising-money-via-illegal-marijuana-plantations-experts-115032100087_1.html.

Maoists want to overthrow Indian state by 2050: Pillai. *The Economic Times*. Available (Consulted 08 September 2024) at: https://economictimes.indiatimes.com/news/politics-and-nation/maoists-want-to-overthrow-indian-state-by-2050-pillai/articleshow/5648211.cms?from=mdr.

May 30, Forty Years Ago: Bihar's Salwa Judum. (2015, May 30) *The Indian Express*. Available (Consulted 08 November 2024) at: http://indianexpress.com/article/opinion/editorials/may-30-forty-years-ago-bihars-salwa-judum/.

Mazumdar C. (1965) What is the source of the spontaneous revolutionary outburst in India? In: Kistler C. (2020) Historic Eight Documents. Paris: Foreign Languages Press.

Mazumdar, C. (1968) Boycott elections: international significance of the slogan. Translated from Bengali text originally published in Deshabrati, 21 November 1968. In: *Liberation* 2(2) ed. Sushital Ray Chaudhary. Available (Consulted 08 September 2024) at: https://www.marxists.org/subject/india/cpiml/liberation/2-2.pdf.

Mazumdar, Charu (1967) Deshbrati, 26 October 1967. In: *Collected works of Charu Mazumdar*. Lokyudh Prakashan.

Mazumdar, Charu (1969) Party's call to the youth and students. *Liberation*, September 1969. Originally published in Deshabrati, 21 August 1969 (translated from Bengali). Reproduced as part of the 40th anniversary year feature of the CPI (ML). Available (Consulted 30 October 2024) at: https://www.archive.cpiml.org/liberation/year_2009/may_09/special_feature.html.

Mazumdar, Charu (1981) Collected works of Comrade Charu Mazumdar. Lokyudh Prakashan.

Menon, S. & Das, K. (2007, September 18) Salwa Judum and tale of 644 deserted villages. *Rediff.com*. Available (Consulted 08 November 2024) at: https://www.rediff.com/news/2007/sep/18naxal.htm.

Miliband, R. (2000) State and revolution. In: What is Maoism and other essays. Kharagpur: Cornerstone Publications.

Ministry of Home Affairs (2025) *Parliamentary reply: QUESENG_08052025.pdf*. Government of India. Available (Consulted 30 October 2024) at: https://www.mha.gov.in/sites/default/files/2025-05/QUESENG_08052025.pdf.

Ministry of Home Affairs (n.d.) *Naxal Management Division*. Government of India. Available (Consulted 21 October 2024) at: https://www.mha.gov.in/en/divisionofmha/left-wing-extremism-division.

Ministry of Home Affairs. (2025, June 3). *Left Wing Extremism Division*. Government of India. Available (Consulted 5 August 2024) at: https://www.mha.gov.in/en/divisionofmha/left-wing-extremism-division.

Ministry of Home Affairs. (2025, June 3). *Left Wing Extremism Division—Schemes*. Government of India. Available (Consulted 08 September 2024) at: https://www.mha.gov.in/en/divisionofmha/left-wing-extremism-division.

Ministry of Rural Development. (2019). *Demand No. 82: Pradhan Mantri Gram Sadak Yojana—Road connectivity project in LWE-affected areas (RCPLWE)*. In *Notes on demands for grants, 2019–2020*. Government of India. Available (Consulted 16 November 2024) at: https://www.indiabudget.gov.in/budget2019-20(I)/ub2019-20/eb/sbe82.pdf.

Mishra, R. (2017, May 10) 25 CRPF men ambushed in Sukma: why the region is a graveyard for forces. *Hindustan Times*. Available (Consulted 18 January 2025) at: https://www.hindustantimes.com/india-news/chhattisgarh-s-death-road-why-this-jungle-highway-is-a-graveyard-of-indian-security-forces/story-LZDTWM1MYc7nEivZ7TEQmL.html.

Mishra, R. (2021, February 14) *Chhattisgarh: Maoists 'threaten' scribes, activists, for alleged corporate links*. Hindustan Times. Available (consulted 19 January 2024) at: https://www.hindustantimes.com/india-news/chhattisgarh-maoists-threaten-scribes-activists-for-alleged-corporate-links-101613287851136.html.

Mishra, R.N. (2008, January 20). *Maoist Menace: Terrorism in India*. Boloji.com. Available (Consulted 31 October 2024) at: https://www.boloji.com/articles/9368/the-maoist-menace-terrorism-in-india.

Mishra, V. (1993) How did our party evolve? Available (Consulted 30 October 2024) at: https://www.marxists.org/reference/archive/mishra/1993/05/x02.htm.

Mitra, P. and Sen, M. (1971) Communist Party and Naxalites. Communist Party Publication.

Mohanty D. (2008, December). Net closes in on Cong MP for Orissa. *Visakeo*. Available (Consulted 25 February 2025) at: https://visakeo.blogspot.com/2008/12/net-closes-in-on-cong-mp-for-orissa.html.

Mukherjee, O., Yadav, H. and Yadav, H. (2023, April 26) *Chhattisgarh blast brings back memories of 2021 Sukma: a list of major Naxal attacks. News18*. Available (Consulted 30 October 2024) at: https://www.news18.com/india/chhattisgarh-blast-brings-back-memories-of-2021-sukma-heres-a-list-of-major-naxal-attacks-7646449.html.

Mukherji N. (2024, January 17). Arma Over People. *Outlook*. Available (Consulted 31 October 2024) at: https://www.outlookindia.com/national/arms-over-people-news-265485.

Mukherji, P. (1983) From left extremism to electoral politics. New Delhi: Manohar Publications.

Mukherji, P. and Chakrabarti, P. (1983) From left extremism to electoral politics: Naxalite participation in elections. New Delhi: Manohar Publications.

Murty, B.V. (2010, September 16) Chandwa town doesn't sleep at 6 anymore. Hindustan Times. Available (Consulted 09 October 2024) at: https://www.hindustantimes.com/india/chandwa-town-doesn-t-sleep-at-6-anymore/story-0Vbgb9V04O0D8Gs5uX5DvJ.html.

My Little Acre. (2007, October 27). *LiveMint*. Available (Consulted 16 November 2024) at: https://www.livemint.com/Opinion/q07QBfB5ziHZ8acX7KNWNJ/My-little-acre.html.

Naik, G. (2019, July 3) The severity of economic impacts of the Maoist Movement. Vivekananda International Foundation. Available (Consulted 15 October 2024) at: https://www.vifindia.org/article/2019/july/03/severity-of-economic-impact-of-the-maoist-movement.

Nair, K. (2024, May 10). *Countering Maoist insurgency: Has Chhattisgarh turned the corner?* ORF Expert Speak. Observer Research Foundation.

Nandini Sundar & Ors vs State of Chhattisgarh (2011, 5 July). *Indiankanoon.org*. Available (Consulted 2 September 2024) at: https://indiankanoon.org/doc/920448/.

Nanjappa, V. (2019, October 22) Stifling the flow of funds: How Modi sarkar is bringing an end to the Naxal movement. *MyNation*. Available (Consulted 19 November 2024) at: https://www.mynation.com/views/stifling-the-flow-of-funds-here-how-modi-sarkar-is-bringing-an-end-to-the-naxal-movement-pzrk8g.

Narayan, J. (2011). *Naxalism in Bihar: A historical perspective*. The Indian Journal of Political Science, 72(4).

Narcotics Control Bureau, Ministry of Home Affairs (2014) Annual Report. Available (Consulted 02 November 2024) at: https://narcoordindia.gov.in/narcoordindia/Periodicals/1656247933-2631-DOC-2014.pdf.

Nash, Andrew (n.d.) Leninism and democracy. *Theoria: A Journal of Social and Political Theory* 76: 19–32.

National Human Rights Commission of India. (2009). *Report 2008–2009*. New Delhi. Available (Consulted 19 April 2024) at: https://nhrc.nic.in/publications/annual-reports.

Naxal affected regions constricted to 38 districts by April 2024: MHA to Lok Sabha (2024, August 6). *The Times of India*. Available (Consulted 08 November 2024) at: https://timesofindia.indiatimes.com/india/naxal-affected-regions-constricted-to-38-districts-by-april-2024-mha-to-lok-sabha/articleshow/112316002.cms.

Naxal problem now confined to only 5 Jharkhand districts: DGP (2024, June 10). *Deccan Herald*. Available (Consulted 2 September 2024) at: https://www.deccanherald.com/india/jharkhand/naxal-problem-now-confined-to-only-5-jharkhand-districts-dgp-3060135.

Naxal violence down by 77% between 2010 and 2023, Govt. tells Lok Sabha. *The Hindu*. Available (Consulted 30 October 2024) at: https://www.thehindu.com/news/national/naxal-violence-down-by-77-between-2010-and-2022-govt-tells-lok-sabha/article66618779.ece.

Naxalism biggest challenge: PM (2006, April 13). *Hindustan Times*. Available (Consulted 08 September 2024) at: https://www.hindustantimes.com/india/naxalism-biggest-challenge-pm/story-WmDgTunxXYDyDsC2z9hwRM.html.

Naxalism vanishing from jungles but taking root in urban centres: PM Modi. (2025, March 6). *The Hindu*. Available (Consulted 14 November 2024) at: https://www.thehindu.com/news/national/naxalism-vanishing-from-jungles-but-taking-root-in-urban-centres-pm-modi/article69301386.ece.

Naxalites recruiting young children in their cadres. (2010, August 17) *The Economic Times*. Available (Consulted 31 October 2024) at: https://economictimes.indiatimes.com/news/politics-and-nation/naxalites-recruiting-young-children-in-their-cadres/articleshow/6324818.cms?from=mdr.

Naxals extort Rs. 140 crore annually from traders, corporates (2016, May 18). *The Hindu*. Available (Consulted 18 October 2024) at: https://www.thehindu.com/news/national/naxals-extort-rs-140-crore-annually-from-traders-corporates/article5680697.ece.

Naxals recruit 4,000 children as cadres. (2013, September 6). *The Economic Times*. Available (Consulted 31 October 2024) at: https://economictimes.indiatimes.com/news/politics-and-nation/naxals-recruit-4000-children-as-cadres/articleshow/22373511.cms?from=mdr.

Naxals recruit 4,000 children. (2013, September 8). *Millennium Post*. Available (Consulted 31 October 2024) at: https://www.millenniumpost.in/naxals-recruit-4000-children-37217.

Naxals recruiting children in Chhattisgarh and Jharkhand: UN. (2017, October 7) *Outlook India*. Available (Consulted 15 November 2024) at: https://www.outlookindia.com/website/story/naxals-recruiting-children-in-chhattisgarh-and-jharkhand-un/302742.

Naxals recruiting children. (2012 October 18) *Hindustan Times*. Available (Consulted 15 November 2024) at: https://www.hindustantimes.com/videos/india/naxals-recruiting-children/video-aMzzrTc77ik5W6RFbnl3gN.html.

Naxals trying to expand to new areas without much success: MHA report (2024, December 31). *Hindustan Times*. Available (Consulted 24 November 2024) at: https://www.hindustantimes.com/india-news/naxals-trying-to-expand-to-new-areas-without-much-success-mha-report-101735647703200.html.

Naxals turn mining mafia in Jharkhand (2010) *NDTV*. Available (Consulted 19 November 2024) at: https://www.ndtv.com/india-news/naxals-turn-mining-mafia-in-jharkhand-415800.

Naxals use children to fight in Chhattisgarh, Jharkhand: United Nations Secretary-General Antonio Guterres (2017, October 7) *The Hindu*. Available (Consulted 15 November 2024) at: https://www.thehindu.com/news/national/naxals-use-children-to-fight-in-chhattisgarh-jharkhand-un/article19818163.ece.

Nepalese hail vote on Secular Status. (2006, May 19) *The New York Times*. Available (Consulted 25 February 2025) at: https://www.nytimes.com/2006/05/19/world/asia/19iht-nepal.html.

Net closes in on Congress MP for Orissa Swami's murder. (2008, December 27). *Hinduism Today*. Available (Consulted 25 February 2025) at: https://www.hinduismtoday.com/hpi/2008/12/27/net-closes-in-on-congress-mp-for-orissa-swami-s-murder/.

NGOs funding Naxals. (2007, March 18) *Naxal Terror Watch*.

No Maoists in Jangalmahal, says Mamata. (2010, October 19). *Rediff News*. Available (Consulted 24 October 2025) at: https://www.rediff.com/news/report/no-maoists-in-jangalmahal-says-mamata/20101019.htm.

No support for Salwa Judum, Centre tells Supreme Court. (2010, September 1). *The Hindu*. Available (Consulted 02 August 2025) at: https://www.thehindu.com/news/national//article61771662.ece.

Over 12,000 killed in Naxal violence in past 20 years (2014, March 12). *The Indian Express*. Available (Consulted 14 November 2024) at: https://indianexpress.com/article/india/india-others/over-12000-killed-in-naxal-violence-in-past-20-years/.

Pande, M. (2016, March 4) *Truthiness Labs: This is how easily TV news got you to hear 'Pakistan Zindabad' in a JNU video. Newslaundry*. Available (consulted 19 January 2024) at: https://www.newslaundry.com/2016/03/04/truthiness-labs-this-is-how-easily-tv-news-got-you-to-hear-pakistan-zindabad-in-a-jnu-video.

Pandey A. (2013, September 25). Naxal menace: Rampant abduction of children has this Jharkhand village on edge. *NDTV*. Available (Consulted 15 November 2024) at: https://www.ndtv.com/india-news/naxal-menace-rampant-abduction-of-children-has-this-jharkhand-village-on-edge-535578.

Pawar, S. (2013, May 30). *Naxalism not just law and order problem: Pawar Sharad*. Business Standard. Available (Consulted 27 October 2025) at: https://www.business-standard.com/article/pti-stories/naxalism-not-just-law-and-order-problem-pawar-113053001229_1.html.

People's Union for Democratic Rights. (2015) *War and the Lightness of Being Adivasi: Security camps and villages in Bijapur, Chhattisgarh*. Available (consulted 19 January 2024) at: https://www.pudr.org/publicatiosn-files/2015-Feb-War%20and%20the%20Lightness%20of%20Being%20Adivasi.pdf.

People's Union for Democratic Rights. (2016) *State of Siege: Report on Encounters and Cases of Sexual Violence in Bijapur and Sukma Districts of Chhattisgarh*. Available (consulted 27 January 2024) at: https://ideas.repec.org/p/ess/wpaper/id11264.html#download.

Phadnis, A. (2013, June 14) State of war. *Business Standard*. Available (Consulted 06 February 2025) at: https://www.business-standard.com/article/beyond-business/state-of-war-107063001016_1.html.

Prakash, O. (2015) Funding patterns in the Naxal movement in contemporary India. *Proceedings of the Indian History Congress*, 76, pp. 900–907.

Press Information Bureau (2019) *Naxal affected districts*. Available (Consulted 18 October 2024) at: https://pib.gov.in/newsite/PrintRelease.aspx?relid=188075.

Press Information Bureau (2025) *Naxalmukt Bharat Abhiyan: From Red Zones to Growth Corridors: India's Decisive Battle Against Left Wing Extremism*. Available (Consulted 22 August 2024) at: https://www.pib.gov.in/PressReleaseIframePage.aspx?PRID=2120771.

Press Information Bureau, Government of India, Ministry of Rural Development. (2011, October 11). *From Tirupati to Pashupati: Some reflections on the Maoist issue* [Sardar Patel Memorial Lecture]. Available (Consulted 02 August 2025) at: https://pib.gov.in/newsite/PrintRelease.aspx?relid=76575.

Press Information Bureau. (2018, April 16). *Government's new policy paying dividends in containing Left Wing Extremism* [Press release]. Ministry of Home Affairs, Government of India. Available (Consulted 2 September 2024) at: https://www.pib.gov.in/newsite/PrintRelease.aspx?relid=178704.

Press Information Bureau. (2024, February 7). *National policy to combat Left Wing Extremism* [Press release]. Ministry of Home Affairs, Government of India. Available (Consulted 2 September 2024) at: https://www.pib.gov.in/PressReleaseIframePage.aspx?PRID=2003503.

Press Information Bureau. (2025, April 10). *India's decisive battle against Left Wing Extremism* [Press release]. Ministry of Home Affairs, Government of India. Available (Consulted 08 September 2024) at: https://www.pib.gov.in/PressReleasePage.aspx?PRID=2120771.

Press Information Bureau. (2025, June 23). *In regions where Naxalism is being eradicated, our government is delivering food, healthcare, education …* [Press release]. Ministry of Home Affairs, Government of India.

Press Information Bureau. (2025, May 14). *Achieving a historic success in the resolve of a "Naxal-free India"*. Ministry of Home Affairs, Government of India.

Press Information Bureau. (2025, May 14). *Achieving a historic success in the resolve of a "Naxal-free India": Security forces kill 31 Naxalites in the biggest-ever operation against Naxalism at Karreguttalu Hill* [Press release]. Ministry of Home Affairs, Government of India. Available (Consulted 08 September 2024) at: https://www.pib.gov.in/PressReleasePage.aspx?PRID=2128736.

Press Information Bureau. (2025, May 14). *Before March 31, 2026, we will eliminate Naxalism from the country* [Press release]. Ministry of Home Affairs, Government of India. Available (Consulted 5 August 2024) at: https://www.pib.gov.in/PressReleseDetailm.aspx?PRID=2101142.

Press Trust of India (2011, December 06). Naxal violence destroys nearly 260 schools in 5 yrs. *News18*. Available (Consulted 16 November 2024) at: https://www.news18.com/news/india/naxal-violence-destroys-nearly-260-schools-in-5-yrs-425813.html.

Prime Minister's Office (2006) *PM's speech at Chief Ministers' meet on Naxalism.* Available (Consulted 08 September 2024) at: https://archivepmo.nic.in/drmanmohansingh/speech-details.php?nodeid=302.

Prime Minister's Office. (2006, April 13). *PM's speech at the Chief Ministers' meet on Naxalism.* Available (Consulted 23 October 2025) at: https://archivepmo.nic.in/drmanmohansingh/speech-details.php?nodeid=302.

Protection of tribals from Naxalism. (2013) *Press Information Bureau.* Available (Consulted 08 November 2024) at: https://pib.gov.in/newsite/PrintRelease.aspx?relid=93525.

Puniyani, R. (2016, August 6) *Should RSS Volunteers Be Permitted To Join Government Services?* CounterCurrents. Available (consulted 27 January 2024) at: https://countercurrents.org/2016/07/should-rss-volunteers-be-permitted-to-join-government-services/.

Punwani, J. (2010). *The Trial of Binayak Sen.* Economic and Political Weekly 45(52).

Puri Shankaracharya calls for ban on conversion. *The Hindu.* (2015, January 20). Available (Consulted 25 February 2025) at: https://www.thehindu.com/news/national/puri-shankaracharya-calls-for-ban-on-conversion/article6785797.ece.

Putul, A. (2025, May 22). *"Warzone": Why Indian forces have launched a deadly assault on Maoists. Al Jazeera.* Available (Consulted 08 September 2024) at: https://www.aljazeera.com/news/2025/5/22/warzone-why-indian-forces-have-launched-a-deadly-assault-on-maoists.

Ramana, P.V. (2013, November 19). *The child soldiers in Indian Maoist ranks.* Daily News and Analysis (DNA). Available (Consulted 16 November 2024) at: https://www.dnaindia.com/india/comment-the-child-soldiers-in-indian-maoist-ranks-1215003.

Ramana, P.V. (ed). (2008). *The Naxal Challenge: Causes, Linkages and Policy Options.* New Delhi: Pearson Education India.

Ramana, P.V. (2014) Understanding India's Maoists: Select Documents. New Delhi: Institute for Defence Studies and Analyses.

Ramanan, N. (2008, October 12). On the other side of the firing line. *The Times of India.* Available (Consulted 08 November 2024) at: https://timesofindia.indiatimes.com/on-the-other-side-of-the-firing-line/articleshow/3585182.cms.

Ranjan, M. (2010, January 6). *Soren contacts Maoist boss does not tell Delhi* (D. Majumdar, Interviewer). CNN–IBN.

Rao, D. (2011, July 13). The Salwa Judum Judgment: Judicial Assertions and Reality. *Swarajya Magazine.* Available (Consulted 08 September 2024) at: https://swarajyamag.com/commentary/the-salwa-judum-judgment-judicial-assertions-and-reality-2.

Rastgar, Hamayon (2016) Continuity and rupture: philosophy in the Maoist terrain. Marx & Philosophy Society. Available (Consulted 14 November 2024) at: https://marxandphilosophy.org.uk/reviews/8221_continuity-and-rupture-review-by-hamayon-rastgar/.

Red Cross and MSF accused of helping India Maoists. (2011, January 21) *BBC News.* Available (Consulted 14 November 2024) at: https://www.bbc.com/news/world-south-asia-12247693.

Reddy, T. (1993) How Indian is the Indian bourgeoisie. In: India mortgaged. Tarimela Nagy Reddy Memorial Trust. Originally published 1978. Available (Consulted 14 November 2024) at: https://www.marxists.org/subject/india/apcccr/india-mortgaged/reddy-12.pdf.

Refworld. (2010, February 10). *Education under attack 2010—India*. Available (Consulted 16 November 2024) at: https://www.refworld.org/docid/4b7aa9e02b.html.

Rogers, H.K. (2015) Before the revisionist controversy. In: *RLE Marxism*. London: Routledge.

Roy, A. & Navlakha, G. (2010, June 4). India's war on people at home. Available (Consulted 14 November 2024) at: https://mronline.org/2010/06/04/indias-war-on-people-at-home/.

Roy, E., & Biswas, P. (2016, March 29). *Mamta Banerjee tells Jangalmahal what she did what the Left Front and the BJP didn't*. The Indian Express. Available (Consulted 17 June 2025) at: https://indianexpress.com/article/india/india-news-india/west-bengal-assembly-elections-2016-mamata-banerjee-jangalmahal-bjp-tmc/.

Roy, M.N. (1987) Selected works of M.N. Roy: 1917–1922. New Delhi: Oxford University Press.

Sahay, M.A. (2005, December 15). *Naxals admit to links with LTTE, Nepal Maoists*. Rediff. Available (Consulted 16 November 2024) at: https://www.rediff.com/news/2005/dec/15bihar.htm.

Sahni, A. (2011, November 22). *A shift too late: Mamata Banerjee's U-turn on Maoists*. Firstpost. Available (Consulted 27 October 2025) at: https://www.firstpost.com/politics/a-shift-too-late-mamatas-u-turn-on-maoists-136673.html.

Saqib, M. (2018). *Recent trends of Naxal violence in India: Need for comprehensive approach from the government*. International Journal of Research in Social Sciences, 8(11). Available (Consulted 07 October 2025) at: https://www.ijmra.us/project%20doc/2018/IJRSS_NOVEMBER2018/IJMRA-14770.pdf.

Satapathy, R., Mandal and C., Ojha, S. (2010, April 10) The Maoist empire: Rs 1,500cr and counting. The Times of India. Available (Consulted 15 October 2024) at: https://timesofindia.indiatimes.com/home/sunday-times/deep-focus/the-maoist-empire-rs-1500cr-and-counting/articleshow/5783114.cms.

SC Extends House Arrest of Activist Gautam Navlakha Till Second Week of January. (2022, December 13). *The Wire*. Available (Consulted 14 November 2024) at: https://thewire.in/law/sc-extends-house-arrest-of-activist-gautam-navlakha-till-second-week-of-january.

Schaff, A. (1973) Marxist theory of revolution and violence. *Journal of the History of Ideas* 34(2): 263–270.

Sebastian, K.S. (2016) Event on Afzal's 'judicial killing' triggers controversy. *The Hindu*, 10, February. Available (consulted 5 September, 2024) at: https://www.thehindu.com/news/cities/Delhi/Event-on-Afzal%E2%80%99s-%E2%80%98judicial-killing%E2%80%99-triggers-controversy/article60573178.ece.

Sen, S., Panda, D. and Lahiri, A. (1978) Naxalbari and after: a Frontier anthology, Vol. 1. Calcutta: Kathashilpa.

Sengupta, T. (2013, June 22). *People's grand alliance will defeat Maoist-Marxist-Congress combine: Mamata Banerjee*. The Economic Times. Available (Consulted 17 June 2025) at: https://economictimes.indiatimes.com/news/politics-and-nation/peoples-grand-alliance-will-defeat-maoist-marxist-congress-combine-mamata-banerjee/articleshow/20715536.cms.

Sethi, A. (2011, July 5). Chhattisgarh SPOs to be confined to camps following SC order. *The Hindu*. Available (Consulted 2 September 2024) at: https://www.thehindu.com/news/national/chhattisgarh-spos-to-be-confined-to-camps-following-sc-order/article2162118.ece.

Sethi, A. (2016, November 7). MSF, Red Cross aiding Maoists, claims Dantewada police. *The Hindu*.

Sethi, A. (2021, November 28). *Chidambaram says no, but troops believe 'Green Hunt' exists. The Hindu*. Available (Consulted 27 November 2024) at: https://www.thehindu.com/news/national/Chidambaram-says-no-but-troops-believe-lsquoGreen-Hunt-exists/article16365253.ece.

Shah, A. (2019). *Nightmarch: Among India's Revolutionary Guerrillas*. Chicago: University of Chicago Press.

Sharma, H. (2013, November 11). *Chhattisgarh polls: Electorate defy Naxals, 67 per cent cast their votes*. News18. Available (Consulted 17 June 2025) at: http://www.news18.com/news/politics/cgarh-polls-650189.html.

Sharma, K. (2010, December 28). *Binayak Sen: India's war on a man of peace*. The Guardian. Available (Consulted 24 October 2025) at: https://www.theguardian.com/commentisfree/libertycentral/2010/dec/28/binayak-sen-india-british-gandhi.

Sheshank, A. (2003, June 16) *Scanner on NGO funds*. The Telegraph. Available (Consulted 02 November 2024) at: https://www.telegraphindia.com/jharkhand/scanner-on-ngo-funds/cid/817299.

Shibu Soren supports Maoists, says Maoism a "people's movement". (2010, December 30). *The Economic Times*. Available (Consulted 07 October 2025) at: https://economictimes.indiatimes.com/news/politics-and-nation/shibu-soren-supports-maoists-says-maoism-apeoples%20movement/articleshow/7189936.cms.

Shukla, T. (2019, November 22). *The Unnoticed "Seeds" of Violence: Child Soldiers in Maoist Ranks*. Centre for Land Warfare Studies. Available (Consulted 16 November 2024) at: chrome-extension://efaidnbmnnnibpcajpcglclefindmkaj/https://claws.co.in/wp-content/uploads/2025/01/IB_199-Unnoticed-Seeds-.pdf.

Shyam Balakrishnan vs State of Kerala, August 2010. (2010). *Indiankanoon.org*. Available (Consulted 14 November 2024) at: https://indiankanoon.org/search/?formInput=Shyam+Balakrishnan.

Singh, A. & Diwan, S. (2010, April 5) Red Money—tracing India's Maoist money trail. *Eurasia Review*. Available(Consulted 12 January 2025) at: https://www.eurasiareview.com/05042010-red-money-tracing-indias-maoist-money-trail.

Singh, A.K. and Diwan, S. (2024, January 17) Red Money: On the Maoist money trail. *Outlook India*. Available (Consulted 22 January 2025) at: http://outlookindia.com/national/red-money-news-264950.

Singh, D.K. (2010, June 11). *NAC meet: Govt faces fire on Maoist policy*. The Indian Express. Available (Consulted 24 October 2025) at: http://archive.indianexpress.com/news/nac-meet-govt-faces-fire-on-maoist-policy/632208.

Singh, P. (1995) The Naxalite movement in India. New Delhi: Rupa & Co.

Singh, P. (1995) *The Naxalite Movement in India*. New Delhi: Rupa Publications.

Singh, Pratibha. (2013, March 28). Naxals target Schools. *Centre for Land Warfare Studies*. Available (Consulted 06 February 2025) at: http://archive.claws.co.in/991/naxal-target-schools-pratibha-singh.html.

Singh, S. (2016, February 23) *Leftists at JNU pose the gravest danger to India*. DailyO. Available (consulted 27 January 2024) at: https://www.dailyo.in/politics/jnu-anti-national-jnusu-umar-khalid-afzal-guru-kanhaiya-kumar-abvp-rss-dsu-communism-9178.

SOG is the mother of Salwa Judum. (2011, July 07). *The Kashmir Times*.

South Asia Intelligence Review (SAIR), Weekly Assessments & Briefings, 7.23. (2008, December 15). *SATP*. Available (Consulted 06 February 2025) at: https://www.satp.org/satporgtp/sair/Archives/7_23.htm.

South Asia Terrorism Portal (2009) Bihar Timeline 2009. Available (Consulted 23 October 2024) at: https://satp.org/terrorist-activity/india-maoistinsurgency-bihar-Oct-2009.

South Asia Terrorism Portal (2010, April 5) South Asia Intelligence Review 8 (39). Available (Consulted 02 November 2024) at: https://satp.org/south-asia-intelligence-review-Volume-8-No-39.

South Asia Terrorism Portal (n.d.) *India Maoist assessment: 2012*. Available (Consulted 14 November 2024) at: https://www.satp.org/satporgtp/countries/india/maoist/Assessment/2012/indiamaoistassesment2012.htm.

South Asia Terrorism Portal (n.d.) Maoist Communist Centre—Left wing extremism, India. Available (Consulted 18 August 2024) at: https://www.satp.org/satporgtp/countries/india/maoist/terrorist_outfits/MCC.htm.

South Asia Terrorism Portal. (2025). *Maoist insurgency timeline—2025*. Institute for Conflict Management. Available (Consulted 16 November 2024) at: https://www.satp.org/terrorist-activity/india-maoistinsurgency.

South Asia Terrorism Portal. (n.d.). *Liberation Tigers of Tamil Eelam (LTTE)—Terrorist group, Sri Lanka*. Available (Consulted 06 February 2025) at: https://www.satp.org/satporgtp/countries/srilanka/terroristoutfits/ltte.htm.

Sundar, N. (1999). *Subalterns and sovereigns: An anthropological history of Bastar 1854–2006*. England: Oxford University Press.

Supreme Court judgment in Salwa Judum case. (2021, November 16). *The Hindu*. Available (Consulted 2 September 2024) at: https://www.thehindu.com/news/resources/supreme-court-judgment-in-salwa-judum-case/article21185766.ece.

Surjeet, H.S. (2000) The CPI (M) programme: updated in tune with changing times. *The Marxist*, July–December 2000.

Surrendered woman Maoist alleges torture by fellow Naxalites. (2010, May 02) Hindustan Times. Available (Consulted 06 February 2025) at: https://www.hindustantimes.com/india/surrendered-woman-maoist-alleges-torture-by-fellow-naxalites/story-uKNBWf3aovt9QlDorvzKeM.html.

Swami Laxmanananda Saraswati death anniversary: A legacy of service and sacrifice. (2024, August 23). *The Organiser*. Available (consulted 21 February 2025) at: https://organiser.org/2024/08/23/253124/bharat/swami-laxmanananda-saraswati-death-anniversary-a-legacy-of-service-and-sacrifice/.

Swami, P. (2013, June 4) *Congress' doublespeak on Maoist terror isn't confusion, it's policy. Firstpost.* Available (Consulted 2 September 2024) at: https://www.firstpost.com/politics/congress-doublespeak-on-maoist-terror-isnt-confusion-its-policy-838797.html.

Swami, P. (2013, June 4). *Congress double speak on Maoist terror isn't confusion, it's policy*. Firstpost. Available (Consulted 17 June 2025) at: https://www.firstpost.com/politics/congress-doublespeak-on-maoist-terror-isnt-confusion-its-policy-838797.html.

Swami, P. (2013, June 4). *Congress double speak on Maoist terror is not a confusion, it's policy*. Firstpost. Available (Consulted 17 June 2025) at: https://www.firstpost.com/politics/congress-doublespeak-on-maoist-terror-isnt-confusion-its-policy-838797.html.

Sweezy, P. (2010) Marxism and revolution 100 years after Marx. In: What is Maoism and other essays. Kharagpur: Cornerstone Publications.

Teens held at Naxalite training camp. (2007, September 16) *Times of India*. Available (Consulted 06 February 2025) at: https://timesofindia.indiatimes.com/city/nagpur/teens-held-at-naxalite-training-camp/articleshow/2373029.cms.

Thakur, R.K. (2021, July 01) *Home Ministry declares six Bihar districts Naxal-free. The New Indian Express*. Available (Consulted 2 September 2024) at: https://www.newindianexpress.com/nation/2021/Jun/30/home-ministry-declares-six-bihar-districts-naxal-free-2323474.html.

Thamizhchelvan (2011). Interfaith dialogues and inculturation: The real face of the Church. Vijayvaani. Available (consulted 21 February 2025) at: https://www.vijayvaani.com/ArticleDisplay.aspx?aid=2087.

The Adivasis of Chhattisgarh: Victims of the Naxalite Movement and Salwa Judum Campaign. (2006, March 17). *Asian Centre for Human Rights*. Available (Consulted 23 September 2024) at: http://sanhati.com/wp-content/uploads/2010/10/achr-report_adivasis_ofchattisgarh-2006.pdf.

The drama unfolds (2003) *Journal of CPI (ML) Naxalbari* 2: 2–22. Available (Consulted 14 November 2024) at: https://www.bannedthought.net/India/CPI-ML-Naxalbari/Naxalbari-Magazine/Naxalbari-02.pdf.

The Proletarian Revolution and Khrushchov's Revisionism (1964) Peking: Foreign Languages Press. Available (Consulted 14 November 2024) at: https://www.marxists.org/history/international/comintern/sino-soviet-split/cpc/prolrev.htm.

The working process of human rights activists & Christians in Nepal. (2011, December 27) *Sri Lanka Guardian*. Available (consulted 21 February 2025) at: http://www.srilankaguardian.org/2011/12/working-process-of-human-rights.html.

Threats persist from left-wing extremism, terrorism: Manmohan. (2011, February 1). *The Hindu*. Available (Consulted 07 October 2025) at: https://www.thehindu.com/news/national/Threats-persist-from-left-wing-extremism-terrorism-Manmohan/article15123957.ece.

Tikku, A. (2013, July 19) *Maoists raise Rs 140–250 crore a year through extortion, protection rackets. Hindustan Times*. Available (Consulted 18 October 2024) at: https://www.hindustantimes.com/delhi/maoists-raise-rs-140-250-crore-a-year-through-extortion-protection-rackets/story-q6IEtckJzYrlUz7KV5sHfJ.html.

Times of India. (2007, June 24). *13 villagers kidnapped by Naxals in Chhattisgarh*. Available (Consulted 06 February 2025) at: https://timesofindia.indiatimes.com/india/13-villagers-kidnapped-by-naxals-in-chhattisgarh/articleshow/2144932.cms.

Tiwari, A. (2008, July 23). *Kalawati, the woman Rahul spoke of in Lok Sabha*. The Times of India. Available (Consulted 23 October 2025) at: https://timesofindia.indiatimes.com/india/Kalawati-the-woman-Rahul-spoke-of-in-Lok-Sabha/articleshow/3266447.cms.

Too Judgmental. (2011, July 8). *The Indian Express*. Available (Consulted 08 September 2024) at: https://indianexpress.com/article/news-archive/web/too-judgmental/.

Trinamool is patronizing Naxals. (2010, August 10). *The Economic Times*. Available (Consulted 24 October 2025) at: https://economictimes.indiatimes.com/news/politics-and-nation/trinamool-is-patronising-naxals-cpm/articleshow/6285255.cms.

U.S. Department of State (2007). International Religious Freedom Report. Available (consulted 28 February 2025) at: https://2009-2017.state.gov/j/drl/rls/irf/2007/9023.

Umar Khalid, 4 others charged with sedition spotted at JNU. (2016, February 22) *Hindustan Times*. Available (consulted 7 February 2024) at: https://www.hindustantimes.com/india/umar-khalid-4-others-charged-with-sedition-spotted-at-jnu-police-reach-campus/story-AsnxdK1Hvo80BMtNnbRj9N.html.

UN concerned over use of children as human shields by Maoists. (2014, July 04) The Indian Express. Available (Consulted 06 February 2025) at: https://indianexpress.com/article/india/india-others/un-concerned-over-use-of-children-as-human-shields-by-maoists/.

Union Budget allocates ₹3,481.27 crore for security & infrastructure in fight against Naxalism. (2025, February 1). *The Economic Times*. Available (Consulted 16 November 2024) at: https://economictimes.indiatimes.com/news/defence/union-budget-allocates-rs-3481-27-cr-for-security-infrastructure-in-fight-againstnaxalism/articleshow/117832702.cms.

University of Regina (1999) Marx on social class. Available (Consulted 15 November 2024) at: https://uregina.ca/~gingrich/s28f99.htm.

Vivekananda, S. (1899). *On the bounds of Hinduism*. Prabuddha Bharata. Available (consulted 28 February 2025) at: https://www.ramakrishnavivekananda.info/vivekananda/volume_5/interviews/on_the_bounds_of_hinduism.htm.

Vyas, S. (2013, May 26). Foreign funds help Naxals to contest polls. *The Times of India*. Available (consulted 28 February 2025) at: https://timesofindia.indiatimes.com/city/mumbai/Foreign-funds-help-Naxals-to-contest-polls/articleshow/20283933.cms.

What is Salwa Judum? (2011, July 6). *India Today*. Available (Consulted 23 September 2024) at: https://www.indiatoday.in/india/photo/salwa-judum-of-chhattisgarh-365831-2011-07-06/1.

What really happened on the night of Feb 9: A JNU student recounts. (2016, February 16) *Hindustan Times*. Available (consulted 7 February 2024) at: https://www.hindustantimes.com/india/what-really-happened-on-the-night-of-feb-9-a-jnu-student-recounts/story-Hz3USZC3NwntZFwKpF2g1M.html.

What was the February Revolution? Imperial War Museum. Available (Consulted 15 November 2024) at: https://www.iwm.org.uk/history/what-was-the-february-revolution.

When the State Makes War on its own People. (2006, May 17). *People's Union for Democratic Rights (PUDR)*. Available (Consulted 23 September 2024) at: https://www.pudr.org/publicatiosn-files/2006-5-when-the-state-make-war-on-its-own-people.pdf.

When the state makes war on its own people: Violation of people's rights during the Salwa Judum campaign in Dantewada, Chhattisgarh. (2006, May 17) *People's Union for Democratic Rights (PUDR)*. Available (Consulted 23 September 2024) at: https://www.pudr.org/publications/when-the-state-makes-war-on-its-own-people-violation-of-peoples-rights-during-the-salwa-judum/.

Why Maoists never attack churches in Chhattisgarh: RSS leaders ask. (2015, November 15) *Hindustan Times*. Available (consulted 28 February 2025) at: https://www.hindustantimes.com/india/why-maoists-never-attack-churches-in-chhattisgarh-rss-leader-asks/story-q7xvFtEoV1GkQ9RmuaVYXJ.html.

Why was Swami Lakshmananda killed? (2022, August 23). *The Organiser*. Available (consulted 21 February 2025) at: https://organiser.org/2022/08/23/92098/bharat/shri-swami-lakshmanananda-sarswati-smruti-din/.

Women Naxals disclose instances of sexual exploitation: Govt. (2012, March 14). *The Times of India*. Available (Consulted 30 October 2024) at: https://timesofindia.indiatimes.com/india/Women-Naxals-disclose-instances-of-sexual-exploitation-Govt/articleshow/12262296.cms.

Zaidi, A. (2007, September 14). *Resisting the rebels*. Indian Vanguard. Available (Consulted 23 October 2025) at: https://indianvanguard.wordpress.com/2007/09/14/page/2/.

Zedong, M. (1965) Selected works, Vol. I. Peking: Foreign Languages Press.

Annex 1

1 Fatalities in Major Incidents

UPA

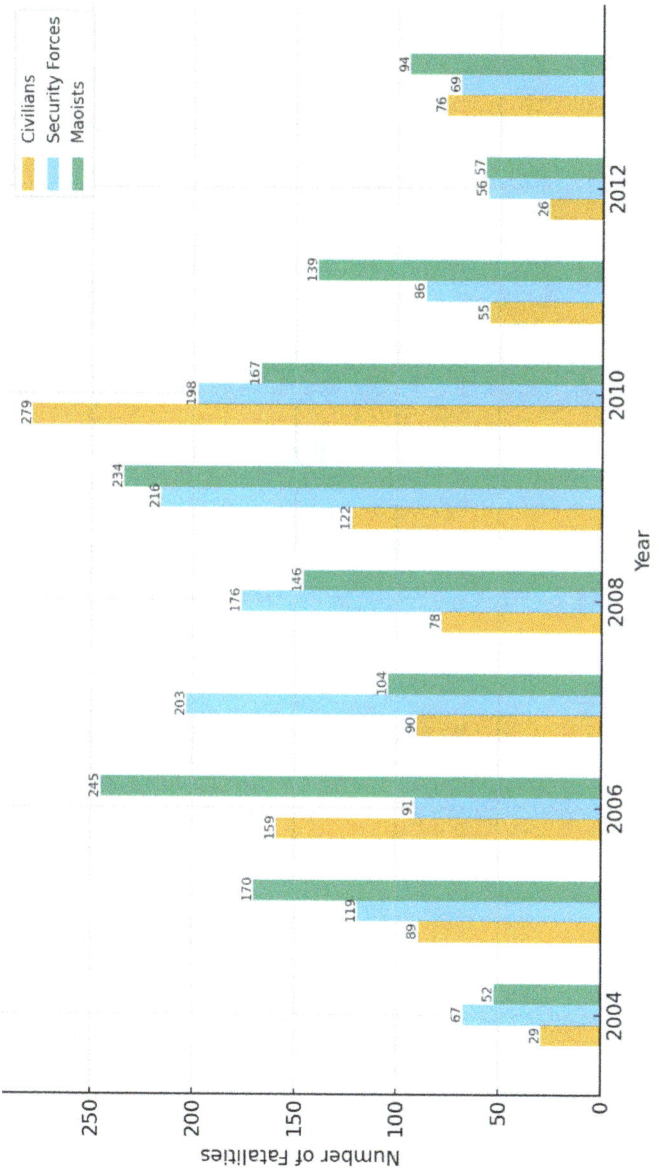

FIGURE 1 Fatalities in major incidents (2004–2013) Source: South Asia Terrorism Portal

 | HTTPS://DOI.ORG/10.1163/9789004765054-016

NDA

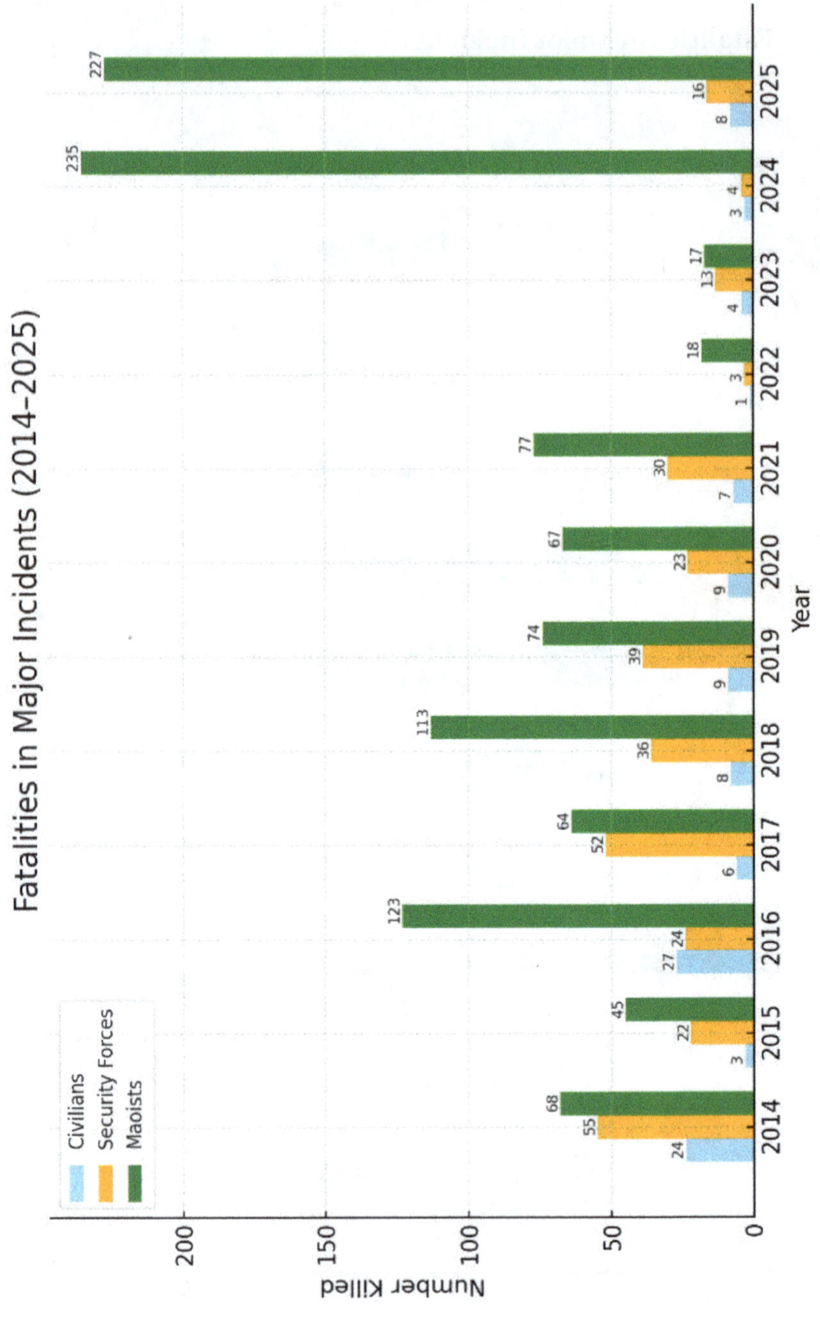

FIGURE 2 Fatalities in major incidents (2014–2025) Source: South Asia Terrorism Portal

2 Suicide Attacks

UPA

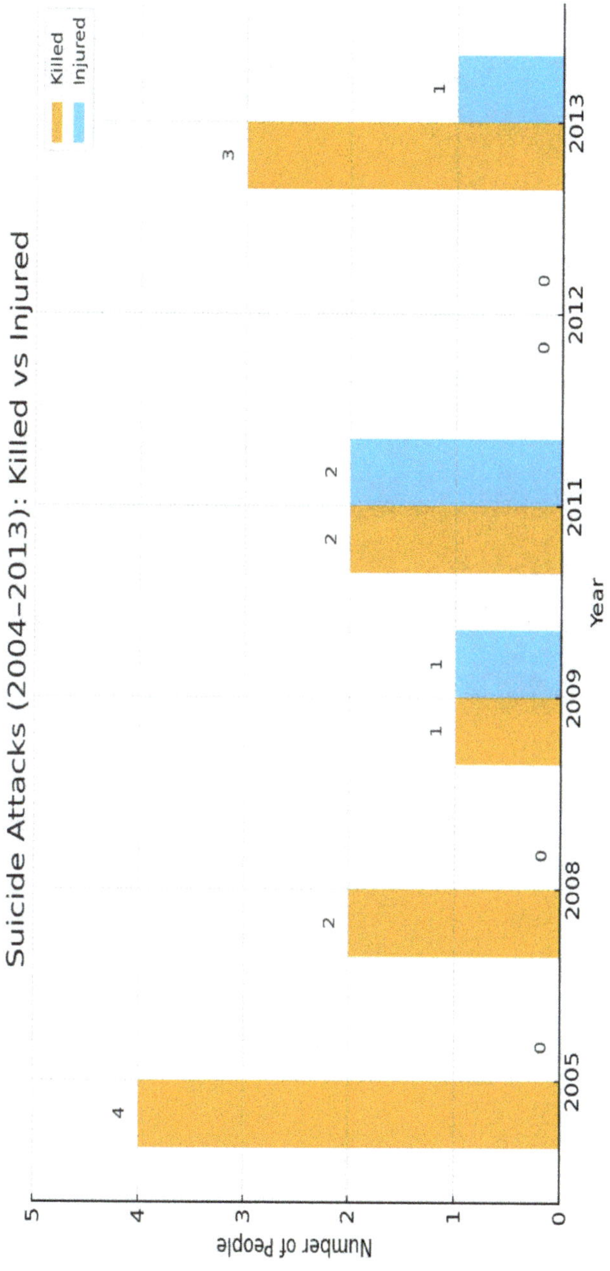

FIGURE 3 Suicide attacks (2004–2013): killed vs injured. Source: South Asia Terrorism Portal

NDA

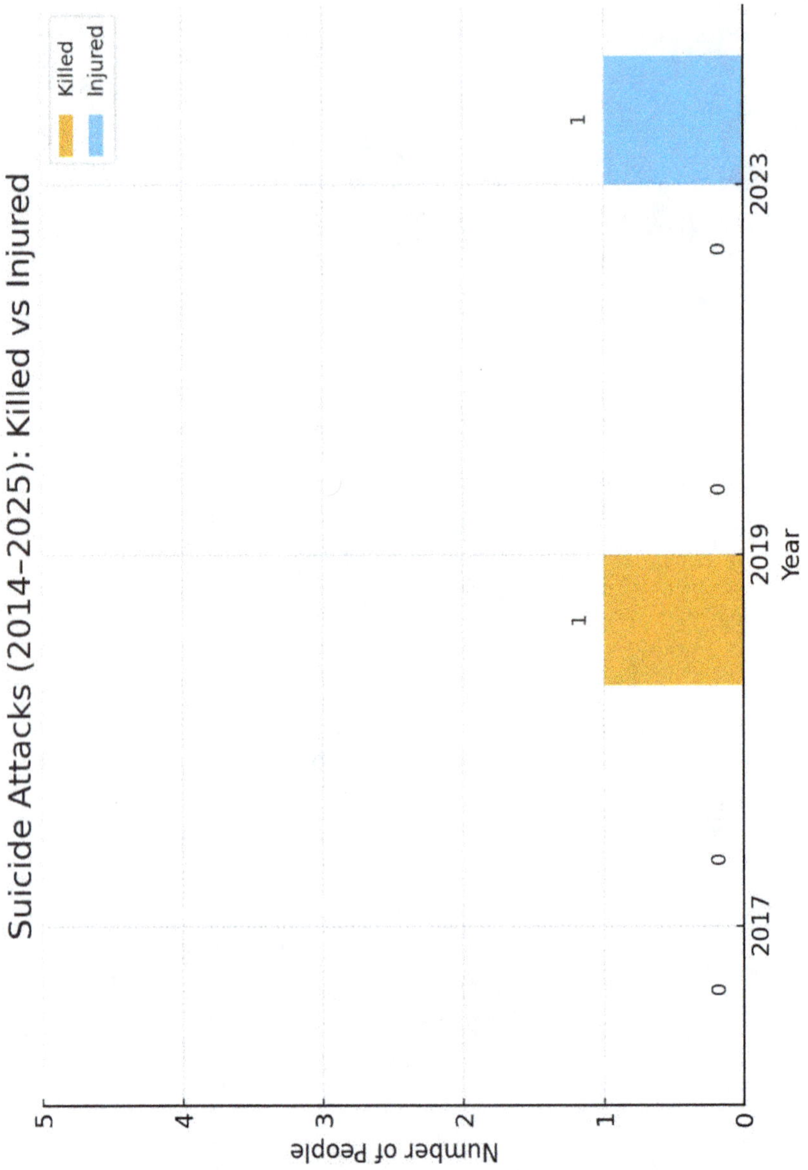

FIGURE 4 Suicide attacks (2014–2025): killed vs injured. Source: South Asia Terrorism Portal

3 Surrender

2004–2005

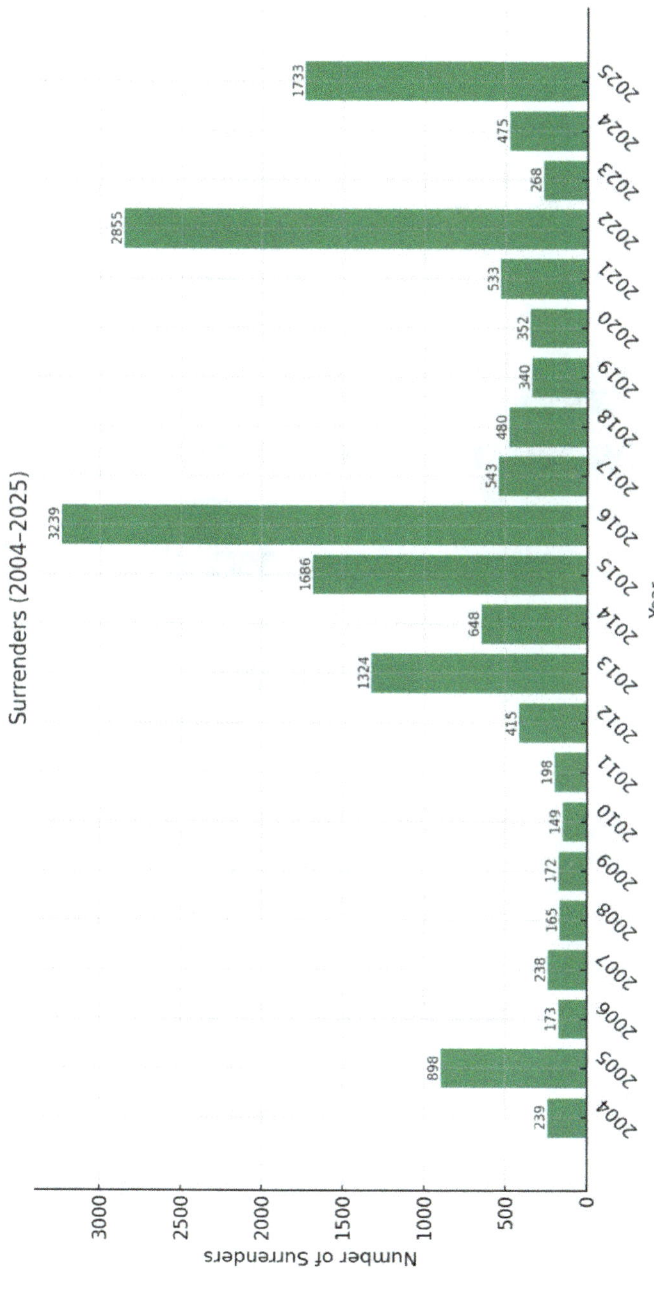

FIGURE 5 Surrenders (2004–2025) Source: South Asia Terrorism Portal

4 Fatalities Due to Explosions

UPA

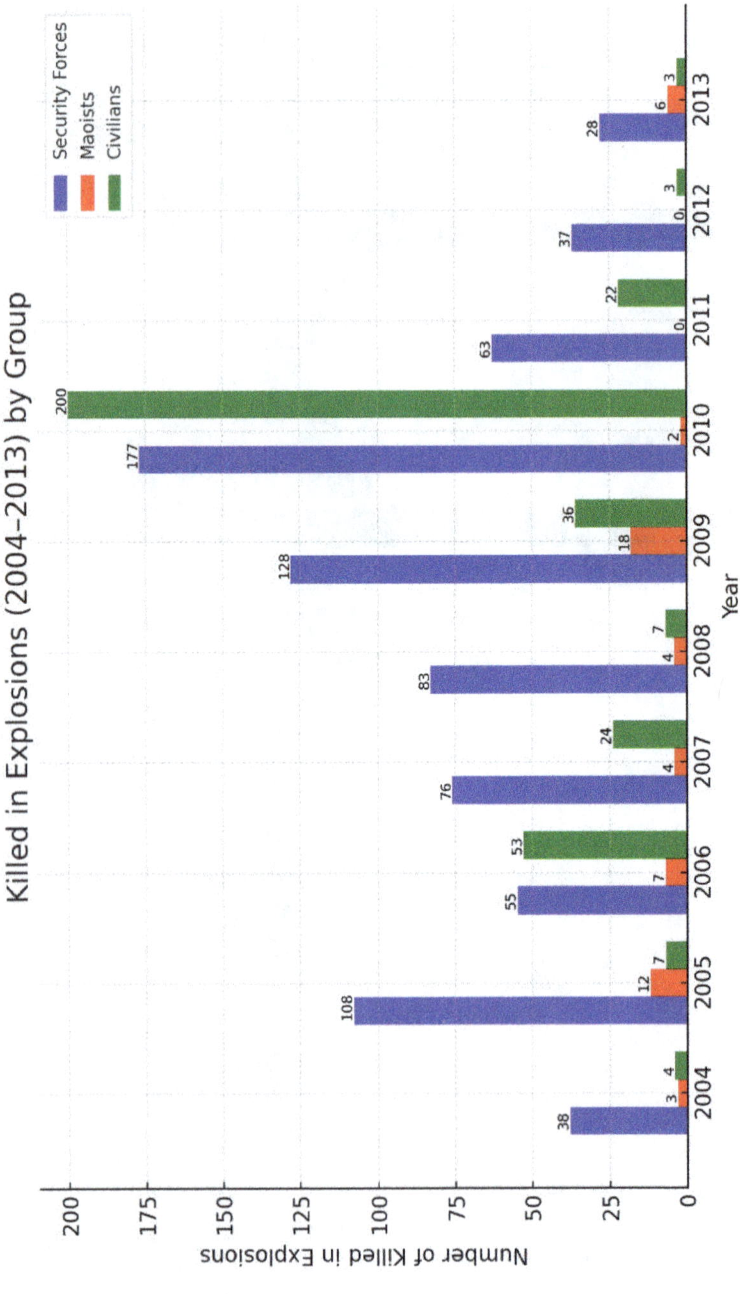

FIGURE 6 Killed in explosions (2004–2013) by group. Source: South Asia Terrorism Portal

NDA

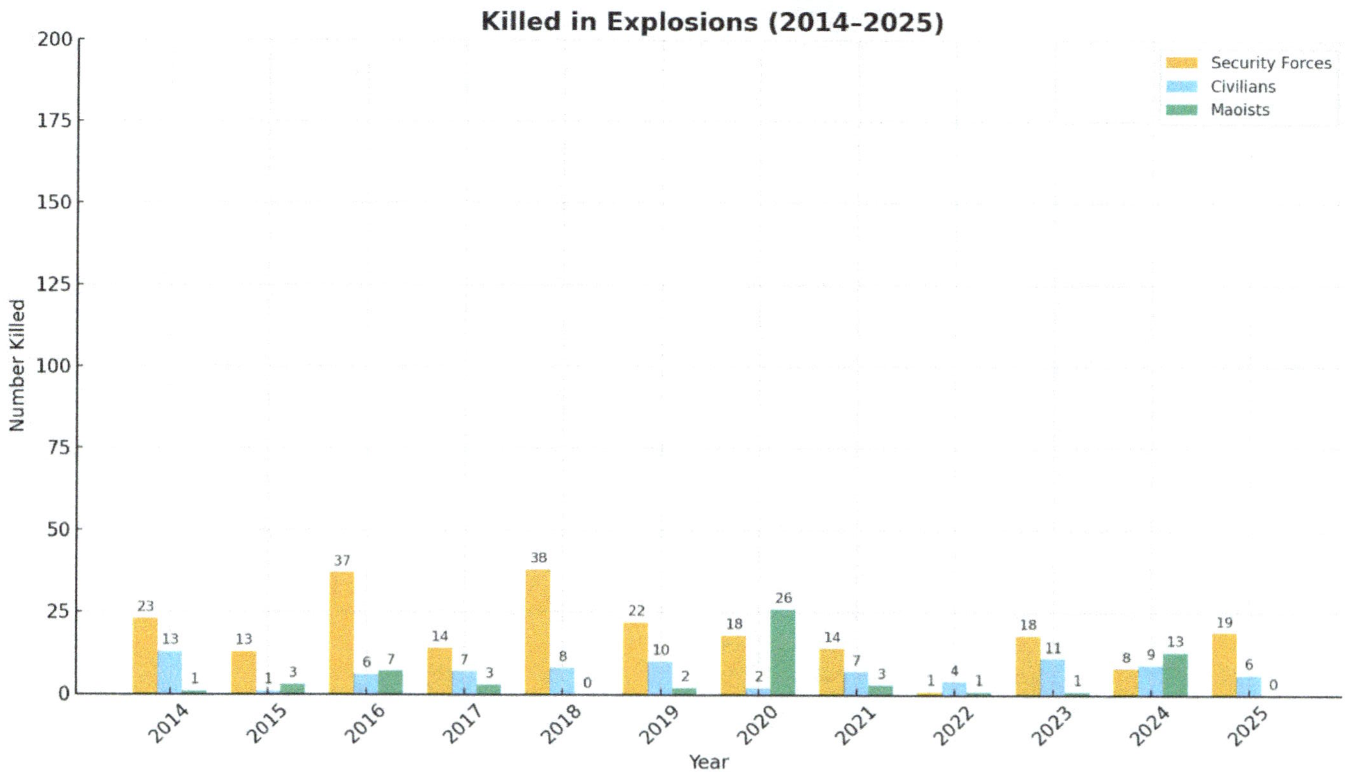

FIGURE 7 Killed in explosions (2014–2025)) Source: South Asia Terrorism Portal

5 Comparative Analysis of Security Forces Injured in Major Incidents

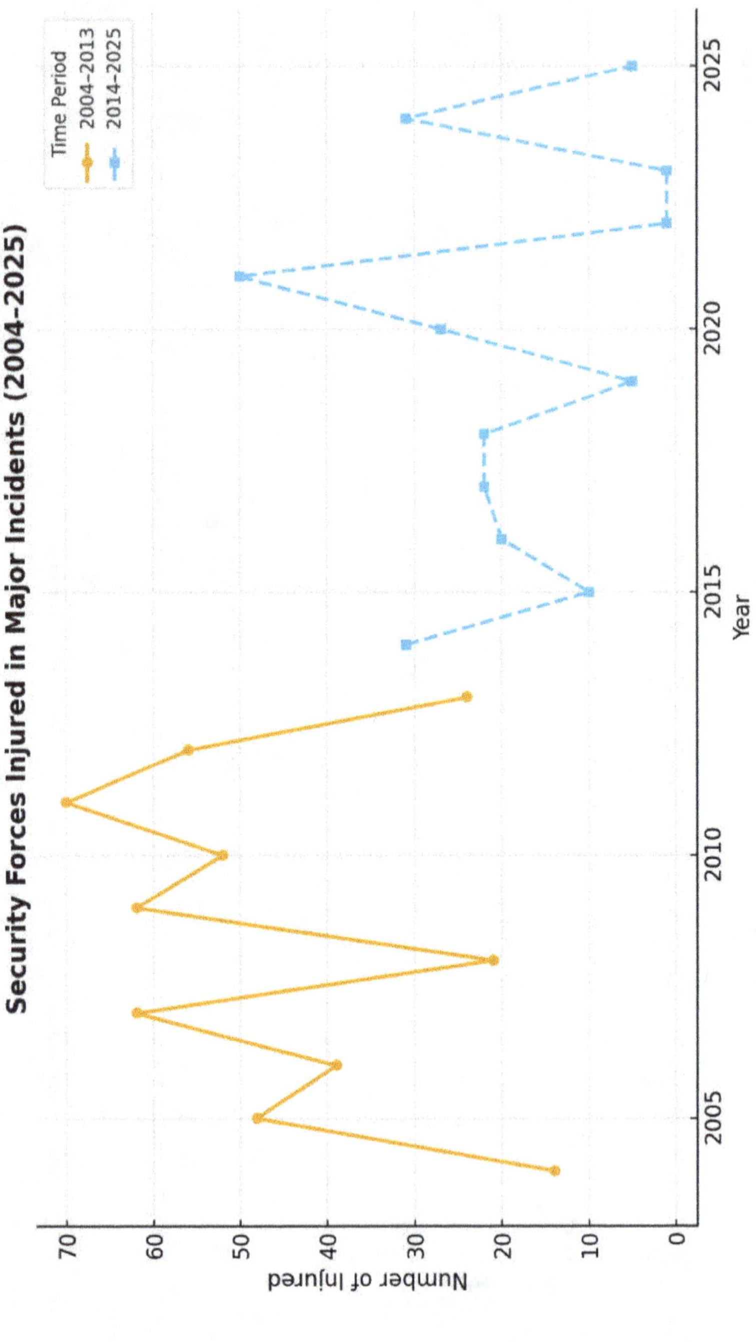

FIGURE 8 Security forces injured in major incidents (2004–2025) Source: South Asia Terrorism Portal

6 Comparative Analysis of Security Forces Killed in Major Incidents

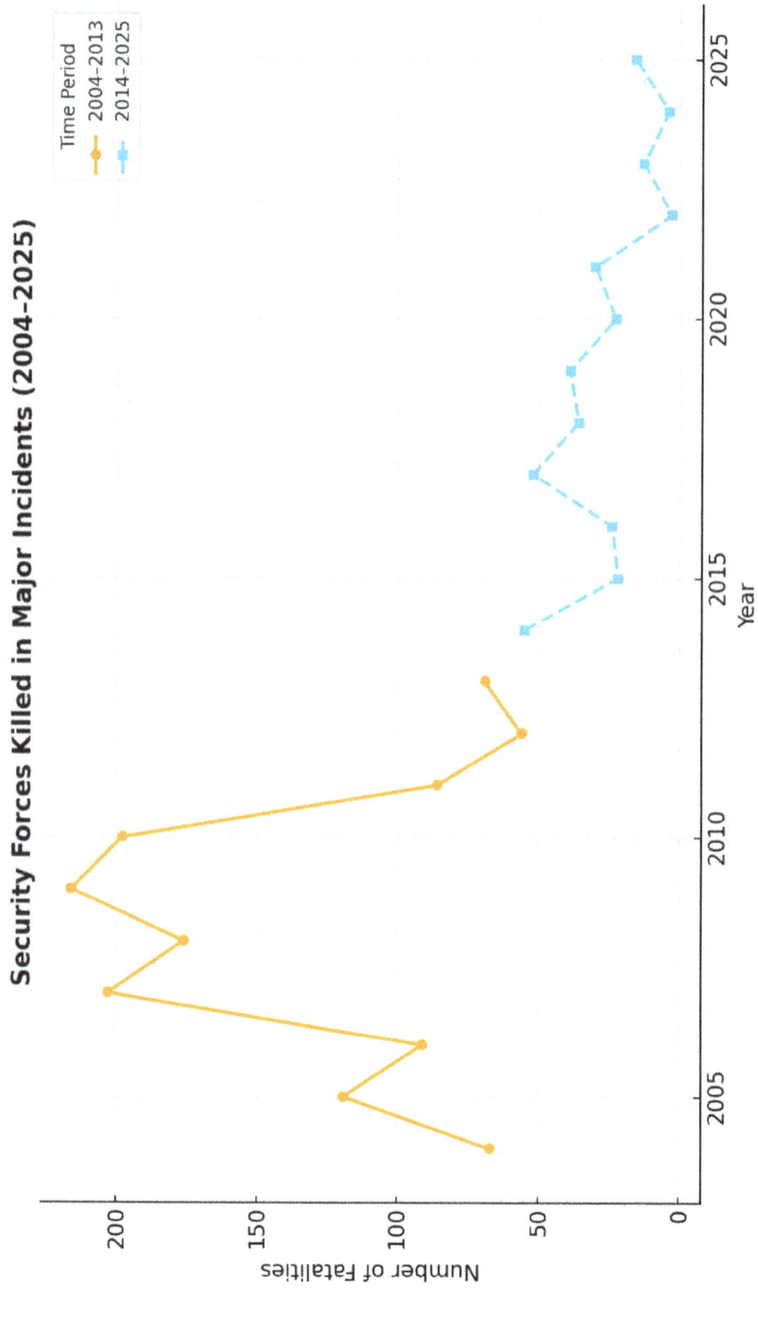

FIGURE 9 Security forces killed in major incidents (2004–2025) Source: South Asia Terrorism Portal)

7 Comparative Analysis of Security Forces Injured in Explosions

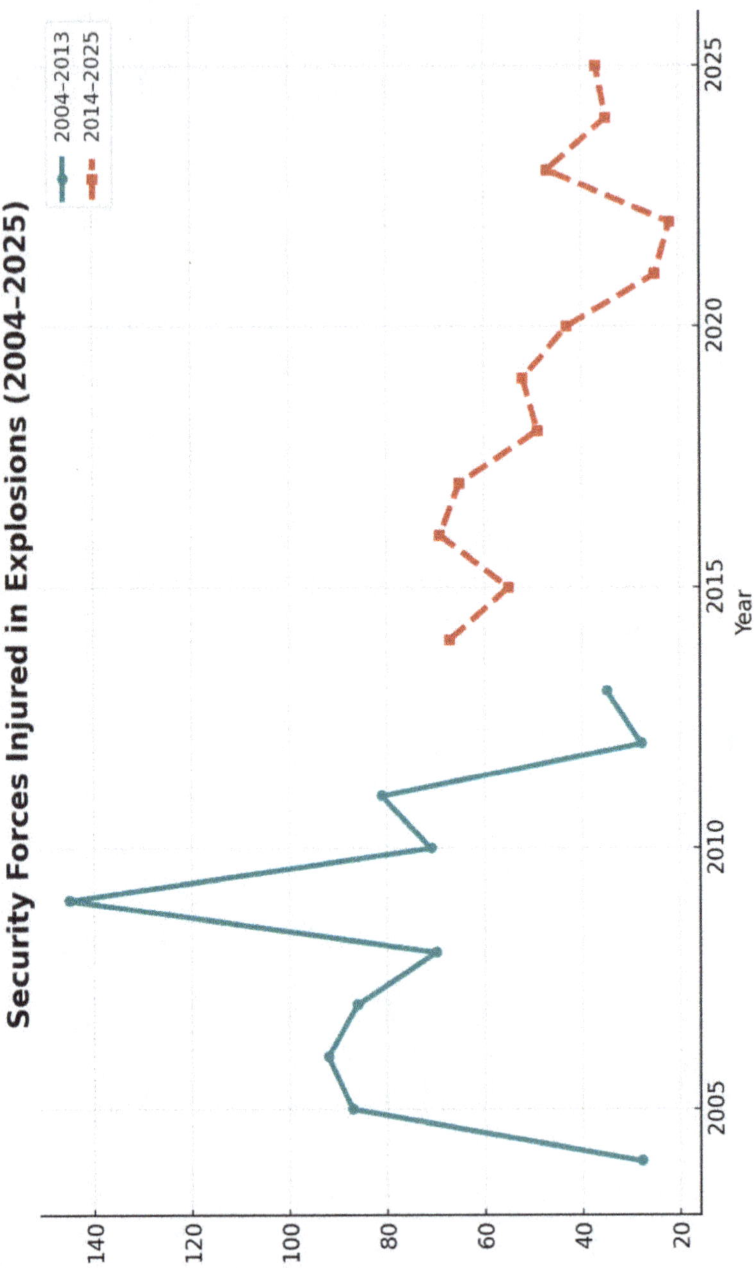

FIGURE 10 Security forces injured in explosions (2004–2025) Source: South Asia Terrorism Portal

8 Comparative Analysis of Security Forces Killed in Explosions

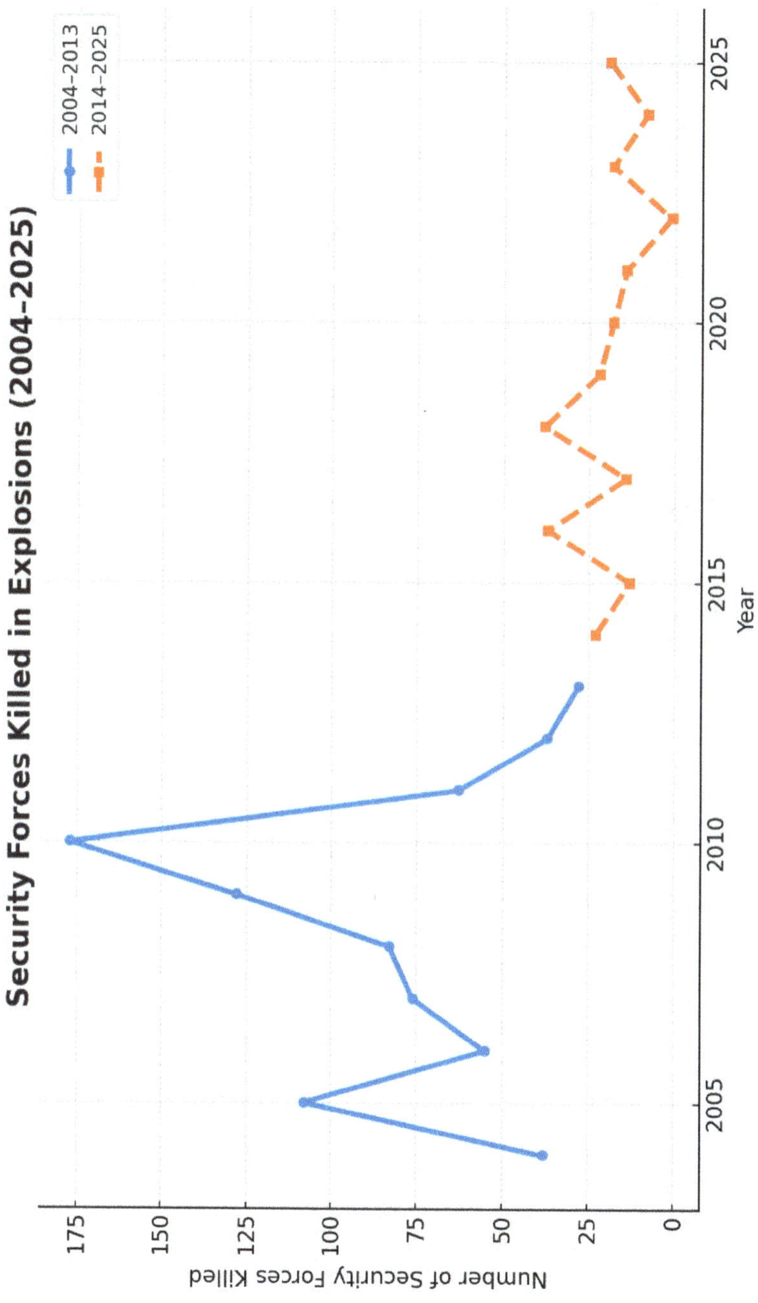

FIGURE 11 Security forces killed in explosions (2004–2025) Source: South Asia Terrorism Portal

Annex 2

Major Maoist Insurgency Incidents (2005–25)

Source: South Asian Terrorism Portal

YEAR-2005:

JANUARY

January 15: As per the Hindu, six Naxals killed in encounter with police in Mahboobnagar, Andhra Pradesh.

FEBRUARY

February 2: Maoist killed a TDP activist in Warangal, Andhra Pradesh on suspicion of being a police informer.

February 11: Six police personnel were killed by Naxalites in Tumkur, Karnataka.

February 22: Five police killed and 12 injured in attack in the Gadchiroli, Maharashtra.

MAY

May 17: Naxalites killed a Congress party activist, in Chikmagalur district,Karnataka.

May 23: Five police personnel were killed in landmine explosion triggered by Maoist Dantewada, Chhatishgarh.

May 30: Seven police and a civilian were killed in landmine blast by Maoist in Gondia Maharashtra.

JULY

July 3: Three police personnel were killed and two injured when Naxalites fired on police patrolling party in Gadchiroli, Maharashtra.

AUGUST

August 9: Maoist killed two persons related to Chhattisgarh's Leader of Opposition in the State Legislative Assembly in the Dantewada district, Chhatisgarh.

SEPTEMBER

September 3: 22 CRPF personnel and two State police were killed in a landmine explosion triggered by CPI-Maoist Dantewada, Chhatishgarh.

September 12: As per PTI, Naxalites killed 15 civilians in the Giridih district of Jharkhand.

September 27: CPI-Maoist shot dead a Congress party leader, Subash Biswal, Malkangiri, Odisha.

OCTOBER

October 8: Thirteen personnel of the state police and central paramilitary forces killed in a bomb blast triggered by CPI-Maoist Chatra, Jharkhand.

 | HTTPS://DOI.ORG/10.1163/9789004765054-017

NOVEMBER

November 12: CPI-Maoist attacked a home guard training centre in Giridih, Jharkhand and shot dead five persons, including four home guards, and injured 16 persons.

DECEMBER

December 26: According to Daily News & Analysis, two police personnel and 4 Naxals were also killed in gun battle in Gadchiroli, Maharshtra.

December 31: CPI-Maoist killed Rabindranath Kar and his wife, Communist Party of India (Marxist) leader in Purulia (WB), according to Times of India.

YEAR 2006:

JANUARY

January 1: According to Hindustan Times, six Maoist killed in encounter with police Maharashtra-Chhattisgarh border in Gadchiroli, Maharashtra.

January 15: According to Press Trust of India, Maoist killed an engineer from Border Roads Organisation (BRO) in Gadhchiroli, Maharashtra.

January 30: According to The Times of India 11 persons, including eight civilians and three CPI-Maoist killed in Maoist attack on a government camp in the Dantewada, Chhatishgarh.

FEBRUARY

February 6: According to Indo-Asian News Service, Maoists killed 13 police personnel, including 10 from the Nagaland Armed Police (NAP), in two separate attacks in Chhattisgarh.

February 28: 25 tribals were killed and 40 injured in a landmine blast by CPI-Maoist Dantewada.

MARCH

March 8: CPI-Maoist killed 4 civilians in Dantewada, Chhatishgarh.

March 24: Maoist shot dead two police personnel and took hostage at least three Government officials in attacks on a police station Gajapati, Odisha.

March 31: CPI-Maoist killed two local BJP leaders in Rajnandgaon, Chhatishgarh.

APRIL

April 16: CPI-Maoist attacked police outpost in Dantewada district and killed 11 police personnel.

April 19: Two police personnel were killed in a landmine blast triggered CPI-Maoist in Gadchiroli, Maharashtra, reported by the Telegraph.

April 29: According to Hindu, Maoist killed 13 of the 52 abducted villagers and released 37 others in Dantewada, Chhatishgarh.

MAY

May 13: Maoists attacked a refugee camp in Dantewada, Chhatishgarh and shot dead four SPOs and wounded five people.

May 16: In a landmine explosion triggered by Maoist, 12 members of a marriage group were killed in Gadchiroli, Maharashtra.

JUNE

June 20: Maoists killed seven persons and injured two others at Chikuarguda in the Konta region, Chhatishgarh, according to Pioneer.

JULY

July 17: According to Hindu CPI-Maoist killed 17 villagers and injured 70, besides kidnapping over 20 people in Dantewada. The Hindu reports that at least 27 tribal activists of the anti-Maoist Salva Judum campaign were killed and 40 others were injured in the attack by CPI-Maoist Dantewada district.

AUGUST

August 18: CPI-Maoist attacked the police station in Nalgonda, Andhra Pradesh and killed a Sub-Inspector (SI), an Assistant SI and a home guard.

SEPTEMBER

September 21: Two police personnel of the Bomb Disposal squad were killed and 29 others, including some senior police officers and journalists, were injured in a land mine explosion by CPI-Maoist Paschim Medinipur, WB.

September 30: New Indian Express reports that three villagers, including a former sarpanch (village head) were killed by Maoist in Dantewada, Chhatishgarh.

OCTOBER

October 22: Hindustan Times reports that Maoist killed three abducted civilians in Bastar, Chhatishgarh.

October 23: A DIG of Police was allegedly killed by CPI-Maoist Rayagada, reports The Hindu.

NOVEMBER

November 9: Maoist shot dead a Congress party leader, in Andhra Pradesh, according to The Hindu.

DECEMBER

December 2: 14 police personnel of the Jharkhand police were killed and three injured in a landmine blast detonated by CPI-Maoists Bokaro, reports The Hindu.

December 13: Four police personnel were killed by Maoist at a relief camp in Dantewada, Chhatishgarh reports Times of India.

December 21: Five persons, including two security force (SF) personnel, were killed and four others were injured when Maoist triggered landmine blasts in the Dantewada, Chhatishgarh, reports Asian Age.

YEAR 2007:

JANUARY

January 16: Seven CRPF personnel were killed in an IED in Kanker, Chhatishgarh, reports DNA.

January 31: Three forest employees were killed by Maoist in the Kandhar forest area of Kankadahada block in the Dhenkanal, Odisha[Times of India].

FEBRUARY

February 27: As The Hindu reported, Maoist killed four police personnel and blew up railway tracks at two places in Lakhisarai, Bihar.

MARCH

March 1: Eight persons, six security force (SF) personnel, were killed in a landmine triggered by Maoist in the Dantewada, on the Andhra Pradesh-Chhattisgarh border.

March 15: Fifty-four persons, including 15 personnel of the Chhattisgarh Armed Force, were killed and eleven persons were injured in attack by Maoist on police in Bastar region, reports The Hindu.

APRIL

April 6: Six people were killed when Maoist CISF camp in Bokaro, Jharkhand.

MAY

May 28: Nine police personnel were killed by Maoist cadres in Bastar, Chhatishgarh, reports The Hindu.

May 31: Maoist abducted and killed three unidentified civilians, alleging to be police informants, in Dantewada, Chhatishgarh, reports Dainik Bhaskar.

JUNE

June 5: CPI-Maoist killed K. Satyam, a Congress party leader, at Chinnamidisaleru village in the Khammam, Andhra Pradesh. Three employees of the Chhattisgarh State Electricity Board were killed and five Special Task Force (STF) personnel sustained injuries Maoist triggered landmine blast in Naryanpur, Chhatishgarh, reports Hindustan Times.

June 7: A local BJP leader, was shot dead by CPI-Maoist in Simdega, reports The Hindustan Times.

JULY

July 9: 24 security personnel and 20 Maoist were killed in a gun battle in Dantewada, Chhatishgarh according to New Indian Express.

July 10: Maoist cadres shot dead a Congress leader in Prakasam, Andhra Pradesh.

July 12: Maoist killed a local leader of Congress party, Khammam district, Andhra Pradesh, The Hindu reports.

AUGUST

August 29: 12 security personnel were killed in an ambush by Maoist in Dantewada district, reports Times of India.

OCTOBER

October 27: 17 people, including the son of former Jharkhand Chief Minister, Babulal Marandi, were killed by Maoist in Giridih reports The Hindu.

October 28: Five people were killed by Maoist in Latehar, Jharkhand, Sify News reports.

October 29: Five SPOs were killed by Maoist indiscriminate fire in Bijapur, Chhatishgarh, reports The Hindu.

NOVEMBER

November 2: Maoist ambushed and killed 16 policemen, including six CRPF personnel, reports The Hindu.

November 12: Maoist ambushed CRPF and killed three of them, in Bijapur district, reports The Hindu.

DECEMBER

December 12: Indian Express reports that three police personnel were killed and another wounded Maoist attack on Police station in the Bastar district.

December 20: According to Times of India, 12 policemen were killed in ambush by Maoist in the Dantewada, Chhatishgarh.

YEAR 2008:

JANUARY

January 1: According to Sahara Samay, four policemen were killed Maoist in the Munger, Bihar.

January 26: Maoist gunned down three persons, accusing them of being police spies, in Karimnagar district, reports Hindustan Times.

FEBRUARY

February 15: 13 police personnel and a civilian were killed when Maoist attacked a Police Training School (PTS) in Narayangarh in Odisha, reported Times of India.

February 18: 13 Maoist and six CRPF personnel were killed in two separate encounters in the Bijapur, Chhatishgarh, according to Times of India.

February 29: Maoist killed an activist of Congress party in Srikakulam, Andhra Pradesh, according to Times of India.

APRIL

April 10: Maoist killed six persons belonging to the Sashastra People's Morcha (SSM) Rohtas, Bihar, reports The Hindu.

April 13: Six persons, including five SF personnel, were killed in an attack by Maoist in Jhajha railway station in the Jamui, Bihar.

April 13: Maoist killed three Communist Party of India-Marxist (CPI-M) in West Midnapore district, reports The Hindu.

MAY

May 8: Three policemen were killed when Maoist triggered a landmine and in Kanker, Chhatishgarh, reports Times of India.

May 15: Maoist shot dead two civilians in the Udupi, Karnataka, PTI reports.

JUNE

June 8: Three CISF personnel, including a sub-inspector, were killed and two others injured in an attack by Maoist in Durg, Chhatishgarh, reports The Hindu.

June 29: Times of India reports that 39 security force (SF) personnel were killed in an attack by Maoist in Malkangiri, Odisha.

AUGUST

August 21: Six policemen, two Maoist cadres and a civilian were killed in an exchange of fire betweem Maoist and police in Gaya, Bihar, reports Times of India.

August 23: Five persons including VHP leader and four disciples, including a woman, were killed in an attack by Maoist in Kandhamal, Odisha, reports The Hindu.

SEPTEMBER

September 4: Indian Express reports that five SF personnel, CRPF, were killed and five injured in attack by Maoist in Sarguja, Chhatishgarh.

OCTOBER

October 20: 12 CRPF were killed and six injured in an ambush by Maoist in the Bijapur, Chhatishgarh, reports Indian Express.

October 22: Three persons, including a doctor of the West Bengal Health Department, were killed in a landmine blast by Maoist in West Midnapore district, reports The Hindu.

October 26: Maoist ambushed and killed four personnel in Gadchiroli (Maharashtra), reports Indian Express.

NOVEMBER

November 5: Maoist killed RSS in Kandhamal (Odisha), reports The Indian Express.

November 9: 2 BJP leaders were killed by Maoist in Dantewada (Chhatishgarh), reports Times of India.

November 15–16: Three villagers abducted and subsequently killed by Naxalites for refusing to pay levy in Jamui (Bihar), reports Times of India.

November 25: 7 policemen were killed when Maoist blew up a bridge in Bastar (Chhatishgarh), The Hindu reported.

DECEMBER

December 5: Maoist killed five policemen in Khunti (Jharkhand), reports Indian Express.

YEAR 2009:

JANUARY

January 3: Five tribals were killed in attacks Maoist Bijapur, Chhatishgarh, The Hindu reported.

January 17: Six Policemen were killed in a landmine blast by Maoist in the Latehar, Jharkhand, reports Times of India.

January 31: Four villagers were shot dead by the People's Liberation Front of India (PLFI) Khuti, Jharkhand, reports IANS.

FEBRUARY

February 1: 15 Police were killed by Maoist in Gadchichiroli, Maharshtra, The Pioneer reported.

February 9: 10 Policemen, SAP were killed by Maoist attack on the Security Force personnel in Nawada, Bihar, Patna Daily reported.

February 18: Three CRPF personnel were killed in an ambush by Maoist in Kanker, Chhatishgarh, reports Indian Express.

MARCH

March 9: Times of India reports that Maoist killed two women and two children of a family by slitting their throat in the Arwal, Bihar.

APRIL

April 12: PTI reports that 11 CISF personnel and four Maoist were killed in a gunfight in Koraput, Odisha. In Chhatishgarh, 10 persons, including six Maoist SF personnel, were killed in three separate incidents, The Hindu reported.

April 16: Five election officials and two CRPF personnel were killed by Maoist in Chhatishgarh, reports The Statesman.

April 23: Times of India reports that four Security Force personnel and a civilian were killed in a landmine explosion by Maoist in Muzaffarpur, Bihar.

April 30: Four persons were killed by Maoist in landmine blast in West Midnapore District, (WB) reports PTI.

MAY

May 6: The Hindu reports that 11 persons, including four civilians and seven security force (SF) personnel, were killed in an ambush by Maoist in Chhatishgarh on a special Police party.

May 11: 12 Policemen and a civilian were killed as Maoist ambushed in Dhamtari (Chhatishgarh), reports The Hindu.

May 21: 16 Police, including five women constables, were killed in encounter with Maoist in Gadchiroli, Maharashtra, Times of India reported.

May 27: Two Police constables, were killed by Maoist in Gadchiroli, Maharashtra.

JUNE

June 3: Three Policemen were killed and two others injured when Maoist ambushed in the Bankura (WB), Times of India reported.

June 20: IANS reports that 12 CRPF personnel were killed in the landmine blast Maoist in Dantewada (Chhatishgarh).

AUGUST

August 1: Maoist killed two local-level politicians, CPI-Marxist from Jharkhand in West Midnapore District (WB), reports Times of India.

August 5: The Hindu reports that Maoist shot dead three in the West Midnapore (WB).

August 11: Two persons, SPO were killed in attacks by Maoist in Bijapur (Chhatishgarh).

August 22: Four Police personnel, including an Assistant Sub-Inspector, were killed by Maoist attack in Jamui (Bihar), reports Times of India.

August 23: PTI reports that Maoist shot dead two activists of the Jharkhand Party-Aditya in West Midnapore (WB).

SEPTEMBER

September 6: Indian Express reports that Maoist killed two supporters of CPI-Marxist in West Midnapore (WB).

September 6–7: Five villagers were shot dead by Maoist in Jharkhand, Hindustan Times reported.

OCTOBER

October 1–2: Maoist killed two leaders of the Jharkhand Janamukti Morcha (JJM) in the West Midnapore (WB), Times of India reports.

October 8: The Times of India reports Maoist killed 18 Policemen, including Sub-Inspector in ambush in Gadchiroli (Maharashtra) and 15 Maoist also killed.

October 29: Maoist killed RSS office-bearer and his two relatives in Dantewada (Chhatishgarh), reports Telegraph.

NOVEMBER

November 8: PTI reports that Maoist killed four Security personnel in West Midnapore (WB).

YEAR 2010:

JANUARY

January 2: Maoists shot dead two CPI-Marxist members after 'kangaroo' court trial in WB.

January 7–8: Two persons were killed in West Midnapore (WB) on January 7 by Maoist, reports The Hindu.

January 27: Maoist killed CPI-Marxist in Bankura (WB), reported Times of India.

January 31: In WB, 10 Police personnel, including a Deputy Superintendent of Police, were injured during an exchange of fire between the Security Forces (SFs) and Maoists.

FEBRUARY

February 1: Maoist killed CPI-Marxist worker in the West Midnapore (WB), reported The Hindu.

February 15: 24 SF personnel, were killed in Maoist attack on SF camp in West Midnapore (WB), reported The Hindu.

February 17: At least 12 villagers, including three women and one child, were killed in Maoist in Jamui (Bihar), reports The Hindu.

February 21: Maoist shot dead two local leaders of CPI-Marxist in Purulia (WB), reports The Hindu.

MARCH

March 23: Three Policemen were shot dead in Gajapati, Odisha by Maoist, reports Indian Express.

APRIL

April 4: Nine personnel of the anti-Maoist Special Operation Group (SOG) were killed in Maoist triggered landmine in Koraput, Odisha, reports The Hindu.

April 6: 70 CRPF personnel were killed in an attack by Maoist in Dantewada, Chhatishgarh, reports Times of India.

MAY

May 3: Four troopers of the Bihar Military Police (BMP) were killed in Maoist firing in Aurangabad (Bihar) on May 3, reported PTI.

May 4: Three persons were shot dead by Maoist in West Midnapore (WB), reported NDTV.

May 8: Seven CRPF personnel were killed as Maoist blew up vehicle in Bijapur, Chhatishgarh, reports The Hindu.

May 27: Two local leaders CPI-Marxist were killed by the Maoists in West Midnapore (WB), reported The Hindu. In Maharashtra, Two Police constables, were killed by Maoist in Gadchiroli District on May 27.

May 28: 65 passengers were killed Maoist triggered blast on railway track causing derailment of Howrah-Kurla Express in West Midnapore (WB), reported Indian Express.

JUNE

June 8: Maoist killed two persons in West Midnapore (WB), reported IANS.

June 16: 12 Maoist dead in encounter Maoist and forces in West Midnapore (WB).

June 27: Forward Bloc party leader from Purulia in WB killed by Maoist, reports Times of India.

June 29: Twenty-six personnel of CRPF were killed in a Maoist ambush in Narayanpur, Chhatishgarh, reports The Hindu.

JULY

July 1: Hindustan Times reports that three civilians were killed by Maoist in Narayanpur (Chhatishgarh).

July 12: A local leader of JMM was shot dead by Maoist in Purulia (WB), reports The Hindu.

July 16: Three persons were killed Maoist in West Midnapore (WB), reports Indian Express.

July 20: PTI reports Maoist killed two activists of CPI-Marxist in Purulia (WB).

July 26: Times of India reports that six cadres Maoist a woman and a CRPF trooper were killed in an encounter in West Midnapore (WB).

July 29: Times of India reports that Maoists shot dead TMC politician in Purulia (WB).

SEPTEMBER

September 1: The Hindu reports that two persons shot dead by Maoist in West Midnapore (WB).

September 8: IANS reports that TMC supporter was shot dead in West Midnapore (WB).

September 24: CRPF and Maoist were killed in an encounter between SF and CPI-Maoist cadres in West Midnapore (WB), reports The Hindu.

OCTOBER

October 4: Times of India reports that a land mine blast triggered by Maoist killed CRPF Inspector, two Sub-Inspectors of District and two Constables, of CRPF in Gadchiroli, Maharashtra.

October 8: Seven persons, including two schoolchildren and three Indo-Tibetan Border Police (ITBP) personnel, were killed in encounters with the Maoist, at Maharashtra and Chhattisgarh border reports Times of India.

NOVEMBER

November 25: The Hindu reports that three persons were killed in a landmine blast by Maoist in Vishakhapatnam (Andhra Pradesh).

November 27: The Hindu reports that five persons, including two women and a three-year-old child, were killed as Maoist blew up an ambulance by landmine blast in Kandhamal (Odisha).

DECEMBER

December 9: The Hindu reports Maoist killed a local leader of CPI-Marxist in Birbhum (WB).

December 17: The Hindu reports that Maoist killed seven Forward Bloc party workers in Purulia (WB).

YEAR 2011:

JANUARY

January 14: The death toll in Maoist violence in West Midnapore (WB) is nine, The Hindu reported.

FEBRUARY

February 9: The Hindu reports that Maoist shot dead an All India Forward Bloc (AIFB) supporter in Purulia (WB).

February 16: The Hindu reports that Maoist abducted District Collector of Malkangiri, Odisha.

February 28: NDTV reports that three Policemen, including an Assistant Sub Inspector, a Head Constable and a Home Guard, were killed in a landmine blast by Maoist in Chatra (Jharkhand).

MAY

May 3: Times of India reports that 11 SF personnel were killed and nearly 40 injured when Maoist ambushed in Lohardaga (Jharkhand).

May 5: The Hindu reports that a landmine blast by Maoist killed six persons of a family in Gadchiroli (Maharashtra).

May 17: Five CRPF troopers were killed and two others injured in a landmine blast by Maoist in Dantewada (Chhatishgarh), reports Daily.bhaskar.com.

May 23: Nine Policemen, including the Additional Superintendent of Police (ASP) were killed in a landmine blast by Maoist in Raipur (Chhatishgarh), reports The Hindu.

JUNE

June 10: Three CRPF personnel were killed when Maoist attacked the CRPF camp in Dantewada, Chhatishgarh, reports The Hindu.

JULY

July 1: Nearly 50-armed Maoist stormed Bangalwa Kareli village in Munger District of Bihar and killed six people and abducted seven others, reports Times of India.

AUGUST

August 4: Maoist killed three villagers in Bijapur (Chhatishgarh) on suspicion of being Police informers.

SEPTEMBER

September 24: Maoist killed Biju Janata Dal (BJD) MLA Personal Security Officer (PSO) in Nabarangpur (Odisha), reports Telegraph.

OCTOBER

October 8: A Police Constable was killed in an encounter with Maoist in Dakshina Kannada, Karnataka, The Hindu reported.

NOVEMBER

November 8: Seven Security Force personnel, five of Jharkhand Jaguar and two of District Police in land-mine explosions by Maoist in Latehar, Jharkhand, reports The Times of India.

DECEMBER

December 3: Ten persons, including eight Policemen, were killed by Maoist as they attacked the convoy of MP and former Jharkhand Speaker Inder Singh Namdhari, in Latehar, Jharkhand, The Times of India reported.

December 30: Four tribals, including a postman, were killed by Maoist in Bastar, Chhatishgarh, for allegedly refusing to follow the Maoist diktat, reports IBN Live.

YEAR 2012:

JANUARY

January 21: Maoist, by landmine blast, killed 13 Police personnel in Garhwa (Jharkhand) reports The Telegraph.

FEBRUARY

February 1: Three Policemen, including an Assistant Sub-Inspector, were killed by Maoist in a landmine blast in Latehar, Jharkhand, reports The Times of India.

February 10: Four personnel of BSF including a commandant were killed in an ambush by Maoist Malkangiri (Odisha).

MARCH

March 14: Three BSF troopers were killed Maoist blew up the vehicle in Kanker, Chhatishgarh, reports The Hindu.

March 18: Two Italian tourists on a trekking tour on the Ganjam-Kandhamal border, (Odisha) were abducted by the Maoists, reports Zee News.

APRIL

April 3: The death toll in the landmine blast by Maoist in Gadchiroli (Maharashtra) totaled 13, reports The Hindu.

April 21: Maoist abducted the collector of Sukma, Chhatishgarh and killed his two body guards, reports Times of India.

MAY

May 14: Seven persons, including six troopers of CISF and a civilian driver, were killed in an ambush by Maoist in Dantewada, Chhatishgarh, reports The Times of India.

JUNE

June 1: The Hindu reports that Ranvir Sena Chief Brahmeshwar Singh was shot dead by unidentified gunmen in Bhojpur, Bihar.

OCTOBER

October 1: Two personnel of CRPF were shot dead by Maoist in West Midnapore, WB, reports The Indian Express.

October 18: Three troopers of CRPF killed as Maoist triggered IED blast in Gaya (Bihar), reports IBN Live.

NOVEMBER

November 9: Three Policemen and a prisoner were killed Maoist attack on on police van in Giridih (Jharkhand), reported The Times of India.

YEAR 2013:

JANUARY

January 7: Seven CRPF were killed and 12 injured in an encounter with Maoist in Latehar (Jharkhand), reports The Times of India.

January 10: The Maoists placed a bomb in the body of dead CRPF trooper that killed civilians in Jharkhand.

FEBRUARY

February 19: Three tribals killed by Maoist in Visakhapatnam, Andhra Pradesh, reports The Hindu.

February 22: Maoist triggered a landmine blast that killed six Police personnel in Gaya, Bihar, reports The Times of India.

APRIL

April 4: Five personnel of the Jharkhand Armed Police (JAP) were killed in Maoist firing in Gumla (Jharkhand) reports The Hindu.

April 12: Four Maoist, a Policeman and two villagers were killed in an encounter between the Maoists and Commandos in Gadchiroli (Maharashtra), reports The Times of India.

MAY

May 12: Four police killed Maoist in Bastar and Sukma (Chhattisgarh), reports The Hindu.

JUNE

June 13: In an armed attack on a train by Maoist Jamui (Bihar) and killed three persons and injuring six passengers, reports The Hindu.

JULY

July 2: Pakur District Superintendent of Police (SP) and four Policemen were killed in an ambush by Maoist in Dumka (Jharkhand), reports The Indian Express.

July 17: Three Special Auxiliary Police (SAP) troopers and two guards of a private road construction company were killed by Maoist in Aurangabad (Bihar) reports The Times of India.

AUGUST

August 13: Three Chhattisgarh Armed Force (CAF) troopers Maoist were killed in encounter between the Maoists and security personnel in Bastar (Chhatishgarh), reports The Times of India.

OCTOBER

October 17: Maoist used IED blowing up vehicle and killed seven in Aurangabad (Bihar), reports The Times of India.

NOVEMBER

November 10: Maoist killed three persons in Gaya (Bihar), reports The Times of India.

DECEMBER

December 1: Maoist shot dead 3 Bihar Military Police (BMP) personnel, reports The Hindu.

YEAR 2014:

FEBRUARY

February 2: Maoist killed JVM-P leader in Giridih (Jharkhand), reports The Times of India.

February 9: CRPF Deputy Commandant and Constable were killed and ten injured as Maoists triggered a blast and fired in Sukma (Chhatishgarh), reports The Times of India.

February 28: Five Policemen were killed and three injured in Maoist ambush in Dantewada, Chhatishgarh, reports The Times of India.

MARCH

March 11: Fifteen SF personnel were killed in Maoist ambush in Sukma (Chhatishgarh) reports The Hindu.

APRIL

April 7: Three CRPF personnel were killed and eight others injured in a landmine blast in Aurangabad (Bihar), reports The Times of India.

April 9: Three personnel CoBRA unit of CRPF were killed in Maoist ambush in Sukma (Chhatishgarh), reports The Hindu.

April 10: Two CRPF were killed and 3 injured as Maoists triggered an explosive in Jamui(Bihar), reports The Times of India.

AUGUST

August 10: Two CRPF troopers were killed by Maoist in Bijapur (Chhatishgarh), reports The Pioneer.

NOVEMBER

November 3: People's Liberation Front of India (PLFI), a faction of CPI-Maoist gunned down seven persons, in Gumla (Jharkhand), reports The Times of India.

DECEMBER

December 1: Maoist killed 14 CRPF personnel & injured 13 troopers in an ambush in Sukma (Chhatishhharh), reports The Hindu.

YEAR 2015:

JANUARY

January 23: As per The Deccan Chronicle, bomb blast in Arrah (Bihar) civil court killed 3 persons including a Police constable.

FEBRUARY

February 24: Two Central Reserve Police Force (CRPF) troopers were killed when CPI-Maoist cadres blew up a mini-bus carrying them in Gaya, (Bihar) reports ndtv.com.

MARCH

March 22: Two Policemen were killed in an encounter between Gadchiroli Police and CPI-Maoist cadres in Gadchiroli (Maharashtra), reports The Times of India.

JULY

July 15: Four auxiliary constables belonging to Chhattisgarh Police were killed by CPI-Maoist cadres in Bijapur (Chhatishgarh), reports Indian Express.

AUGUST

August 26: Three Border Security Force (BSF) personnel and a civilian were killed in a CPI-Maoist ambush in Malkangiri (Odisha), reports The Hindu.

OCTOBER

October 9: A SPO was shot dead in Gadchiroli District of Maharashtra by CPI-Maoists.

YEAR 2016:

JANUARY

January 8: Two Border Security Force (BSF) personnel were killed by CPI-Maoist in Koraput (Odisha), reports New Indian Express.

January 26: CPI-Maoist cadres killed a junior Police, identified as Girija Paswan in Aurangabad (Bihar), reports Deccan Herald.

MARCH

March 30: Seven jawans (troopers) of the Central Reserve Police Force (CRPF) were killed by Maoist led explosion in Dantewada (Chhatishgarh), reports The Hindu.

APRIL

April 2: A leader of the BJP youth leader, was shot at by CPI-Maoist in Bijapur (Chhatishgarh), reports The Hindu.

April 14: A Policeman was killed when CPI-Maoist cadres opened indiscriminate fire at a function in Gadchiroli (Maharashtra), reports The Hindu.

April 16: CPI-Maoist cadres have executed, a school student, in Balaghat (MP)on April 16, reports, The Times of India.

AUGUST

August 1: A college student was killed by Maoist cadres in Gadchiroli (Maharashtra), reports The Hindu.

YEAR 2017:

JANUARY

January 12: Two civilians, were killed by CPI-Maoist cadres in Gadchiroli (Maharashtra), reports The Hindu.

January 26: CPI-Maoist cadres killed a junior Police, in Aurangabad (Bihar), reports Deccan Herald.

FEBRUARY

February 1: At least eight Police personnel were killed by CPI-Maoist cadres in Koraput (Odisha), reports prameyanews7.com.

APRIL

April 8: A Sub-Inspector (SI) and a Policeman were killed by CPI-Maoist, in Simdega (Jharkhand) reports Hindustan Times.

April 24: 26 personnel of 74th Battalion of Central Reserve Police Force (CRPF) were killed by CPI-Maoist, in Sukma (Chhatishgarh), reports PTI.

MAY

May 3: A Security Force (SF) Personnel was in Gadchiroli District, reports Indian Express.

AUGUST

August 6: A Police Sub-Inspector (SI) and a Constable were killed by CPI-Maoist cadres in Rajnandgaon (Chhatishgarh), reports The Pioneer.

NOVEMBER

November 24: A Policeman on duty was killed and a policewoman seriously injured when CPI-Maoist cadres triggered a blast in Gadchiroli (Maharashtra), reports Business Standard.

November 26: A Central Reserve Police Force (CRPF) jawan, was killed by CPI-Maoist cadres in Gadchiroli (Maharashtra), reports The Hindu.

YEAR 2018:

JANUARY

January 2: A CRPF jawan, was killed by Maoists at hills in Gaya (Bihar) reports The Times of India.

FEBRUARY

February 18: Two Policemen were killed by CPI-Maoist in Sukma (Chhatishgarh) on February 18, reports Business Standard.

MARCH

March 3: Two civilians, CPI-Maoist in Jamui (Bihar)on March 3, reports The New Indian Express.

March 13: Nine CRPF personnel were killed by Maoists in Sukma (Chhatishgarh), reports The Telegraph.

MAY

May 20: Seven Security Forces were killed Maoists in Dantewada (Chhatishgarh), reports The Asian Age.

OCTOBER

October 30: A Doordarshan (DD) cameraperson along with two Policemen were killed by Maoist in Dantewada (Chhattisgarh), reports Hindustan Times.

NOVEMBER

November 8: Four civilians and a CISF were killed by CPI in Dantewada (Chhattisgarh), reports The Hindu.

November 11: A BSF Sub-Inspector was killed by Maoist at Kanker (Chhatishgarh), reports The New Indian Express.

YEAR 2019:

JANUARY

January 22: Three villagers were killed by Maoist, in Gadchiroli (Maharashtra), reports The Hitavada.

FEBRUARY

February 1–2: Two villagers were shot dead by Maoist cadres, in Gadchiroli (Maharashtra), reports The Indian Express.

February 14: A CRPF SI was killed in a landmine blast triggered by Maoist in Gaya (Bihar), reports The New Indian Express.

APRIL

April 4: Four BSF personnel were killed by Maoist cadres in Kanker (Chhattisgarh), reports The Hindu.

April 9: Five persons including the BJP legislator from Bastar region, and his four security personnel were killed by Maoist in Dantewada (Chhattisgarh), reports The Pioneer.

MAY

May 1: At least 15 SF, and one civilian driver were killed by Maoist in Gadchiroli (Maharashtra), reports The Pioneer.

JULY

July 10: Two wanted cadres of Maoist, were shot dead in Balaghat, Madhya Pradesh, reports News18.

July 27: Maoist involved in the killing of five Policemen in Seraikela-Kharsawan (WB)reports, The Week.

AUGUST

August 23–24: All Jharkhand Student Union (AJSU) leader, was killed by Jharkhand Sangharsh Jan Mukti Morcha (JSJMM) cadres in Latehar (Jharkhand), reports Hindustan Times.

OCTOBER

October 4: Maoist killed two Policemen in Ranchi, Jharkhand, reports The Tribune.

NOVEMBER

November 22: Maoist killed four Police personnel in Latehar (Jharkhand), reports The Times of India.

DECEMBER

December 12: Two women cadres Maoist were shot dead in Balaghat (MP), reports The Times of India.

YEAR 2020:

FEBRUARY

February 10: Two CRPF personnel and a Maoist cadre were killed in an exchange of fire between in Bijapur (Chhatishgar), reports The Times of India.

MAY

May 17: Two Police personnel were killed by Maoist in Gadchiroli (Maharashtra), reports The Times of India.

JULY

July 10: Maoist killed a civilian, in Gadchiroli (Maharashtra) on July 10, reports Outlook.

AUGUST

August 14: A Police Constable was killed while another Constable, was injured by Maoist in Gadchiroli (Maharashtra), reports The New Indian Express.

SEPTEMBER

September 11: A Forest Ranger, was hacked to death by in Bijapur (Chhattisgarh), reports The Pioneer.

NOVEMBER

November 28: An Assistant Commandant of Central Reserve Police Force (CRPF's) was killed and seven others were injured in a blast by Maoist in Sukma (Chhatishgarh), reports Hindustan Times.

YEAR 2021:

FEBRUARY

February 12–13: Two Maoist, including a woman, were killed in an exchange of fire with Security Forces in Mandla (MP), reports The Pioneer.

MARCH

March 23: Five Police personnel of the District Reserve Guard (DRG) were killed and 13 others injured after Maoist exploded the bus in which they were travelling in Narayanpur (Chhatishgarh), reports The Pioneer.

APRIL

April 3: At least 22 Security Force (SF) personnel were killed and 30 others injured in an encounter with Maoist in Sukma (Chhatishgarh), reports CNBCTV18.

MAY

May 17: Three People killed in an exchange of fire between the CPI-Maoist cadres and SFs at Silger in Sukma (Chhatishgarh), reports NDTV.

AUGUST

August 24: Maoist killed two members of a family in Jamui (Bihar), reports The Times of India.

NOVEMBER

November 13: 26 Maoist cadres were killed in an encounter in Maharashtra, reports rediff.com.

YEAR 2022:

MARCH

March 21: A territorial army was shot dead by Maoist in Kanker (Chhatisgarh), reports livehindustan.com.

JUNE

June 20: Three Maoist were killed by Madhya Pradesh Police in an encounter in Balaghat, reports The Indian Express.

June 21: Three CRPF personnel were killed by Maoist in Nuapada (Odisha), reports oneindia.com.

AUGUST

August 29: Maoist killed deputy of Kurnapally Gram Panchayat in Kothagudem (Telangana), reports Telangana Today.

NOVEMBER

November 30: Two Maoist cadres were shot dead in an encounter with the Security Force (SF) personnel in Balaghat (Madhya Pradesh), reports The Free Press Journal.

YEAR 2023:

FEBRUARY

February 20: Two Police personnel were killed by Maoist in Rajnandgaon (Chhattisgarh), reports The Print.

APRIL

April 26: Ten Security Force personnel of the District Reserve Guards (DRG) and a civilian driver were killed in blast triggered by Maoist in Dantewada (Chhattisgarh), reports The Quint.

YEAR 2024:

JUNE

June 23: Two personnel of CRPF were killed by Maoist in Sukma (Chhattisgarh), reports wionews.com.

NOVEMBER

November 21: Maoist hacked to death two villagers in Mulugu (Telangana), reports Telangana Today.

YEAR 2025:

FEBRUARY

February 1: Eight Maoists were killed by the Security Forces (SFs) in Bijapur (Chhattisgarh), reports The Hindu.

February 3: Maoist killed two villagers, accusing them of being 'police informers, Bastar (Chhattisgarh), reports NDTV.

SEPTEMBER

September 11: Security Forces killed at least 10 cadres of Maoist Gariabandh, Chhatishgarh, reports Ommcom News.

September 17: Twelve Maoist surrendered before SP, Narayanpur District in Bastar division of Chhattisgarh, reports Daijiworld.

September 24: Seventy-one CPI-Maoists urrendered in Dantewada Chhattisgarh, reports The New Indian Express.

OCTOBER

October 2: 103 Maoist surrendered in Bijapur District, Chhattisgarh, reports ETV Bharat.

October 8: Sixteen Maoist surrendered before the Police in Narayanpur District Chhattisgarh, under the state's rehabilitation drive 'Poona Margham', reports Hindustan Times.

October 15: 78 Maoist surrendered in three districts of Chhattisgarh on October 15, reports NDTV.

October 17: 210 Maoist surrendered in Bastar, Chhattisgarh on, reports The New Indian Express.

Index

Amnesty International 86, 170–171
Andhra Pradesh 1, 4, 18, 33–37, 47, 52–53, 55, 56, 68, 69, 77, 88–90, 92, 94, 162, 175, 210–212, 232, 233
Anti National 41, 79, 144, 170, 180, 212
Anti- Naxal Operations 49, 86, 189
Armed Forces 12, 48, 52, 56, 59, 89, 95, 96, 101, 124, 126, 128, 158, 165, 171, 174, 190, 195–196, 199, 201, 213
Armed Militia 61
Armed Naxals 169, 173
Armed Rebellion 114, 176
Armed Revolution 3, 13, 34, 83, 206
Armed Struggle 1, 4, 13, 17–18, 21, 23–24, 27, 31–33, 36–37, 42, 61–62, 65, 73, 115, 178
Arms 2, 9, 11, 37–38, 51, 57, 59, 66, 70, 79, 81, 82–83, 91, 120, 124, 128, 131–133, 135–136, 138, 143, 154, 162, 164, 166, 170, 172–173, 175, 178, 179, 203, 233–234
Aspirational District Programmes 3, 11
Assam 34, 70

Baal Sangathans 90
Baal Sangham 89–90
Baby Brigade 89
Bailadila 77
Banerjee, Mamta 196, 201–205
Bengal (West) 1, 4, 10, 19–21, 33–35, 38, 47, 52–57, 67–69, 80, 84–85, 87, 89, 145, 150–152, 161–162, 174, 180, 195–196, 198–199, 201–205, 212, 217, 232–233
Bengal Uprsings 21
Bernstein 18
Bhumi Uchhed Pratirodh Committee (BUPC) 203
Bhumihars 38, 207
Big Bourgeoise 18–19, 28–29, 45
Bihar 1, 10, 30, 33–38, 48, 52–53, 56–58, 67, 70, 75–78, 80, 87, 100, 118, 122, 135, 173–175, 177, 202, 205–208, 233
BJP 2, 9, 10, 12, 47, 48, 108, 110, 112, 123, 128, 135–136, 142, 147, 150, 154, 159, 166, 171, 180, 194–195, 203, 205, 207–211, 213, 223, 226, 229–231, 233
Bolsheviks 15, 73
Britain 30, 114, 116
Bureaucratic Capitalism 22, 62

Capitalism 14–15, 17, 22, 28–29, 41–42, 44, 51, 81, 107, 112, 152, 174, 231–232
Chaitanya Natak Manch 91
Chandra, Satish 148
Chaudhary, Shubhranshu 123
Chhattisgarh 1–2, 4, 7, 9–10, 12, 35, 37, 47–48, 52–53, 56–58, 66–70, 77, 85–88, 90–93, 98, 110, 112, 116–117, 120–123, 130–131, 133–138, 140, 143, 158–159, 161–167, 170–172, 174, 176–178, 181–182, 187, 190, 193–196, 198–202, 205, 209–210, 213, 218, 222–223, 225–226, 229–230, 232–234
Chidambaram, P. 2, 49, 193, 199, 200, 211, 218–220
China 4, 13, 15–17, 19–24, 27–29, 31, 33, 43–44, 60–61, 114–115, 142, 153, 232
Chinese Communist Party 17, 20–21, 33
Chinese Revolution 13, 24, 29
Christianity 6, 44, 79, 105–112, 114, 115, 229
Civilians 1, 5, 12, 48–49, 50, 84, 90, 120, 130, 132, 157–159, 180, 195–196, 201, 204, 221, 233
Class-Consciousness 14–15, 17
Common Minimum Programme 215
Communism 13–14, 16, 21, 23, 39, 43, 104, 212, 231–232
Communist Party of India (Marxist) 1, 18, 27, 28
Comprador 23, 28–29, 39, 40–42, 45, 58, 62
Comrades 17, 29, 39, 42, 45, 60, 75, 80, 100, 114, 153, 171, 192
Congress 2, 7, 17, 19, 24, 27, 40, 52, 56, 106, 122–123, 142, 145, 148–149, 150, 154, 177, 193–201, 207, 209, 211–212, 214–215, 217–219, 223, 229, 231
Counter-insurgency 3, 11, 120, 133, 138, 163–166, 170–174, 198, 214–215, 217–218, 220–221, 223–226
CPI 4, 13, 18, 25–26, 42, 78, 150–151, 180, 199
CPI (M) 20, 25, 28, 30–31, 33, 38–45, 56, 60, 66, 97, 162, 203–205, 215, 217, 218

 | HTTPS://DOI.ORG/10.1163/9789004765054-018

CPI Maoist 37, 39, 42, 44–45, 60–61, 81, 105, 122, 208, 216, 224, 227
CPI(ML) 1, 4, 20–21, 23, 25, 28, 30–31, 33–38, 54, 206, 208, 212, 233
CPM 1, 4, 10, 19, 20, 29, 39, 52–55, 145, 151, 180, 195–196, 198–199, 201–204, 213, 230, 232
Central Reserve Police Force (CRPF) 48, 68, 121, 143, 201, 205, 210, 221–223, 227
Cultural Ambassadors 97
Cultural Revolution 23–24, 28

Dakshin Desh 38
Dandakaranya 47, 122
Dantewada 19
Dange, S.A. 48, 56–57, 68, 77, 90, 98, 116, 122–125, 130, 134, 136, 143, 191, 210, 218, 224, 227
Delhi 35, 70, 80, 86, 135, 144–146, 148, 151, 154–155, 157, 161, 163, 169
Delhi University 144, 148, 151
Democratic Revolution 17, 27, 41

Economic Exploitation 52, 133
Engels 13, 24
Essar 57, 68, 69, 70, 161, 200
Extortion 5, 12, 51, 57, 66–68, 70, 72–77, 81, 82–83, 86, 94, 96, 136, 139, 159, 162, 181–182, 184–186, 191–192, 195, 224

Father Xavier Manjooran 118
Fedudalism 14, 41, 45, 62
Feudal 1, 11, 14, 17–18, 23–24, 26, 28, 39–42, 58, 61, 64

Gandhi (M.K) 40, 72, 109, 111
Gandhi, Rahul 145, 197, 199, 211–212, 219
Gandhi, Sonia 2, 197, 200, 215, 219
Garhchiroli 56–57, 95
Gaya 34, 38, 57, 78, 80, 206–207
Guerrilla Zone 59
Guerrilla War 2, 18, 23
Guerrilla Warfare 13, 35, 39, 58–59, 86, 206, 221
Gujarat 118, 156, 174

Harmad Vahini 202
Haryana 35, 86
Hezbollah 88
Himachal Pradesh 86
Hindu 6, 7, 60, 63, 104, 106–115, 119, 146, 149, 153, 169–170, 212
Hindustan Times 169
Hindutva 7, 44, 62, 106, 108–109, 111
Historically Obsolete 13
Human Rights 2, 6–10, 12, 45–46, 60, 84–86, 89–91, 96, 102, 117, 120–121, 126, 132–136, 138, 145, 156–159, 162–163, 165–166, 170–171, 173, 175, 179–182, 184, 188–189, 192, 196, 199, 213, 220, 223, 225–226, 230
Human Rights Watch Groups 84–86, 162

Imperialism 17, 19, 23–24, 28, 31–32, 39, 41, 44–45, 62, 107, 217
India 1–6, 8–12, 15, 18–36, 39, 40–49, 51–55, 59–61, 63–65, 68–69, 79–83, 85–86, 89–94, 96, 101–102, 104, 106–110, 114, 116–118, 120–121, 133–134, 136, 141, 143–150, 152–154, 156, 162–163, 166, 169, 171, 174, 176–182, 193–194, 198, 200, 204–205, 209, 211–212, 214–216, 218, 223, 224–225, 228–232
Indoctrination 2, 94
Integrated Action Plan 220
Internal Conflicts 24
Internal Security 2, 49, 178, 200, 215, 217, 221
Islam 44, 107, 146, 229

Jagdalpur 91, 186
Jaish-e-Muhammad 89
Jal, Jangal, Jamin 2, 57
Jammu and Kashmir 60, 173–174, 193
Jan Adalat 127, 130, 185, 191
Jan Jagran Abhiyan 183
Jangal Mahal 38, 53–54, 56, 203–205
Jangal Santhal 20, 33, 152
Jawaharlal Nehru University (JNU) 141–148, 154–155, 169
Jehanabad 34, 38, 77, 118, 206–207
Jharkhand 1, 4, 10, 34, 37–38, 47–48, 53, 56–58, 67–71, 74–75, 79, 80, 85, 87, 90, 92–93, 97–98, 101–102, 175, 197–198, 201–202, 205, 207–208, 211, 218, 223, 229, 233–234
Jharkhand Mukti Morcha 202
Jungle Bachao Andolan 196

Karat, Prakash 215, 217
Kashmir 8, 45, 60, 63–64, 108–109, 135, 142, 145–146, 148, 153, 171, 173–174, 180, 193
Kashmiris 8, 152–153
Kautsky 26
Kerala 1, 4, 35, 53, 99, 109, 136, 150, 162, 175, 177, 180, 193, 195–196, 210, 233
Khrushchev's revisionism 20
Khrushchev's policy 20
Khrushchev's alliance 24
Kishanji 203, 205
Krantikari 39, 90, 94, 154

Lalgarh 196, 203
Landlords 23, 27, 39–41, 52, 58, 66, 72, 83, 94, 102, 150, 152, 175, 206–207
Lashkar-e-Taiba 88, 218
Leadership 2–5, 13, 17–20, 32–33, 35, 38, 40, 44, 51–52, 55, 61, 73, 78, 80, 96, 99, 103, 121, 123–124, 196–197, 202, 207, 209, 212, 214, 217–218, 221, 224, 227, 229–230, 233
Left Liberal Intelligentsia 86, 136, 163, 166, 168, 175, 179
Left Wing Extremism (LWE) 5, 11, 48, 215, 216, 218, 220–222, 224–227, 229, 233
Left Intelligentsia 8, 135, 196
Left Wing Terrorism 198
Lenin 13, 15, 17, 24, 26
Leninism 21
Leninism-Stalinism 4
Liberation 17, 34, 62, 64–65, 146–147, 152, 208
Liberation Tigers of Tamil Eelam (LTTE) 39, 88–89

Madhya Pradesh 1–2, 35, 37, 51, 53, 80, 152, 162, 209, 229–230, 232
Maharashtra 1, 4, 35, 53, 56–57, 68, 78, 90, 118–119, 151–152, 154–155, 174, 178, 210, 218, 226, 228, 233–234
Malkangiri 57, 76, 80–81, 88, 93
Mandal, Esha 118
Mao 1, 4, 13, 15–17, 22–25, 28, 31, 33, 39, 42, 56, 61, 63, 232
Maoism 1, 3, 10–11, 13, 18, 21–23, 32, 41, 44, 108, 114, 161, 166, 174, 176–177, 180, 201, 205, 230, 232
Maoist 1, 2, 4–6, 8, 10–11, 28, 32–33, 44–45
Maoist Communist Centre (MCC) 36, 38–39, 41, 52, 56, 77, 206–208
Maoist Cultural Wing 85
Maoist-Leninist 1
Maoist Movement 4, 7–8, 18, 36, 56, 68, 96, 151, 156, 180, 218, 234
Marxian Lexicon 18, 25
Marxism-Leninism 14, 20–24
Marxism-Leninism-Maoism 21–22, 41
Marxism 4, 13–14, 16–17, 20–27, 30, 39, 41, 107, 113, 152
Mazumdar, Charu 19–20, 22–23, 33, 152
Ministry of Home Affairs 3, 48–49, 53, 216, 224, 226
Missionaries 6–7, 79, 104–116, 118–119
Modi, Narendra 3, 10–11, 65, 79, 82, 141, 145, 178–179, 199, 214–215, 217, 219, 221–223, 225–230, 234

Naidu, Chandrababu 52
Nandigram 54, 203
National Human Rights Commission 2, 9, 50, 131, 157–158, 179, 181–185, 187, 189, 191–192, 231, 234
Nationalist Bourgeoisie 17, 26–29, 60
Naxal-Free 3, 53, 228
Naxal Infested 7, 12, 47–49, 53, 55, 65, 69, 71–74, 90, 170, 180, 185, 200–201, 210, 233–234
Naxalbari 1, 4, 20–21, 23, 33, 55, 89, 151–152, 214
Naxalism 1–3, 10–13, 47, 49, 52, 63, 93, 103, 107, 176, 179, 181, 198, 204, 210–211, 214–217, 219, 221–225, 229, 230–233
NDA 3, 11, 145, 221–223, 225, 227
Nehruvian Socialism 27
Neo-Colonial State 28, 30
Neo-Colonial 2, 28, 30, 40, 99
Neo-economic 170
Neo-Liberal 9, 168–169, 173–174, 217
Nepal 7, 32, 39, 80, 82, 88, 114–116
New Democratic Revolution 22, 37, 41, 61
Non Governmental Organizations (NGOs) 5, 7, 31, 66, 78–79, 81–82, 84–85, 102, 104, 116–117, 119, 126, 134, 136, 141, 162, 180–181, 196

Odisha 1, 38, 48, 53, 68–69, 76, 80, 85, 87–88, 90, 98–100, 104–105, 118, 218, 222–224
Operation Green Hunt 2, 65, 200, 202, 211–212, 218, 220, 229, 231

Paralakhemundi 118
Parliamentry Elections 26, 35, 201, 209
Parliamentry Politics 1, 13, 17, 19, 24, 34–35, 40, 151
Patna 80, 96, 135, 151, 173, 207
Patekar, Medha 196
Peal of Spring Thunder 21
People's War Group 36–37, 39, 88–89
Peru 32
Peruvian Communist Party 22
Philippines 43, 114, 118
Prahar 222, 227
Predatory Capitalism 168
Proletarian 4, 14–16, 18, 25, 28, 41, 99
Proletariat 13, 15, 22–23, 25, 41–42, 49, 60, 85, 143
Propaganda War 12, 91, 111, 133, 135
Protracted Armed Struggle 1, 18, 31, 73
Punjab 34–35, 86, 173–174
People's Union for Civil Liberties (PUCL) 90, 122, 133–134, 157–159, 180, 213, 223
People's Union for Democratic Rights (PUDR) 90, 122, 138, 140, 157, 158–159, 161, 170, 180, 212

Rajputs 38, 207
Red Corridor 1, 5, 12, 47, 214, 218, 226, 230, 233
Reddy, Chandrafulla 36
Reddy, T.N. 36
Red Flag 34–35
Revisionists
Revolutionary International Movement 21
Roy, Arundhati 108, 135, 180, 224
Roy, M.N. 17
RSS(Rashtriya Swayam Sevak Sangh) 6, 105–106, 109–112, 150, 229
Russia 15–16, 20, 22, 24, 28

Salwa Judum 2–3, 7, 8–10, 52, 65, 98, 120–140, 156–164, 166, 170–171, 173, 178–179, 181–184, 186–193, 195–200, 209, 213, 229–230, 234
Salwa Juroom 121
Sanyal, Kannu 20, 33, 35–36, 152
Singh, Manmohan 2, 49, 134, 199–200, 211–212, 215, 217, 229–230
Singh, Mahendra Karma 52, 121–123, 131, 140, 195
Singh, Rajnath 221–222
Singh, Satyanarayan 33
Secular 106, 111, 114–116
Separatists 8, 45, 108, 135, 142, 145–146, 180
Shah, Amit 3, 47, 224–225, 230
Shiv Sena 194, 213
Singur 54, 180, 203, 213
Socialism 4, 13–14, 16, 23, 25–28, 30–31, 33, 37, 41–42, 44, 49, 130, 148, 174, 231
Soren, Hemant 201
Soren, Shibu 201
Soviet Communist Party 21, 24
Soviet Union 20, 31, 43–44, 148–149, 232
SPOs (Special Protection Officers) 7, 10, 102, 120, 128–129, 131–132, 134, 136, 138, 164, 170–171, 173–174, 177, 184, 190–191, 193–194, 200, 234
Stalin 24, 29, 44, 56, 63
State Apparatus 1, 4, 11, 53, 98, 180, 230
State Terrorism 154
Students 1, 13, 22, 29, 60–62, 64–65, 75, 98–99, 121, 141–147, 150–152, 154, 155–156, 169, 184, 224
Students Islamic Movement of India (SIMI) 218
Sukma 48, 52, 56, 68, 112, 158, 186, 201–202, 213, 222–224, 227
Sen, Sun-Yat 17
Sen, Vinayak 156, 194, 196
Sunder, Nandini 135, 163, 181
Supreme Court 9, 54, 120, 127–128, 134, 136, 140–141, 163–164, 170–171, 175, 177–178, 182, 192–193, 196–197, 230–231

Tata 43, 54, 57, 69–70, 137, 161, 200
Telangana 1, 18, 23, 36–37, 40, 47, 53, 55–56, 161, 226
Telegu Liberation 34
Terrorism 2, 44, 90, 113, 130, 134, 174–175, 219
The People's Daily 21
The Times of India 85, 91–92, 101, 169
Third International 16, 24

Third World 15, 17, 20, 33, 44, 171
Three World Theory 31
Tiananmen Square 60, 142
Trade Union Centre of India 35
Trinamool Congress (TMC) 54, 196, 201–205
Turkey 32

UPA 9, 10, 114, 195–200, 215–218, 221, 230
Urban Naxal 65, 141, 179, 223, 233
USA 30, 110, 113
Uttarakhand 86

Vanvasi Kalyan Ashram 6, 106, 110–111, 113
Veermata 100
Veerpatni 100
Violent uprisings 117
Vishakhapatanam 55–56, 68
Vishwa Hindu Parishad (VHP) 104

Xiaoping, Deng 31

Yechuri, Sitaram 145, 215
Yogi, Ajit 196, 209, 219

Zamindari 55

www.ingramcontent.com/pod-product-compliance
Lightning Source LLC
Chambersburg PA
CBHW071248230926
51849CB00001B/266
9789004765047